Political Traditions in Foreign Policy Series
Kenneth W. Thompson, Editor

The values, traditions, and assumptions undergirding approaches to for-eign policy are often crucial in determining the course of a nation's his-tory. Yet, the interconnections between ideas and policy for landmark periods in our foreign relations remain largely unexamined. The intent of this series is to encourage a marriage between political theory and foreign policy. A secondary objective is to identify theorists with a con-tinuing interest in political thought and international relations, both younger scholars and the small group of established thinkers. Only oc-casionally have scholarly centers and university presses sought to nur-ture studies in this area. In the 1950s and 1960s the University of Chi-cago Center for the Study of American Foreign Policy gave emphasis to such inquiries. Since then the subject has not been the focus of any major intellectual center. The Louisiana State University Press and the series editor, from a base at the Miller Center of Public Affairs at the University of Virginia, have organized this series to meet a need that has remained largely unfulfilled since the mid-1960s.

Traditions and Values
in Politics and Diplomacy

Kenneth W. Thompson

TRADITIONS AND VALUES
IN POLITICS AND DIPLOMACY

Theory and Practice

LOUISIANA STATE UNIVERSITY PRESS
Baton Rouge and London

Copyright © 1992 by Louisiana State University Press
All rights reserved
Manufactured in the United States of America
First printing
01 00 99 98 97 96 95 94 93 92   5 4 3 2 1

Designer: Glynnis Phoebe
Typeface: Times Roman
Typesetter: G & S Typesetters, Inc.
Printer and binder: Thomson-Shore, Inc.

Library of Congress Cataloging-in-Publication Data

Thompson, Kenneth W., 1921–
    Traditions and values in politics and diplomacy : theory and
practice / Kenneth W. Thompson.
        p.   cm.—(Political traditions in foreign policy series)
    ISBN 0-8071-1742-0 (cloth).—ISBN 0-8071-1746-3 (paper)
    1. United States—Foreign relations—Philosophy.   2. International
relations—Philosophy.   3. United States—Foreign
relations—1945–1989.   I. Title.   II. Series.
    E183.7.T47   1992
    327.73—dc20   91–39876
                                                                    CIP

The author is grateful to the editors and publishers of the following journals for permission to reprint the following chapters, which first appeared, in a somewhat different form, as essays in the journals noted: "The Religious Transformation of Politics and the Political Transformation of Religion," *Review of Politics,* L (October, 1988), 545–60; "History as End Point or New Beginning?" *Mediterranean Quarterly,* I (Winter, 1990), 111–26; "Power," *Society,* XXVIII (November–December, 1990), 56–65.

    Chapters 4 and 23 are adapted from the following articles in *Ethics and International Affairs,* published by the Carnegie Council on Ethics and International Affairs, New York: "Peace Studies: Social Movement or Intellectual Discipline?" IV (1990), 163–74; "The Decline of International Studies," V (1991), 233–46.

Dedicated to the memory of
my father and mother
and to a third generation,
Ken, Paul, and James

Contents

Preface

Studies of politics and diplomacy especially in the late twentieth century have tended to ignore traditions and values. One reason for the neglect is the dominance of change in contemporary national and international life. Most of us have learned to recite phrases such as "change is the first law of the universe." What is true of axioms in general, however, is true of verbal reminders of change. As in the counseling of young people, the message is brought home not in homely phrases but in tradition-shattering events such as the revolutions of 1989 or the destructive political movements that brought on World War II.

Yet change requires a standard and in politics and diplomacy finds it in traditions and values. Traditions provide the road map of where a society has been and what its center of gravity continues to be. Values give content to changing traditions that might otherwise deteriorate into offering little more than justifications of the status quo. Traditions provide chronologies of where a society has been. Customs and practice help us to trace the main outlines of a society's traditions. Values enable society to distinguish good and bad, justice and injustice, or virtue and cruelty. Traditions and values blend, the one describing the main course a society has followed, the other introducing an evaluative principle. The former asks what and when; the latter asks why. Traditions are shaped by history, language, culture, and legend. Values are a product of moral reasoning using philosophy, religion, law, and ethics. This book is about their intersection.

Remembering the patterns of the past and society's present norms and values and reflecting on their interconnections are a preparation for discussing politics and diplomacy. Yet politics is not just one more aspect of social life. For Plato and Aristotle it is the path to self-realization and virtue. Christian thought from Saint Augustine to Reinhold Niebuhr views politics in more ambiguous terms: government is for brigands and robbers, Augustine declares. From the classical to the contemporary era, diversity reigns in discussions of politics. Politics for some is the struggle for power, for others, the good life, and for behaviorists, the authoritative allocation of values.

A general treatise on traditions and values in politics and diplomacy cannot resolve all these controversies and issues. It can, however, illuminate the areas where debate is most continuous. Thus far, the series *Political Traditions in Foreign Policy,* published by the Louisiana State University Press, has dealt with particular controversies and debates: idealism versus realism, Hans J. Morgenthau and his critics, Antonio Gramsci and the Socialists, the founding fathers and values expressed in policy problems such as immigration and Indochina, China, and presidents and foreign policy making.

The present volume is an attempt to review, reexamine, and synthesize these and other contributions to the main themes of the series. It sets forth general principles directed toward the quest for an informing theory on traditions and values. It also warns of the pitfalls and limitations of theory. The goal of such an inquiry is to identify the possibilities and constraints of political theory in international relations addressed quite specifically to traditions and values. It examines the contemporary relevance of political theory. Finally, it offers some summary views that may have validity in the discussion of a variety of more specific inquiries into problems involving traditions and values.

Traditions and Values
in Politics and Diplomacy

Introduction

Most discussions of traditions and values begin with Judaeo-Christian and Graeco-Roman thought, and this study is no exception. Within a framework of philosophy, religion, and ethics, it reconsiders historic concepts of the polity, of the idea of authority and competing views of rulers as robbers and brigands or as men of virtue, of two perspectives on human nature, and of the transcendent and the relative in moral standards. It should come as no surprise that the two leading streams of Western thought are religion and philosophy. Successive generations of political philosophers have repeated Alfred North Whitehead's words that all philosophy since Plato is a footnote. In much the same way, religious and ethical thinkers return to Saint Augustine and Saint Thomas Aquinas. Thus, this study takes the classical and Christian traditions as its point of departure and goes on to consider more current issues.

A second theme appropriate to philosophy, religion, and ethics is the controversy over the rise and fall of moral standards. Enlightenment thought is unqualifiedly optimistic about the rise of moral and political standards, but its heirs are confronted by the harsh realities of two world wars and a great depression. Drugs, poverty, and unimaginable cruelties and killings mar the Enlightenment picture of a kinder and more moral world. The judgment of history, therefore, is more mixed than either a too optimistic or a too cynical perspective would suggest. Man still remains "his own most vexing problem," as Niebuhr wrote.

Four decades of international relations theorizing provide subject matter for a tour d'horizon of the field. Diplomatic historians, international lawyers, and political scientists have contributed to new perspectives in the field. Such theorizing contributes elements essential to a tradition in international thought.

Peace studies is only the most recent attempt to eliminate or defuse international conflicts and to demonstrate the people's commitment to harmony and peace. The debate over peace studies revolves around whether it should be evaluated as an intellectual discipline or as a political and social reform movement. It will stand or fall according to the standards by which it is judged.

Finally, the relationship between religion and politics is fundamental to a normative tradition. A perennial issue that has come to the fore is whether we seek the religious transformation of politics or the political transformation of religion. The consequences that flow from such a choice are bound to be far-reaching. This discussion completes the book's first section, which is intended to define the relationship between philosophy, religion, and politics.

If Part I focuses on the broadest and most inclusive issues of tradition and values, Part II addresses complexities, obstacles, and constraints to values in politics. It treats the time-honored concepts of realism, power, and national interest in seeking to bring the precepts of philosophy, religion, and ethics down to earth. It examines the application of values in practice as contrasted with theory.

However, purpose is no less central to political reality than power, and for Americans purpose has taken the form of freedom and equality or, stated more specifically, equality pursued in freedom. In politics, men and nations pursue more than one goal, and statesmen must balance purposes such as equality and freedom. If power is considered as the means, purpose defines the ends of politics. This section is meant to link these two dimensions, which are sometimes treated separately and apart from one another.

Devotion to purpose in political theory requires the beliefs of which Abraham Lincoln spoke when he warned of a people "bereft of faith and terrified by doubt." The belief of the founders in the Constitution is a historic example of purpose; faith in the nation takes the form of patriotism. Belief in the political realm is corrupted, however, by true believers who hold only to their own true beliefs, which they equate with the nation's purpose and the creed of its citizenry. They would condemn other beliefs to the fire and the sword.

Part III asks if values that were once an integral part of the political process can be reinstated in the 1990s in politics and diplomacy. Can the marriage of values and politics be restored to American life? Toward this end, I discuss moral values and international politics, followed by approaches to power and morality in an increasingly complex world. Because leaders make decisions on war and peace in the shadow of nuclear conflict, a new way of thinking may be required. This section closes with some more positive reflections on the meeting or convergence of ethics and diplomacy.

Two sections introduce case studies, first, Part IV on persistent problems such as human rights, disarmament, and human survival, and second, Part V on presidents and the conflicts of values they face in the decision-making process. The problem with most discussions of human rights is that they are approached as essentially rational enterprises. But those arguments that defend human rights on the basis of reason or oppose them on grounds that can never be consistently followed on any kind of universal basis largely ignore the role of the contingent in history. Thus, certain human rights involving freedoms of speech and of assembly in the Soviet Union took on new life with Mikhail Gorbachev and *glasnost*. Contrariwise, the political rights that were supposed to follow greater economic rights in China were thwarted by the savagery of Tiananmen Square. Human rights draw their meaning and define themselves in the realm of experience.

Efforts to reach agreements on arms limitation invite a discussion of the question of why we pursue disarmament and arms control. By focusing on the thinking of a few extraordinary statesmen, such as Winston Churchill, we may be helped to answer a more basic question: What lessons does history teach on the priorities that statesmen should give to direct approaches to disarmament contrasted with prior attempts to deal with political and regional differences? Which comes first, security or disarmament?

Human survival transcends every other issue in international relations. Mankind, which reformist thinkers believe was moving toward the elimination of war, has reached a point where universal destruction for the first time is possible. Here the question worth asking is how human survival can be assured. Should we all join in a noble crusade, or is a coherent plan the prerequisite to human survival? Issues such as these deserve the most careful thought and discussion.

The implementation of traditions and values is sometimes uniquely the task of American presidents. Two chapters in Part V deal with presidential faith and politics, on the one hand, and the dilemmas and antinomies of leadership, on the other. Religion and civic culture are interconnected but are not identical. We speak of the imperatives of leadership quite confidently at times, but we know that opposite imperatives may come into play at other times and in other places. This section concludes with two quite specific case studies. John F. Kennedy's presidency involved a contest between activism and pragmatism as the basis of moral and political choice. Richard M. Nixon's foreign policy was a study in values posed in terms of continuities and contradictions. These case studies of respected presidencies in which the clash of values was present help to illuminate the subject matter of the book.

A concluding section, Part VI, is addressed to the question "Whither men and nations?" The 1980s, which leaders had heralded as an era of transformation, restoring hope for the individual and respect for the nation, ended with serious questioning about the future. A State Department official wrote a much discussed paper proclaiming the end of history. A Yale University historian published a best-selling volume on the decline of the two most powerful nations, the superpowers after World War II, the Soviet Union and the United States. Curiously, the euphoria that accompanied Ronald Reagan's presidency was replaced overnight by anxious warnings about the decline of nations and the end of history that even a victorious war could not erase. Those who had criticized talk of malaise in Jimmy Carter's administration were confronted with reflections on decline by members of successor administrations.

It should be obvious with the freeing of the nations of Eastern Europe and hopeful developments elsewhere in the world that the times are not ones of unrelieved despair. Serious crises appear and reappear in the Middle East and elsewhere. A concluding essay invites greater efforts by all to learn to live with uncertainty. If anything is clear about the future, it is that uncertainty will accompany us into the twenty-first century.

Part I

Tradition in Philosophy, Religion, and Ethics

1

The Classical and Christian Traditions

The dual source of the American tradition of values in politics and diplomacy is the convergence of the classical and Christian traditions. The former derives primarily from Greek political philosophy, and the latter is the product of the Christian religious heritage and of Christian social and political ethics. The one traces the pathways through which the individual realizes his true nature within the state, whereas the other looks beyond history for the meaning of life. Political philosophy is the quest for virtue and justice in the polis, whereas the Christian tradition looks for the ground of being in an ultimate point of reference.

The Classical Tradition

The roots of political reflection in the West go back at least to the sixth century before Christ. Interest and speculation about politics, which is sometimes ascribed to the influence of the Renaissance and the Reformation, was actually in full flowering two thousand years earlier. Not only is the concept "political" derived from the Greek polis, or city-state, but the major unsolved problems of justice, law, and power with which every society must wrestle were explicitly formulated by the Greeks. Therefore to discover the beginnings of Western thought and concern for political decisions we must consider some of the more salient characteristics of Greek political philosophy, especially as represented in the writings of Plato (427 to 347 B.C.) and Aristotle (384 to 322 B.C.).

Before we enumerate the particular principles of Greek political philosophy that have been a part of the Western legacy, it is essential to refer to a problem basic to all social science. One of the greatest of contemporary philosophers, as we have seen, declared that all philosophy since Plato has been essentially a footnote, even though Plato wrote and reflected under circumstances that politically, socially, and morally were radically different from our own. We would hardly expect someone embarking on the study of the physical or natural sciences to go back to the chemists, physicians, or physicists of Plato's time, and yet it can be argued that nothing new in basic and fundamental problems has been discovered by political scientists since the fourth century B.C.

Whitehead's viewpoint has been sharply challenged by a new and aggressive trend in social thinking. Social scientist spokesmen for this trend charge that any reference to the Greeks or the ancients is a sign of backwardness and that unless the social sciences rid themselves of their antiquarianism they can never hope to match the accomplishments of the natural sciences. However, this recent trend in social thinking has not proved fully satisfying or convincing. We have seen a counterreaction against the behavioral school that would fashion the study of man from the methods employed in the study of nature.

Within recent decades, writers such as Reinhold Niebuhr and Hans J. Morgenthau have argued that progress in social science is qualitatively different from progress in the physical sciences. Therefore, they say, it is logical even today to study Greek political philosophy because Plato and Aristotle dealt with human nature with its recurrent ambitions and drives and with the problems growing out of man's relations with other men. Such issues as justice, political power, and revolution are as basic in our own day as they were for our precursors. It should be the task of social science to separate what is most enduring in Greek writing and experience from speculations relevant only to the unique conditions that prevailed at the time. Yet this task is impossible if the Greek interval in world history is appraised and evaluated exclusively in terms of the standards drawn from other periods in history, as, for example, the standards of nineteenth-century liberalism. The confidence of some moderns that they can look at the past in their own terms and thereby understand it better than it understood itself has not contributed to man's fund of knowledge about either the recurrent or the unique elements in history. To understand philosophy we must approach it on its own terms.

Four general principles or beliefs constitute the pillars on which Greek political philosophy was founded. The first is a belief in the existence of objective truth. The second is the proposition that the individual can realize his true nature only through association with his fellows in the state. The third is an unwillingness to distinguish, as have modern philosophers, between facts and values, holding to the view instead that politics is a part of applied ethics. The fourth is the acceptance of an essential dualism in human nature.

The first of these principles emerged as a reaction to the precepts of the philosophical school of Sophism. Sophism was then the dominant trend of philosophy, and mention of the Sophists as a community of scholars carried almost none of the negative connotations the name subsequently acquired. Plato and Aristotle, however, found themselves in opposition to this group, which maintained that law and justice were mere conventions. The Sophists had claimed that the state and human society were mere artifices of man and thus were relative to his whims and caprice. Thrasymachus, when asked in the dialogue of Plato's *Republic* "What is justice?," replied that it was the right of the stronger. Justice, according to Sophists like Thrasymachus, depended solely on ever-changing power relationships. Political beliefs were wholly subjective creations of man bearing no resemblance to any underlying principles of truth.

Plato and Aristotle in answering these claims sought to discover an objective basis for the concepts and institutions of political life. The Sophists had argued that forming the state was essentially the same as producing a pair of shoes created arbitrarily by each man for his own use. Plato and Aristotle, in disputing this viewpoint, contended that the state as a natural phenomenon was both objective and necessary. In other words, the state as *physis* was an objective reality with criteria and standards that transcended the will of the majority of the people. The task of the political philosopher was to undertake to discover the essence of the true state, reflected in current, visible states. The aim of classical thought was to establish a system of thought explaining the political reality that existed beyond the illusion of merely visible reality.

In explaining this search for reality, Plato used the figure of the cave. Most men who observed the functions of their states were like slaves chained to the wall of the cave. The shadows they saw on the wall of the cave were mere reflections of the events taking place in the sunlight outside, that is, images and reflections of reality.[1] A few in the cave could discover reality through reason, by turning from the wall of the cave to the sunlight outside. These few were the political philosophers. Most, by reason of their physical nature, would remain chained to the wall inside.

Objective reality, insofar as the state was concerned, was not a utopia. That was because a great gulf existed between the ideal state and the historic state of experience. The perfect state was a concept of higher political reality, and only by accident or through grace could it be achieved. For Plato there was an even more unbridgeable chasm between the real, or true, and the visible states than for later Christian philosophers between the City of God and the City of Man, which were at least commingled. In Saint Augustine's system the final transformation depended not on accident but on salvation through God's grace.

There is another way in which the ideal is related to the visible. For Plato a recognition of injustice points to a standard of justice against which every instance of imperfect justice may be measured. It should be the task of the political philosopher to determine the objective relationship between visible reality and the essential reality of politics. The historic state should be conceived in light of the objective and ideal state as well as in terms of its own particular historical circumstances.

When we consider the questions that are uppermost in the minds of modern political philosophers, this interest appears to have almost disappeared. Contemporary philosophers are concerned with relations between the state and the individual, not between the state and its essence or ideal. Questions about the absolutely best political order or the best possible political order are no longer accepted as an appropriate concern of political philosophy. For Americans no inquiry is needed. Democracy is the best.

The second general principle of classical philosophy relates to the individual. For the Greeks there could be no existence as such for the individual outside the state. Only with the appearance of Stoicism and Christianity was there an emphasis on individual rights independent of and outside the state. If the individual could realize his true nature only in association with others

---

1. The men chained in the cave actually see only shadows of the things on the ledge behind them, which in turn are reflections of the world outside, so they are seeing at a third remove. See Plato, *The Republic,* Book VII.

in the state, he nevertheless did not, as he does in the totalitarian state, exist only for the state. For the state is a partnership in every mode of life. Life for the ancient Greeks had an intimacy made possible by the size and structure of the city-state. Art, religion, politics, and ethics were centered in the state, and the sharp divisions or compartments into which modern society has been fragmented were not present. Thus, life in the state comprised all aspects of life in common, and individuals who were outside the state were considered not harmless but useless. Political science was concerned with the wise handling of concrete, immediate situations in the common political order. In the pursuit of communal life the individual gave expression to values that transcended his mere biological needs. The state is not a necessary evil, as liberalism and Marxism assume, but an ethical and moral relationship in which individuals are able to realize their virtues.

A third principle central to the classical outlook is the belief that questions relating to values should not be excluded from political philosophy. Political philosophy was assumed to have its point of origin at the center of political life, where intelligent men asked questions regarding the good life and the best political order. Thus the philosopher might ask ultimate questions—questions beyond those asked in the sphere of practical politics—but he must not abandon faith in the orientation of politics as such. When the value distinctions being made by statesmen and politicians were judged to be mere ideologies and not intrinsically a part of the essence of politics, the philosopher's orientation in politics was breached and destroyed. Political life and its observance lead to philosophy, and though philosophy is primarily concerned with those virtues that are good for all communities, political science involves the practical virtues that are best for the governing of a particular community. Method in these terms is subordinate to virtue and wisdom.

The fourth principle is the belief that man is to be understood primarily from the standpoint of his rational faculties. What is unique in man is essentially his capacity for thought and reason. The dualism of classical political thought results from an identification of the body with evil and of the mind with the ideas of goodness and universality. Since the body alone is corrupted and corruptible, classical philosophy assumes an optimistic frame of mind in regard to what man can accomplish through reason. Here the Greeks part company with many of the great religious and political systems that consider man as fallen and incapable of doing more than mitigating his political and social problems. The rationalism and dualism of classical thought deprive it of the tragic sense, and, in certain respects, of the insights some other philosophies have attained.

Christian Thought

Christian thought from the standpoint of politics and the state had its origins with the bishop of Hippo, Saint Augustine (A.D. 354 to 430). Augustine lived in the transition between the classical civilization of Greece and Rome and the Christian civilization of Western Europe. As has been true throughout history, new political traditions appear in times of troubles. The classical era that Plato and Aristotle represent was a period marked by the dissolution of traditional institutions and beliefs. The Athenian polis was in crisis, as was the Spartan state. Conflicts between rich and poor were sources of dissension in most of the Greek city-states. Failure to resolve the conflicts among the city-states led to a series of wars culminating in the Peloponnesian War. Nor were later historical periods any more stable, as with the Renaissance when Niccolo Machiavelli wrote about political realities, the Civil War in seventeenth-century England when Thomas Hobbes called for a great Leviathan to restore order and stability, and the years leading up to the French Revolution when Jean-Jacques Rousseau expressed dissatisfaction with the ancient regime.

The age in which Augustine lived and wrote, the late fourth and early fifth centuries, was a similar time of troubles. Augustine was heir to the classical tradition, but he was also one of the most original Christian philosophers and theologians. He held to certain traditional ideas, while helping to create the political and religious thought relating Christianity to a changing social order. The transition between the two civilizations was not abrupt. The barbarians who moved across Europe were in part Romanized. They used Roman titles and the fruits of Roman education and its bureaucracy. Nevertheless, society for Augustine was in flux. Power began to flow from the established institutions, including the institutions of imperial taxation that functioned to support the army and the bureaucracy. Barbarian forces, including the Visigoths and the Ostrogoths, overran Italy's heartland. The Sack of Rome symbolized the turmoil and the changes that were taking place.

Yet the picture of Christianity as a revolutionary social and political movement of the poor and the enslaved seeking to overthrow the Roman Empire is false. Christians awaited the Messiah's return, and this spiritual orientation encouraged an attitude of indifference to power and to political opposition that could lead to revolution. The guide for Christians was still the injunction "Render to Caesar the things that are Caesar's and to God the things that are God's." The state was accepted as the best available instrument for the preservation of order. It was also the chief agency for the punishment of evil doers. Despite all the persecution the church suffered at the hands of the Roman state from the time of Nero, Roman emperor from A.D. 54 to 68, to Diocletian, emperor from A.D. 284 to 305, in the beginning of the fourth century Christians still held to a dualistic view of church and state. They still believed that they were obligated to obey the state. They supported this view even though they half accepted, half rejected, the state as the main object of their loyalty. Then in 312, nine years after the beginning of the Diocletian persecution of the Christians, which lasted from 303 to 305, Emperor Constantine converted to Christianity. By the time Constantine died in 337, Christianity was one of two official religions. In 380 it became *the* official religion.

In this historical setting, Augustine fashioned a view of the state and society that to the present day we characterize as political realism, or Christian realism. On the one hand, Augustine didn't ignore or discard the classical view of the state. He conceived of the state much as his classical forerunners had done, as the highest and noblest human community that could bring citizens happiness and fulfillment. On the other hand, the full realization of the fruits of such a community awaited the City of God, the *civitas Dei.* The true city was not of this world. Only in the City of God could men realize the goals proclaimed by Plato and Aristotle.

At another level, Augustine chose to look at actual states and ask what they could do and could not do and how far they could go. Actual states exist in the *civitas terrena,* or *civitas mundi,* that is, the city of this world. This world was created by God but is not eternal. It had a beginning and will have an end. Man was created good but fell from grace. The story of human nature is the story of the Fall. Man, though created in God's image, is not incorruptibly good. Man is possessed of free will and the power to obey or disobey. Thus sin is a matter of privation; it involves turning away from God. The city of this world is dominated by self-love to the point of contempt of God. The City of God is dominated by love of God to the point of contempt of self.

For Augustine, in contrast with classical thinkers, the city of this world is not some small city-state but rather the whole of humanity. It involves the three communities of man's natural existence: the family, the commonwealth, and the world. Augustine's conception of the world is far removed from the conceptions of the stoics and modern idealists, who stressed a world of justice and harmony. Instead he maintains that the world community has more imposing dangers, just as "the greater sea is more dangerous." One source of danger is that men speak in different languages. Two men who are ignorant of each other's language discover that "dumb animals, though of a different species, [can] more easily hold intercourse than they, human beings though they be."[2] Thus, common linguistic and cultural forces, which historically bring unity and coherence within the state, are sources of division and disunity on the wider regional and worldwide stage. The assumption of the idealists that common humanity or common reason can easily produce a world community is belied by history.

Moreover, the City of Man for Augustine is rent by tensions, frictions, competitions of interest, and conflict even at the level of the family. Its rulers are bands of robbers. The picture Augustine paints is harsh and dispiriting. He notes that even in the family, trust and community are threatened; the family is endangered, "seeing that secret treachery has often broken it up." In language that is uncompromisingly realistic, Augustine speaks to the problems and difficulties of societies that are separated by a millennium and a half. Nonetheless, his words have unmistakable contemporary relevance. He provides a corrective to the too sanguine picture of rational societies and commonwealths, which, Marcus Tullius Cicero explained, required simply "a compact of justice." In fact, commonwealths are bound together more often by elements of coercion and power, forces that almost inevitably are accompanied by injustice. Augustine explains it in these words: "Without injustice the republic would neither increase nor subsist. The imperial city to which the

2. Saint Augustine, *De Civitate Dei*, 19.7.

republic belongs could not rule over provinces without recourse to injustice, for it is unjust for some men to rule over others."[3] Governance involves "lording it over others" and therefore brings injustice.

In this regard, Augustine in his realism was ahead of his time. In calling attention to the role of coercion and power he anticipated political thinkers such as Moisey Ostrogorski and Vilfredo Pareto, who described the inescapable tendency toward oligarchy even in the most democratic political movements. Politics exemplified the iron law of oligarchy. In the ancient empires of Egypt or Babylon or Rome, some smaller unity or city-state provided the organizing power for the establishment of empire. Within larger political systems, unity derived from the likely influence of some city or state. Augustine saw in political unification not "a compact of justice" but political injustice even when power was exercised in the name of justice. In emphasizing coercion, he ran the risk of not distinguishing between government and slavery or between a commonwealth and a robber band. Both systems involve the rule of man by man, and both are founded on collective interests. "For even thieves must hold together or they cannot effect what they intend." Yet not power alone but a sense of justice was present, for example, in the constitution of Rome or in a democracy, where each group receives some approximation of the good through the workings of a separation of powers.

In Augustine's political thought compared with classical political thought, the root cause of sin and conflict is self-pride. Sin is disobedience and a revolt against God. Man rebels against accepting his status as creature; he rejects subordination to God. In his prideful self-centeredness, he makes himself the hub of the universe. He seeks to dominate other men and use them as means to his ends. Original sin came with the Fall. With it the human race is "sick and sore . . . from Adam to the end of the world."

Classical thought assumed that order and justice in the polis and virtue for the individual would be realized when reason had brought nonrational forces under its control. Augustine maintained that the forces in human life that offered resistance to universal ideals and norms were not readily controlled in this way. Not only are social factions and competitions, which are present in every level of the community, resistant, but so are certain stubborn

3. *Ibid.*, 19.5.

traits in man himself. Men hide their self-centeredness in moral pretense and claim more virtue than they can achieve. Self-centeredness and moralism reside in the contradictory nature of man, yet the sources of self-centeredness and self-interest are offensive to man's concept of social obligation. Therefore, he cloaks his self-interest in assertions that he is pursuing nobler ends in serving his family, the state, or the world.

Classical rational thought defined human nature as comprised of mind and body, the mind being the source of virtue and the body the cause of evil. Through the mind, the person has the ability to bring under the control of reason the drives and impulses that lead men astray. From the body derive those "lusts and ambitions" that generate evil. By contrast, Augustine declared the unity of both mind and body was determined by the self. It is the self that controls mind and body, not the mind that rules the body. Augustine explains: "These three things, memory, understanding, and love are mine and not their own, for they do what they do not for themselves but for me; or rather I do it by them. For it is I who remember by memory and understand by understanding and love by love."[4]

Augustine derives the concept of self from biblical not philosophical sources. His notion can be comprehended only in what has been called the dramatical-historical mode of apprehension of the Bible. Classical thought undertook to fit the mind into a system of universal mind and the body into the system of nature. Contemporary thinkers in the social sciences seek to reduce human selfhood to the criteria of a system of nature, seeking, for example, to isolate some natural impulse such as "aggression" and thereby to manage it. What Plato and Aristotle sought to do through the concept of disinterested reason, moderns seek to do through the scientific method. They underestimate the spiritual dimension of man's inhumanity to man or the corruption of reason by self-centeredness. The power of self-love is more spiritual than the lusts of the body, and it manipulates them to its ends. It rules the processes of the mind more than the classical philosophers recognized.

There are, however, residual elements of classical thought in Augustine. Man is a social being, and the *ecclesia,* a society of believers. Society is natural to man, and the legal order can be remedial. God created Adam, a

4. Saint Augustine, *De Trinitate,* 15, 22.

solitary man, so that men might learn the value of society. Some seek applause, but true virtue requires humility, not pride. Augustine tells the nuns of Hippo that "pride is seen . . . in your good works." True righteousness based on the love of God is different from virtue that seeks the praise of men.

Nonetheless, distinctions between Augustine's Christian perspective and the major classical philosophies persist. Virtue for Augustine is the perfect love of God manifested in the four human virtues of temperance, fortitude, justice, and prudence. By contrast, virtue is the quest for fulfillment and self-realization through reason for Plato or through nature for Aristotle. In Augustine's thought, the perfection of virtue is possible only in the life to come. For the Christian, true justice consists not only in equity and fair dealing, as for the classical writers, but in true benevolence. The Christian message is to love all men even though one is not able to do good to all men. A clear sense of the inward misery of the wicked man is evident in his unending search for human satisfaction outside himself.

Peace for Augustine is unattainable in the City of Man. Its realization is possible only in the City of God. Yet in his references to war, one finds no trace of militarism or any glorification of overt conflict. Augustine speaks of war in sorrow, not in the spirit of praising it. When he died, the city of Hippo was under siege by invading Vandals. He asks concerning war what it gains the conqueror or the conquered except the "inane pomp of human glory." At the same time, he acknowledges that wars are inevitable, given human greed, avarice, and lust and given the fallen state of man. Wars, he seems to say, will be with us forever. Wars will not cease until the end of the world. Peace is a mere truce between wars.

On the subject of justice, there is controversy over the proper translation of a passage in Book 5 of the *City of God*. Three versions are put forward. One translates: "A kingdom without justice is like a band of robbers." Another: "Since justice is absent, kingdoms are bands of robbers." The third reads: "If justice is absent, kingdoms are bands of robbers." Depending on the translation, Augustine's view of the state can be interpreted as more or less pessimistic concerning the possibility of justice within earthly kingdoms. Whatever the interpretation, Augustine in comparison with classical thought views justice as stemming less from some rational system of coherence and more from the convergence of interests and a certain equilibrium of power. He remains to the end the political realist.

The Two Traditions and American Democracy

The strength of American democracy is a reflection of the unique relationship between classical and Christian or Graeco-Roman and Judaeo-Christian thought. This fact throws into question the rather extravagant claims of both secular and religious thinkers on the origins of our political system. Those who see our strength as rooted in political and legal ideas inherited from the Greeks and Romans are quick to point to the polis as the forerunner of our representative assemblies and Roman law as the cornerstone of the rule of law. Although such claims have validity, they must be weighed against the contribution of the Christian and Jewish faiths to respect for the dignity of the individual. Democracy demands the highest evaluation of man if he is to resist being made the means to the ends of successive political programs or social movements. Religion provides this evaluation in its concept of all men having been created in the image of God. Since the essence of American democracy is equality pursued in freedom, the sanctity of the individual as enshrined in Judaeo-Christian thought is an indispensable ingredient of the American political vision. Religion protects not only the rich but the poor, not only whites but blacks and Hispanics, not only men but women, from becoming instruments for society's ends, however benign.

On the other side, democracy must be on guard against the false sanctities and idolatries that religion can import into politics. The founding fathers were successful in preserving the separation of church and state. Where separation is absent, it is true that religion historically has been a means of buttressing sometimes tyrannical regimes. Traditional societies have used religion to cloak patterns of domination. Religious men engaged in politics are endlessly tempted to frame their practical programs in the absolute language of religion. Once policies are defined in such terms, the political process breaks down. Compromise and give-and-take are impossible when political debate takes on the character of absolute right and wrong or of good and evil. An example of such a breakdown that threatened the Union was the debate over slavery between North and South. Not ultimate ends but immediate political proposals are the stuff of politics. The "limited warfare" of parliamentary politics requires political competition over programs and values that are soberly and critically assessed in the political process.

In fact, American democracy is saved from the excesses of each of its constituent sources by a fortunate confluence of the two traditions. The classical tradition is more disposed to view politics as a practical endeavor in which politicians must cope with variant and changing forces in the interest of justice. It is philosophy and religion that provide the invariant principles and the forces that affect the broad social and political environment. The classical view is better able to hold fanaticism in check, though secular traditions sometimes take on a quasi-religious character (communism became in the postwar era a political religion). But Greek and secular thought are less able than Christian thought to provide a view of man on which democracy ultimately must rest. We are led to the conclusion that democracy is the fortunate result of a convergence of religious and secular forces.

2

The Rise and Fall of Moral Standards:
Renewal or Retrogression?

Making the transition to twentieth-century America requires a leap of the imagination. The connections between classical and Christian thought and the present will emerge only as we examine in some detail the rise and fall of moral standards in the postwar era. Beginning in the late 1960s and 1970s, concern with moral and normative issues in public discourse came to the fore, and thinking about right and wrong in politics and society took on new life. Half a dozen factors contributed. Specific events and social forces crisscrossing society shattered what had been a reign of silence in the 1950s, at least among particular groups. A succession of controversial events sparked moral debate. Significant trends and tendencies left their mark on men and nations, especially those in the vanguard of social and political change. The personalities and perspectives of public figures had their impact on renewal, even though the full measure of their influence still awaits the judgment of history. Observers noted the breakdown of older values and the discovery of new standards. How lasting and deep-rooted such new values might be was debated even at the time. What was clear was that disillusionment with ancient and traditional norms and values had set in. Leaders and followers of widely different generations and backgrounds rushed in to fill the void.

One approach to understanding the influence of the myriad factors that came together to influence the rise and fall of moral standards is to try to reconstruct what happened. For those who remember the times, it may be sufficient to recall what transpired and how we responded at the time. Others are dependent on the American equivalent of the oral history tradition characterizing tribal societies, in which recollections are passed down from one generation to another. With the benefit of hindsight we may be able to judge more clearly the nature and full consequences of the changes that swept across the historical landscape in the 1960s and 1970s, reinforcing the process of change in moral values.

For most young Americans in the 1960s and 1970s, Vietnam was and remains a watershed in their thinking about moral and political values. Two generations tended to view history in diametrically different ways. The generation that had fought World War II internalized a few relatively simple values. They believed in the principle of collective security, or of "one for all and all for one." The lessons of the events that led up to World War II were imprinted indelibly on the minds of a senior group of American policy makers. Failure to oppose Adolf Hitler when the Wehrmacht moved into the Rhineland and across central Europe had proven to be the most egregious error in both the theory and the practice of American foreign policy. The lesson of the interwar period was that aggression had to be stamped out at its source. Otherwise like a forest fire it would spread across the international landscape, destroying the last trace of free and independent nations in its wake.

The Munich syndrome became the symbol of a failed approach to foreign policy. Compromises such as British prime minister Neville Chamberlain made with Hitler in 1938 when he forced Czechoslovakia to cede the Sudetenland to Nazi Germany were denounced by the architects of postwar American foreign policy. In Dean Rusk's words: "My generation of students was led down the path into the catastrophe of World War II, which could have been prevented. We came out of the war thinking that collective security was the key to the prevention of World War III." Moreover, it was collective security worldwide that was the goal. As Secretary Rusk acknowledged, "It was written strongly and plainly into Article 1 of the United Nations Charter, reinforced by the Rio Pact in this hemisphere, by NATO [North Atlantic Treaty Organization] across the Atlantic, and by certain treaties across the Pacific." The words of these treaties as conceived by their drafters reflect not a highly pragmatic and selective viewpoint. Rather, they are an expression of a universalist philosophy of "all for one and one for all." They revived the inspiring creed that had captured the moral imagination of Rusk's generation, harking back to Woodrow Wilson. "Never send to know for whom the bell tolls; it tolls for thee," penned the poet John Donne. To the biblical question "Am I my brother's keeper?," the response was "I am." Wartime experience and a political tradition that many Americans had momentarily embraced and then rejected when the Senate turned down membership of the United States in the League of Nations comprised a noble legacy that offered hope to the world. For many young Americans, however, and for some foreign policy analysts it was a fateful tradition that led inevitably to Vietnam.

Americans, at least in the twentieth century, have been slow to anger and often the last to enter the struggle. Whatever the strategic views of their leaders, the American people have fought wars as moral crusades. Once victory was won and virtue had triumphed, they laid down their arms, confident that peace had been restored. One reason limited wars are difficult for most Americans in contrast, for example, with the British and the French, whose struggles in colonial areas were sustained over long periods of time, is the difference in perspectives on war and peace. For Carl von Clausewitz and many Europeans, war is a continuation of politics or diplomacy by other means. As a nation's people pursue politics for certain political aims, wars are fought for strategic and territorial purposes.

The problem with the Vietnam War for many Americans was that neither moral nor political objectives were clearly defined. Secretary of State Rusk, who towers above many others responsible for the conduct of the war, including both the handful who defended it to the end and those who changed their stripes when defeat was in sight, acknowledged that he and his colleagues underestimated the tenacity and determination of the North Vietnamese, "who kept coming," and overestimated the patience and resolve of the American people. The two mistakes for which Rusk accepted responsibility, however, are symptoms and not causes. Underlying the symptoms are questions such as why our adversary kept coming and why the American people lost their resolve. Ironically, it had been leaders like Rusk who had warned fellow policy makers against being swallowed up in an endless war on the mainland of Asia against the vast forces of Asian nationalism. He had also cautioned his colleagues that the war must not become an American war. The North Vietnamese kept coming because they were fighting for nationalism and for what they imagined was their national survival. Pursuing the dictates of collective security, Americans were fighting for an abstract principle to which only a fraction of the American people were committed. The war against Hitler and a Japanese aggressor who brutally bombed Americans at Pearl Harbor had been a war for moral objectives as World War I had been a war to make the world safe for democracy. It was one thing for Americans to show resolve in such a struggle but another to expect them to fight in a far-off land in the name of collective security. Whatever patience existed with this view was bound to erode after nearly sixty thousand Americans were killed in almost a decade and a half of grim and grueling jungle warfare. More important, policy makers were never able to demonstrate convincingly to the American people that the defense of Southeast Asia was a vital interest. As a result, public and congressional reaction to reliance on armed force in Vietnam was half-hearted and less deeply rooted than in Grenada, Panama, or the Persian Gulf.

Secretary Rusk offered two reasons for the erosion of support for collective security. He explains: "First, new generations . . . arrived on the scene who did not experience and cannot remember the events of the postwar years, when we built the United Nations, the Marshall Plan, NATO, and the entire postwar structure of collective security. Like any new generation, they won't take answers automatically from an older generation." For anyone who has experienced the vacant and uncomprehending stares of a roomful of students when early postwar events are discussed, Secretary Rusk's explanation is credible, but if the polls can be trusted, scores of older Americans also lost faith in Vietnam. Rusk has a second explanation: "The American people have taken almost five hundred thousand casualties in dead and wounded since the end of World War II in support of collective security. . . . If collective security means fifty thousand American dead every ten years, and it is not even collective, maybe that is not a very good idea."[1] In Korea, Americans supplied 90 percent of the non-Korean forces and in Vietnam 80 percent of the non-Vietnamese forces. Rusk's two reasons are an important part of the story.

Yet two other reasons deserve mention, and the second may be more important than the first. First, the administration invoked the Southeast Asia Treaty Organization (SEATO) collective security treaty in justification of American involvement in Vietnam. If we failed to meet our responsibility under the treaty to defend South Vietnam, an independent nation threatened with aggression in Southeast Asia, the treaty for signatories and others would become a worthless scrap of paper. Trust in the United States and other instruments of collective security would evaporate.

The second reason goes to the heart of the problem. For the thousands, even millions, of Americans who turned against their policy makers, Vietnam became a moral issue. War for most Americans has always been an overt

1. Dean Rusk, *As I Saw It*, ed. Daniel S. Papp (New York, 1990), 503.

moral issue, except perhaps in struggles to preserve and defend the Union. The morality or lack of it of the Vietnam War swept over the consciousness of millions graphically night after night as television brought the conflict into family living rooms. The public's concern multiplied as a whole generation revolted against the culture and folkways of their parents and grandparents. Opposition to Vietnam and what has been called the countercultural movement were mutually reinforcing, and the rallying cry for young people became a call for ethics in American society and Vietnam.

If Vietnam was a moral issue, so was Watergate, which led to the first resignation of an American president. Europeans asked why there was such a fuss. Weren't all governments corrupt at some time or another? Nixon, throughout his long and often fruitful political career, had polarized Americans. The end came for him not only because of the break-in at Democratic party headquarters by Nixon campaign operatives in search of damaging information concerning Nixon's political adversaries but because of his own protracted denial of any knowledge of the act. When he lied to his own closest allies, Barry Goldwater and Hugh Scott in the Senate, the jig was up. Moreover, Watergate and Vietnam simply confirmed for young Americans in revolt that something was fundamentally wrong morally and politically with the system. The more militant among them rejected the urging of moderates "to give the system one more chance."

Not young people alone but the American electorate had earlier grown concerned about politics and campaign abuses, and this concern was to persist into the 1990s. Groups such as Common Cause called for electoral reforms especially affecting the problem of money in politics. Even earlier the target of reform was the committee system in Congress, with chairmanships long having been the monopoly of southern congressmen, who enjoyed the longest seniority and who blocked civil rights legislation. However, congressmen were not only objects of reform. They also spearheaded efforts to police themselves and their party colleagues as in ABSCAM, which led to the expulsion and imprisonment of a senator from New Jersey. Congress, through the Senate committee chaired by Senator Frank Church, undertook oversight of the Central Intelligence Agency (CIA). All these efforts were part of a renewed effort to restore morality to government.

Looking back, we can see that reformist actions spread across the whole of American society, reflecting an intensity of concern not fully comprehended by everyone at the time. Business practices involving mergers, junk bonds, and questionable influences on leading congressmen came under increased public scrutiny, culminating later in the fateful savings and loan crisis. Once again, as with Vietnam and Watergate, the media's reports aroused a public that might otherwise have remained somnolent. Investigative reporters were tireless, if ruthless, in pursuing those suspected of moral dereliction. Actions and events in the name of morality were being initiated on a broad front from antiabortion or anticommunist campaigns to crusades for civil and human rights and equal opportunity. Issues that had been considered the province of individual Americans were politicized. Single-issue groups that judged politicians by but one litmus test sprang up overnight, and the political process became more and more divisive as the early postwar consensus on questions such as foreign policy dissolved. Few were conscious at the time of the number of events that involved profound moral concerns. Taken together, these events sensitized a growing number of Americans to leading moral issues, however defined.

Not events alone, however, but certain underlying trends and tendencies heightened moral consciousness. The American electorate seemingly moves from periods of political reform to years of political consolidation, from an era of progress to a pause, and from change to retrenchment and back. Thus, the public supported the New Deal and the Fair Deal with Franklin D. Roosevelt and Harry S Truman but then turned to eight years of consolidation under Dwight D. Eisenhower. Following Eisenhower, the pendulum brought back the FDR cycle with Kennedy and Lyndon B. Johnson. In the 1970s, it returned to conservatism with Nixon and Gerald R. Ford but followed them with Jimmy Carter, who on civil and human rights in particular was liberal. With Reagan, a conservative trend was reintroduced, followed by the more moderate conservatism of George Bush. That two contending views of American politics have competed for dominance in American political thinking has prompted the raising of moral issues. That one trend of political thinking has been up and another down at any given time in American history assures the presence of what Walter Lippmann called "the indispensable opposition," each challenging the moral and political assumptions of the other. Hence the cyclical nature of American politics has contributed to moral discourse.

Further, the lessening of the most intense phase of ideological competition with communism occurring in the 1950s and the 1970s and again in the mid-to-late 1980s and 1990s had the effect of promoting moral reasoning. After each great political upheaval throughout history, years in which leaders sought to be more discriminating in moral reflections have followed ones of intense ideological competition. Thus, the writings *following* the Crusades, the French Revolution, the Russian Revolution, and the American Revolution display an increase in moral and political discrimination, for the last most notably in the writings of the authors of the *Federalist Papers*. A similar pattern is evident in the history of the Cold War. When Americans assumed that answers to every political problem could be found in the book of anticommunism, their zeal for thinking based on moral and political discrimination diminished. They were wholly dependent on the axioms of a narrow, self-contained ideological system. The periods of the most intense ideological competition in Soviet-American relations, including from 1946 to 1955 and from 1980 to 1985, were hardly years of great intellectual flowering in political ethics. The literature tended to be declaratory and rhetorical, whether for confronting the enemy or justifying particular foreign policies, such as containment or the Reagan Doctrine or the transforming of political or military institutions. However successful policies such as the Truman Doctrine or the Marshall Plan have been, we remember them as concrete actions and reactions or responses to crises, not as timeless statements or profound analyses of American values.

A notable dissenter to the view that ideological competition is not productive of moral reasoning is Senator Daniel Patrick Moynihan of New York. In opposition to the view that moral reasoning is more likely in postrevolutionary periods, Moynihan has argued that ideological confrontation becomes increasingly evident in a time of detente. When military and political tensions abate, nations, especially in their international relationships, are more likely to turn to vigorous ideological competition. However, Moynihan confuses ideological and political debates with moral and political reasoning. We remember Thomas Paine not for the profundity of *Common Sense* but for its call to action. By contrast, *Federalist* 51 remains a classic statement on the moral foundations of the idea of the separation of powers and checks and balances. The senator's dissent is an expression and rationalization of his own highly personal approach to foreign policy rather than an enduring statement of political truth.

A third development in American politics ironically enough has generated a modicum of normative thinking despite contributing to the breakdown of political consensus. The rise of special interest groups in American politics has enlivened political debate on issues such as abortion, gun control, and the environment. At the same time, it has divided the electorate in potentially damaging ways inasmuch as these issues have become litmus tests for the qualification or lack thereof of candidates for political office. Single-interest groups have caused the fragmentation of political coalitions within and between the major political parties. That some of the groups engaged in single-interest politics had previously been isolated from the political process led to a broadening of concerns of the electorate. Their participation also required them to make more explicit the ethical assumptions that had led them to conclusions on abortion, protecting wilderness areas, aid to distressed cities or industries, the Equal Rights Amendment (ERA), and gun control. Although they remained isolated from the mainstream of political thought in American politics, they provoked others to think more seriously about the ethical implications of their particular single issue. Their approach fell short of moral reasoning, which weighs ethical alternatives and hierarchies of values, but they did sensitize others to particular moral concerns linked to the special interest with which they were seized.

Fourth, another trend or tendency much debated in American society arises from the crisis in Western society. Philosophers of history beginning with Oswald Spengler and Arnold J. Toynbee have written about the decline of Western civilization. Their views have generated continuing debate among historians who have either embraced or criticized philosophical and historical views of decline. Setting aside for history's judgment the final resolution of the debate, these prophecies have revived discussion of the ancient proposition that the owl of Minerva is most often heard not at the beginning but at the end of civilization. Moral and political discourse is most intense in a time of troubles. A society in crisis generates the most searching examination of moral issues. The deepest reflection may foreshadow either the rise of a new civilization or the decay of an old one. A civilization or a great religion may be a carrier of the values of one civilization across historical distance to another. In President Carter's fateful "malaise speech," he offered a modest version of the idea of decline, which, however, led to much political debate over the causes, sources, and substance of the malaise. There followed the later discussions of decline by the historian Paul Kennedy. The focus in the 1970s was moral decline, whereas in the 1980s it was industrial and strategic decline due to civilizations outreaching themselves. We shall return to these issues in the concluding section.

Individual personalities and public figures contributed to a moral reawakening in significant ways. Jimmy Carter inspired wide public interest in human rights and in some of the themes that Woodrow Wilson had introduced into American politics. Although critics took exception to the moralistic strain in Carter's approach to politics, few would question his influence in reviving moral concerns in politics. Other leaders inspired attention to moral issues with other dimensions. Despite his role in Watergate, Nixon called attention to a neglected group in American politics, "the silent majority," who have rights. Moynihan spoke in the United Nations for the United States as "the party of freedom." Reagan appealed to simple values and truths that helped restore American self-respect, however they may or may not have influenced policy. Earlier John Kennedy had caught the imagination of "a new generation of Americans." Taken together, these leaders and others, including Martin Luther King, Jr., Robert Kennedy, and Lyndon Johnson, in areas such as civil rights and education enhanced moral sensitivity across the land.

The change that went beyond personalities and leaders was the change resulting from a sweeping cultural revolution in the 1960s and 1970s. It stemmed from the breakdown of old values and the accompanying attempts to institute new values or restore older ones. An example of the latter was the revolt against modernity that has continued into the 1980s and has found political expression in movements such as neoconservatism. The argument against modernity centered on the charge that it had wrought destruction of ancient traditions and truths that were an integral part of the classics. In the 1960s, University of Chicago professor and political philosopher Leo Strauss called for the restoration of political philosophy. Nearly a quarter-century later, one of his students, Allan Bloom, renewed his mentor's appeal in a best-selling book, *The Closing of the American Mind*. As Strauss had urged a search for the true meaning of the early texts in political philosophy and their reinterpretation, Bloom warned that education had abandoned the study of the enduring truths of the classics in exchange for catering to the frivolous and transient interests of each individual student. Whereas Strauss and Bloom provided philosophical underpinnings for neoconservatism in politics, humanist and literary scholar E. D. Hirsch, who is a dedicated political liberal, reinforced Bloom's appeals by calling for a return to the classics in the struggle for cultural literacy in American education.

More far-reaching perhaps than the Straussian criticism of modernity were popular responses to the crises in values and in culture and to the attacks on the regnant values controlling particular institutions. The revolution that surrounded the countercultural movement of the 1960s is even now difficult to assess and explain. Neither critics nor defenders were explicit about the basis for change or the basis for preserving the traditions of the past. Change in the 1960s apparently was an outgrowth of broad social, intellectual, demographic, and economic forces in society at large. It involved a profound transformation in the relationship between generations and social groups. Today's analysts ask how far-reaching such change could have been since the movement dissolved and disappeared as suddenly as it appeared. Yuppies replaced revolutionaries and protagonists of change seemingly overnight. They quickly accepted the dominant mores and standards of the selfsame society whose social and cultural patterns they had criticized so vehemently only a short time before.

Scholars who have dealt with social and cultural change, such as the late Margaret Mead, defended through a lifetime of research and study the proposition that when change is gradual and not too far-reaching, the new social groups end by becoming the carriers of old values from one society to the next. Immigrants who migrated to this country bringing with them alien languages and diverse cultures tended to accommodate their former culture to the new one. They prided themselves on being Americans. While struggling to maintain their native languages and cultures, they embraced the language and culture of their newly adopted country. They did so despite the inevitable competition between a younger and an older generation, the former being more predisposed and positioned for change. The respected scientist and university leader Harrison Brown illustrated such continuity by saying he was closer to his immigrant father, who spoke no English, than he was to his son, with whom he shared a common language. When asked how this could have happened, analysts point to a complex of factors, including the isolating in the son's generation of a critical mass of the population of significant size and coherence, the intensity of the new beliefs, the harsh criticism of the values practiced as contrasted with the values professed by the parent's generation, and the worldwide nature of cultural and political changes.

Writers seeking to assess the extent and character of such changes note first the size of the group proposing the overthrow of old values. History echoes to the revolt of generations in conflict with one another; there is nothing new about generational differences. The dynamic of the countercultural movement in the 1960s, however, was a product of numbers. Universities that experienced the greatest turbulence and the most violent uprisings, such as Cornell, were institutions where the groups in revolt were both more numerous and less integrated into any of the older traditional groups, including rising minorities who were third- and fourth-year students. Moreover, the revolutionary groups displayed clearly visible cultural identities, including common life-styles, art, dress, music, and hairstyles.

Thus, the revolution of the 1960s drew its strength from the appearance as well as the reality of countercultural unity and goals. Not only unity but the intensity of attitudes and beliefs gave the movement its impetus and character. That intensity was reflected in attitudes toward the traditional family from children of upper- and middle-class families who were reacting to the gap between the values professed and those practiced by their parents. The ability of young people to pursue lives of protest and cultural isolation also resulted from postwar affluence in the United States. Even with our having enumerated the factors that led to social change, it continues to be difficult, if not impossible, to put them all together to account for the extent of the revolution in values.

Moreover, the revolt was as much international as it was national. Institutions that were confined within national boundaries felt the impact of change, but so did regional and worldwide institutions. Western civilization was challenged by a new nationalism and by non-Western cultures. The specter of mutual annihilation challenged the historic role of force as a credible and legitimate instrument of international order and stability. Terrorism and continuing intervention in the affairs of other states threatened long-established principles of international law and precepts of national security and domestic jurisdiction. The possibility and the very prerequisites of national security came under review. Not only the conflict between democracy and communism but vast differences between rich and poor countries led to a breakdown in moral and political consensus, affecting stability in the international community.

Global change had begun with an emerging disillusionment with certain international goals and purposes that dominated international relations thinking at the turn of the century. The arbitration movement, which eventuated in the Hague Peace Conferences of 1899 and 1907, offered hope of new concepts and norms for the resolution of international disputes. Secretary of State William Jennings Bryan was so inspired by the new approach that he left the administration of the normal business of the Department of State to others. Wilson's Fourteen Points and his vision of a League to Enforce Peace carried the introduction of new standards in international relations even further. With Wilson's defeat, the intellectual community in the interwar years took upon itself the responsibility of sustaining his ideas. Every major chair in the field in all the leading universities was defined as requiring both the promotion of the study and the outright reform of international relations. The occupants of these chairs, primarily international lawyers, sought to join the principles of international law with those of international organization. Together, reformers were determined to prevent the United States from ever again turning its back on international cooperation. Participants in the Carnegie Endowment Conferences on International Law and Related Subjects joined proponents of international organization in offering the world a new and better form of international relations than traditional international politics.

The common fate of each of these reform movements was failure, at least in terms of any immediate change. Each fell short of realizing its goals. Disillusionment set in as reformers became victims of a crusade that suffered from euphoria and overselling. Hitler and World War II shattered the belief that a peaceful and harmonious world order was within reach. In the 1970s, a similar fate befell the foreign policy of detente, highly publicized by President Nixon and Secretary of State Henry Kissinger. Excessive advertising of the successes of accommodation and normalization invited a reaction that consultants such as Hans Morgenthau had warned Kissinger was likely to occur. (Scholarly consultants seem to be recruited more often to silence their criticism than to gain their objective counsel.) History demonstrates that policy makers must walk a fine line between the legitimate defense of their policies and extravagant public relations campaigns. Overselling in the age of mass media has become a social disease in American society, and it is not surprising in a consumer culture that public policy is as subject to being overturned as are products for which too much is promised.

The lesson of history that emerges from the succession of examples enumerated above is that established norms and values tend to break down in every era of revolutionary change. With their breakdown, policy makers and the citizenry make their choices in a void as new standards and values that are operationally relevant are slow in taking the place of old values. A profound change in leadership accompanies the rise of mass societies replacing long-established organic societies. Whereas the older societies have had at least a small group of well-accepted leaders who speak for them, the question of leadership in revolutionary societies is continuously in flux. An example of the competition that goes on is the succession taking place in the Soviet Union or in Eastern Europe.

Change is evident at every level in every community undergoing change here and abroad. New York City was once ruled by a select fifty families, whose values became the values of the city. Today scores of ethnic and minority groups struggle for control, and no one can any longer identify the fifty or some other number of dominant families. Congress was once ruled by clear majorities with the support of minority leaders, both of whom were able to deliver large blocs of votes as policy interests required. In the 1950s, congressmen like Speaker of the House Sam Rayburn of Texas and the majority leader in the Senate, Lyndon Johnson, controlled the Congress. The small group of senators and congressmen who at the end of a day's congressional business joined one another for drinks in Rayburn's office called themselves the "Board of Education." (Vice-President Truman was relaxing with such a group late one afternoon when he received word Roosevelt had died.) Committee chairmen in both the House and the Senate were leaders with long seniority and often came from southern states. Their power in committees such as the Rules Committee enabled them to keep legislation bottled up for years on end. By the 1970s, a new Congress with some 120 subcommittees transferred influence and public visibility to almost any member who aggressively sought it. The day of the Board of Education had passed.

Internationally, similar changes were taking place. The leaders of the Grand Alliance in World War II were Roosevelt, Churchill, and Joseph Stalin. In 1955, the Bandung Conference found a wholly new group of leaders of nonaligned countries moving onto the international scene. Gamal Abdel Nasser of Egypt, Tito of Yugoslavia, Jawaharlal Nehru of India, and Sukarno of Indonesia were a new breed of revolutionary figures who sought to avoid too close an identification with either the Soviet Union or the United States. Within the United Nations, new elites began appearing, brought together for a time in the so-called Committee of 77, representing essentially Arab and African countries. In the early years of the United Nations, the United States had been able to dominate the proceedings through support from the Latin American and European states. The change begun in Bandung reached its climax in the Reagan era, when United Nations Ambassador Jeane Kirkpatrick sometimes found herself voting alone.

It became clear that the most effective leaders in the United Nations from countries that had lost their dominance were those still able to steer a quiet, steady course in a radically new and changing political and social environment. British diplomats, westernized Asian leaders, and Latin American spokesmen such as Alberto Lleras Camargo of Colombia accommodated to a changed set of circumstances and sought points of convergence between their values and those of the Third World countries. They discovered how to be at least marginally effective in what was called the "New United Nations." Without rejecting norms from the past, they sought to adapt them to a new international environment. They were able to work with United Nations secretaries-general, whose succession symbolized the shift in power within the United Nations: Trygve Lie, Dag Hammarskjöld, U Thant, Kurt Waldheim, Javier Pérez de Cuéllar, and Boutros Ghali. By the time the Swedish leader Hammarskjöld had come to power, it had become clear that the Americans and the Europeans could no longer mold international institutions to suit their purposes. Indeed, Hammarskjöld spoke of exercising leadership in the international community as being like guiding a vehicle with no more than the light touch of a finger on the wheel. Leadership required not forcing history but trying to keep it on course whenever possible. The New United Nations, however, did not transform the nature of politics among nations. Influence and power were not eliminated; they had merely been redistributed.

If everything examined in this discussion of the renewal and reinterpretation of values points in the direction of the enduring, though changing, character of moral purpose, the question remaining concerns society's retrogression in the realm of other values. Can we identify trends in our societies that point to the outright repudiation of values? Are we seeing the reversal of moral standards? Every newspaper provides evidence that makes this a serious and relevant question. A woman jogger is brutally attacked, raped, and left for dead in Central Park in New York City. Her alleged assailants describe her as an "it," not a person; they view their victims as the "other," not human beings. They consider violence as "wilding" and "having fun." Arsonists set fire to schools and churches, including the very ones meant to guide and direct their lives along more hopeful and constructive channels. Protesters destroy those who try to help them. Blacks rob and kill other blacks, and blacks and whites drive one another into the path of death-dealing traffic on highways and subway tracks. Even in quiet university towns, crowds of two hundred or more gather after midnight for acts of violence and vandalism. Drugs have become the scourge of the cities, and drug dealers accumulate massive profits while wreaking havoc on society and officials standing in their way.

In the 1960s, George F. Kennan in describing the youth revolution criticized it primarily on two counts. First, it lacked a sense of history; human experience was seen in isolation from what had gone before or might come after it. Second, the countercultural philosophy, Kennan argued, was essentially nihilistic. It saw society as a great void of nothingness. Individuals were tossed about like atoms careering against one another without rhyme or reason. If life had any meaning, nihilists asserted, it was beyond human capacity to comprehend such meaning.

Somehow, for many Americans life in the 1990s has become as meaningless as the nihilists portrayed it in the 1960s. Especially the poor and the oppressed approach life with a sense of quiet desperation. The underclass exists lacking purpose and meaning. When my own life's story is empty and purposeless, I cannot impute meaning and purpose to the lives of others. If I look upon another human being as "the other," that judgment reflects a void in my quest for my own identity. Nihilism begins with man's view of himself. Inevitably, it broadens out to encompass man's view of others. A void in the one makes likely a wasteland of respect and concern for others.

Thus if regression or reversion is an apt description of the decline in values that leads to increased violence and lawlessness in society, the root cause goes back to loss of faith in oneself. And such loss of faith in turn is a product of the decline in conditions that promote self-respect. All levels of the human community are in jeopardy. From broken families to a war-torn world, reflected in the lives of the homeless and the occupants of overcrowded jails, the human drama is played out in the cold emptiness of vacant scenes that yield only despair. Life is passing through turnstiles into unpeopled subway tunnels that are damp and deserted.

However, this dark chapter is only one aspect of the human drama. Fortunately, for most it remains part of a wider story. The renewal, rediscovery, and revival of values is equally part of the human drama. Renewal is the road to overcoming nihilism and social decay. Potentially it can bring hope, whereas nihilism brings only despair. The present state of the nation is the scene of a struggle between renewal and retrogression in fundamental values, with the outcome still in doubt. In a certain sense, such struggles have been part of the nation's history from the beginning. The United States is a nation whose progress and strength have been assured through continuing change and revolution. If history is any guide, the republic may again transcend threats to its standards and its very existence through the effects of its unfinished revolution.

3

Four Decades of International Relations Theorizing

If we look back on the past four decades of international studies, what is most striking is the seemingly endless repetition of intellectual and philosophical debates rooted in profound differences in methodological approaches and views of man and politics. Theories and schools of thought come and go, but underlying attitudes and perspectives persist. This scenario is true of the origins of theorizing, the forms and types of theorizing, and the consensus or lack of it regarding the uses and limitations of such theories.

It should come as no surprise that the discussion of theory is always influenced by the spirit of the times. The national mood and popular psychology touch international relations thinking no less in international than in domestic politics. The years from 1945 to 1970 witnessed the beginning of the end of the age of American omnipotence. Following World War II, the United States had been catapulted into a position of world leadership that it neither sought nor fully comprehended. One would have difficulty proving that many of its leaders believed the United States should rule the world. Only a small group of influential publicists and unreconstructed policy makers spoke openly and consistently of an American century or of our ability to police the world. Empires, however, are born "in a fit of absentmindedness," and it was the objective world situation that invited the illusion of omnipotence. We were, after all, one of two great powers to emerge following World War II. The United States saw itself not only as a world power but also as the trustee of a political creed that had drawn the world's peoples to our shores from nations everywhere as if by a magnet. To test this proposition, one has only to reflect on the number of constitutions rather slavishly modeled after the American Constitution, some drafted before World War II. Yet we and others were to discover that the social and political circumstances that gave birth to our system were lacking in other societies, for example, the Weimar Republic and some Latin American states.

Our sense of omnipotence had other roots. Postwar America was an island of plenty in a sea of great poverty. Given the puritan ethic and the deeply ingrained view that outward success was a reflection of inner virtue, it was natural to conclude that American power stemmed from American virtue. Otherwise how could one explain why a nation that had eschewed entangling alliances and denied itself the trappings of power had become the world's greatest empire, capable of influencing nations anywhere in the world?

Another "grand illusion" was the belief that new international institutions would transform overnight the nature of international politics. Many saw the United Nations as essentially the United States writ large. The preamble of its charter and Articles 1 and 2 expressed for the world a faith in due process, in the consent of the governed, and in the rights of man, derived from the United States' founding constitutional documents and the Declaration of Independence. Secretary of State Cordell Hull, on his return from the Moscow Conference, announced to the world that the United Nations was putting an end to power politics and war among nation-states. But early in its history the United Nations found, as our friends in Britain had prophesied, that it was destined to play a more limited and modest role, serving as a forum for harmonizing the differences among contending nation-states. Its power to make laws and to bring about peaceful change was far less than that of national legislatures.

Another illusion had roots in a too simple view of the nature of the conflict. Given the postwar struggle for power between the Soviet Union and the United States, it is not surprising that Americans viewed the conflict as quite simply a struggle between political ideologies and systems, or between communism and freedom. Forgotten was the fact that the United States and the Soviet Union had coexisted for decades not because communism had changed its spots but because in the years more immediately before World War II, communism was less explicitly and actively linked with historic Russian imperialism. By the end of the war communism's position at home was more secure, and its leaders could turn their attention to external problems. Following World War II, the dynamics of world communism and the tendency of the Soviet Union to fill power vacuums wherever they existed lent credence to the dogma of anticommunism as a basis of policy formulation. The USSR occupied the heart of Europe, dominated its East European satellites, held sway over the Communist parties in France and Italy, and gained control of substantial new territories. More specifically, the Truman Doctrine, defined as the keystone of American foreign policy, was based on the proposition that the underlying purpose of American policy was resistance to the spread of communism everywhere in the world. Slowly and almost imperceptibly, thinking changed and influential policy makers came to recognize that Russian imperialism and expansionism were the threat, not communism alone.

The final illusion was the belief that peoples everywhere, if given a chance, would choose the idea of freedom in economics and in politics and the structure of parliamentary democracy. This optimistic view ignored the residual impact of traditional values and the persistent influence of deep-seated cultural factors on the shape of political systems. A neutralist Third World opposed both East and West, preferring to pattern itself after indigenous models rather than imported ones. Furthermore, the hesitation, ambivalence, and uncertainty of the United States in coming to their aid led the Third World nations to think more about self-help and self-defense and less about indissoluble links with one or the other of the great powers.

These factors combined to influence approaches to international relations theory and the successive stages through which such theory has developed. They created a climate of thought that led to a changing emphasis meriting review and analysis.

The Origins of Theory

There are three major approaches that one can identify in the study of international relations in the Western world and, in particular, in the United States. If one excludes the discipline of history, then the legal approach is undoubtedly the first great effort to come to terms with both problems of American government and problems of international affairs. This point of view dominated the early stages of thinking on foreign relations in virtually every developed country, and its sources of influence are obvious. As we compared national and international life, the missing elements on the international scene appeared to be law and government. The implicit theory of most international lawyers, who moved self-confidently to fill the void, was that only by substituting law for lawlessness could the unhappy circumstances of international life be rectified.

Lawyers are not hesitant to serve as innovators by stepping in when others are ignoring current problems. In the study of American government, the first comprehensive framework for the study of current problems was a legal framework. In the 1930s, this viewpoint became dominant in the foreign relations field. In appearing to cope with the rather alien, ambiguous, and disillusioning sector of international politics, this approach appealed to the moral impulses of the American people. Lawyers were part of a long and respected heritage (the subject of a brilliant analysis prepared for discussion by the British Committee on the Theory of International Politics by the late professor Martin Wight of Sussex University), dating back to international lawyers in the seventeenth and eighteenth centuries, who contributed to a more ordered and rational world outlook.

In revisiting the legal approach, one is struck by its prevailing oversimplification in at least three broad phases of its development. In the 1930s, its main thrust was in outlawing and legislating against war. The Pact of Paris, or the Kellogg-Briand Pact, and the instructions of Andrew Carnegie to the trustees of the Carnegie Endowment, suggesting they first address themselves to eliminating the problem of war and when they had done away with it turn to the next most urgent problem, are representative of this way of thinking. Beginning in the 1930s and 1940s, the study of law merged with the study of organization and, more specifically, the League of Nations. Scholars with extraordinary talents turned to international organization. A sense of guilt coupled with a liberal humanitarian outlook led observers to ask why the United States had failed to throw its weight behind the new international institution.

Since World War II, international law studies have shifted from an interest in broad theoretical problems to increasing concern with ad hoc problems and issues, though there are exceptions in the writings of such men as Judge Charles de Visscher and Julius Stone. A growing interest has been manifested in what law could contribute to the resolution of the daily problems of industry, finance, and agriculture as they span national boundaries. The acquisition, use, and disposal of property and its legal aspects became a concern of the law. Specific problems have been addressed, such as why, when no guarantees against risk were offered for private investment, investment nevertheless flowed to certain countries and why, in other instances, despite explicit guarantees, investment failed to materialize. These and similar issues have become the focus for many who study and deal with international legal issues across traditional disciplinary lines.

Since World War II, the multiplication of international organizations and institutions, each with its own legal personality, has led to the creation of a new branch of international law. More recently, human rights has constituted the focus for research at Columbia University and the University of Maryland and for individual scholars and policy makers emphasizing the status of the individual as a subject in international law.

The great contribution of the legal approach results from its quest for a constitutive international order and its effect on a more rational way of thinking about international problems. It also serves to carry men beyond the status quo through anticipating and regulating those disturbing tensions that lead to war.

Yet international law has failed in its quest for a theory, partly because its own theoretical presuppositions have so little relevance to many of the more urgent and tragic problems of conflict in international society as a whole. Where it succeeded, it has tended to deal with areas peripheral to war and peace, for example, the Universal Postal Union, but it has failed almost completely in its many attempts to regulate and control conflict and armaments. It has paid too little attention to the inescapable relation between political objectives or national interests and the willingness of nations to abide by principles and rules of law. The non-Western world views law as a Western product, leading to its rejection by nations emerging from dependency allegedly maintained by legal principles.

Another major approach, with origins in the post–World War II period, has been the political approach. Here one finds students of international relations searching for a new point of focus and finding it in the existing discipline of political science. The political approach is an attempt to discover a core, or center, for the subjects that make up the totality of international relations. International politics is an effort to order and relate the elements of international society to some overarching set of concepts, problems, and questions.

In terms of field theory, what questions of primary concern and interest does one ask as one considers the varied and changing play of forces within a given system? This basic issue must be faced in any attempt to construct a theory. The questions, though theoretically unlimited, must reflect the urgent needs and problems of the day. The overall interest in the political approach stems in part from the orientation of students after World War II. The postwar generation, schooled in a certain way of looking at international problems, experienced the pathos of World War II and learned that earlier approaches to the world were insufficient. Treatises by Professors Morgenthau, William T. R. Fox, and Frederick S. Schuman had as their objective the regrouping and clarification of those aspects of international studies that they saw as most relevant to contemporary needs and as requiring more rational and systematic treatment. They placed stress on the analysis of the relationships between power and policy, diplomacy and military strength, and statecraft and popular support for policy. A whole clustering of issues not commonly dealt with by those with primarily legal concerns prompted attention to political and sociological problems and led to the political approach.

The stages in the development of this approach are readily identified. The initial stage was one in which survey courses laid the groundwork for subsequent works and in which the great enabling documents were issued in the form of original and creative texts. For this field, as for the study of economics, where the writings of Paul Samuelson and others were formative, seminal texts had the effect of ordering the data and reorienting the thinking of serious students and observers, including some not fully aware of the shift in their viewpoint (Quincy Wright is one example).

A second phase came with the merging of the interests of a wide variety of people representing a variety of disciplines and approaches. It involved a marriage of interests between political philosophers, theorists, policy planners, columnists, and observers, who addressed themselves to the basic issues of international politics. It was an outgrowth of the work of theorists and practitioners who came together quite unexpectedly in the postwar years.

A subsequent development, less amenable to simple generalization, was the growth and proliferation of specialized and fractionalized interests within this wider approach. Research institutes sprang up to deal with military problems, civil-military relations and defense policy, behavioral studies of the role

of the actor and decision maker in foreign policy, traditions of political philosophy and their implications for theory, and game theory and conflict resolution at centers such as Harvard University and the University of Michigan.

There are now signs that scholars and practitioners are turning to the
application of general principles to specific emergent problems in foreign relations, to the analysis of modes and forms of diplomacy, and to the testing
and use of overall theories. This way of looking at foreign relations can be a
means of injecting greater realism into foreign policy analysis and of helping
to understand the dilemmas and problems of those who daily work at the
tangled skein of foreign relations. Ironically, it has also served to knit contemporary foreign relations studies more closely to the past, because if one assumes that the world is not utterly new, one then perceives the value of a
study, say, of diplomatists such as Viscount Castlereagh or George Canning
grappling with recurrent problems in an earlier historical era.

As an organized body of knowledge has evolved from interest in international politics, this focus has served to reunite policy makers and scholars.
However, there remain certain troublesome problems inherent in this approach. Barely hidden from view is the inescapable risk of making norms out
of past and current practice. It is tempting to argue that what is must always be.

Beyond this temptation, the difficulty presents itself of adapting any
general theory to researchable problems or of giving content to broad categories that set boundaries to the field but do not necessarily help in asking
specific, crucial questions at the center of policy making. Economists may
have had an easier time, for example, working within a cost-benefit frame of
thought or in using the idea of economizing as a theoretical framework to
move to the consideration of data strikingly amenable to statistical and quantitative analysis. Therefore, they and their "trade" have become more "operationally relevant" to their consumers. The data of international relations
may be too intractable for this kind of theorizing.

A third overall approach to international relations is through the study
of international institutions. Here the data include the multiplication of international institutions and the evolution of more regularized patterns of discussion in international affairs, beginning with the Hague Peace Conferences, if
not with the Congress of Vienna. The rise of representative national governments and their preference for the familiar institutions and processes of do-

mestic governments have spurred the scholar and citizen alike to support this approach. The impact of the United Nations idea, coupled with the desire of new nations to be numbered among those who participate in the community of nations, has given additional impetus and force to this perspective. For the great powers, it has provided opportunities for marshaling support. For the smaller states, there is evidence that the canceling out of disparities of power and influence is more likely within than outside an international institution.

The institutional approach has moved from the 1920s and 1930s, when scholars were heavily preoccupied with building their own models of an ideal international community, to a changing emphasis on institutional description and analysis. In the 1930s, it involved assessing the role of the League of Nations Secretariat, the changing concept of the office of the secretary-general, the unique structure of the International Labour Organization (ILO), and similar questions.

Later, in the late 1930s and 1940s and 1950s, political science entered the field more aggressively with studies of the relation between foreign policy and international organization by Arnold Wolfers, Morgenthau, Walter Schiffer, and Rupert Emerson. These inquiries dealt some with the structure and functioning of institutions but went on to relate them to the great forces and political movements that influenced states within and outside the organization.

In the 1950s and 1960s, growing attention was directed to the techniques and methods of parliamentary and multilateral diplomacy. These investigations sought to impose on the study of international institutions some of the time-honored concepts and questions with which scholars of international politics have for decades been concerned but to do so within an institutional framework.

A companion interest was the determined search for wider theoretical formulations of the principles of international organization. This search involved efforts to impose some kind of orderly framework on the study of international organization. In the same general category are studies that call attention to the relation between responsibility and representation within international bodies. It has been estimated that, at most, 10 to 20 percent of the positions taken on issues and resolutions in the United Nations are put forward on the basis of instructions to delegates by home governments. For some of the new nations, the size of their delegations to the United Nations exceeds the number of people in the foreign ministries that they serve. Thus the uninstructed are uninstructed because there is no one left to instruct them. Moreover, many of these delegates have had no particular experience or training in foreign affairs. Therefore, conventional concepts of responsibility for policy within an international body become increasingly complex and even meaningless.

The contribution of the institutional approach has been to focus on a very vital and significant trend. It has inspired reflection on evolutionary developments in world institutions. It has provided rough guidelines for practitioners and offered clues on the relations between continuity and change. The Trusteeship Council and other bodies in the United Nations have often mirrored and sometimes augmented the great social revolutionary movements in Africa and Asia. In this respect, what was happening in the United Nations has kept scholarship riveted on an important but otherwise neglected problem.

However, as with other approaches, this outlook has bred its own problems. A too passionate dedication to the defense of the subject has sometimes misled and confused the scholar. The very proliferation of study material has made research difficult. The tendency to concentrate on organizational structures rather than on political realities and groupings inside and outside the organization has forced discussion into sterile and formalistic molds. Finally, the lack of a clear and accepted point of focus contained in an ordering theory has limited the enduring value of research and writing.

In more recent times, the institutional emphasis has shifted to nonstate actors within the international system. Multinational corporations dwarf small- and even medium-sized states in power and influence. Labor unions, church groups, foundations, and scientific bodies span national boundaries. On numerous specific issues such organizations may weigh in and tip the scales where decisions affecting their interests are involved. With the communications and transportation revolutions, their impact may be as great as or even greater than the influence of nation-states. Theorists postulate that economic unities in the world draw international business and philanthropic bodies into international relations in an interdependent world.

What one can say as one surveys these varied approaches is that implicit theories underlie almost every discussion of international relations. In order of concern with theory, the political approach ranks first, partly because it has been the most self-conscious about its interest. The legal and institutional approaches follow in that order. Interdependence theories bring together economic and political perspectives. This ranking may be debated, especially by some of the emerging theorists of international institutions, but the evidence of their importance over time is reasonably conclusive.

The Philosophy of International Relations

Within the context of emerging theories of international relations, we can ask the further question of what place a philosophical approach to the subject should have. In the 1950s and 1960s, a score of political thinkers in the United States and Britain contributed in rather significant ways to international theory. Prominent among them was Hans J. Morgenthau, whose graduate seminar on the philosophy of international relations at the University of Chicago had a lasting effect on his students. Although the course never led to a separate publication, Morgenthau often suggested that a volume introducing the major thinkers whose work could be called philosophical was needed. He had in mind especially theorists such as Niebuhr, Lippmann and Louis J. Halle, Jr., whom he cited as the most important influences on contemporary thinking.

With Morgenthau's encouragement, I prepared the text *Masters of International Thought*, published by the Louisiana State University Press in 1980, with what I hoped were concise and coherent summations of the philosophies of eighteen significant writers, taking the form of personal and intellectual profiles. What distinguished the eighteen master thinkers from many other students of international relations was the breadth and generality of their thought. Almost without exception, they sought to link the thinking in contemporary international relations with traditional political theory. Thus Plato and Aristotle, Augustine and Aquinas, Machiavelli and Hobbes, and Adam Smith and Hugo Grotius provided foundations for contemporary thinkers about man, politics, and society. Because the core problems in the philosophy of international relations concerned power and morality, authority and order, and justice and equality, it was not surprising that classical political philosophers were invoked. Although not every master thinker linked his thought as closely with earlier philosophers as Niebuhr did with Augustine or Father John Courtney Murray with Aquinas, the recourse to the classics was a singular characteristic of virtually every one of the eighteen thinkers. For this reason their work can appropriately be designated as the philosophy of international relations. Technical international law studies and the prevailing institutional analysis that characterized much of the writing on international institutions paid less attention to philosophical issues. Indeed, one behavioral political theorist scornfully commented that political philosophy was irrelevant because it concentrated on "the writings of dead men," who presumably had little to say about the present. Philosophers of international relations set out to refute this critical view of political theory.

What was it about the postwar period that generated such interest in political philosophy? How are we to account for the revival of philosophy as an approach to international relations? First, World War II and its aftermath plainly were factors. The intellectual migration of European thinkers before and during the war had a profound impact. Scientists and scholars in search of freedom and survival had migrated to the United States before, as had intellectuals of widely differing national origins. However, viewed in the context of successive waves of migration, few social movements had as much importance for international thought as the one occurring in the 1930s and 1940s with the flight of intellectuals from Hitler's Germany. Some found their way directly into science and government, and others, into business and academic life. It is fair to say that the Manhattan Project, based under Stagg Field at the University of Chicago and leading to the discovery of the atomic bomb, would not have been possible without European scientists. In the humanities and social sciences, the graduate school of the New School for Social Research in New York provided an academic home for some of the best minds of Europe, including Leo Strauss, Hans Spier, Arnold Brecht, Kurt Riessler, Hans Jonas, and Erich Hula. Many of the most original thinkers in the social sciences in postwar America were refugees from Hitler and are esteemed to this day for original contributions to American social thought.

No other field or discipline profited more from this migration of talent than international studies and certain related sectors of political thought. One group constituted the most important figures in political philosophy: Strauss, Hannah Arendt, Jonas, and Eric Voegelin. Another included major theorists of comparative government: Carl Joachim Friedrich, Franz and Sigmund Neumann, Otto Kirchheimer, former German chancellor Heinrich Brüning, and Waldemar Gurian. International law received new impetus from Leo Gross and Hans Kelsen. Other legal scholars remained in England, including George Schwarzenberger and Hersh Lauterpacht, and still others chose to continue their work in Spain and Switzerland. History, sociology, economics, and literature claimed their share of leading European thinkers such as Jacob Viner, Friedrich A. von Hayek, Karl Mannheim, and Joseph A. Schumpeter. It would be difficult to find a comparable migration of human talent in all of intellectual history. Fortunately, American universities were receptive to influences from those British and European scholars, many of whom were sympathetic to broad philosophical approaches. As graduate students in the early postwar period, my fellow students and I partook of a veritable intellectual feast at the University of Chicago, served up by thinkers who were exemplars of this viewpoint. I cannot think of a situation before or since that can match the immediate postwar years.

Second, the nature of international politics invited an approach that was attuned to the historical relations among independent and sovereign political units. It was the group of European-American and certain British scholars who insisted on a world view that emphasized the importance of power in politics. For nearly two centuries, Americans had been shielded from the harsh realities of power politics because of the nation's isolation from Europe and the surrogate role played by the British navy in protecting U.S. interests, particularly across the seaways of the Atlantic. By contrast, Britain and the states of Europe for nearly four hundred years had accepted the fact of power politics. For them, as for the founding fathers, who were children of European thought, power was seen as a perennial factor in government and politics, unlikely to disappear even with a new international order. Postwar Americans were more likely to be children of Woodrow Wilson in his more reformist and evangelical phase and were, therefore, more optimistic about international law and organization as substitutes for power politics. Wilsonians, in opposition to much of European thought, prophesied that archaic international political practices, such as alliances and the balance of power, were being replaced by new institutional structures reflecting the common interests of mankind.

Not surprising, the interconnection between the reformist view of international relations and the more newfangled approaches to political science, on the one hand, and the historic European view of international society and traditional political philosophy, on the other, persisted through most of the mid–twentieth century. Therefore, those European-Americans who maintained that power was a perennial reality were also those who clung to the concepts and methods of political philosophy. Thus Niebuhr could describe Wolfers as more a political philosopher than a political scientist. Writing in the preface to the latter's *Discord and Collaboration: Essays on International Politics*, Niebuhr observed: "He is a 'philosopher' in that he scrutinizes and weighs the validity of various theories, concepts and presuppositions and discusses the larger patterns of international relations. But as any good philosopher, he is also a scientist in the sense that empirically ascertained facts serve him as the final criteria for the adequacy of general concepts or for the validity of general suppositions." For both Niebuhr and Wolfers, philosophy was joined with politics and power in theorizing. Niebuhr put it this way: "The issues discussed by Dr. Wolfers are by no means 'academic.' They go to the heart of many of the burning problems of contemporary foreign relations." His former students gave this summary of Wolfers' contribution: "[He] has excelled in making theory relevant to policy and in making the analysis of policy yield insights that further refine theory."[1]

Third, the normative perspective is central to the philosophy of international relations and has occupied a conspicuous place in the philosophical approach of the postwar period. For those approaches that were dominant in the first half of the twentieth century, the normative question had presumably been answered. In its simplest form, normative thinking entails an inquiry into the "is" and the "ought" of political relationships. The "ought" in the first four decades of the century was unequivocally internationalism and international law and organization. Observers of the international scene thought

---

1. Arnold Wolfers, *Discord and Collaboration: Essays on International Politics* (Baltimore, 1962), viii; Roger Hilsman and Robert C. Good, eds., *Foreign Policy in the Sixties: The Issues and the Instruments: Essays in Honor of Arnold Wolfers* (Baltimore, 1965), xi.

in terms of "good internationalism" (the League of Nations) and "bad nationalism" (Hitler's Germany). Few, if any, thinkers concerned themselves
with "bad internationalism" (the quest for domination by the Communist
International) or "good nationalism" (the Good Neighbor Policy).

If we look back to the thinkers who sought to return normative thinking
to its historic moorings, the majority are found among philosophers of international relations. Niebuhr, Morgenthau, and Sir Herbert Butterfield undertook to instruct their contemporaries on the complexities of moral choice,
quoting Justice Oliver Wendell Holmes, who observed that some people ad-
mire the man of principle but he respected the man who could find his way
through a maze of conflicting moral principles. In international relations, the
goals of peace and order compete, as do stability and change. Domestically,
freedoms of speech and assembly, the Supreme Court has decreed, give no
one the right to cry "Fire!" in a crowded theater. Moral judgments in foreign
relations by national leaders are often premature, in part because of what
Butterfield described as the idolatrous worship of some superperson, society,
state, or other large-scale organization. Normative thinking for Butterfield
requires walking alongside the actors in history, placing oneself in their position, seeking to recapture their perception of events and striving to understand the problems with which they had to cope and the standards they sought
to uphold.

Opposed to this method is the tendency for every contemporary leader
to be locked into systems of national self-righteousness, which make difficult
the weighing of choices in a process of moral reasoning. When Butterfield
founded the British Committee on the Theory of International Politics, he
stated its purpose as the *study* of "the nature of the international state-system,
the assumptions and ideas of diplomacy, the principles of foreign policy, *the
ethics of international relations and war* [my emphasis]." He explained that
the concern was more "with the historical than the contemporary, with the
normative than the scientific, with the philosophical than the methodological,
with principles than with policy." Sustaining the work of the committee was
a pervasive moral concern that he summarized thus: "The underlying aim . . .
is to clarify the principles of prudence and moral obligation which have held
together the international society of states throughout its history, and still hold
it together." The international realm is the political order of "the contingent

and the unforeseen, in which the survival of nations may be at stake, and agonizing decisions have to be made."[2]

Children of World War II and Philosophy

For the children of World War II, the philosophy of international relations has strengthened their capacity to cope with the postwar world. For most returning service personnel, one illusion has given way to another along the path to greater understanding of the world. American innocence about the world led some to assume we could have as much or as little to do with the world as we chose. Thus, it would be possible to accept responsibility or not for the defense of vital interests or to remain aloof following a great war, much as we had held to isolationism before the conflict broke out. An opposite illusion was belief in the American Century or, more recently, in a New World Order wherein the writ of the United States would be made to prevail throughout the world. From the illusion that we could abstain from the practice of power politics, we embarked on a crusade to establish and maintain democracy everywhere through our new role as world policeman. Having denounced alliances and the balance of power, we had by the mid-1950s negotiated some forty separate security pacts with nations around the globe.

The function of a philosophical viewpoint of international relations has been to help balance illusions and possibilities, innocence and hope. If philosophy is defined as an unusually stubborn attempt to think clearly, then a comprehensive approach to world politics can help us rediscover our place in history. Perhaps that is why so many who served in a worldwide crusade to subdue Hitler and Japan and who returned to a nation bent on achieving a utopian world order turned to the philosophy of international relations. It enabled them to recover hope in the face of profound anxiety. Having moved

2. Herbert Butterfield and Martin Wight, eds., *Diplomatic Investigations: Essays in the Theory of International Politics* (Cambridge, Mass., 1966), 11, 12, 13.

from illusion to disillusionment, mature Americans regained some modicum of confidence through philosophy.

What of the Future?

The lessons of this experience are that intellectual history is relevant to the study of international politics and that present thinking will more likely flourish if rooted in the philosophies of the past. One strength of the philosophical approach is its relative immunity from the fads and fashions of a transient present. It also provides a grounding for the examination of such perennial issues as power and morality or peace and order. Such foundations are especially vital where the temptation is ever present to turn to nostrums and panaceas to relieve the gravity of harsh conflicts that may lead to war. In different eras in recent times, proponents of far-reaching changes in the international system have argued that "Change x is necessary and is therefore possible." A return to past philosophies is a hedge against such wishful thinking.

The other contribution from the past is that of first-rate minds grappling with grave issues of war and peace. Former president of Brown University Henry Wriston was wont to say, "First-class problems attract first-class minds." As the history of thought makes clear, master thinkers in international relations have emerged in past decades in part for this reason. We ought to return to their work to reinvigorate present thinking as we confront a whole array of challenging new problems.

4

Peace Studies:
Social Movement or Intellectual Discipline?

The study of international relations is replete with examples of changing patterns of thought in disciplinary and reformist approaches to human problems. It comes then as no surprise that a recent group of claimants promises new light on the nation's most urgent problems. There are precedents for such claims, both from those who have sought to advance understanding and from those who seek primarily to bring about reform. The twentieth century is a history of one established intellectual discipline following another in successive attempts to make thinking in international relations more coherent and relevant. International law and organization studies supplanted diplomatic history as the dominant approach in the 1930s and 1940s, and international politics and theory came into its own in the postwar period. Much as governments hailed the study of politics, with its focus on the political process within the nation-state, as an advance over constitutional law, postwar students of international politics announced that power, its determinants, and the normative and political constraints on power were essential for understanding the international political process. Domestic and international politics sought an organizing principle and found it in interest and power, however defined. In national politics, the focus is on political parties and interest groups. For international relations, it is the national interest and national power and prestige.

International relations thought demonstrates the intermingling of the search for understanding or coherence and the quest for reform or improvement. From time to time one or the other tendency appears dominant. Each reformist group entertains the view that only it embraces the possibility of lasting improvement and unquestioned change. In the 1930s and 1940s, law and organization were the focus of reform. Most university chairs in international law and organization carried provisions that the responsibilities of chairholders were something more than the mere search for understanding. Beyond pursuit of scholarship, each occupant also accepted responsibility for transforming the international environment and mankind's thinking about it. International lawyers and students of international organization conducted their research and teaching all the while harboring a sense of guilt over the nation's rejection of membership in the League of Nations. One of the missions of professors of international law and organization was to assure that never again would the United States turn its back on international cooperation.

The reformist enthusiasms of academics were lukewarm by contrast with the messianic and crusading spirit of outsiders. Emery Reves brought the idea of peace through law into every socially conscious community group and into many liberal arts college classrooms. Carl Van Doren's *The Great Rehearsal* became a textbook for applying the wisdom of the founding fathers to the world scene, an undertaking that a group of philosophers, humanists, and lawyers, led by Robert Maynard Hutchins at the University of Chicago, carried even further to the drafting of a world constitution. The United World Federalists inspired other movements and leaders like Clarence Streit of Union Now to seek legislative support for their proposals. To say that reform was the governing purpose of their work is not to discredit their intellectual competence. Indeed the superior mental powers of Hutchins and Giuseppe Borgese or Grenville Clark and Louis Sohn or Streit and Norman Cousins hardly require defenders. Yet their primary aim, like the aim of Marxists, was not to understand the world but to change it. In Hutchins' memorable phrase, repeated in a series of debates with the realist Niebuhr, "Because world government is necessary, it is therefore possible." In pursuit of a new and better world, they sought to leave behind any trace of the world as it was.

Peace Studies as Reform

The present reformist movement in international relations that invites comparisons and contrasts with postwar reformist movements is peace studies. Because of its claims, it must be judged as a reformist movement, at least in the first instance. Its defenders and spokesmen, including some of history's most belligerent pacifists, would doubtless quarrel about a reformist designation and not necessarily with the calm and grace of Kenneth Boulding's "twelve friendly quarrels" with Johan Galtung. They would argue that peace studies is legitimately the newest, most comprehensive, and best approach to understanding international relations. Yet the burden of evidence makes clear that peace studies is inextricably linked with the prevailing social climate in international affairs. It began at a few smaller liberal arts colleges, most of them with religious affiliations (the first serious program in the United States appeared in 1948 at the Brethren's Manchester College in northern Indiana) and spread throughout the nation only after Vietnam and the antinuclear movements, including the movement for a nuclear freeze, in the 1970s and 1980s. The peace studies approach was and continues to be an activist response to the nuclear problem and to associated threats to human survival existing throughout the world. Even though peace studies has merged with earlier approaches such as conflict resolution, expanding interest in it and related fields coincides with the mounting concerns of the nuclear age. Peace studies is fueled by the nuclear crisis, and without that crisis it might have remained the province of a small band of college teachers rather than expanding to attract activists and reformers.

Professor Neil H. Katz, who is director of the Program in Nonviolent Conflict and Change at Syracuse University's highly respected Maxwell School, writes that "academia has not led the rush into this field [peace studies]."[1] The dynamics of peace studies is illustrated in two noteworthy events, one, the World Game, a nuclear attack and social injustice simulation organized for a hundred people in a Syracuse, New York, community college, and the other, a 1987 Great Peace March for Global Nuclear Disarmament, involving five hundred walkers in a 3,700-mile walk spanning an eight-and-a-half-month period. Coming at the close of his discussion of peace studies, Katz's evaluation gives priority to the dependence of peace studies on the peace movement. Peace students can validate themselves through the strengthening of the movement.

Others go further and equate peace studies with the goal of the university's changing its character and responding as a corporate body to the nuclear threat. In a paper entitled "University Education for the Nuclear Age," Professors Walter Kohn and Lawrence Badash of the University of California at Santa Barbara warn that "unless there is a radical change in direction, going far beyond the recent Intermediate-range Nuclear Forces (INF) Treaty . . . a

---

1. Neil H. Katz, "Conflict Resolution and Peace Studies," *Annals,* DIV (July, 1989), 21.

nuclear war is all but certain to break out, if not in our lifetime, then in the next one or two generations."[2] Yet universities, with a few notable exceptions such as the land-grant state colleges in agriculture and the mechanical arts established by the Morrill Act of 1862, have not often responded directly to social needs. Another exception may prove to be the multicampus organization the University of California Institute on Global Conflict and Cooperation, created in 1983 to advance the prevention of nuclear or other global conflicts. While teaching and research are included in its mandate, the institute also sponsors statewide extension activities, colloquia, and meetings and summer teaching seminars aimed at promoting the prevention of nuclear war. However, its main emphasis has been on study groups and colloquia in international relations.

For still others, peace studies in its broadest terms is education in nonviolent social change. Advocates—and advocacy is apparently a requirement of peace studies—quote a favorite phrase by A. J. Muste: "There is no way to peace; peace is the way." Peace studies "enables one to act, to live in a fully human way." Peace studies liberates one from historical and geographical prejudices. It marks out clear pathways to a conflict-free world. It proceeds on the premise that war and destructive violence are pathological, not normal. Psychologists and educators have undertaken to demonstrate that men and women have different attitudes toward violence because boys and girls are educated differently. The efficacy of organized violence is overrated, and nonviolent sanctions are underrated. Such efforts as Bill Moyers' Social Movement Empowerment Project provide an eight-stage strategic framework for social change, including steps involving the failure of institutions, powerlessness, movement takeoff, and continuing struggle. According to Kathleen Maas Weigert of the University of Notre Dame's Institute for International Peace Studies, peace studies as a movement seeks to make use of a variety of such models. In Moyers' words, they have "lifted morale, helped activists recognize their movement's successes, restored energy and helped develop strategy for moving ahead."[3] It is significant that the space given in Weigert's essay to Moyers' model exceeds that given any other analytical model, sug-

2. Walter Kohn and Laurence Badash, "University Education for the Nuclear Age," *ibid.*, 23.

3. Kathleen Maas Weigert, "Peace Studies as Education for Nonviolent Social Change," *ibid.*, 45.

gesting that peace studies as a movement is more important than is the study of peace.

Through all the discussions of peace studies as a social movement, references to social activism appear and reappear. Anthony Bing, who is director of peace and global studies at Earlham College, maintains that "no experimental dimension to peace learning, nor other serious academic work, will be educationally sound without an affirmation of this thinking-acting link." The key to education, we are told, is education for transformation, or the transformation of new comprehension into action. Comprehension in itself will not suffice. Impetus for peace studies comes from belief in transformative values. Marie A. Dugan, director of the Consortium on Peace Research Education and Development (COPRED) states: "Many believe, and I agree, that without a strong value orientation a program is, by definition, no longer a peace studies program."[4] By definition, peace studies is the advancement of peace in the world and must be judged as such.

Finally, a recurrent theme in most peace studies literature is the cry for influence from those who consider themselves bereft of a voice in policy making. In the words of Barbara Welling Hall of Earlham College, "peace studies has been the intellectual domain of outsiders." Thus, one of the goals "of the peace study community has been to empower the powerless." Diplomats and Sovietologists are examples of conspicuous insiders. They are professional elites wedded to the status quo and oblivious to the winds of change. They lack the creative imagination "to envision a future world in which conflicts and disputes are resolved without violence, hegemony is replaced with respect for diversity, basic . . . human needs are met, and nuclear weapons are abolished."[5] Who can question such goals?

Having demonstrated the commitment of peace studies to influencing society, we must ask what the criteria are for measuring the impact of the movement. If "peace is breaking out around the world," is peace studies responsible and, if so, in what ways? What is striking is that despite peace studies' reformist character, the writings by leaders in the movement stress more its contributions as an intellectual discipline than its success in the fur-

4. Anthony G. Bing, "Peace Studies as Experimental Education," *ibid.*, 52; Marie A. Dugan, "Peace Studies at the Graduate Level," *ibid.*, 76.

5. Barbara Welling Hall, "Peace Studies as if Soviet Studies Mattered," *ibid.*, 108, 109.

therance of peace. An impressive curriculum guide, containing histories of peace studies and a variety of course outlines, is now in its fifth edition. A political and social science journal contains essays on teaching and research. Most interpretations of the influence of peace studies emphasize its effects on the educational process. As with education in general, however, peace studies is viewed as long-term, and thus its influence can only be measured in the future.

Professor Chadwick Alger of Ohio State University's Mershon Center is an exception to most writers on the influence of peace studies. In discussing the wide array of grass-roots peace movements, Alger argues that people in a society that no longer believes in "the mythology of the state system" are increasingly skeptical that "only a few experts in the national capital are competent to define the national interest" and "at the grass roots now dare to become their own experts on specific kinds of weapons systems." It is people at the grass roots who "are formulating plans for conversion from military to peaceful production" and who "work for the release of political prisoners in distant lands [Reverend Jesse Jackson], offer sanctuary to those denied it by their government, and establish nuclear-free zones in towns and cities." It is people at the grass roots, too, who "have created a people's foreign service, through which thousands of people have visited Central America, the Soviet Union, and other critical areas to view conditions for themselves."[6] It is people who have brought about change in U.S. policy toward apartheid and people who forced a change in the standards of the World Health Organization for controlling the marketing of the infant formula produced by the Nestle Corporation. In Third World countries, it is people at grass-roots levels who are resisting militarization and development programs determined and controlled by the state.

Even if such grass-roots activity is accepted as important, the question of what its relationship to peace studies is must be asked. Professor Alger's response is that international studies must be transformed from efforts to understand traditional international relations problems to efforts to observe and interpret grass-roots peace activities. The people and the peace researchers must become coinvestigators of the problems that preoccupy ordinary people in their grass-roots activism. They must join together at the crossroads of

6. Chadwick F. Alger, "Peace Studies at the Crossroads: Where Else?," *ibid.*, 123.

action and research. Until the emergence of peace studies, international relations studies at most sought opinions from the public through social surveys and opinion polls. But traditional international studies, with its focus on statesmen and diplomats, rarely, if ever, considers the participants in the grass-roots peace process as actors. New concepts and paradigms for study are needed. Peace studies must help break down the emphasis on foreign policy as primarily an activity of state officials and shift the focus to the people in their grass-roots activities.

What peace studies can do in an activist, as distinguished from an intellectual, sense is illustrated by the United Nations. The great weakness of such international bodies results from their being cut off from the people of the world. A network of bureaucracies and national officials stands between the people and the ideals of the United Nations. Covenants, conventions, and treaties enacted by multilateral bodies remain unratified. In the meantime, most people at the grass roots are not even aware of the existence of such international instruments. It should be the mission of peace researchers to bring to the people an understanding of provisions like those contained in the preambles to the United Nations' Covenants on Civil and Political Rights and on Economic, Social, and Cultural Rights. Defenders of peace studies insist that the individual has responsibility to strive for the promotion and observance of human rights contained in such covenants.

The responsibilities of peace studies so defined are thus reformist but primarily in an intellectual sense. Few of the advocates of peace studies encourage young men and women to join the Foreign Service or even the Peace Corps. Most of the high-risk responsibilities in foreign policy, including national policy making and administration in international organizations, inspire more critical than favorable comments by these advocates. Moreover, peace researchers are encouraged to play activist roles more as advisors and interpreters than as decision makers. If this approach is reformist, it is reform in the spirit of the 1930s and 1940s, when international law and organization professors sought through teaching, research, and service to change the environment of international thinking. It is as outsiders looking in that those pursuing peace studies become insiders. Professor Alger's advice to peace researchers and peace educators is to find a place at the crossroads of education, research, and action. First, they should engage in a dialogue with activists, especially at the grass roots. Second, they should encourage both negative (prevention of war and violence) and positive (justice and human improvement) peace approaches. Third, they should widen their peace paradigm to include the concerns of the growing array of peace movements in local communities. Fourth, they should be a bridge for mutual awareness between local movements and global institutions.

Peace Studies as Intellectual Discipline

If the purpose of peace studies is to reform and restructure international relations by being its advisor and interpreter, the issue of the intellectual foundations of the field comes once more to the fore. How are we to judge peace studies as an intellectual discipline? Two sets of answers are possible for peace studies, as for any organized field of study. They are, first, the answers of the advocates or protagonists and, second, the answers of outside observers and authorities seeking light shed on and understanding of the discipline.

The first answer that advocates of peace studies give is quantitative in character. Running through most of the literature on peace studies are claims made for the veritable population explosion in the number of peace studies programs. We are told that a mere handful of programs existed in the 1950s and 1960s. In 1971, the Institute for World Order, which supported and initiated peace studies, reported programs on 50 campuses. By 1978, COPRED identified 80 institutions with programs. In 1986, the same organization could point to 100 undergraduate and graduate programs. The editors of the 1989 edition of *Peace and World Order Studies: A Curriculum Guide* listed 185 undergraduate and 75 graduate programs. COPRED, in announcing its latest directory, promised descriptions of more than 200 actual programs. Although the number of programs is impressive, the argument and controversy that follow the aphorism "lies, damn lies, and statistics" are possible. One year after the Institute for World Order made its estimate of 50 programs, Marie Dugan, who was to become director of COPRED, could find only one degree-granting program in peace studies, at the University of Pennsylvania.

A second answer of the advocates is financial, again quantitative in character. The Ford, MacArthur, and Sloan foundations and the Carnegie Corporation, plus numerous smaller foundations, have given generous support to peace studies. For example, the MacArthur Foundation, following the work of a two-year commission convened jointly by it and the Carnegie Corporation, awarded and committed grants for studies in peace and international cooperation estimated at approximately $65 million. Its "funds supported more than 350 students and 140 faculty members . . . [and] nearly 80 major faculty research projects." If money follows ideas, such commitments suggest the emergence of a fundamentally new area of study. The MacArthur allocation, however, invites rather dramatic comparison with the commitment of a little over $1 million by the Rockefeller Foundation in the 1960s in an individual grant program that gave assistance to a significant number of younger scholars who were to become the leading figures in international relations in the 1970s and 1980s. How, though, is one to compare the two efforts? Do their breadth of vision and possibility of long-term impact compare? Perhaps even more intriguing and important, What does either effort tell us about the expansiveness of the spirit of the times?

A third answer proponents give is to point to the multidisciplinary character of peace studies. In the 1960s, the major disciplines in international relations were political science, international law, history, economics, and certain physical sciences. By contrast, the architects of the MacArthur program take pride in the fact that a host of new disciplines have been supported, including "discourse analysis and interpretive work, game-theoretic approaches and public opinion and survey projects."[7] Again, the proof will be in the pudding resulting from this effort.

A fourth answer, by Elise Boulding, puts stress on a vast number of new paradigms for the study of war and peace. She mentions "retooling" in new disciplines, the concept of *alternatives* applied to *alternative* security, nonviolence theory, the role of women, the role of teachers and of religious and ethical perspectives, the conditions of peace approach, social impact assessment, nonoffensive defense (NOD), civilian-based defense, environmental impact assessment, and a multidisciplinary issues group on peace. Professor Boulding summarizes her views: "The very rise of concepts such as the international information order and the international cultural order, to

7. Kennette Benedict, "Funding Peace Studies: A Perspective from the Foundation World," *ibid.*, 93, 94. .

say nothing of the international economic security and environmental orders, reflects new understanding."[8]

The contrasts between peace studies as an intellectual discipline and traditional international studies are dramatic. In the 1950s, as we have seen in Chapter 3, political scientists took note of the first signs of an emerging field of study in international politics. They identified half a dozen characteristics that set their field apart. First, they were able to point to a group of major text writers whose works delineated the boundaries, the core, and the periphery of the field. What the contributions of these text writers had in common was certain defining principles and informing theses that brought unity and direction to the discussion of the international political process. The authors were able to distinguish their area of inquiry from other fields of study such as international law and international organization. The most important outcome was a body of material for inquiry and study inside the classroom and outside in discrete application of their findings.

Second, clustered around the work of the text writers was an equally important body of literature that reinforced and deepened their findings. The subject matter of treatises and monographs went beyond the texts and took the form of such works as Nicholas J. Spykman's *America's Strategy in World Politics*, E. H. Carr's *The Twenty Years' Crisis*, Wolfers' *Britain and France Between Two Wars: Conflicting Strategies of Peace*, and John H. Herz's *Political Realism and Political Idealism*. Each of them became the focus of discussion and debate undertaken in relationship with one another and with the major texts of such neighboring disciplines as international law.

Third, a literature on the intellectual forerunners of the new field of international political studies began to appear. American and British writers sought to draw connections between present-day writers and those who had gone before. Whereas the reformist literature, especially of outsiders, undertook to leave behind the legacy associated with power politics and war, the founders of the new school reintroduced Plato, Aristotle, Machiavelli, David Hume, and Edmund Burke. The pursuit of such inquiries continues down to the present day in such studies as the examination of the European and

8. Elise Boulding, "Introduction," in *Peace and World Order Studies*, ed. Daniel C. Thomas and Michael T. Klare (5th ed.; Boulder, 1989), 7.

German background of Hans J. Morgenthau's thought by the Swiss scholar Christoph Frei.

Fourth, the fateful separation between theory and practice was broken by a burgeoning literature on principles of foreign policy and international politics. Diplomats and policy makers, including Kennan, Halle, C. B. Marshall, Paul H. Nitze, Dean Acheson, and Dorothy Fosdick, to name but a few, enriched and enlivened the discussion. In much the same way that the essays, speeches, dispatches, and memoirs of past leaders such as Otto von Bismarck, Canning, and Robert Gascoyne-Cecil, Marquis of Salisbury had offered insights and ideas for international theory, the reflections of Kennan and Acheson and the writings of Halle and Marshall brought theory down to earth. They kept the doctors of international politics close to the patient in the bed of contemporary diplomacy.

Fifth, the concentration on a single ordering discipline such as political science brought with it certain unifying ideas that are often lacking in multidisciplinary study. From political science, international relations appropriated concepts and core principles that a broadly eclectic perspective denies the scholar. My first mentor was Quincy Wright, and the educational experience he offered me and countless others had inestimable value. In his *Study of War* and *Study of International Relations*, he drew on virtually every humane and scientific discipline, thus introducing his students to a breathtaking and encyclopedic sweep of knowledge. But to the end, Wright lacked the focus and unifying principles that became the hallmark of international politics. He never discovered the informing theory that might have brought deeper meaning and purpose to his quest for understanding. He provided all the components of an international theory but stopped short of constructing a theory of his own. International politics in contrast, by subordinating a vast array of data to a few unifying concepts, contributed a logically coherent and empirically based theory.

Finally, the new field of international politics beginning in the 1950s took on certain defining characteristics not as political theory in general but as theory applied to international relations. It undertook to relate national interest and power. It examined the determinants of national power, as in Spykman's study of geopolitics and power, the Sprouts on the foundations of power and Carr, Morgenthau, and Niebuhr on realism and idealism. That each successive contribution in theory led to the expanding of core ideas and to the generating of debate was evidence of the interrelatedness of knowledge in international politics. Through all the "great debates," new ideas appeared and were refined around the unifying principles that anchored the discipline from its earliest formulation. More specialized areas of study such as national security and strategic studies were spun off from the core ideas, and revisionist thinking found a place in the theories of neorealism.

Conclusion

It should be evident, then, that a comparison of the histories of peace studies and of international politics reveals more differences than similarities. Their beginnings and evolution as intellectual disciplines follow diverse paths that cannot be equated. Each quite possibly expresses the dominant needs of its time. The birth and growth of international politics coincided with the Cold War and the arrival on the world scene of the two superpowers. Peace studies received its impetus from the nuclear age and the threat of nuclear annihilation.

Yet their beginnings and their relationship with a prevailing international environment only partly explain the differences. The one, international politics, followed the more or less traditional pattern of the birth, growth, and maturing of most established intellectual and scientific studies. The other, peace studies, is a product of deep-seated anxieties and concerns, leading to a profusion of varied activities whose importance tends to be judged more in quantitative than in qualitative terms. Peace studies has been driven less by the existence of controlling or dominant theories and ideas, which has characterized the history of political science, economics, and history, and more by the infusion of large-scale financial assistance. Its development has been a story less of ideas attracting money than of money in search of ideas. Closely related are two further defining characteristics, in particular for peace studies: the proliferation of disciplines, each contributing some segment of interest and knowledge, and the promise of new paradigms of thought, which thus far remain largely a promise. The principles that have emerged are the result of large-scale international institutional efforts, usually taking the form of announcements at international professional meetings. It would be difficult to think of many past efforts by large part-time associations that have resulted in new paradigms of thought. Individuals, not organizations, are normally the authors of new ideas.

Nevertheless, peace studies has touched a nerve in American higher education and may have served an important purpose in stimulating thought on all-important problems. Clearly, it expresses the nation's optimism that an organized and collective approach to any problem can lead to its resolution. It has enlisted in a good cause some of society's most tireless reformers. Further, peace studies contributes a needed balance to war studies and large-scale inquiries on national security and defense. However, it is necessary to ask if the prevailing intellectual framework has become too restrictive, if it addresses idiosyncratic and esoteric interests more than important dimensions of the international problem such as the role of power, and if it mistakenly believes that only peace studies advocates are engaged in the quest for peace. Yet because vast human energies and considerable talents are committed to peace studies, even its critics must welcome the effort. We shall be able to judge more responsibly the lasting consequences of peace studies sometime in the future, perhaps in the twenty-first century. For now, an interim report must characterize its accomplishments as modest, whether it is judged as social movement or as intellectual discipline. Quite likely, future critics will say that peace studies suffered most from the fact that it pursued simultaneously two goals, or objectives, that by their very nature are in tension, if not war, with one another.

5

The Religious Transformation of Politics
and the Political Transformation of Religion

The Religious Transformation of Politics

From its founding, the American republic has provided a testing ground for the relating of religion to politics. It is surely the case that religion was present in the minds of those who drafted the Constitution. It is no less true that certain founding fathers never stopped urging the separation of church and state. The concept of separation as checks and balances permeates American constitutionalism. A century and a half after the country's founding, Justice Louis Brandeis was to write, "The doctrine of the separation of powers was adopted by the Convention of 1787 not to promote efficiency but to preclude the arbitrary exercise of power—not to avoid friction but by means of the inevitable friction incident to the distribution of governmental powers among these departments to save the people from autocracy." [1]

In New England and Virginia alike, not only secular thinkers but religious leaders were attuned to the problem. Society is indebted to Calvinist theologians such as John Cotton, who warned, "Let all the world give mortall man no greater power than they are content they shall use for use it they will." The "great blasphemies" of which such men might be guilty led jurists and theologians to warn against abuse of power by both political and religious leaders. Even a staunch Enlightenment figure such as Thomas Jefferson could write in the last article of the Kentucky Resolutions of 1798: "Confidence in the men of our choice . . . is . . . the parent of despotism: free government is founded in jealousy and not in confidence. . . . In questions of power then let no more be heard of confidence in man, but bind him down from mischief by the claims of the Constitution."

Yet historians point to another side of Jefferson's political thinking, formed by the Enlightenment and by a Deist faith that in turn was shaped in

1. Brandeis dissenting, in Myers v. United States, 272 U.S. 52, 293.

part at least by the rationalism of the French Enlightenment. For Jefferson, the American experiment clearly represented a new beginning. The colonists had shaken the dust of Europe from their feet. They boasted that the thirteen colonies knew nothing of European feudalism and tyranny or of divisions of class and ethnic groups. The American Zion was "a City on a Hill," which Saint Matthew records in Chapter 5 of his gospel, beckoning to all mankind. Nearly a century later, Lincoln was to speak of "something in that Declaration giving liberty, not alone to the people of this country but hope to the world for all future time." The common people of America had reached a high ground that Europeans had not attained in a thousand years with all their division into rich and poor, wolves and sheep. "Here are not aristocratical families, no courts, no kings, no bishops, no ecclesiastical dominion," wrote John de Crevecoeur. "We have no princes for whom we toil, starve and bleed; we are the most perfect society now existing in the world."[2] The idea of perfectibility was always present in the American political experience.

Moreover, God was never absent from this picture. If Calvinists and Deists were divided on certain religious truths, they were united in the faith that the new nation was an "American Israel." Religiously, "the influentials" displayed the marks of utopianism. The same was not true politically. Neither the Calvinism of New England nor the Deism of Virginia held out much hope for the religious transformation of politics. Calvinists took a pessimistic view of human nature. Man was burdened by original sin, and society's political task was to provide for political arrangements that held evil in check and channeled virtue toward good social ends. It is true that Puritanism left room for election day sermons, but such appeals in churches on the eve of balloting were timed to coincide with the closing days in the electoral process. It is also true that some forms of the religion of New England went far toward affirming the title that Edward Johnson gave his book in 1650, *Wonder Working Providence of Zion's Saviour*. The emphasis, however, was primarily on religious purity, and Johnson proclaimed that "Jesus Christ had manifested his kingly office toward his churches more fully than ever the sons of men saw." The individual and his church might be transformed in the New World but not politics as such.

2. *Collected Works of Abraham Lincoln*, ed. Roy P. Basler (9 vols.; New Brunswick, 1959), IV, 240; Hector St. John de Crevecoeur, *Letters from an American Farmer* (New York, 1912), 39–41.

For Jefferson and the Deists, transformation would come about, if ever, through the intervention of reason and the interplay of a natural harmony of interests. It was reason and the American experience that possessed a transforming power, not religion. The frontier and a preference for rural life were more likely to foster the ideal community. Jeffersonian reform was a goal to be sought through the broadening of political and economic opportunity, not something that had deep religious roots. For Jefferson, education was the road to a new and better life. Progress was inherent in human nature and would be neither produced nor obstructed by "nature's God." Yet present-day heirs of Jefferson who are Christians quote the ancient dictum "Work as though everything is up to you; know that everything depends on God." The search for the balance between individual responsibility and God's transforming influence is endless in human history.

In the late 1970s and 1980s, we have witnessed a change in these historical and philosophical perspectives. In the 1950s and 1960s, a school of thought that many called Christian realism was dominant, especially among Protestant thinkers. Its influence was mediated through teachers of the era's political leaders and reformers. Christian realism provided a background and an intellectual framework for the political actors of the time. It never pretended to provide the answers for specific policies or concrete policy choices, and in the 1970s even some of its more activist adherents departed from it for this reason. Realism was not activist enough. Indeed, those who were caught up in the prevailing mood of social criticism and counterculture were found lacking in almost every form of historical realism and idealism. By the mid- and late-1970s, however, Christian realism was experiencing a resurgence.

Throughout the 1950s and especially the first three-quarters of the 1960s, the influence on politics of Christian realism, while significant, was almost always indirect rather than direct. Historically, this fact has been true of most religious and intellectual movements. Realism, like other philosophical approaches, has never claimed to offer copybook answers for politicians. More than the movements that preceded and others which followed it, Christian realism has remembered Christ's words: "My Kingdom is not of this world." Niebuhr, Butterfield, and Toynbee emphasized the differences between the vocation of the theologian or historian and the vocation of the politician.

The 1950s and 1960s witnessed mounting awareness of civil rights in the forefront of the nation's unfinished business. The preeminent civil rights leader was Martin Luther King, Jr. As with many other civil rights leaders, King's teacher was Spellman College president Benjamin Mays, one of America's greatest educators. It was Mays who spoke in the language of Christian realism, pressing home the goals of the civil rights movement but with a keen understanding of the alliances that were essential and the obstacles that had to be overcome. Mays's realism frustrated militants such as Vincent Harding, who imagined that the movement could realize its full program here and now. I recall visiting Atlanta University and Spellman College in the 1960s, when the militants had locked Mays in his office as a protest against his more pragmatic approach. Not long afterward, a political leader who had been for many years the symbol of American liberalism, Hubert Humphrey, received lukewarm support at best from liberal groups in his 1968 race for the presidency. Julian Hartt and Charles Garretson have shown that Humphrey's mentor, insofar as the former vice-president did any systematic thinking on religion and politics, was Reinhold Niebuhr. The ideas of Christian realism, then, were transmitted by great teachers to political figures who reformulated the ideas to meet what they saw as the challenges of the day.

The central thesis of Christian realism is that the relation between religion and politics in the United States rests not on their being identical but on their having mutual strengths and reinforcing qualities. The health of the relationship is threatened when either seeks to rule and overwhelm the other. Religion lives in the realm of moral absolutes and transcendent justice. It provides an overarching spiritual environment for society. It represents a higher order of lasting truths about God and man that fallible human beings only dimly perceive. Lincoln had described Providence's scroll unfolding toward an indeterminate end that no human being could fathom but that was a reality nonetheless. Some aspects of spiritual truth remain forever in the higher order of a *mysterium tremendum,* where they constitute objective truth. To the extent men catch a glimpse of such truths, they do so as shadows on the wall of a cave or through revelation as understood by theologians. Religion is the order of a higher truth.

Politics, by contrast, is the realm of proximate truth. The vocation of politics demands willingness to accept compromise and adjustment Lincoln was a sad man, John F. Kennedy once remarked, because he learned that in politics no one can have everything he wants. Politics means living with half a loaf. It seldom, if ever, is a matter of all or nothing. The political process breaks down when one or both sides call for total moral victory without appreciation of what the other's identity and self-preservation demand. The breakdown becomes inevitable when political valuations are made in the name of absolute right and wrong, as was the case in the Civil War. It might have been possible for the North and the South to compromise on questions of relative political influence in the new states or on the need for a particular organization of the economy. Questions of power or efficiency are measured by the yardstick of more or less. Once the issue becomes the righteousness of a cause or God's will expressed in a given political arrangement, there is no escape from the impending conflict. Compromise and give-and-take become impossible when either side sees its own cause as wholly righteous and the other's as altogether evil. In rough terms, this situation occurred in the war between the states. Politics came to an end, and a holy war took its place. Was this scenario true also of the war in the Gulf?

Christian realists warned in the 1950s and 1960s of the fateful tendency of religious men and women to invest their own political ends with religious or quasi-religious sanctity. It is true that life is raised above the level of brute existence by the higher ends mankind pursues, even when men fail to reach the heights. Religion assures a sense of the holy and the sacred in life that for an individual can bring transforming power. However, when every proximate political goal from electoral reform to a host of single-interest group policies, for example, gun control or prayer in the schools, is sanctified, prospects for a working democracy are weakened, if not destroyed. At its best, religion can work a profound civilizing influence on politics, but Christian realists are too sensitive to history and too understanding of the nature of man to imagine that religion can transform the political process. One of them warned: "Christians ought to be a little shy of identifying their faith with particular parties and policies . . . especially as in the realm of politics and public affairs, so many things depend on inferences from complicated sets of political data." What religionists neglect to measure is the consequences of one course of policy against another, or, as Butterfield put it, of "stretching the elastic too far, or producing unpleasant results in some different realm which one had forgotten to take into account." They neglect the possibility of accidents and consequences they haven't taken into account. Saints, by their nature, are not very good at political calculation. "Real statesmanship . . . requires the ability to hold in one's mind a whole jungle of relevant details, a whole forest of complicating inconsistencies."

By the late 1960s two social and political movements were beginning to challenge Christian realism. Viewed in the light of intellectual history, that these two constituted major challenges is ironic. From the standpoint of coherent thought, other movements, such as pragmatic pacifism or Catholic just-war theory, were more worthy of critical thought and popular response.

The first challenge had roots in the countercultural movement and the youth revolution. It was a response more to events than to ideas: Vietnam, Watergate, and the assumed passivity of citizens, intellectuals, and "the establishment." In one sense, the revolt of young people against society was an event waiting to happen. The consensus on which postwar American foreign policy had been based was in part political, involving the cooperation of Truman Democrats and Vandenberg Republicans, and in part intellectual, involving the thinking of a generation of "wisemen" schooled in the harsh realities of war. Following Vietnam, when events soured as was inevitable given the intractability of human affairs, countervailing political movements were bound to arise. Critics were waiting in the wings for postwar leaders to stumble.

The intellectual revolt, while largely secular and sometimes antireligious, challenged Christian realism and every other form of prudential outlook that demonstrated some respect for the political process. Realism in all its forms was not sufficiently activist. Its stress on ambiguity and complexity obscured the need for far-reaching changes in society. While acknowledging the possibility of giving the system one more chance, leaders in the movement, whose outlook reflected a curious blend of utopianism and mild anarchism, mobilized followers bent on transforming politics. To the extent the movement was based more on blind faith than on political reason, "make love not war," it took upon itself the marks of a quasi religion. In the reformers' minds, not only politics but the flawed society of their parents' and grandparents' generations had to be transformed. Because the numerical strength of the movement was substantial and its comprehensive makeup all-inclusive, including the faithful's music, dress, and overall life-style, the revolt, however short-lived, had far-reaching effects. For segments of the population, the youth revolution led to the transformation of politics, in ways quite unforeseen, including the enfeeblement of one of the two major political parties, the Democratic party.

If the first challenge to the existing political system calling for the transformation of politics was only quasi-religious, the second was an explicitly religious movement. If the first represented a challenge from the left, the second came from the far right. What the two shared in common was a commitment to a radical reorientation of politics. One assumed that politics would be different if leadership were to pass to more young people on the left, the other, to more older people on the Christian right. One spoke in the language of reform or withdrawal, the other, in the language of long-range transformation not of politics as such but through the legislating of a social and fundamentalist agenda. Both movements put stress on using the blunt instrument of coercion, as distinguished from consensus building, in politics. Neither showed much tolerance for the politics of inclusion. Their most conspicuous lack, when compared with Christian realism or Catholic just-war theory, was the absence of any preeminent theorists or intellectual spokesmen. It was as though American constitutional thought had rested exclusively on the ideas of Paine or Patrick Henry, the provocateurs, rather than James Madison or Jefferson, the builders. Both countermovements involved the politics of political protest rather than the politics of political theory or governance. They both had extensive lists of what they were against. Whereas Christian realism can point to Niebuhr and Butterfield and Catholic just-war theory to John Courtney Murray, historians continue to ask who the intellectual leaders of either of these protest movements were and whether as a result of the movements anyone gained some measure of respect across the political spectrum. Did someone bequeath a legacy in political thought that endures for thinking men and women in society at large?

Not surprising, neither movement brought about a lasting political transformation. The successors of the protesters on the left became yuppies, hardly a transforming force in American politics. On the right, the enduring contribution is more modest still. Even the most conservative postwar American president, Reagan, showed little willingness to commit his political capital to the enactment of radical social programs of the religious right, and his successor has shown even less. Given the media visibility of the movement, it is instructive how few of their social programs were enacted into law. If one compares the legislative results, say, of the New Deal of Roosevelt with the enactments of friends of the Moral Majority of Jerry Falwell, the differences are stunning. Beyond any comparisons measured by laws and policies enacted, the more important conclusion has to do with political transformation. If the goal of the two, the religious and the quasi-religious movements, was to transform politics and the political system, purging it of certain undesirable features and restoring lost values, the evidence of results is virtually nonexistent. Some residual signs of each movement persist in the 1990s, and some of its considerations are traceable in local political contests and conventions. But ongoing political struggles are taking place in a political setting not fundamentally different from that of the 1950s and the first three-quarters of the 1960s, in which traditional politics prevailed.

The Political Transformation of Religion

If the absence of the promised religious transformation of politics in the past decade confirms the judgment of the Christian realists, the results of efforts seeking the political transformation of religion support the realist viewpoint even more. Serious writers have long been cautious about the transformation of religion. Butterfield's thoughts are an expression of Christian realism: "Clearly, the political notions and policies that we adopt as Christians, are liable to be entangled (without our ever realizing it) in our patriotic fervor, or our vested interests—all this mixed together with no end of wishful thinking."

Two competing views of religion shape the conclusions that historians reach about the political transformation of religion. The one perspective conceives of religion as an end in itself, the other, as a means to certain mundane ends that religion is capable of serving. On this issue, Christian realists group themselves together in one school of thought, however they may differ on decisions in practical politics. The quasi-religious and religious movements discussed above are part of an outlook that views religion largely in utilitarian terms. Niebuhr is especially critical of those Christians who are forever "lobbying for special favors in the court of the Almighty." Butterfield is even more caustic in writing that "it isn't the function of religion or the church to solve the problems of diplomacy or to tell governments how to balance their budgets." The uniqueness of the church is found in its affirming and sustaining a spiritual dimension at the heart and soul of a nation's life and nurturing a deepening of man's inner life.

Having recognized what sets religion apart, the realists emphasize the immensity of the terrestrial consequences of religion, most being unanticipated and even unintended. The Protestant Reformation, for example, was more instrumental than most Protestants acknowledge in the rise of the all-powerful sovereign nation-state. Butterfield points to an analogy between science and religion, quoting Lord Ernest Rutherford, who, after the success of his experiments, declared: "Thank God. They will be of no utility to anyone." If he were to return to this life, Rutherford would confront the shattering results of his labors, of nuclear physics threatening the survival of the world. The monastic movement devoted itself to prayer and meditation but became as well the intermediary for transmitting to a semibarbaric world the civilizations of Greece and Rome, which might otherwise have disappeared. Looking back, economic historians trace the growth of the wool trade to the English monasteries. It was John Wesley and his lay preachers, beginning in the eighteenth century, who planted seeds of respect for each individual human being, precious in God's sight however downtrodden, and who were to be the forerunners of those who spearheaded the trade union movement. Precursors of modern international law such as Francisco de Vitoria and others, who were basically monks, argued that even the illiterate and pagan Indians in South America, who were objects of Spanish conquests, had certain rights because they were the children of God's creation. Butterfield once noted that friends were forever telling him that a man couldn't be a true Christian unless he was a socialist or unless he was a conservative. To this he responded: "Too often, people are waiting to subordinate their religion to some mundane course or other. They don't quite realize how significant Christianity appears to us when we see in every age where its own principles have taken men." [3]

The contrast could not be greater between this view and the ideology of those who call for the political transformation of religion. Many who call for such transformation have their own hidden political agenda. They seek to

3. Herbert Butterfield, "Religion and Politics" (Unpublished paper in my possession), 3, 4, 7.

impose on religion in general and on Christianity in particular their own pe-
culiar brand of religion, in the most recent years the religion of the Christian right.

There is special irony in all this because of the present state of religion
in America. We live in a society marked, as never before, by religious plural-
ism. Social scientists count the number of so-called religions in the thousands.
This is the reality. Yet we are exposed to an unending stream of religious
discourse that equates family and virtue or religious and political salvation
with what is in fact only one form of one particular Protestant denomination.
New York *Times* religion columnist Kenneth A. Briggs writes: "Fundamentalists and their somewhat more moderate evangelical brethren believe that
moral degeneracy and court decisions, especially those against school prayer
and Bible reading and in support of abortion, have undercut America's divinely sanctioned mission." [4] Another commentator suggested that fundamentalists were acting as though they were "a state religion."

Christian realism embraces a view of religion and politics that is essentially different from present-day fundamentalism. The realists maintain that
the world of politics and the world of religion are not the same world, a view
that orthodox Christianity has always held. The two cannot be merged into a
single union; their values never completely overlap. The ultimate end of religion is a purpose beyond all human purposes, whereas the ends of politics are
most often power as a means to order and justice. Politicians seek to harmonize interests and adjust differences; they are the bargainers and horsetraders.
Their particular temptation is to emphasize means over ends and to place
success ahead of virtue. Some religious leaders suffer from the opposite ex-
cess. They tend to become moralists who are forever preening themselves
over the righteousness of their cause but in the process hardly at all help
struggling humanity in coping with a harsh world. They have no understanding of the virtue that is the hallmark of statesmanship, prudence. It is a virtue,
in the form of political wisdom, that joins together the morally right with the
politically possible and labors to apply ethical principles within the circumstances of competing interests and diverse aims.

Columnist Doug Bandow has written: "The spectacle of clerics using
the Gospel to promote their ideological preferences is not pretty. Thus centu-

4. Kenneth A. Briggs, New York *Times*, September 9, 1984.

ries ago those who desired to freely worship God crossed an ocean to found what became a new nation; today those who claim to follow God drag him into disputes over gambling." At one level, the struggle is being waged within religious bodies themselves. Denominations in which opposing trends have long coexisted are now locked in self-described holy wars. Their struggle is one of total war. Fundamentalists and theological moderates face one another across a deep spiritual chasm, as in the Southern Baptist Convention. One religious writer quoted Baptist moderates as saying that "fundamentalism is not so much a doctrinal position as it is a style of life that is negative, judgmental and suspicious of anyone who doesn't agree with the way they see things." One moderate seminary president went further and spoke of "unholy forces . . . at work in our midst" and "campus subversives" recruited and indoctrinated by the fundamentalists. Conservative leaders revel in their recent political gains and predict a takeover of all the church's institutions in less than a decade. Defending themselves, the moderates are shifting to a year-round strategy, as contrasted with an annual convention, to counter the fundamentalists.

Where is all this leading? For some, religion and politics appear to be merging into what one church historian, George Marsden of Calvin College, calls "shallow folk religion." For others, the casualty is religion itself. However, it is difficult to measure the effects on religion as such. Thirty years ago, the United States appeared to be witnessing the greatest surge of churchgoing in its history. In contrast to nations with an official state church, membership and church attendance were high. A record level of 49 percent of the population attended weekly church services. By the mid-1980s, the level had dropped below 40 percent.

A group of Protestant and Catholic leaders recently hired George Gallup to repeat a survey conducted ten years ago of those he describes as the "unchurched," namely, persons who are neither members nor regular participants in services at some church or synagogue. The findings are not encouraging for the health of organized religion. Some 78 million adults, or 44 percent of the population of the United States, said they did not regularly attend a church or synagogue, compared with 61 million, or 41 percent, ten years ago. Their reasons were not lack of religious faith (88 percent said they prayed to God). The most common complaint was that churches spend too much time worrying about money, influence, and organization. Others objected to too much

dogma or to church teachings that are too narrow and negative or to the hierarchy telling people what to do or think. A recent news article was entitled
"Many Shun Church for Other Acts of Faith." A growing number have turned
from religion to secular activities that they find spiritually more fulfilling.

Most would agree that the data are not conclusive on the effects on
religion of the political activism of certain religious sects. The place of religion in the public square and its concern for human life, rooted in the Bible,
deserves a hearing no less than does the Humanist Manifesto. Yet its guidelines for politics are unclear. Columnist Bandow concludes his critique: "But
while the Bible—the most important sacred text in a nation where Christianity is the predominant religion—tells us a lot about right and wrong in
dealing with God and our neighbors, it says much less about the role of
the state."[5] Ancient Israel as a covenant nation bears little resemblance to
today's secular political systems. No religion offers a coherent list of divinely
ordained public policies. The religious texts we revere were written in a
time of sheep and shepherds, not big government, big labor, and powerful
corporations.

Early in his career, Billy Graham rather incautiously proclaimed that if
all men were Christians there would be no nuclear problem. Niebuhr, who
found the young Graham personally engaging, responded, "Not if we fail to
develop a viable nuclear policy." Archbishop Desmond Tutu may be wiser
than the young Graham, for he repeatedly affirms, "I am a pastor, not a
politician." With the gravest political problems, the hope must still be that
when the moment for conflict resolution arrives, churchmen, and especially
those who seek to convert politics into religion or religion into politics, will
step aside and let the politicians do their work, as in the last two years of the
Reagan administration.

Conclusion

Fortunately, democracies have been saved by the generous admixture of two
traditions that enrich and strengthen one another. The religious tradition is the

5. Doug Bandow, Washington *Post,* August 3, 1988, p. A17.

Judaeo-Christian tradition, which provides fundamental values on which a free society can be based. Religion permeates American government, especially through the dignity it accords the individual. The state exists for the individual, not the individual for the state, as in totalitarian societies. It is fair to ask if there would be any first ten amendments to the Constitution if there were no higher law on which the Constitution rested. As Edwin Corwin and others have demonstrated, the higher law is essentially a political expression of the Judaeo-Christian tradition. Justice, or giving each person his or her due, is a practice derived from broad concepts of equality going back to the idea that all men are equal in God's sight. Values are part of the American political heritage; their roots go back to the Judaeo-Christian tradition. They stand apart from every notion of hierarchy and class structure that undertakes to freeze American society at some arbitrarily chosen point in time.

Counterpoised with this two-thousand-year-old tradition is the Graeco-Roman legacy, which bequeathed ideas of law and politics to American society. If the Judaeo-Christian tradition affirms certain substantive propositions about man and the state, Graeco-Roman thought provides concepts regarding the legal and political process. If the former provides the moral and political underpinnings of the American constitutional system, the latter teaches what is needed for the functioning of the legal and political system. Law gives the order and predictability that holds society together. It protects society against the centrifugal pressures of influence by too many single-interest groups. What united Rome and preserved Roman civilization was Roman law and the confidence every Roman felt in being a Roman citizen (*civis Romanus sum*). The Greek tradition of politics assured both respect for political experience—the experience of men reaching self-fulfillment through participation in the political life of the polity—and an honest recognition that politics was not religion or philosophy but without them was bound to become an order of brigands and robbers. The Aristotelian study of political systems offered distinctions between the absolutely best, the best under particular circumstances, and the corrupted political systems.

The dual legacy of Judaeo-Christian and Graeco-Roman thought assured that two important strains of thinking would continue down to the present in the American political system. The two protected the colonies and ultimately the Union from both utopianism and cynicism. Because the Judaeo-Christian tradition put the individual at the center of the political universe, sanctified by a relationship with God, no tyrant's strategy is defensible if it sacrifices individual rights to some collective or ideological goal. Thus the religious tradition protects us against cynicism. From the Greeks, Americans learned that politics, though worthy of respect, was neither the highest nor the lowest form of experience. It partakes of a certain moral dignity, however, because men are able to learn virtue through politics. It is a realm of trial and error, of light and shadows, of shades of grays more than of unquestioned right or wrong. Above all, politics is essential in the City of Man, even as religion is the cornerstone of the City of God. Seemingly, present-day political and religious figures have either forgotten or never known these ancient truths. They seem oblivious to their meaning when they seek the religious transformation of politics or the political transformation of religion. Their mission is hardly designed to bring health to the relationship between religion and politics.

Part II

Complexities and Constraints:
The Realities of Practice

6

Realism

Some forty years ago, George F. Kennan sought to define the national interest by discussing what it was not. By boxing in the concept and excluding broad areas that extended beyond the national interest, he reasoned that he might possibly contribute to improved understanding. He explained his rationale: "Concepts and ideas are sometimes like shy wild animals. You can never get near enough to touch them and make exact measurements of them, but you can round them up and gradually pen them in." Kennan's method was argument by exclusion. Ideas such as national interest were too rich in meaning, too many-sided, for any single explicit and narrow definition. By confining the scope and content of a concept, we are able to approach its meaning more fully, not by definition but by exclusion.

To illustrate, Kennan pointed to three things the national interest is not. First, it is *not* "a detached interest in our international environment *for its own sake*, independent of our own aspirations and problems." A nation's values, history, geography, and international relationships are aspects of national interest. Second, national interest does *not* consist in the pursuit of abstractions, such as peace or a just peace or other legal definitions. Third, it is *not* "primarily a question of purpose or of objective but rather "a question of method"; that is, it "is a question of the 'how' rather than the 'what.' " Thus, national interest is an approach to the conduct of foreign policy. On this third point, Kennan explained: "A study of the great decisions of national policy in the past leaves the historian impressed with the difficulty of analyzing the future clearly enough to make really reliable calculations of the consequences of national action. It also reveals that too often the motives of national action are ones dictated for government by developments outside of its control. Its freedom of action, in these cases, lies only in the choice of method—in the *how* rather than the *what*." [1] In excluding from the meaning of the national

1. George F. Kennan, "The National Interest of the United States," *Illinois Law Review,* XLV (January–February, 1951), 730, 736, 738.

interest mere abstractions and concepts divorced from the traditions, the history and values of a particular nation, and thinking that ignores the question of style and methods, Kennan sought to give direction to foreign policy actions. It may be that a comparable approach to the subject of political realism can perform a similar function.

It can be said, first, that realism is *not* the glorification of force and violence. It is *not* German romanticism or unchecked militarism. Although some who emphasize the role of conflict equate force with power, the premier political realists from Machiavelli to Morgenthau most decidedly do not. They draw rather sharp distinctions between the political process at work and its breakdown in civil war when force and violence take the place of power. Competition for influence and power is essentially a psychological relationship. By contrast, force and violence involve physical relationships between individuals, groups, and nation-states. Because the goal in political contests is the control of one mind or a group of minds over others, the most subtle of all forms of psychological relations comes into play. Give-and-take, compromise, and concessions are at the heart of the political process.

Second, realism is *not* the antithesis of morality. The writings on international politics by realists such as Niebuhr, Morgenthau, and Butterfield are dominated by a profound concern with morality. However, they address morality not in the abstract but in relationship to political action and, in particular, international political action. That relationship is one of tension because the facts of politics impose sometimes inescapably hard choices in morality; political choices are a blending of moral choice and political necessity. Moral commands offer standards that are oftentimes in conflict with the requirements of political success. On the level of international relationships among nation-states, universal moral standards are rarely applicable directly to the actions of those states but must be filtered through the circumstances of time and place in which nations find themselves. Ethics judges human action by its conformity with the moral law: "Thou shalt not kill." Political ethics, especially as expressed in the ethics of responsibility, judges action by its political consequences: "Thou mayst kill in defense of thy country." In the relationship between morality and politics, prudence, because of the inherent tension between moral and political imperatives, becomes the instrument of mediation and thereby the supreme virtue.

Third, moral judgment is *not* exhausted in the moral purposes and goals of a particular nation, even though throughout history nations have been tempted to identify their moral aspirations with universal moral purposes. What the Germans proclaimed in the particularly self-righteous phrase "Got mit uns" (God is on our side) has in varying degrees marked the national self-righteousness of nations throughout history. Butterfield writes of nations being locked into their own particular forms of national self-righteousness. Rather than helping them to attain greater virtue, it prevents their recognizing the virtue and the interests of others.

If realism is neither the glorification of force and violence nor the antithesis of morality nor a recognition of the universal righteousness of a particular nation—my nation—what is it? Once we have boxed in the meaning of realism by invoking the principle of exclusion, what remains? A rather frivolous answer might be "A great deal." The history of mankind harking back to classical and biblical times is essentially a chronicle of the interplay of change and recurrence in political life. Two overarching theories offer explanations of this history. One school of thought sees man irresistibly on the move. The account is familiar and reassuring. Optimists proclaim man's conquest of nature and ultimately his conquest of himself. History is on the march. Progress is occurring across an ever-widening front. Ancient rivalries and struggles for power are seen as becoming things of the past. New laws and new institutions are molding and fashioning "the new man." In the same way that American society rooted out slavery in the nineteenth century, it will eliminate war in the twentieth century. By whatever name proponents identify themselves and their world view, the essential features of the new utopia are not difficult to discover. Its mood is one of unquenchable optimism. Its faith reposes in novel institutions, changed human nature, and a unilinear theory of progress. It looks forward to a kinder, gentler world in which ambition and alliances, self-interest and balances of power, will fade away and no longer threaten peace and tranquillity.

Realism, by contrast, insists on the need to deal with the world as it is. Realists don't deny that the scale and setting of international politics may some day change. Present-day nations quite possibly will be superseded by larger, more comprehensive political units better suited to meet and solve such problems of late industrial societies as nuclear conflict, environmental deterioration, or the population explosion. However, even if the players in the drama of world politics change, the play will go on much the same as it has for hundreds of years. The main actors in the drama will continue to play out their roles of competition and cooperation. Competition will express underlying social forces, such as nationalism and imperialism, which in turn are the expression of yet more basic aspects of human nature. The struggle for power and peace is driven by the dynamic of underlying social forces that are inherent in human nature. To improve the world, leaders must work with such forces, seeking to bend them to the most constructive ends. As for cooperation, its cornerstone is the convergence of interests of nations and groups who come together because of expected benefits and rewards more often than from noble goals or transcendent purposes alone.

Realism approaches international politics in the same way it approaches human relations: as the arena where self-pride and self-interest comingle with high purposes. Man is a curious and contradictory blending of selfishness and virtue. Philosophers who talk only of man's selfishness fail to explain how we are able to recognize self-centeredness in the absence of a sense of virtue and otherness. On another ethical plane, without some measure of good how do we perceive evil? Is it not self-evident that men need at least to glimpse the good in order to recognize evil? Yet those thinkers who praise the good and see man as basically virtuous ignore the distance separating the affirmation of the good from its practice. It will not do to describe man as either wholly good and virtuous or totally depraved and evil unless philosophy wishes to divorce itself from the vast array of evidence from historical experience.

Once men and nations are perceived as inescapably good and evil, or on another plane self-interested and altruistic, realism sets out in search of the proper political order. It discovers, at least in the West, such an order in a political system that holds man's selfishness in check through countervailing balances of power while seeking to channel both self-interest and virtue to the most practical and realizable good ends. Significantly, the greatest contemporary realists have been democrats who have celebrated the American political order of separation of powers and checks and balances. Equally noteworthy, the supreme hero of realists such as Niebuhr and Morgenthau is Abraham Lincoln, who, though he exercised emergency powers with seeming disregard for legislative authority in suspending habeas corpus and raising an army, went on to seek early ratification by a returning Congress. The two realists often paraphrased founding fathers such as Madison, saying that if men were devils no government would be possible and if they were angels no government would be necessary. However, because man is such a complex intermixture of good and evil, realists must be schooled in managing both the selfish and virtuous aspects of human nature.

Moreover, the constraints of realism can be as great for highly virtuous men as they are for selfish men. The theologian Niebuhr was wont to speak of the hazards of religion and philosophy that lead men to claim they are more virtuous than they really are. The political scientist Morgenthau warned of the need to hold good men in check. He wrote of men and women who consider they are so good that they stand above all rules of the political order. They are the Fawn Halls of the international order. Like Ms. Hall, who was Colonel Oliver North's secretary at the time of the Iran-Contra crisis, they claim they are following a law higher than the Constitution, just as she did when she shredded the Iran-Contra documents. Whereas society has found ways to take the bad man in stride and protect itself against those who know the rules of the political game only too well and use them to the detriment of society, it also needs protection from men who are so good that they suffer no external rules or constraints.

Realism lays stress on learning to put oneself in the statesman's shoes and walking alongside him in the choices he must make. What is required of the observer is, in a certain respect, what we expect of the diplomat or statesman. Professor Morgenthau put it best: "What is required of the statesman is, first of all, to see clearly: himself, the enemy, and then himself again as the enemy sees him. To see clearly means to see without passions, without the passion of pride, of hatred, and of contempt. The statesman must master the paradox of wanting passionately to win over an enemy to whom he feels passionately superior, and of having to view his relations with the enemy with the detachment and objectivity of the scholar." [2]

Realism also seeks to provide a road map of the factors that the statesman must weigh and evaluate. Foremost are considerations of interest and power. Realism's central concern is the need for unifying concepts and for a theory of politics, whether domestic or international. For a general theory of politics, interest defined as power provides the type of unifying focus that income or profits provide for economics and that social class once provided

2. Hans J. Morgenthau, *Politics in the Twentieth Century: The Decline of Democratic Politics* (3 vols.; Chicago, 1958), I, 338.

for sociology. The test of such a theory is not whether it gives ready-made and universally accepted solutions to foreign policy problems but rather whether it is logically coherent and empirically consistent with the facts of history on which it is based.

Historically, support for such concepts may be found in the writings of philosophers and statesmen. For Thucydides, the history of ancient Greece demonstrated that "identity of interests is the surest of bonds whether between states or individuals," and in the nineteenth century Lord Salisbury found evidence that "the only bond of union that endures" among nation-states is "the absence of all clashing interests." Our first president, George Washington, went further in laying down the general principle:

> A small knowledge of human nature will convince us, that, with far the greatest part of mankind, interest is the governing principle; and that almost every man is more or less, under its influence. Motives of public virtue may for a time, or in particular instances, actuate men to the observance of a conduct purely disinterested; but they are not of themselves sufficient to produce persevering conformity to the refined dictates and obligations of social duty. Few men are capable of making a continual sacrifice of all views of private interest, or advantage, to the common good. It is vain to exclaim against the depravity of human nature. . . . The experience of every age and nation has proved it and we must in a great measure, change the constitution of man, before we can make it otherwise. No institution not built on the presumptive truth of these maxims can succeed.[3]

Woodrow Wilson, idealist though he was, wrote of the double temper of Americans and illustrated it with the example of Jefferson:

> "Peace is our passion," he declared; but the passion abated when he saw the mouth of the Mississippi about to pass into the hands of France. Though he had loved France and hated England, he did not hesitate then what language to hold. "There is on the globe," he wrote to Mr. Livingston at Paris, "one single spot the possessor of which is our natural and

3. *The Writings of George Washington,* ed. John C. Fitzpatrick (39 vols.; Washington, D.C., 1931–44), X, 363.

habitual enemy. The day that France takes possession of New Orleans seals the union of two nations, who, in conjunction, can maintain exclusive possession of the seas. From that moment we must marry ourselves to the British fleet and nation." Our interests must march forward, altruists though we are; other nations must see to it that they stand off, and do not seek to stay us.[4]

The concept of national interest has sometimes been compared with the "great generalities" of the Constitution, such as the general welfare and due process clauses. The core, or residual, meaning of national interest is determined by factors such as the vital interests the nation seeks to protect in order to maintain its security, the political environment within which it defends its interests, and the rational necessities that limit the choice of ends and means by all actors on the stage of international politics. Those necessities include the necessity of choice not between absolute good and evil but between competing goods. National interest requires that decision makers establish hierarchies of interests and goals. Further, it demands that leaders distinguish between personal moral sympathies and the nation's political interests that must be defended. Lincoln called attention to such differences when he spoke of his *official* duty to preserve the Union and his *personal* wish to see universal moral values prevail. The individual has a right to sacrifice himself in defense of a moral principle. The statesman has no moral right to act in defense of a universal moral principle, say, of liberty, if the nation's survival is in jeopardy.

National interest is comprised of a series of relatively permanent and variable elements within the framework of a political approach to foreign policy. The survival of the nation or, at other points in time, of any political unit is the irreducible minimum of the national interest or interest in general. The content of such an interest encompasses the nation's territorial integrity, the preservation of its political institutions from external threat, and its history and culture. The variable elements of national interest include crosscurrents of thinking among leading personalities, public opinion, sectional interests, partisan politics, and changing folkways. The unfolding of the national interest in practice is a product of the movement of thought and action between

4. Woodrow Wilson, "Democracy and Efficiency," *Atlantic Monthly,* LXXXVII (March, 1901), 293–94.

the core and the periphery, the relatively permanent and the variable elements of national interest.

Whenever nations seek to realize their goals in international politics, including the safeguarding of the national interest, they do so by striving for power, which can be defined as "man's control over the minds and actions of other men." Political power involves "the mutual relations of control among the holders of public authority and between [them] and the people at large." [5] It also involves the mutual relations among nations pursuing their national interests.

The link between power and national interest is in one respect a relationship between means and ends. Through power, men and nations seek to safeguard and realize their interests. The quest for power and security, however, is bound up with man's anxiety and insecurity. Men are anxious about their insecurity and secretly fearful of their limitations. They feel vulnerable in the presence of the power of others. Therefore, they endlessly search for power over others as the road to greater security. The more they gain power, the more they contribute to the insecurity of others. Children seek security and self-esteem by reaching out for independence and autonomy within the family. Parents strive to preserve their authority and to maintain family values and control. Thus, personal growth for children is in tension with family stability. Throughout society, men seek power over their fellows in order to achieve self-realization and to overcome social anxiety. They endeavor in a multitude of ways to subdue others lest they be dominated in turn.

The struggle for political power is only one example of the rivalry played out at every level of human life. It manifests itself in the relations of husband and wife, of parents and children, of the new spouse in the family and the mother-in-law, and of children, step-children, and remarried parents. The best witnesses to power are step-children and mothers-in-law because they may alternately be both victims and wielders of power. For example, one parent may treat a step-child as inferior, or the child may seek to influence its own parent against a new spouse. In national politics, power is present in the struggle between national governments and the champions of states' rights, among the three branches of government, executive, legislative, and judici-

5. Hans J. Morgenthau and Kenneth W. Thompson, *Politics Among Nations* (6th ed.; New York; 1985), 32.

ary, and between majority and minority ethnic groups. On the international scene, it is a perennial feature in relations and rivalries between France and Germany, Russia and Germany, the Soviet Union and the United States, and the Soviet Union and China.

Because family and great power struggles involve psychological elements that stem from human anxiety, they are raised to the level of spirit, where the quest for influence and power becomes limitless and insatiable. Man, being more than a natural creature, is not interested merely in physical survival but seeks prestige and social approval. Thus, while he shares with the animals their natural appetites and desires and, not least, the impulse for survival, man seeks something more. Having the intelligence to anticipate the perils in which he stands, he seeks security by enhancing his power, individually and collectively. In so doing, he places in jeopardy the security of others, who in turn seek greater power, which then becomes threatening to still others. By casting the quest for power in terms of spirit and ideology, nations find themselves in the grip of a nearly insoluble conflict.

This terrible human predicament, or deadlock with one's neighbors, is the fateful security-power dilemma. Weak men and weak nations assume that if they had more power, they would be more secure. However, the more power (or missiles or territory or bases or allies) an individual or nation acquires, the more its individual or collective life impinges on the lives and security of others. Thus, more wisdom is required to bring it into some kind of decent and viable harmony with others. All social and political groups in the political arena, though, are motivated, half-consciously at times, to seek dominion over others. Labor seeks dominion over management, and management over labor. Every collective or corporate entity competes for security and power in the manner of the individuals who comprise it. The intensity of group conflicts grows out of their tendency to express both the virtue and selfishness of the group's members. Nationalism in particular unites the self-sacrificial loyalty to a given nation-state with the frustrated aggression of the masses who seek through their nation to achieve the supremacy denied them as individuals in mass societies.

Is there an escape from this dilemma? Realists maintain one escape exists in the restoration of diplomacy and the return to foreign policy based on the national interest. Such a return is capable of bringing moderation and a less messianic style to the conduct of foreign policy. Nations can induce greater mutual respect for the interests of others simply by becoming more self-conscious of their own interests. International politics needs to be freed from the crusading spirit. Once all come to accept the fact that nations must base their policies on interest defined in terms of power, they can move away from the terrible human predicament of spiraling power and ever-intensifying ideological conflicts. Such is the realist hope.

If we were to write a postscript to all the early debates over realism, we would be surprised at how the focus of criticism and apparently of thinking in international relations has shifted. The debate is no longer over how nations behave. It is all too apparent that present-day nation-states put their own interests first and that they seek power and influence through alliances and arms buildups. This description fits both the new nations who form themselves into power blocs, such as the Committee of 77 in the United Nations, and those who commit serious violations of international law, as in Iraq's invasion of Kuwait. International law goes unrespected not alone by the new nations who have criticized it as a product of western political thinking but by the United States, who in the 1980s breached it in the mining of the Nicaraguan harbor. Thus, the utopian vision of an international society ordered by international law with law-abiding states has lost at least some of its credibility. The attitudes and beliefs of the 1930s and 1940s have lost much of their appeal and in their place realism increasingly provides a more coherent system of thought.

Surprising as it seems, the new criticism of realism is directed at flaws in the self-executing character of its principles. Apparently, some believe that realism, in contrast with conservatism or liberalism or any other past political or normative theory, must provide universally agreed upon answers and policies for successive foreign policy problems. Failing that, realism's validity is in question. It is as if one were to argue that the general welfare or due process clauses of the Constitution ought automatically to give not only a broad standard embodied in a general principle but a ready-made policy answer on which everyone agreed with respect to every problem. Yet we know that not even our highest judges agree, as is reflected in the multitude of five-to-four judgments by the Supreme Court.

No one of right mind and sound judgment would claim that a concept such as national interest can do everything for foreign policy. Free political choice, politics in a democracy, and issues requiring on-balance judgments, to mention only three among many factors, preclude ready-made answers. What a "great generality" such as national interest assures is attention to core concerns that a nation's leaders ignore at risk of the nation's survival. National interest provides a rational map for the preservation of a nation's security. Implementing and realizing such requirements are no simpler than agreeing on the requirements of the general welfare. Policy makers pursue such ends in a world of light and shadows. Shifting forces on the periphery influence action. Without some map of political imperatives, however, action has no guideposts. Like a pilot's checklist as he prepares to launch an aircraft into flight, the core elements of national interest guide the statesman in the hard choices he must make. To expect more of a theory is to reduce decision makers to automatons, without all the variations in temperament and psychology that characterize them in living societies. Thus, political realism offers pointers for thinking about foreign policy but not fixed solutions and answers. It provides signposts, not simple answers.

Another illusion is the view of so-called friendly critics that the failure of some of the acknowledged leaders in realist thought to arrive at the same policy conclusions for a given foreign policy problem proves the insufficiency of the realist paradigm. This criticism ignores the interplay of the many factors that influence conclusions on particular issues, whether made by policy makers or by theorists. The example of Vietnam in the 1960s and 1970s is a case in point. Some who harbored doubts about U.S. policy in Vietnam nevertheless supported that policy, provisionally at least, as a way of maintaining the solidarity of Franco-American relations in Europe. Others who were privy to information about early U.S. initiatives for negotiations with the Vietcong were more sympathetic to U.S. policy in Vietnam than those who had no such knowledge. However strongly held our views might have been on the need for peacemaking, the troublesome question "What do you want me to do tomorrow morning?" remained. This question was what Secretary Rusk asked his critics over and over again. Basically, he was asking, "How do we get from here to there?" A host of variable factors clustering around the core aspects of the national interest influence the perspectives on policy and help form the judgment of leaders who otherwise share a common philosophy of international politics.

None of these variations in thinking or differences in tactics can excuse theorists or policy makers from failure to weigh the principal elements that should have made up the central question: Is U.S. policy in Vietnam based on U.S. national interest? It is significant that critics and defenders alike either ignored this question or answered it in the negative but still went on to justify continued U.S. action in Vietnam on other grounds. To claim that the theory of the national interest was responsible for such an evasion of political judgment is hardly reason for dismissing the theory. Moreover, the strongest proponents of national interest among American theorists, whether Morgenthau, Niebuhr, or other realists, were generally united in agreement on the errors of U.S. policy for that troubled land.

Therefore, the foremost realists dismiss criticisms that seek to make the point, first, that realism almost always leads some individuals to different policy conclusions and, second, that on highly contentious issues such as Vietnam it can provide no fixed solution or absolute policy guidance. Most leading realists, in fact, had early on reached consensus on Vietnam. The problem with Vietnam was not that the national interest approach was tried and found wanting but rather that it was never tried by those who were responsible for American foreign policy. Their answer was no, the United States had no direct and immediate national or strategic interest in Vietnam but yes, we should commit 500,000 men to its defense on grounds of collective security or the domino theory. That formula is reminiscent of the three-step logic Churchill applied in questioning his government's policy over the Italian invasion of Ethiopia. The government, he said, had declared that "sanctions meant war" and "we reject war," but "we must apply sanctions." The logic of policy in Vietnam followed a similar course, however much that policy might have been defensible on humanitarian or other grounds. The example puts to rest the most recent criticism of national interest voiced by newcomers to the debate, most of whom have been far removed from the conduct of foreign policy in this or any other country.

7

Power

Thinking about power, especially as an aspect of international politics, has been influenced by four historic attitudes in Western society. The first treats power as man's highest end in life and the noblest expression of his potential. It is a viewpoint that sanctifies and glorifies power, whether for the individual or the group. The individual's fulfillment and self-realization are dependent on his ability to dominate other men. It is in man's nature to seek domination. The best in human nature emerges when one person seeks dominion over others. History's most compelling lesson, thus, is the survival of the fittest. However, the German romantics and certain philosophers who hold to this view of power assert that religion and culture stand in the way of the attainment of the deepest attributes of man's nature. Religious and humanitarian creeds shelter and protect the weak and perpetuate the lives of the infirm and the disabled. Even the Good Samaritan does a disservice by sustaining those who lack the inner resources to maintain themselves. This version of power, which some have called the idolatry of the strong, reached its most powerful expression philosophically in the writings of Friedrich Nietzsche. Its most blatant form is extreme crusading nationalism. Its ultimate corruption came with the doctrine of National Socialism and Hitler's conception of a superior Teutonic race. The Führer went Darwinism one better by not only celebrating an existing superior people but calling for artificial and coercive methods for breeding a new super race. Hitler freed his followers from all the restraints of religion and culture and gave them incentives to rise to ever higher levels of self-realization. As for the state, the great German philosopher Georg Wilhelm Friedrich Hegel had argued earlier that "the root kernel of the doctrine" was "the idea of a state, which ought to form one nation . . . [and] should be brought to realization by . . . *all the methods necessary for that purpose* [my emphasis]." [1]

1. Friedrich Meinecke, *Machiavellism: The Doctrine of Raison d'Etat and Its Place in Modern History,* trans. Douglas Scott (Boulder, 1984), 358.

A second attitude toward power has been particularly popular at various times in American history. In effect, it represents a denial or outlawry of power and power politics. It sees political power as an archaism or a transient condition of politics. Modern reformist and rationalist thought looks down on power politics as a product of the European state system, a condition of nations crowded together in a conflict-ridden continent. This view of history as a morality play separates the actors into two sets, Europeans and Americans. An attack on the practice and reality of power politics comes naturally to Americans, who have escaped the Old World and seek freedom in the New. They have shaken the dust of Europe from their feet and begun a new life. They see themselves as a chosen people arriving on the shores of a land that for them was a New Jerusalem. Early on, their leaders had warned of becoming embroiled in Europe's ancient struggles and conflicts. Their first president, but others as well, had spoken out against "entangling alliances." Europe's affairs were not their affairs and its historic rivalries were not their concern. They were shielded from danger by a vast ocean and by the protection of the British Navy.

A century and a half later, Secretary of State Cordell Hull on returning from the Moscow Conference heralded the United Nations as a new international institution that would do away with alliances, balance of power, and traditional power politics. He explained that he had studied the history of international relations and believed it was power politics that had brought about conflict and war. In a new and better world, ancient forms of international relationships would be eradicated by a system of law and world order.

A subtler, less direct approach to the denial of power and power politics coincided with the rise of the middle class in modern industrial societies. Representatives of the middle class were proclaimed the carriers of democracy and freedom. They had triumphed over the aristocracy. It seemed plausible, as one looked back, to suggest that power politics belonged to the aristocracy and aristocratic government. The greatest practitioners of diplomacy and power politics had, after all, been aristocrats. With the supplanting of aristocracy by democracy, power politics would thus come to an end.

A third attitude is one that sees power as wholly a result of economics. Marxists have argued that power politics is the product of the underlying means of production. In the feudal era, lords and rulers exercised dominion over their vassals. Later, the bourgeoisie in the name of capitalism dominated the working class. As the historical process unfolds, the proletariat will re-place the bourgeoisie, just as the bourgeoisie took the place of feudal lords. Once communist means of production have supplanted capitalist means of production, the state will wither away and a classless society will be ushered in. In Karl Marx's oft-quoted phrase, the domination of man by man will yield to the administration of things. Power in our day is therefore a product of capitalism.

A fourth attitude views power as essentially an ongoing type of psycho-logical relationship. Power is universal in the political relations of men and nations. Whatever man's ultimate ends, he uses power in organized society to seek that end. Power can be channeled within a constitutional framework, where it can be held in check through the separation of powers and counter-vailing power. However, power as such does not disappear. It is present at every level of society and in all the communities of mankind. It is a perennial factor in politics and except for remote primitive societies is omnipresent, for no one has found a way to translate that kind of indifference to power into the world of the modern nation-state system. Power manifests itself in the relation of mind to mind or will to will. It is a universal relationship among men and nations.

Thus, power is said to be universal in modern societies. Scholars write of the ubiquity of power. It takes on at least four manifestations that analysts and statesmen have identified and evaluated. First, power is fundamental in the human condition. The quest for dominion is deeply rooted in human striv-ing. It is associated with creativity, dynamism, strength of character, and personality. Power is a product of the spirit and creatureliness of man. It comes into play when soaring dreams and vaulting ambitions confront prac-tical realities. Power mediates between them.

"Pride and ambition," Winston Churchill explained, "are the prod of every worthy deed." The quest for dominion is the pathway to realizing val-ues and goals and to controlling one's environment. In the simplest language, power involves "taking charge." The violinist Isaac Stern was asked the se-cret of the great creative performing artist. He responded that he must domi-nate his audience. Stern went on to say that from the moment the artist ap-pears on stage, he must help the audience to know that he (or she) is in command of himself, of his music, and of them. If they have any doubt of his competence or his confidence, his presence must reassure them.

In politics, we speak of the charismatic leader. He is someone who is in command. Wherever such a person is found, all eyes turn to him (or her). Whenever he is present, he takes a place at the center of the discussion. Conversation flows to him rather than leaving him on the fringes of the group. (One criticism, whether justified or not, of the outstanding Democratic candidate for president in the 1950s, Governor Adlai Stevenson of Illinois, was that often in a group he found himself on the periphery of discussions rather than being unmistakably at the head of the table.)

For the commanding leader, an element of mystery surrounds his power. As a speaker, he may not employ perfectly correct grammar. For example, President Eisenhower's press conference answers often appeared garbled and confused. He may not be the most experienced executive or the best-educated person, at least as measured by formal education. Friends marveled at the warm and admiring relationship between the largely self-educated Truman and his Groton-educated secretary of state, Dean Acheson. Yet anyone who was present when the president, following his retirement from office, recounted the story of his political career to a group of some of the most powerful men in America at the New York Council of Foreign Relations soon discovered the sources of his strength. At first his audience of the powerful and the mighty, bankers and businessmen, and diplomats and scholars sat back in their chairs, a little embarrassed by his simple, unabashed story of a first visit to Europe following his presidency. He talked with childlike simplicity of being greeted by the Italian people. He was amazed at the respect and affection they had shown him. Then he began describing the great foreign policy decisions he had made in that famous fifteen-week period in 1946, and all of them—bankers, scholars, and university presidents—leaned forward in their chairs. At that point, they discovered why Acheson and all his colleagues had such respect for the little man from Missouri who knew instinctively when and where the buck stopped.

Casting the net more broadly, however, the mystery still remains. Some of America's greatest leaders, including its first president, have resisted the ascent to power and turned power aside after briefly exercising it. Others such as Richard Daley, Chicago's longtime mayor, have tried to avoid tests of power and are remembered for such homey phrases as "Don't make no waves; don't rock no boats." Some presidents, including Jimmy Carter, have come from small states without much national experience or power, and others,

such as the actor Ronald Reagan, have had unusual backgrounds in preparation for political power. Apparently neither youth, for John F. Kennedy, nor
old age, for Reagan, qualify or disqualify men and women from the exercise
of power. Nevertheless, culture and circumstances may shape the environment within which power holders are chosen, as in China, where ancestor
worship and respect for the elderly influence public attitudes toward aging
leaders. Leadership and success in the acquiring of power sometimes move in
cycles. It seems that for everything there is a time and a season. Kennedy's
call for a new generation of leaders to take the torch of power followed the
era of an aging hero-president, Dwight D. Eisenhower. Harold Nicolson in
The Portrait of a Diplomatist tells of an eighty-six-year-old ancestor who
grew increasingly blind and deaf and painfully arthritic. He remained quietly
in the corner of his room, yet enfeebled as he was, he invariably became the
center of any discussion. Before they left, visitors always turned to him for
his wisdom. At eighty-six, he had become the commanding presence.

A second manifestation of power is in its link with anxiety and insecurity. We seek power in order to overcome fear and anxiety. Power is a function
of man's response to powerlessness. Men and nations are anxious about their
insecurity and secretly fearful of their limitations and vulnerability. The
macho image and the cultivation of feminine charms are especially visible
responses to anxiety. Men and women search for security through power and
its manifestations, hoping thereby to enhance self-esteem and individual autonomy. The search is unending and the dilemma insoluble throughout life.
Children seek security by reaching out for greater independence and power to
find an answer to the timeless question "Who am I?" Parents respond with
efforts to preserve their authority and maintain family values and controls. A
child's personal growth is almost always in some kind of tension with family
stability and the status quo. Even the most powerful feel insecure in the absence of the last measure of power they seek.

To overcome social anxiety and achieve self-realization, then, persons
seek power over others, endeavoring in a multitude of ways to subdue them
lest they themselves be overcome and dominated. The struggle for political
power among the holders of political authority and between them and the
people is but one example, though a particularly poignant one, of the rivalry
that goes on at every level of human life. As we have noted above, the struggle for power manifests itself in relations between husband and wife, parents

and children, spouses and in-laws (the classic rivalry between new spouses and mothers-in-law), children and remarried parents, and children and step-children. In the United States, contests for political power occur among ethnic groups, between advocates of states' rights and national governments, and among the three branches of government. The struggle for power is also a perennial feature of international politics, involving a long succession of countries, each moving to the center of the international stage at different times in history: France versus Germany, the Soviet Union versus the United States, China versus the Soviet Union, and tripolar and multipolar patterns of power. In the Cold War, the Soviet Union sought control of Eastern Europe, while the United States extended its influence into Europe and the rimland of Asia. Far from disappearing, power rivalries have persisted with ever greater intensity in the postwar era, that era Secretary Hull had prophesied would see their demise.

A third manifestation of power in the postwar world is expressed in the truth that the struggle has been raised to the level of spirit, where contests become limitless and the appetite for power insatiable. As I argued earlier, man is interested in more than mere physical survival; he also seeks prestige and social approval. Possessing the intelligence to anticipate the dangers surrounding him, man seeks safeguards against those perils by amassing power. Thus men, individually and collectively, jeopardize the security of their fellows to achieve their own security. They couch the quest for power in the language of spirit and in ideologies so all-embracing and controlling that they are unable to retreat from them.

Domestically, minority groups who have been abused and persecuted for generations also raise the struggle for autonomy and well-being to the level of spirit, thus threatening those who were earlier their sponsors. The intensification of the conflict may take the form of a holy war between two largely spiritual versions of politics, each seeking supremacy without compromise. The surge of one crusading vision is met by the backlash of another: blacks versus white ethnics, women versus the opponents of ERA, pro- and anti-abortion movements, and a host of other struggles. Whoever the participants, the struggle manifests itself in appeals to the hearts of men. Within the White House, members of the staff "struggle for the mind of the presidency." If it remains at the level of spirit and with the suspension of the political process becomes no longer susceptible to compromise and give-and-take, the struggle can be beyond resolution.

A fourth manifestation of the problem of power is the security-power dilemma. Mankind is caught in a terrible human predicament. The security-power dilemma is the most fateful and tragic expression of international politics. Nation-states find themselves in deadlock with their neighbors. The process ever recurs.

The source of the security-power problem is capable of definition. Contempt for another group, whether family or nation, is the pathetic form that respect for one's own frequently takes. For families, the tender emotions that bind members of the same family together are sometimes expressed as indifference and distrust for others. It is often true that the more I love and protect my own children, the more I am tempted to overlook the needs of others. The quest for the strengthening of ethnic groups at a subnational level may produce national disunity. Not my country first but my family or ethnic group first becomes the rallying cry. Professor O. D. Corpuz of the University of the Philippines tells the story of a certain president of the Philippine republic. When President Carlos Garcia was charged with having diverted funds from the public treasury to members of his extended family, he responded that he lived under two laws of morality: responsibility to his family and responsibility to the state. When the two conflicted, he said, family responsibility came first. Corpuz described these two laws as the two faces of Philippine morality. Not only family interests but special interest groups gain priority over national interest, illustrating the fourth problem.

Contemporary nationalism is by far the most serious manifestation of the security-power dilemma. Nations seek power and threaten other nations, which then increase their own power, thus threatening others. One nation builds up its armory of weapons to assure its security, generating a response in kind from its principal rival. The full force of the security-power dilemma stems from a mixture of psychological factors. A self-sacrificial loyalty to the state, when conjoined with the frustration and aggression of the masses, who seek through the nation to achieve the supremacy denied them as individuals, produces a dangerous strain of nationalism. In an increasingly mechanized world individuals may be deprived of the rewards that personal growth and fulfillment can bring. Historically, the example of the displaced middle class in Hitler's Germany is the most fateful and dramatic. Driven down into the lower class by the ravages of inflation, the so-called lumpenproletariat helped to fuel the sinister campaigns of the Führer. Because they had lost pride and any sense of fulfillment in their own unhappy lives, they sought it in the conquests of National Socialism. They rallied to the harsh cries of Hitler because he promised what they imagined was their rightful dominion over others. The full fury of the German pursuit of security and the quest for power at the expense of almost every humane value found justification in the psychology of the German people.

In our attempt to understand the reality of power, it is important that we consider not only prevailing attitudes toward power and the most significant manifestations of power but also its root causes and its more important components, whether for individuals or nations. Writers on power alternately seek to condemn and deny power or to glorify and defend it. At some point the student of power is driven back to consider such fundamental puzzles as the nature of man and the nature of the international system. Yet the problem for the political scientist in addressing a discussion of root causes is profound and may be insoluble.

For almost two decades I worked overseas alongside agricultural and medical scientists—scientists for whom I came to feel growing admiration mixed with much awe and a little envy. As a group, they expressed an overwhelming conviction that what they were doing mattered. They were single-minded in their concentration on what they called "the core problem." They united with fellow scientists, whatever their nationality or politics, in a spirit reminiscent of wartime camaraderie. As one of them put it, they had confidence they could "turn around" the agricultural or health delivery system of any country. They believed they could transform such systems. Their approach and dedication, I hoped, might be transferable to educational assistance in the developing countries, which was my responsibility. Two lessons or guidelines emerged for me from their approach to science: first, seek to identify the most urgent problem or problems in any society; second, look for its root cause, not merely the symptoms.

These precepts of the natural sciences face resistance in the human sciences. Human and psychological obstacles stand in the way. All of us construct our own little escape mechanisms when asked to face our most urgent problems. Denial is an ever-present reality in life. Infants react in rage when sources of comfort or gratification are absent or removed. Implicitly, they blame parents or an unfriendly world or both. Child psychologists and counselors explain they must begin their first counseling sessions with the words "Excuses, excuses, excuses." On a less serious note, in an inner office on the entrance to his door a famous adult psychiatrist has a sign that reads: "Stop, think twice. This is expensive. You may really be inferior."

Why don't men face their problems? Turning for an answer to philosophy and religion, we find that one response is the mixture of mortality and immortality in the spirit of man. The perplexities and contradictions of life make up the human condition. We are all children of nature, subject to the limitations of every living thing seeking to survive. One aspect of the human problem is that we are mortal. For men, as for animals, life has a beginning, a middle, and an end. This sequence is the essence of all finite life. Yet as men and women, we are also unique among all living beings in the extent of our possibilities and potential. We are finite yet also infinite in our views of ourselves, of society, and of our destiny. Every religion and philosophy of any worth acknowledges the dualism in man's nature.

Reinhold Niebuhr began the Gifford Lectures by asking this question: "Man has always been his own most vexing problem. How is he to think of himself?" [2] First of all, we are creatures hedged in by circumstances and limits. We are caught up in the search for security and the lust for power. Our biological and intellectual limits are determined by our brute nature. The call for rationality in any classical and objective sense is denied us by the passions and vitalities of our lives.

At the same time, man is also creator and spirit, a creature who dreams of the infinite, constructs visions of himself and the future, and pushes himself toward unending progress while imagining himself god or seeking to make himself godlike. Man is both rational and irrational, both good and evil, capable of the most demonic acts but also of sympathy that knows no bounds. Man's dual nature poses a host of questions and contradictions. If we say that man by nature is essentially good and attribute all evil to his environment or to historical or social causes, we beg the question, because it follows that such causes must be the result of some human force. Traced back, we con-

2. Reinhold Niebuhr, *Human Nature* (New York, 1941), 1, Vol. I of Niebuhr, *The Nature and Destiny of Man*, 2 vols.

clude, they are the product of man in history and therefore of human nature. But, as we discussed above, if we attribute all evil to human nature, how are we to explain how such a frail and fallible man, bereft of all virtue, is capable of judging between good and evil? How can we recognize evil without knowing the good, and if we can recognize the good, can we not be said to possess some good? Neither nihilism nor neutrality between good and evil can provide answers to this dilemma. Yet how much simpler our discourse would be if man were unequivocally good or evil.

Having accepted, then, the dualism of man's nature in preference to any other explanation, we are still left with the problem of relating man's possibilities and his limits. The deeper paradox of human life results from the fact we are suspended perilously between freedom and finiteness, or spirit and nature. Through spirit and human freedom we are able to soar in our imagination, to transcend our limits, and to survey the heights as no other living being, forgetting thereby the limits of our creatureliness. Yet because reason is finite and spirit infinite, we cannot know our limits; and not knowing them, we become anxious, troubled, and insecure. Animals whose lives are under the sway of self-regulating mechanisms are not cursed by the consequences of man's genius. It is man alone who is endlessly tempted to deny the limits that offend the human spirit and to shy away from the implications of painful human problems. Because of anxiety man excuses himself and accuses others to justify his shortcomings and keep alive the hope of progress. It is because I have a vision of the whole that I am so often troubled by all my fragmentary strivings. Dreaming of perpetual health, I shrink from incurable illness. Hoping for long life, I pull back from the sense of my own mortality reflected in the sickroom and the lives of the aged and the infirm. Believing in perfect harmony, I prefer eternal peace to continuing rivalry and conflict. Yearning for tranquillity, I reject all force and violence.

One other factor in modern life has sharpened the conflict between what is finite and what is spirit. The tempo of human existence has shortened the time frame of life. With the lessening of the public's faith in life after death, human consciousness has been compressed into a frantic pursuit of instant gratification and immediate utopias. We resist living with uncertainty. All our towering dreams are reduced to solving immediate problems and ending insecurity. Yet true security requires expressions of the spirit that narrow problem solving is unlikely to bring.

It is one thing for the plant pathologist, free from the public spotlight, to work five long years in his laboratory searching for new varieties of basic food crops to feed the world. It is another thing for the hard-pressed diplomat or statesman to be given time to discover the root cause of conflict in Lebanon or Iraq or of East-West tension or of building new universities or educational programs that can produce national leaders for early progress in nation building in East Africa. Compounding the pressures of time, intense nationalism, and competing goals, the diplomat or policy maker grappling with social and political questions is himself part of the problem. For the scientist in his plant pathology laboratory, his own personal or social attitude toward high-yielding varieties of rice or wheat or corn is essentially irrelevant to his research, as it is for the biologist searching for answers to the eradication of cancer. The same is not true for the social scientist, whose social and political philosophy and attitudes are inseparable from his "scientific" findings. Thus, the Marxist economist, whatever his scientific pretensions, is fundamentally committed to demonstrating the deficiencies of capitalism. The monetarist or free-enterprise economist, however rigorous his methods, is equally committed to the preservation of capitalism and freedom. The architects of grand designs for global peace look at the world through lenses different from those the theorists of protracted East-West conflict use. Intellectual and moral allegiances affect the "science" of the social scientist.

Solutions in the social sciences, then, reflect the scientist's personal preferences and goals in a way that is not normally the case in the natural sciences. For all these reasons and more, the search for the root causes of war or depression or social misunderstandings or tensions by the social and humane scientist is encumbered by ideological presuppositions and social pressures from which the natural scientist is more nearly free.

To be more specific, the root cause of power, and especially power in international politics, is determined in large part by which one of four viewpoints or perspectives the social scientist adopts. The four perspectives are the geographic, the economic, the military, and the political. Each deserves attention and analysis.

The geographic viewpoint defends the importance of power, first, in terms of the international system. Nicholas Spykman explains the basis of this perspective: "International society is . . . a society without central authority. . . . The result is that individual states must make the preservation and improvement of their power position a primary objective of their foreign policy." Writing at the time of World War II, Spykman found that the interventionists and isolationists represented two distinct geopolitical schools of thought. In World War II, the interventionists saw the first line of defense for the United States in a balance of power in Europe and Asia, with a second line of defense in the western hemisphere. The isolationists, who had been dominant before World War I, proceeded from the principle that only the western hemisphere mattered. However, the size of the geographic area making up the hemisphere expanded from the boundaries of the United States to the Caribbean littoral and then to the whole of the hemisphere. Spykman described this expanded view as a streamlined version of the old isolationist position. The defense of the hemisphere through hemispheric isolation was the American strategy at the time of the Monroe Doctrine. By World War II, though, interventionism or internationalism had won out.

What is power viewed from a geographic or geopolitical perspective? Spykman's response is: "Power means survival, the ability to impose one's will on others, the capacity to dictate to those who are without power, and the possibility of forcing concessions from those with less power." The basic objective of any foreign policy in the modern state system is the preservation of the territorial integrity and political independence of the state. Some observers suggest that power depends solely on military forces, but the geopolitical thinkers disagree. Rather, they say, the relative power of a state is largely determined by "size of territory, nature of frontiers, size of population, absence or presence of raw materials, economic and technological development, financial strength, ethnic homogeneity, effective social integration, political stability, and national spirit." Although geostrategic approaches often view power as broadly as suggested in Professor Spykman's list, which goes well beyond geographic factors, he elsewhere narrows his list to a handful of factors such as size and breadth of territory, location, topography, and relation to the oceans.

Thus, power according to geopolitics is a function of geography. The entire earth's surface is a circle, and every nation is encircled by other groups of nations. The western hemisphere is encircled by Eurasia, which constitutes the primary security problem in American foreign policy. Sir Halford John Mackinder had asserted that "whoever controls the Heartland controls the world," with the Heartland extending along a large plain from Siberia through

Germany to the North Sea, bounded on the south by the Alps, the Balkans, and the Himalayas. Spykman modified Mackinder's axiom to read that "he who controls the Rimland controls the Heartland and thereby controls the world," with the Rimland extending from France through the Middle East to South Asia and China. The Rimland also controls the oceans and gives access to any part of the world. Britain with 20,000 ships held strategic entrances to the Mediterranean at Gibraltar, at Suez, and through islands such as Malta. When it lost these key points, it lost the geographic locations on which its power was based, despite its navy remaining intact. Spykman concludes that Britain's power was even more geographic than it was naval before World War II.

If one sentence can summarize the major concept that underlies the geographic conception of power, that sentence is a phrase Spykman composed in 1941 at the height of the Era of Good Feelings with the Soviets: "A Russian state from the Urals to the North Sea can be no great improvement over a German state from the North Sea to the Urals."[3] Nothing ran more counter to popular thinking at the time as good will for the Soviets prevailed, yet Spykman as a geostrategic thinker recognized that Russia was destined to emerge as the strongest power in Europe, with China and Russia also threatening to achieve dominance in Asia. The balance of power, therefore, required the active participation not only of the United States but of Britain and France, joined by Germany, in Europe, with Japan in Asia prepared to throw its weight into the balance. He saw this as a clear geostrategic imperative. No one could afford to be oblivious to the reality of power in the postwar world.

The economic viewpoint substitutes economics for geography as the main determinant of power. In the nineteenth century and the opening decades of the twentieth century, the dominant philosophies that shaped thinking about power were liberalism and Marxism. For liberalism, the individual rather than the collectivity or the group was the more important. Education and reform held out the promise of an escape from the toils and burdens of power. The middle class, which had taken the place of the aristocracy, was the carrier of a world view offering assurance of the peaceful milieu of economics and commerce in place of the struggles of rivalry and power. It was the aristocracy

3. Nicholas J. Spykman, *America's Strategy in World Politics: The United States and the Balance of Power* (New York, 1942), 7, 18, 19, 460.

that had perpetuated contests for power, but with the aristocracy's having yielded to the middle class, power had disappeared. The lessons of history confirm what economic theory postulates, it was argued. The struggle for power lost its purpose with the rise of the middle class.

It is true, broadly speaking, that the commercial and trading class strives to preserve peace and harmony when conflict and war threaten. Trade and commerce depend on a predictable environment, and war and the struggle for power substitute chance and indeterminacy for order. Obscured, though, is the fact that the middle class owes its dominance to a victory over the feudal class, which had earlier triumphed over the universal religious community, whose sacerdotal authority had long gone unchallenged. The business viewpoint that prevails in certain segments of society, even in the 1990s, and draws strength from its claim to be apolitical and opposed to all but the most minimal functions of government is a more recent expression of liberalism justifying the interests of a particular segment of society.

Marxism has provided a similar ideological facade by which it obscures and conceals contests for power. The paradox of the Marxist view of power is classic. On the one side stands the Marxist prophecy according to which the dialectic of history will bring about the withering away of the state. The administration of things will take the place of the domination of man by man. On the other side, the existing communist regimes, particularly over the past forty years in the Soviet Union and China, testify to the illusions of Marxist utopianism. Far from witnessing the disappearance of power, the Soviet and Chinese experiences with communism reveal some of the more grotesque consequences of the merging of economic and political power. Power that had been held in check through various balances in noncommunist regimes, burst the bounds of civilized usage in Stalinism as it had in Nazism. Thus, two philosophies that once offered hope for a respite from power have themselves produced ideological rationalizations for the excesses of power.

Another approach is Hans Morgenthau's view of "the military displacement of power." He chose as one example the contrast between military and political thinking in Britain and the United States at the end of World War II. Churchill argued unsuccessfully for the political significance of military action. Neglecting Clausewitz's dictum that war is a continuation of policy by other means, American military thinkers chose as their objectives goals such as unconditional surrender rather than the formulation of political and territorial aims. In April of 1945 the issue came to a head. Churchill and others urged that military strategy be closely linked with military advances in the interest of political advantage. They argued that the goal should be the liberation of Czechoslovakia, in particular Prague, by General George Patton's army. General George C. Marshall transmitted Churchill's proposal to General Eisenhower, saying, "Personally, and aside from all logistic, tactical, or strategical implications, I would be loath to hazard American lives for purely political reasons." The following day, Eisenhower replied to Marshall, "I shall not attempt any move I deem militarily unwise merely to gain a political advantage unless I receive specific orders from the combined Chiefs of Staff." In his memoirs General Omar Bradley challenged another of Churchill's proposals, which had urged the Americans to continue their advance to Berlin before the Russians reached that city: "As soldiers we looked naively on this British inclination to *complicate* [my emphasis] the war with political foresight and non-military objectives."

Professor Morgenthau asked what lessons might be drawn from these differences and observed that "to win a war without regard for the political consequences of the victory may create political problems as serious as, or worse than, those that the victory was intended to settle." A successful policy must always involve the right admixture of power and suasion. Americans, he pointed out, have allowed themselves to gravitate from one to the other at the expense of a sound foreign policy. Having relied on suasion alone in relationships with Stalin in the wartime and early postwar period, they came to rely exclusively on force as a deterrent. They forgot that force is a means to the end of accommodation with other powers. In the 1920s and 1930s the United States underestimated the use of force in international relations. By the late 1940s and after, it turned to playing the role of the international policeman. In Professor Morgenthau's words, "having realized the error [in the 1930s] of fighting for nobody but one's self, Americans are now willing to fight for anybody threatened by the common enemy." Collective security was the new version of foreign policy that based intervention on global rather than national interests.

Was there ever an alternative? Is the criticism of the kind of apolitical thinking Morgenthau singles out merely negative thinking after the fact, or can he and others point to a better approach to foreign policy? Having denounced the military displacement of politics, what can the analyst put in its place? Morgenthau concludes: "For Sir Winston, the war was a military means to a political end, and the influence of the political end upon the military means was to increase with the speed with which the Armies of the Allies were approaching military victory. For the United States, the war was essentially a self-sufficient technical operation to be performed as quickly, as cheaply, and as thoroughly as the technical rules of warfare would allow." [4] The American view of warfare was apocalyptic: war was a thunderstorm darkening a peaceful scene and an interruption of the normal state of peaceful international relations. For Churchill, the causes and manifestations of war were part of the natural environment of nations, and its consequences flowed from strategies followed during the war. Churchill's thought was both political and military, and he viewed the objectives of the war in this light. Even on the eve of the Potsdam Conference, he questioned the American decision to withdraw troops to the zonal boundaries accepted at Quebec and Yalta. Thus, he assigned primacy to foreign policy objectives, whereas most Americans believed that bringing the war to a prompt conclusion would assure peace in the world and harmony with the Russians.

Churchill is therefore the foremost contemporary exemplar of the political view of power. All political action represents an attempt to influence human behavior. Individuals or groups seek to exercise dominion over others, who seek to exert influence in return. Neither can be oblivious to the role of power; each must determine the right quantity and quality of power to serve his ends. The process of gaining and preserving power and of maintaining at least a rough equilibrium with a potential aggressor goes on unceasingly. Geographic, economic, and military factors are part of the equation but not the fundamental element on the world scene. The political factor is all-important in the statesman's and the public's calculations of the behavior of nations.

In the end, power involves relationships. Recognition of this fact brings us to "the core of the problem" and perhaps to its root cause. Although power cannot be studied in the same way that biologists study cancer, seeking to control if not eliminate it, students of power can nevertheless endeavor to understand it. In doing so, they recognize that whatever the ultimate goal of a political act, attaining some worthy end in politics requires the use of power.

4. Hans J. Morgenthau, *Dilemmas of Politics* (Chicago, 1958), 257, 258, 261, 267–68.

At root, acquiring or maintaining power involves the imposing of a person's or a nation's will on another or others. Whatever the ultimate aim being sought, the quest for power is the process through which that aim is pursued.

As we have seen, Abraham Lincoln in a speech on April 14, 1864, at the Sanitary Fair in Baltimore spoke of freedom and power, explaining, "With some the word liberty may mean for each man to do as he pleases with himself, and the product of his labor; while with others the same word may mean for some men to do as they please with other men and the product of other men's labor." We perceive power relationships and praise or condemn them depending on the perspective from which they are viewed. In Lincoln's words: "The shepherd drives the wolf from the sheep's throat, for which the sheep thanks the shepherd as a *liberator*, while the wolf denounces him . . . as the destroyer of liberty, especially as the sheep was a black one." Lincoln found precisely this same difference among the citizenry, all professing to love liberty. Yet as thousands escaped slavery, some hailed the slaves' being freed as "the advance of liberty" while those who lost power called it "the destruction of all liberty." Perspectives on freedom, as on other goals and values, are shaped by whether we are the holders or the objects of political power.

Morgenthau wrote of another interrelationship, widely misunderstood in the modern world, the connection between power and love. Whereas Morgenthau saw the two as organically interconnected, both having roots in loneliness, modern thought, with its exclusive emphasis on but a few aspects of relationships, such as sex and gregariousness, views love and power primarily at surface levels. Attempting to understand their root cause, Morgenthau observed: "Of all creatures, only man is capable of loneliness because only he is in need of being alone, without being able in the end to escape being alone. It is that striving to escape his loneliness which gives the impetus to both the lust for power and the longing for love, and it is the inability to escape that loneliness, either at all or for more than a moment, that creates the tension between longing and lack of achievement, which is the tragedy of both power and love." Awareness of insufficiency drives man to achieve with others what he cannot realize alone. In a memorable phrase, Morgenthau explains that mortal man seeks the extension of himself "in offspring—the work of his body; in the manufacture of material things—the work of his hands; in philosophy and scholarship—the work of his mind; in art and literature—the work of his imagination; in religion—the work of his pure longing toward transcendence."

What then are the similarities and differences between love and power? For Morgenthau, one similarity is the effort to increase love or power through the duplication or, for nations, the multiplication of individuality. The differences between the two are recorded in poetry and prose. Love is a relation of spontaneous mutuality, power, a union through "unilateral imposition." Ideally, love comes to man as a gift of nature, a union that makes man and woman whole. Power is the result of an individual's imposing his will on another so that the other mirrors him. What is common to love and power, however, is that an element of the one is always found in the other. In common experience, love is power and power is love. "Power points toward love [or some other ultimate moral purpose] as its fulfillment, as love starts from power and . . . is corrupted by an irreducible residue of power." Herein resides the tragedy of love and power.

Love in its purest form is symbolized by complete and spontaneous mutuality. Yet because of the inevitable frustration and transience of love corrupted by power, "the lover behaves as the master and the beloved as the object of the master's power." Thus, love as the reunion of two persons tends to be short-lived. It is the paradox of love that in seeking the reunion of two persons, it attempts to preserve their individuality, only to lose it to the workings of power. Lovers in the end turn to power to do what love cannot do. Power becomes a substitute for love. What mortal man cannot accomplish for any length of time through love he seeks to do through power. Morgenthau explains the relationship further: "Power tries to break down the barrier of individuality which love, because it is love, must leave intact. Yet in the measure that power tries to do the work love cannot do, it puts love in jeopardy. An irreducible element of power is required to make a stable relationship of love . . . [and] without power love cannot persist, but through power it is corrupted and threatened with destruction."

In politics, the same ambiguous relationship between power and love manifests itself. Political stability depends in part on the submissiveness of the ruled toward the ruler, but a political order based only on threats and promises will always be precarious. Therefore, political rulers seek legitimacy through the consent of the governed and approach it through appeals to the love of the subject for the ruler. The love of the people for a monarch is thus the source of the monarch's legitimacy. By ritual and ceremony, Nazism and Stalinism sought to depict their leaders as beloved. Failing to earn the love of their subjects and aware that love was beyond their reach, rulers from Alexander and Napoleon to Hitler and Stalin sought compensation in the accumulation of more and more power. Morgenthau describes the downward spiral of the ruler: "From the subjection of ever more men to their will, they seem to expect the achievement of that communion which the lack of love withholds from them. Yet the acquisition of power only begets the desire for more; for the more men the master holds bound to his will, the more he is aware of his loneliness. His success in terms of power only serves to illuminate his failure in terms of love." He ends by experiencing frustrated love that breeds hate and distrust of men. Paranoia sets in. A beleaguered ruler seeks to close ranks, purging his inner circle of advisers of all but those who claim to love him. Their loyalty, however, gives little satisfaction. They are sycophants whose attachment inspires contempt more often than love.

Morgenthau's conclusion is sobering: "The loneliness of men is, then, impervious to both love and power. Power can only unite through . . . subjection. . . . Love can unite only in the fleeting moments . . . [of] spontaneous mutuality. . . . Thus in the end, his wings seared, his heart-blood spent, his projects come to nought—despairing of power and thirsting for, and forsaken by, love—man peoples the heavens with gods and mothers and virgins and saints who love him and whom he can love and to whose power he can subject himself spontaneously because their power is the power of love. Yet whatever he expects of the other world, he must leave this world as he entered it: alone." [5]

5. Hans J. Morgenthau, *The Restoration of American Politics* (Chicago, 1958), 8, 9, 10, 12–13, 14, Vol. III of Morgenthau, *Politics in the Twentieth Century,* 3 vols.

8

Freedom and Equality:
A Discourse on Purpose

Although 216 years have passed since the birth of American independence, we still ask the same timeless questions: What is America? Democracy? What are freedom and liberty? Equality and justice? What was governance then and what is it now, for ourselves and for others? What is our special heritage, and what do we share with mankind everywhere? Anxiously, we sense that the task of merely coping in this complex world day after day through the last decade of the twentieth century crowds out reflection on these deeper concerns. Our leaders lament they have little time for thought. Increasingly, we are preoccupied with terrorism, violence, and drugs; the clash of contending world powers; and the conflicts of ethnic and national groups. Freedom and equality are being advanced, but they are also threatened by deep-running tides of history. Politicians claim the triumph of democracy, but the struggle for freedom continues.

Naïve as it may sound, the process of asking questions and searching for answers about enduring values and the resulting political order remains the bedrock of America. It towers above building missiles or satellites, winning wars or augmenting the gross national product. Moral and political reasoning is the republic's unique and priceless heritage, more long-lived than those shifting elements of influence and national power we are forever quantifying and measuring. On all sides, we are surrounded by change and flux. The nation is powerful but not all-powerful. Military success and economic miracles come and go. The rest of the world does not stand still. From holding 50 percent of the world's productive capacity, we have fallen to less than 25 percent. We no longer have a monopoly on atomic or nuclear weapons; realism dictates that we and the Soviets must control strategic nuclear weapons. We know that our unfinished experiment is endangered. We are no longer a creditor nation. Trade surpluses have become trade deficits. We spend more than we take in. As we look to the future, the nation's destiny, and its best hope despite our recurring temptation to proclaim ourselves number one, is equal and fair competition, not dominance. Yet political rhetoric lags behind reality, especially in election periods. In the actual, as compared with the imaginary, world, change is an ever-present companion.

What does not change is the national purpose, the American dream of equality pursued in freedom. The United States is not alone in linking governance with some transcendent purpose. Pericles declared of Athens: "Our form of government does not enter into rivalry with the institutions of others. We do not copy our neighbors, but are an example to them." Rome was the cradle of rational government, the rule of law and of empire. What sets the United States apart from Greece and Rome, France and Britain, is that for America discourse and reflection on the national purpose preceded, rather than followed, the nation's birth.

The high point in moral and political reasoning came with the founding fathers. The historian Charles A. Beard was able to find no other example of leaders as rich "in political experience and in practical knowledge, or endowed with a profounder insight into the springs of human action." More remarkable still, our early leaders emerged from a population of little more than four million. They appropriated political ideas from the Greeks, the Romans, and eighteenth-century Europeans but gave them new meaning in a new society. Their practical wisdom made possible the balancing of opposing principles and contradictions. Although they were propertied men, Madison could warn that "various and unequal distribution of property" was the most common source of factions. They were religious men but saw strife in "frivolous and fanciful distinctions." They favored majority rule but feared overbearing majorities. Learning from the early confederation, they saw need for a stronger national government but protected the individual with the Bill of Rights. Even those who praised democracy cautioned against its "turbulence and follies." We inherited a strain of antileadership thought from our experience with the British monarch and governors-general. They believed America should have no permanent rulers or permanent subjects, but they sought ways of assuring a government of talents. They understood that freedom and equality without constitutional purposes and process would be empty, shapeless, and merely procedural concepts. The political process in

America took on deeper meaning from its relationship with higher purpose. The founders asked, "Equal and free for what?" They were as concerned about followers as they were about leaders.

The earliest American immigrants helped forge the answers, and they were threefold: equality and freedom provided an ideal, an example, and a means of reconciliation. What was the ideal? The Puritans who sailed from England to Cape Cod carried memories of oppression and dreams of an ideal political order. In search of a new beginning, they organized a political system based on equality of opportunity with a minimum of political control. Because of the Puritans' vision of a new order, today's historians write that the true American revolution began in 1620, not in 1776. With the peopling of North America, certain Old World patterns would dissolve; the seeds of new ideas were planted. There followed migrations that carried the vision across the country's regions and frontiers to the Pacific. The first settlers fashioned in their minds bold outlines of a new society and set out to build it. The ideal came before the act.

Second, what was the example? The Declaration of Independence, as Lincoln proclaimed nearly a century later at Independence Hall, embodied "a great principle . . . giving liberty, not alone to the people of this country, but hope to the world for all future time." Assuming it prospered and survived, democracy would be an example to mankind throughout the world. However, not military intervention but America as a model would lead others to democracy. Throughout the nineteenth and early twentieth centuries the United States sought influence in the world less from its power than from its example.

Third, what was the reconciliation process? From the founding, the existence of multiple and plural purposes and principles made conflict and tension inevitable between competing ideas such as freedom and equality. Even to this day, we continually ask the important questions: What is liberty? What is equality? Where does either begin and end? How are they related? Who shall bring about their reconciliation?

The most poignant example of an ongoing debate over principles that erupted in conflict is the Civil War. North and South spoke to one another in the language of two competing concepts of freedom. They saw liberty as having two opposing meanings. Lincoln's words at the Sanitary Fair, which I noted earlier, explain the conflict eloquently: "With some the word liberty may mean for each man to do as he pleases with himself, and the product of his labor; while with others the same word may mean for some to do as they please with other men and the product of other men's labor." These clashing principles were encased in holy writ, reconciliation was undertaken but failed, the political process broke down, and the war came.

What Lincoln and the founders sought to leave us was a mediating and reconciling process and a capacity to weigh and consider great principles in competition with one another. There are limits in the application of some principles. A reconciling process guided the Supreme Court when it found that freedoms of speech and assembly do not give the right to cry "Fire!" in a crowded theatre. Reconciliation gave us a committee and conference system in the Congress. It provided checks and balances within the executive and between the branches. It prepared us for the clash of goals and principles in the rest of the twentieth and the twenty-first century.

As we approach the twenty-first century, what is possible and within reach for us is not an easy answer to mounting problems but rather hard choices requiring on-balance judgments: between freedom and order, liberty and justice, national security and the first amendment, prolife and prochoice, a flag amendment and the first amendment, equal opportunity and economic productivity, responsibility and individual rights, military preparedness and a healthy economy, arms limitations and military superiority, war and non-military sanctions. We cannot be certain of final answers, but we can take confidence in the political process. Life's choices involve not absolute right or wrong but rather more of this, less of that. We strive to reconcile the morally desirable with the politically possible. Yet popular leaders are often-times prone to mislead us by framing the most difficult choices in the simplest terms of right or wrong, black or white, good or evil.

What we must seek in the days ahead therefore is not premature answers or a flaunting of our omniscience but the wisdom of minds such as Judge Learned Hand, who wrote this meditation on liberty:

> What then is the spirit of liberty? I cannot define it; I can only tell you my own faith. The spirit of liberty is the spirit which is not too sure it is right. The spirit of liberty is the spirit which seeks to understand the minds of other men and women. The spirit of liberty is the spirit which

weighs in their interests alongside its own without bias. The spirit of liberty remembers that not even a sparrow falls to earth unheeded. The spirit of liberty is the spirit of Him who, near [sic] two thousand years ago, taught mankind the lesson it has never learned, but has never quite forgotten; that there may be a kingdom where the least shall be heard and considered side by side with the greatest.[1]

Or we need the insights of E. B. White, who, when asked to define the meaning of democracy, responded: "It is the line that forms on the right. It is the don't in Don't Shove. It is the hole in the stuffed shirt . . . the dent in the high hat. Democracy is the recurrent suspicion that more than half of the people are right more than half of the time. It is the feeling of privacy in the voting booths, the feeling of communion in the libraries, the feeling of vitality everywhere."[2]

Some would have us rededicate ourselves. Some call on Americans to be militantly positive, others, belligerently negative. Yet we are also free to raise our eyes to more distant horizons. If we do, we may find that what is lasting in the heritage and relevant for the future is less the dragons we slay than the principles we exemplify. It is deeds more than words. "Democracy is an idea which hasn't been disproved yet," while most competing ideologies, including notably and especially in 1989 communism, are, if not in their death throes, certainly in profound disarray. Democracy is "a song the words of which have not gone bad." We ought to sing it, believe it, and live it without harping endlessly on the flaws of others and their false chords. A staunch anticommunist, former president Richard Nixon counseled: "We talk endlessly about communism. The communists at least talk about their problems." So perhaps do others in the countries of Eastern Europe as they strive for new identities.

Through renewing our commitments to the most enduring of all living political traditions, both the process and the purpose, we gain unexampled resources to face future problems. A wartime prayer of a great theologian resides at the heart of democracy, far profounder than the creeds and nostrums

1. Learned Hand, *The Spirit of Liberty*, ed. Irving Dillard (3rd ed.; New York, 1974), 190.
2. E. B. White, *The Wild Flag: Editorials from "The New Yorker" on the Federal Government and Other Matters* (Cambridge, Mass., 1946), 31.

of self-appointed prophets and more in keeping with our American heritage: "God give us grace to accept with serenity the things that cannot be changed, courage to change the things that should be changed, and the wisdom to distinguish the one from the other."

9

Beliefs, True Beliefs, and the Constitution

The believer seeks to reconcile good ends and the social and political order. For the true believer, the means and the social order are often hostage to an altogether good and absolute end. The late director of the CIA William Casey allegedly told Washington *Post* columnist Bob Woodward, "I believed." According to Woodward, one of the first foreign intelligence estimates the director saw in assuming his office in the Reagan administration was entitled "Libya: Aims and Vulnerabilities." To his mind, it was "written by equivocators for equivocators." It was full of "coulds," "mights," and "possibles." Of this document and Casey's response to it, Woodward writes: "It put the intelligence agencies in the bureaucratically secure position of being able, no matter what happened, to dust off the estimate and say, 'See, we told you, we said that *could* happen.' To say everything was to say almost nothing, Casey thought." [1]

"Truly believing," the title Woodward gives to Casey's philosophy, means combining absolute commitments and taking risks. Others in the Reagan administration, even some purporting to embrace the definition of communism as evil empire, shrank from Casey's philosophy and plan of action. Mere ordinary believers, like Secretary of Defense Caspar Weinberger, simply followed their leader, first in Sacramento, later in Washington, D.C. They took fewer risks. By contrast, the full-fledged true believer, such as Casey, possessed the instincts of the venture capitalist prepared to gamble not with money but with human lives. CBS News Pentagon correspondent David C. Martin wrote that if Woodward's account was correct, "Casey's penchant for running risks cost 80 innocent people their lives when an 'off-the-books' attempt to assassinate Sheik Mohammed Hussein Fadallah, the spiritual leader of Hezbollah, Lebanon's Party of God, misfired." In March, 1985, a car bomb intended for the militant Shiite leader wrecked a building in Beirut and killed 80 people.

1. Bob Woodward, *Veil: The Secret Wars of the CIA, 1981–87* (New York, 1987), 96.

Further, gaining the information necessary for intelligence required lying and the protection of intelligence sources. Woodward explains: "To lie was nothing, even to lie in public or under oath was perhaps insignificant compared to the risks the source had taken."[2] Where certainty about true beliefs obtains, the use of any means needed to safeguard or realize truth, whether by lying, coverups, or illegalities, is justified. We remember in this connection the testimony of Admiral John M. Poindexter, presumably a righteous, religious, and upright man, at the Iran-Contra hearings. Denial and lying become interchangeable parts of strategic thinking.

Over much of American history, the debate in American politics has been about beliefs and true beliefs. In the fifteen weeks of preparation that led up to the great policy decisions of the Truman Doctrine, the Marshall Plan, and NATO, Senator Arthur Vandenberg warned President Truman and Secretary George C. Marshall that the American people would rise to resist Soviet expansion only if the issue was framed in terms of the worldwide threat of communism. Meeting with congressional leaders, Secretary Marshall had spoken of humanitarianism and reconstruction as objectives in helping Western Europe's economic recovery. Vandenberg responded that Americans would not sacrifice and pay the price unless something more than economic, political, and strategic interests was at stake. Someone had to tell the grim story of worldwide communist expansionism, so Assistant Secretary Dean Acheson stepped into the breach. From 1946 to the present, the controversy has continued over the nature of the threat, over what Americans should be told to inspire them to action, and over the methods by which we identify and respond to worldwide adversaries and enemies.

It is curious that despite all our differences we and the Soviets have something in common here. They, too, have struggled to define their belief system and what they see as a threat to their interests. That effort continued down to the seventieth anniversary of the Bolshevik Revolution. A New York Times dispatch from Moscow, dated October 31, 1987, reported, "The Soviet Union enters its eighth decade under Communism . . . in a state of transition, wary of its past and uncertain about its future." What has historically been seen as proof of Soviet prestige and power has been questioned in Mikhail Gorbachev's life and works, especially in his book *Perestroika: Restructur-*

2. *New York Times Book Review*, October 18, 1987, p. 43.

ing or New Thinking for Our Country and the World, first excerpted in the November 9, 1987, issue of *U.S. News and World Report*. In *Perestroika* Gorbachev places emphasis on outcomes, not beliefs. He indicts the Soviet economy for not growing enough crops, not producing enough washing machines that work, and not giving enough medical care to the Soviet people. He states that their "rockets can find Halley's comet and fly to Venus with amazing accuracy" but "many Soviet household appliances are of poor quality." He proposes capitalist-style incentives and "self-financing" to strengthen the industrial economy and "more glasnost," or openness. Even in an area that the Soviets have touted as one of their most notable success stories, having "the largest number of doctors and hospital beds per 1,000 of the population," Gorbachev acknowledges "there are glaring shortcomings in our health services."[3] The challenge he is throwing out is reminiscent of Nikita Khrushchev's earlier declaration that the Soviets and East Europeans needed not more ideology but more goulash.

What no one can assert with any assurance is whether Gorbachev will succeed. The danger for the innovator or the improvising leader is that he tends to be judged largely by results. History can be more forgiving and long-sighted in judging the leader who personifies a creed or a doctrine, for its unfolding tends to require generations. Events show that not Gorbachev's ideology but his actions and the pace of his reforms have been the object of sharpest criticism in disputes in the Central Committee. In early meetings between the then–Moscow party chief Boris Yeltsin and Yegor Ligachev, the number two man in the Kremlin, evidence of conflict was already present. In an opening speech to the committee, Gorbachev had criticized the management of Moscow's governing body for failing to keep up with the necessary pace of reforms. Yeltsin blamed senior party officials, some by name, for the delays. A debate ensued, and some commentators explained Gorbachev's reluctance to approve an early summit conference as a direct outgrowth of the conflict.

It is still too early to determine with any finality the relative emphasis that will be put on problem solving versus the forging of a new ideological framework. So far as outsiders can tell, the debate in the Central Committee has been largely over tangible improvements and standards of living. Talk in

3. New York *Times*, November 1, 1987, p. 1.

the party has been about decentralization of economic management with some minimal encouragement of individual enterprise. Gorbachev's agenda has included installing quality controls in major factories, getting more food into the shops, building more housing, increasing the availability of medicines and consumer goods, and improving health services. Some say he has placed too much emphasis on capital development compared with consumer goods. The main items in his program have more to do with actions than with true beliefs. What happens in the cities and countryside, not some grand ideological vision in the sky, is the testing ground for Gorbachev. The late Andrei D. Sakharov once explained the problem: "I have a great deal of hope in Gorbachev's policies and in him. I think perestroika is a historical necessity. . . . [However,] there is a clear distinction between what Gorbachev says and what a Central Committee approves, and a still greater gap between what they approve and what happens in real life." Thus, the accent for Sakharov as for Gorbachev has apparently been on deeds more than on words. Since the death of Sakharov, this concern has not abated.

At the same time, it would be illusory to suppose that only actions mattered in a society founded on Marxist-Leninist beliefs, to which Gorbachev still pays allegiance. In preparing his seventieth anniversary text, he enlisted a team of advisers to help provide a historical and ideological framework for his policies. While he has appeared to offer reforms without anchoring them in a clear statement of political philosophy, he has reminded the West that he is and will remain communist. Ironically, the seeming irrelevance of the Marxist creed for urgent contemporary problems has led both technocrats like Leonid Brezhnev and improvisers such as Gorbachev and Khrushchev to pass over the need for continuing refinements in a coherent system of beliefs.

To approach the problem in more universal terms, the great task in politics is to hold beliefs and actions in some kind of balance. Grand designs and comprehensive systems of thought normally exceed the grasp of practical men of politics. Alexis de Tocqueville describes the politician's attributes:

> The man of action is frequently obliged to content himself with the best he can get. . . . He has . . . occasion to rely on ideas which he has not had leisure to search to the bottom; for he is much more frequently aided by the opportunity of an idea than by its strict accuracy. The world is not

led by long and learned demonstrations: a rapid glance at particular incidents, the daily study of the fleeting passions of the multitude, the
accidents of the time, and the art of turning them to account decide all
its affairs.[4]

Tocqueville appears to be saying that even when ultimate beliefs are
knowable, the man of action has small chance of appropriating them. Denied
to the leader is the luxury of meditation. He must act with the hounds of time
snapping at his heels. For him, information can never be complete. He must
choose, though knowing that he can never comprehend the full dimensions of
present problems, let alone foresee the contours of the future. Yet societies
lacking in values and beliefs threaten the personal security and collective well-
being of their people, who are vulnerable to becoming, in Lincoln's phrase,
"bereft of faith and terrified by doubts." When nations and civilizations find
themselves stripped of their ancient faiths, they are weakened if certain ideological vacuums are not filled. Thus, modern Turkey, with the disintegration
of the Ottoman Empire, was ripe for Kemal Atatürk to plant the seeds of
Turkish nationalism. More generally, European nationalism reflects the outward thrust of certain political societies, like Prussia, that became the carriers
of nationalism. History abhors a vacuum, and a society without beliefs is open
to the spread of more dynamic ideas that will fill the vacuum.

Beyond the likelihood that ideas and beliefs will be set in motion to fill
political and social vacuums, the history of politics makes it plain that no
people have ever completely divorced politics from ethics. Men seek to con-
form to standards more inclusive than success. Political actors must justify
themselves in moral terms within most societies and cultures. They pay tribute to some kind of moral order, with fateful consequences both in words and
deeds if there is no connection between ideals and realities. In politics, therefore, a striking dialectical movement occurs between expediency and morality. Politicians articulate practical political moves often with an eye to
moral principles. In however limited and fragmentary a way, acts of political
expediency are seen to carry forward aims of justice and the common good.
Thus, political morality forces the statesmen who would link expediency with

4. Alexis de Tocqueville, *Democracy in America*, trans. Henry Reeve (2 vols.; New York,
1961), II, 50.

ethics to choose political measures that enable the practical and the moral to march hand in hand.

Certain basic assumptions undergird American constitutionalism and a system of checks and balances that rests on a balancing of power. One such assumption is the belief that the maintenance of a pluralistic society is preferable to its destruction. Leaders around the world even in the poorer countries have been echoing this idea as they call for the creation of democratic regimes. Another assumption is that some type of orderly and peaceful change is more desirable than radical and disruptive change. To the extent that the individual is considered to be of primary importance in politics, individual rights are more likely safeguarded under divided government. Harking back to the Greeks, we define balance and moderation, rather than domination and extremism, as political virtues. Not only the individual but political and social minorities are safeguarded by checks and balances. The author of *Federalist* 51 (Alexander Hamilton or Madison, according to different historians) recommended this course of action: "Comprehending in the society so many separate descriptions of citizens . . . will render an unjust combination of a majority of the whole very improbable, if not impracticable. . . . The society itself will be broken into so many parts, interests, and classes of citizens, that the rights of individuals, or of the minority, will be in little danger from interested combinations of the majority."

It is the union of the concepts of absolute virtue and political power that betrays true believers, whether in the East or West. In politics, as distinct from philosophy, the attainment of virtue and truth is always mixed with political striving. When the true believer looks out on the world, his will to act soon becomes intertwined with self-interest and self-pride. Those who see their vision as at most an approximation of truth strive to open every available channel for political expression in the political system to majorities and minorities. True believers, by contrast, try to narrow the decision-making process to fit their version of ultimate truth. Lack of recognition for other viewpoints characterizes their thinking. For the true believer, all virtue and truth tend to be comprehended in a single vision of the world.

The founding fathers had a mistrust not only of monarchy but of a strictly hierarchical structure of government. Rather than accept hierarchy, they thought in terms of parallel powers and truths and separate but overlapping powers. Their mistrust of concentrated power was best formulated in

John Adams' phrase: "Power always thinks it has a great soul . . . and that it is doing God's service when it is violating all His laws." The founding fathers were nothing if not political realists, and their conceptions of power and truth were firmly planted in the ground of politics in history and practice.

The separation of powers in the Constitution was one expression of the concept of checks and balances espoused by the founders. The division of powers among the executive, legislative, and judicial branches of government imposed limitations on the exercise of power. The doctrine of separation of powers was intended to provide a check against what the author in *Federalist* 51 called "a gradual concentration of the several powers in the same department." Because tyranny was feared most by the founders, he wrote of "contriving the interior structure of the government as that its several constituent parts may, by their mutual relations, be the means of keeping each other in their proper places." The founders went back to the classical writers in search of the intellectual foundations for their politics.

Deserving special emphasis, however, is the fact that the separation of powers reflects not a static condition but a political situation in more or less continuous flux. Foreign observers of American decision making from Tocqueville to the present have searched in vain for a fixed point of authority, especially in foreign policy, at any given time. They ask who has the controlling power. They speak of tumult and confusion and of everything being in motion. They remark on shifting alliances and changing consensus among "opposite and rival interests." The consequences of the separation of powers and of "leaderless government" are an almost continuous fluctuation of authority from one branch of government to another, leaving outsiders who are more at home with centralized political systems in a constant state of uncertainty and confusion. As vice-president of a large private foundation, I welcomed a stream of foreign visitors who invariably asked, "Who has the power?" More often than not, they left the country without having found the answer.

At another level of understanding, however, foreign observers point to the American government as an outstanding modern example of a political system whose stability is dependent on an equilibrium of power among the branches of government. At the forefront of those observers is Lord James Bryce, who delineated the system in this way: "The Constitution was avowedly created as instrument of checks and balances. Each branch of the government was to restrain the others, and maintain the equipoise of the whole. The legislature was to balance the executive and judiciary both. As the equilibrium was placed under the protection of a document, unchangeable save by the people themselves, no one of the branches of the national government has been able to absorb or override the others. . . . Each branch maintains its independence and can, within certain limits, defy the others."

Bryce viewed politics in considerable measure as a struggle for power. His perspective diverged from the view that political life was more and more dominated by reason and that conflicts could be supplanted by the attainment of an easy harmony of interests. Having described the constituent elements in the political system, he went on to say:

> There is among political bodies and offices (i.e., the persons who from time to time fill the same office) of necessity a constant strife, a struggle for existence similar to that which Mr. Darwin has shown to exist among plants and animals; and as in the case of plants and animals so also in the political sphere this struggle stimulates each body or office to exert its utmost force for its own preservation, and to develop its aptitudes in any direction where development is possible. Each branch of the American government has striven to extend its range and its powers; each has advanced in certain directions, but in others has been restrained by equal or stronger pressure of other branches.[5]

Such a view of politics, enshrined in American constitutionalism and well described by Lord Bryce and the authors of the *Federalist Papers*, has not gone unchallenged. Jefferson, despite his recognition of the need to control the ambitions of individuals and groups, could also declare himself unable "to conceive how any rational being could propose happiness to himself from the exercise of power over others." Isolationism in foreign policy appears at first glance to be a noncompetitive policy based on an abstention from the struggle for power, which paradoxically is also the view of crusading internationalism. Wilson gave eloquent expression to his conviction that selfishness and power rivalries could be banished from the relations among nations. He called for, "not organized rivalries, but an organized common peace." In proclaiming government by the consent of the governed at home and around

5. Lord James Bryce, *The American Commonwealth* (2 vols.; New York, 1891), I, 390–91.

the world, Wilson, the liberal true believer, declared: "These are American principles, American policies. . . . And they are also the principles and policies of forward looking men and women everywhere, of every modern nation, of every enlightened community. They are the principles of mankind and must prevail." [6] Yet in failing to take account of the separation of powers, President Wilson saw his vision of a brave new world and a League of Nations defeated by the Senate as it rejected American participation in the league. Looking back on the work of the framers, Charles Beard came to this conclusion: "The framers understood that government in action is power. They tried to pit the ambitions, interests, and forces of human beings in the three departments against one another in such a way as to prevent any one set of agents from seizing all power, from becoming dangerously powerful." [7]

The founders, then, were believers but believers at the most profound level. Running through their political writings and those of political thinkers who come later are certain clear, if sometimes competing, views of human nature. The one view is based on a conception of man that stresses the duality of human nature. Man is neither wholly good nor wholly evil, neither rational nor irrational, neither altruistic nor selfish. Human nature has not changed fundamentally over the centuries. To reiterate, if men were angels, the founders had written, government would not be necessary; if men were devils, government would not be possible. Possessing a spark of the divine intermixed with a trace of the demonic, man requires government to channel virtue and hold selfishness in check.

An opposing view of human nature prophesies the emergence of the new man. For Marxists, the new man awaits only the creation of a genuine socialist order. For the children of the Enlightenment, the triumph of reason awaits the universal spread of democracy and education. The presence of rivalries and conflicts in an earlier era is no more than a passing stage in man's evolution. The struggle for power and the clash of rival and opposite interests in politics, to the extent they persist at all, represent a cultural lag in mankind's irresistible march from a primitive to a modern scientific age.

6. Woodrow Wilson, *The New Democracy: Presidential Messages, Addresses, and Other Papers, 1913–1917*, ed. Ray Stannard Baker and William E. Dodd (6 vols.; New York, 1926), III, 410.

7. Charles A. Beard, *The Republic* (New York, 1944), 190–91.

Further, man pursues a double standard of conduct in private and public life. Privately, man is honest and ethical; publicly, he covers his political acts with rationalizations, lies, and deception. Man's virtue in personal relations is an outgrowth of the conquest of culture over barbarism and of a moral over an immoral age. Early in man's evolution, his conduct in private affairs was corrupted by strife and violence. Today, through reason, he has progressed from conflict to cooperation in personal relations and, to a lesser extent, in organized domestic politics. Only the arena of international politics displays a cultural lag, and even this is in the process of being eradicated. The same conception of ethics that determines the conduct of individuals in interpersonal relations is capable of transforming the way nations behave in a universal and interdependent world community. The forward march of history is raising nations from the level of primitive rivalries into new and enlightened standards of relations in which private norms will become public rules.

Viewed from the perspective of the political realist, such a belief in the transformation of human nature is erroneous and misplaced. Man's ambition for influence and power, and hence the enduring character of competition with his fellow man, is inherent in the human condition. It is utopian to assume that men or nations will abandon old forms of politics and of world politics without having something else to put in its place. A wide gulf remains between political actions and the ideological rationalizations in which they are cloaked. National leaders declare that their aim is to offer freedom or communism to the rest of the world. Power is essential to this end. Yet in the process, one nation's power inspires fear and anxiety in other nations, which seek their own preservation and survival. Because of a Hobbesian fear, nations in their quest for security achieve power and influence at the price of security in other groups. Tragically, there is no alternative to the morally hazardous quest for security through power, even though for each generation the hope persists.

Within and among democratic states, it is fashionable to deny the central place of political rivalries and power conflicts. Some of the culture's wise men have dreamed of a purely rational adjustment of interests in society or have looked to the assuagement of rivalries and differences through scientific solutions or by sharp definitions of and distinctions between justice and injustice. From time to time, a chasm has appeared between the shrewd concepts of practical men of affairs and the vapid speculations of utopian philosophers. By contrast, the early founding American statesmen were imbued with a greater measure of political and historical insight concerning power and the balancing of it.

From the standpoint of the realists and their conception of human nature and politics, the separate units in all societies composed of autonomous members owe their existence primarily to the success of the balance of power and a system of checks and balances. Unless one component unit is prevented from gaining ascendancy over the others, the overall political system will ultimately be shattered or destroyed. It is common to human existence and to animal life in general that when any member or group seeks to increase its influence and power beyond the point where equilibrium with its rivals can be preserved, either the rivals will give way and disappear or else, by combining, will keep the expansionist force in its place. With animal life, the process is often unconscious and automatic, but in politics and diplomacy, effectiveness depends on those sharp discriminations and informed calculations by which the statesman perceives crucial changes in the equilibrium of power. A steady view of human nature, the recurrent patterns of political rivalries, and the necessity to keep political competition in check all point to the perennial need for balance of power and checks and balances in politics.

The founding fathers were men of large political convictions who had a keen sense of political reality. They formed a system that reflected their beliefs and rested on their conceptions of human nature and politics. Those leaders in contemporary American political life who take satisfaction from the constitutional system share in part the founders' political philosophy. Going beyond such practical and realistic beliefs, the question that can be asked is whether true beliefs are compatible with constitutionalism.

What is obvious from events of the 1980s is that true believers find constitutional restraints discomforting. Belief in the rightness and justice of their cause soars above precepts of law and principles of compromise. Moreover, the American constitutional system presupposes that no single person, political party, or branch of government has comprehended the whole truth about politics. Thus, constitutionalism demands the accommodation of my truth and your truth. In constitutional politics, fragmentary truth is a given. If any comprehensive political truth is to emerge, it is more likely to occur where two or three come together than from one leader's obiter dicta.

The world of politics, therefore, is often an uncongenial world for true believers, who are impatient with men of lesser faith. Having arrived at their own definition of truth, they suffer anguish in a world of bargaining and "trimmers." The world of revolution is more suited than is the world of governance to the life of the true believer. One explanation is that struggles in warfare and in social and political revolutions tend to be resolved in clear-cut victory or defeat. Conflicts in politics, however, are seldom, if ever, settled once and for all. Disputes lead to concessions, and those who succeed learn to live with half a loaf and the continuation of the struggle. President Reagan's secretary of state George Shultz caught the spirit of politics when he complained that "nothing is ever settled in Washington."

The true believer has the capacity to spawn a revolution and incite others to action. This is why we remember and celebrate Thomas Paine. His role and the roles of those who followed him were to sound the alarm, not to write a constitution or form a government. The drafters of the Constitution who held fast were believers, not true believers. They were men, such as Madison and Benjamin Franklin, who had settled convictions but looked more for convergences of interest that made agreement possible than for any final truth in politics. In our day the most constructive voices in negotiation sessions on the budget deficit are Madison's heirs, not true believers whether on the right or the left.

Believers in governance are more inclined to weigh costs and benefits against the damage that may come from radical social and political change. At the same time, they recognize that all-out resistance to change can be harmful when large-scale change is needed. A well-known political writer observed that in politics power must be weighed out ounce by ounce, and the same is often true for political transformation. It is this view of power and beliefs, tentative and cautious but realistic, that distinguishes the believer from the true believer.

A contemporary political philosopher has written, "Men have thoughts; ideas have men." The power of ideas, values, and beliefs in determining the course of history cannot be questioned. Democracy, freedom, and equality are writ large in every enduring chronicle of political history. Much as Western man goes back to the ideas of the Renaissance and the Reformation to take his bearings, we look to the large ideas that drive the tides of history in every subsequent historical era.

However, we are also increasingly constrained to point out differences between believers and true believers or between traditional political parties and present-day special- or single-interest groups proclaiming one all-consuming purpose. The two sides reflect the different aims and methods groups or persons apply in politics. The American political process has been successful precisely because believers embrace a variety of sometimes compatible political, economic, and religious beliefs that have the effect of broadening and civilizing everyman's perspective. Thus, the liberal Democrat may be a conservative Episcopalian and a member of a middle-of-the-road chamber of commerce and therefore more likely to be a believer than a true believer. The conservative may be anticommunist ideologically but may support East-West trade. A diffusion of beliefs erodes some of the fanaticism and fury that can sweep across a political scene dominated by true believers. The political process broke down in the Civil War when believers North and South became true believers convinced of the absolute righteousness of their course, whether as abolitionists or secessionists. That is the threat democracies must avoid in seeking a resolution of their problems. Accommodation of competing beliefs must be put above sanctifying any one belief.

Why all this emphasis on differences between believers and true believers in politics, the reader may ask. To what extent is such discourse a mere intellectual exercise, and to what extent does it point to certain fundamental truths? What connection, if any, is there with the present crisis? At the risk of engendering controversy, let me try to be more specific.

First, it seems clear that one source of the problem of the budget deficit in the 1990s is the interplay between true beliefs and prevailing fiscal problems and policy of the 1980s. We have it on the authority of Attorney General Edwin Meese that Reagan throughout his political career was flexible and pragmatic on every issue but two: opposition to tax increases in a free economy and uncompromising anticommunism. The former was an outgrowth of his unexpected wealth as a rising movie star and the heavy toll that taxes exacted from his income. It may tell us something about the exigencies of foreign policy that the president was prepared to compromise on anticommunism but not on taxes. Yet from the start of the Reagan administration most economists warned that vast increases totaling two trillion dollars in military expenditures were impossible in the absence of substantial revenue enhancement. President Eisenhower understood this exchange when he resisted the programs of his own military that would have increased expenditures at the cost of damaging a healthy economy. With Reagan, true beliefs about taxes and spending overpowered the tradition of leaders such as Eisenhower. A personal dogma overrode political and economic prudence.

Second, President Reagan and his secretary of defense defended their true beliefs about the Strategic Defense Initiative (SDI) by asserting that defensive weapons are always morally superior to offensive weapons. A realist believer in national defense would pose three questions about such a viewpoint, all directed at possible consequences. The first question worth asking is actually a set of technical ones. What is technically possible, when is it possible with innovations such as SDI, and how should that affect the United States' negotiating posture? A second question is strategic. What will be the effect of moving to an offensive-defensive weapon mix, especially in a transition period? The third query is economic. What is the cost in billions of dollars? The believer is more likely than the true believer to look at such dimensions of a foreign policy problem, earning Justice Holmes' expressed admiration for "the man who can find his way through a maze of conflicting principles." The true believer holds to his dogma.

Third, it is clear that we live in a world in which true beliefs are increasingly attractive and popular. Television has brought new life to a group tendency H. L. Mencken identified long ago when he said, "For every problem there is a solution which is simple, appealing and wrong." In certain vital areas this tendency is reinforced by the very urgency of our problems. Since 1947, the United States has looked to the strengthening of a national security state as the one overarching requirement of society, sometimes at the expense of concern for civil liberties, a healthy economy, and the maintenance of an effective constitutional system that gives the president and the Congress responsibility for foreign policy. The traditional believer would ask if we are being tempted to neglect the human agenda because of the priority of national defense. Or if we have been promising ourselves limitless personal satisfactions at the expense of the common good. The true believer tends to brush aside such questions and concerns.

The founding fathers were pluralists, not monists, and believers, not true believers, in morality and politics. They understood that most important advances in politics are for multiple, not singular, goods and that those ends are more likely to be achieved with lasting results through long-established constitutional and political procedures. The grand simplifiers may have the first word, but the practical moralists who balance the desirable with the possible are likely to have the last one.

Part III

Reinstating Values in the Practice of Politics and Diplomacy

10

Moral Values and International Politics

It is illusory to think that politics can be free of values. Those spokesmen of realpolitik whom we read long after the passing of their historical era called not for the repudiation but for the reinterpretation of values. Machiavelli wrote of "virtù," Rousseau of "the noble savage," and the nationalists of "national glory." The debate over values, despite the claims of so-called value-free social science, has never been between one school of thought espousing values and another rejecting all values. Rather, almost always it involves two groups with different sets and concepts of values—different perspectives on the nature and content of values. No one who lives in a human community can be wholly amoral if he seeks the trust and cooperation of others. We recall the reference by Sir Harold Nicolson to the classic definition of the diplomat as a man sent abroad to lie and deceive in the interest of his country. Yes, said Nicolson, but he must also return to negotiate another day.

Part of our problem in gaining clarity on values in international politics is that most of us are endlessly tempted either to inflate or to disparage the role of morality in politics. Thus, we fall prey at opposite extremes to moralism or cynicism in our views.

Moralism and Cynicism

The moralist inflates the place of values by sanctifying short-term and parochial interests, absolutizing higher goals into rigid principles that obstruct the political process, and raising moral formulations to the level of irrelevance. No moral disease is more commonplace than the imputing of final virtue to immediate and practical measures. Although every action in statecraft, as in workaday life, has its worth, the moralist errs by elevating the routine to the same level as objective truth. In statecraft, there are countless procedures and acts, such as issuing visas or preparing protocols, that are a vital part of the diplomatic process. What is to be gained by pretending that these important measures, which are part of the day's work, are sacred to the point of being beyond criticism and change? If we are wrong to deny the dignity and worth of the workaday world, we also err in equating that world with all truth and justice, placing it beyond all possibility of change. There is too much arrogance in maintaining that every pragmatic move we make is endowed with some kind of ultimate virtue.

A more serious failing of the moralist, particularly in the United States, is to absolutize particular ends and values, thus elevating them beyond the political process. Whenever political goals are cast in the language of absolute right and wrong, implementing them through the democratic process becomes difficult, if not impossible. As I noted previously, the most fateful example of this rigidification is the breakdown of the democratic process that happened at the time of the American Civil War. Once each side had framed the issue in terms of its total righteousness and the complete depravity of the other, the workings of democracy, with the necessary play of compromise and adjustment, became impossible. The wars of religion are another historical example of absolutizing particular ends; history attests that man is never so cruel and intractable as when he becomes a crusader for moral and religious goals. If liberals are more prone to sanctify certain immediate political and social interests, the religious and moralistic have historically been prime offenders in absolutizing values and goals.

As the doctrines of moralists can lead to rigidity and brutality, their habits and style can lead to irrelevance. For moralists are wont to raise ends and values to such towering heights as to give them a quality of irrelevance in respect to all those practical and pressing choices that confound men in daily life. Thus, it was noble to talk, following World War I, about a new and better world, but for those who sought to hammer out the peace in Paris, the exalted doctrines of Wilson bore little, if any, relation to the harsh issues the negotiators were struggling to resolve.

Cynics are no less misguided and destructive than the moralists when they approach issues of values. They are misled by the discovery that men are never as virtuous as they claim to be and interpret this fact as proof that in man there is no virtue. Sociologists such as Max Weber identify the taint of deception in every virtuous act. They find we cover our self-interest with a tissue of self-justifying ideological rationalization. We do everything as individuals or nations not for our own good, we say, but for the good of others or as part of history's unfolding process. There are some blatant examples of this self-deception: Stalin's liquidating of the kulaks as a necessary and inevitable step in the history-fulfilling design of communism; Hitler's cremation of so-called inferior races as a necessary hygienic measure to assure continued Teutonic superiority; and some of the banishments of deviationists taken in China during the Cultural Revolution.

However, the less blatant examples may be more significant and all-pervasive. Whenever men and nations act, their claims of morality are larger than their actions warrant. If such claims are deception, they are an almost inevitable form of self-deception since nations, no less than individuals, must persuade themselves that their deeds are legitimate because consistent with some larger frame of value. The parent never disciplines the child except for its own good. The powerful nation never goes to war except in the interests of peace and justice. The problem about these actions is not that they are devoid of all justice or that the claims of goodness never serve to lift men and groups above the selfish and the mundane. It is rather that we are almost never as moral as we claim to be, whether as self-righteous individuals or when we speak for the nation as a whole.

The irony of self-righteousness is that there is virtue in our very self-deception as to our righteousness. Hypocrisy is the tribute that vice pays to virtue, for by claiming some form of virtue for himself or his acts, the selfish man reaches up at least a little toward a goal that is higher than his narrow selfishness. Thus, the cynic who finds total depravity in man's self-righteousness is as deluded as the moralist who sees nothing but shining virtue and goodness in man. The reductio ad absurdum of cynicism is the response of a diplomatist who, on learning of the death of a fellow diplomatist, asked, "What can have been his motive?"

The Moral Problem

The difficulty we have in talking about values arises from the fact that there is not one morality but many. Morals and values, at every level, cluster, compete, and are in conflict. Most debates about values are not debates between right and wrong but between right and right, which makes their resolution endlessly complicated. Thus we believe in freedom of speech, but what about crying "fire!" in a crowded theater? We have faith in freedom of inquiry and science, but does this extend to a graduate student building a nuclear weapon in his kitchen? We strive for social justice and equality, but what do we do when, as in Lebanon, systems of order and social stability crumble? In developing societies, how do we reconcile the goal of the civil society with the need, temporary and in the name of order, for a military regime? The moralist may take satisfaction from proclaiming to the hard-pressed citizen leader that there are obvious and clear-cut moral answers to such choices. The cynic, in turn, may find an opposite way out by boasting that he knows there are no moral answers. Caught up in the problem and the need for policy, not rhetoric, the rest of mankind can indulge neither of these luxuries. They must find the best possible answers, knowing, with Friedrich Meinecke, that "every authentic tragedy is a shattering demonstration that moral life cannot be regulated like clockwork and that even the purest strivings for good can be forced into the most painful choices."

The facile optimism of political and social scientists that models can be found for resolving problems at every social level is nearly as mischievous as the attitudes of the moralist and the cynic. We are involved in human endeavors in which the tragic element of life plays a part. The human mind is at best a fragile guide. For all the power of systematic and disciplined scientific studies, we are dealing with stages in the historical process and individual acts that involve hubris. There are fatal flaws in our ability to choose; our best wisdom falls short of what is required. Raymond Aron quoted Montesquieu in a commentary on Henry Kissinger, applying Montesquieu's "Even wisdom has its excesses" to Kissinger's valiant efforts to open up United States foreign policy to contacts with China. Aron asked Kissinger if he didn't feel that in reaching out to his enemies he was forgetting his friends; according to Aron, Kissinger admitted there was that risk.

Yet even the fact of tragedy will not excuse us from acting. Perhaps the first step on the thousand-mile journey toward grappling with moral problems is understanding that violence is most often born of a single-value orientation. This form of seduction is a constant companion of all those who face moral choices. Whenever complexity exists, we seek to reduce it by focusing sharply on a single value. In the 1930s, following the most painful economic depression in our history, reformers proposed that economic security would assure happiness and well-being for all the people. Intellectuals and scholars were urged to concentrate on business cycles and the needs of economic man, and the best and brightest minds of the day assumed that progress on this front would be sufficient. The problems of the 1960s and 1990s dramatize the fact that the economic advancement of the 1950s and 1980s were "necessary but not sufficient."

We turned from economics in the 1950s to programs of national security and defense, long absent from prewar national policy in a nation isolating itself from the struggles in Europe until the eleventh hour. Yet national defense and international security systems cut adrift from cultural and political moorings are bound to flounder. We discovered in Vietnam that neither collective security nor military defense is sufficient if we fail to link them to knowledge of political movements and the cultural context.

The lesson for international politics is that even for security policies cultural factors may be more important than raw power. What is vital in international politics is our perception of ourselves and our interests as a people and a nation, of the interests and commitments of others, and of our common interests. These perceptions are determined not by interests alone but by the cultural and value context for ourselves and others. For large countries, this awareness is no less important than it is for small countries. There is danger in war gaming, both in the academy and in international politics. All too often, it can give false assurance and false security; and we must be on guard against it. The best way to be prepared is to keep our eye on values and the cultural context as we think about the moral problem.

Moral Dimensions

These patterns of thought lead to a final word. There are levels and dimensions at which the moral problem can be brought into focus. One is the level of certain minimum needs and concerns for moral discrimination. Failing here, we destroy ourselves and society. On the positive side, responses to the needs of blacks, women, and other minorities long the victims of discrimination illustrate what a nation must do. On the negative, there are certain things a civilized people, whatever the ambiguities and pressures, must not do. The Watergate conspiracy and the Iran-Contra affair are tragic symbols for this kind of mistake. If doubts arise that we are measuring up to a minimum standard, we have destroyed trust and confidence, the cement that holds us together. The international equivalent is a decent respect for the opinions and fundamental human rights of mankind.

A second level in focusing on the problem is to seek common interests, even in areas where values inevitably differ and conflict, which constitutes the moral problem in foreign affairs. The values of individuals and groups or collectivities are subject to different constraints. In the words of Camillo Benso, conte de Cavour, "If we had done for ourselves what we did for the state, what scoundrels we would have been." The triumph of the Marshall Plan was possible because for a historical moment moral and political interests drew Western Europe and the United States together. Today we talk of a wider European community in 1992, of trilateralism (Europe, Japan, and the United States) and of North-South interests in helping and learning from each other. What goes on at this level suggests that where interests converge in the face of burgeoning problems, there are possibilities for peoples of very divergent systems and ideologies to come together to grapple with these problems and needs.

A final level of the moral problem is present in more intimate communities where values and interests converge. The family is the classic example, but so is the human community at large. We need one another, yet we fear one another; and in fearing, we hurt one another. If the years before and immediately after World War II were filled with moralistic illusions about the similarities of all people, we may in the postwar era have become too cynical about the consequences of all our differences. The 1972 report entitled *Reconstituting the Human Community*, of which Ambassador Soedjatmoko and I were the principal authors, discusses the new attitude required in international relations:

> Recognizing all mankind's differences, there are still unities from which
> we derive strength, as does the world community. This unity is a different
> sort than that which was talked about in too simple terms twenty-five
> years ago. It is a unity which assumes and takes advantage of lesser

unities, such as constructive regionalism and the struggle for recognition by smaller groups within societies. They are unities which those outside a particular unity or unifying tradition have to learn to respect and to esteem, without envy, whether included or not. There will be unities within a country. And the West, particularly the affluent West, must learn to recognize and welcome, as a sign of true progress, worthy of support, the growth of self-confidence and self-reliance in nations and societies elsewhere in the world and their search for new directions. This, after all, is one aspect, varying in time and place, of the growing fabric of the desired human community.[1]

When we wrote those words we had in mind especially the emerging societies of Asia and Africa. With the restoration of freedom to the countries of Eastern Europe, the "search for new directions" in these nations is no less vital. Their "self-confidence and self-reliance" will require unities transcending ethnic and nationality struggles, and their strengthening may be the foremost challenge in the realm of moral values and international politics.

1. *Reconstituting the Human Community* (Report of Colloquium III, at Bellagio, Italy, July 17–23, 1972, for the Program of Inquiries, Cultural Relations for the Future, sponsored by the Hazen Foundation), 50.

11

Power and Morality:
Approaches and Problems

The fundamental problem in all discussions of morality and international relations is determining how to deal with the problem of power. The difficulty is intensified by certain deeply ingrained tendencies in society to seek to approach it through one or the other of three modes of thought: the *progressive*, the *scientific*, or the *power-glorification* approach. Not only does each of these ways of thinking misunderstand the problem, leaving it unresolved and unexamined, but each also contributes to an accentuation of certain inherent difficulties in understanding and coping with power.

Throughout most of the interwar period and the years immediately preceding it, the progressive outlook held sway. It persisted in the postwar period even when overtaken by events. It reflects a dominant way of thinking in the late nineteenth and twentieth centuries. At its center, the progressive perspective sees power as yielding to the irresistible and uninterrupted march of mankind onward and upward through human history. Man is on an escalator that is propelling humanity ever upward. In the same way that society has thrown off the shackles of slavery, human progress assures the substitution of reason for the quest for power in politics. Education is liberating man from the debasing struggle involved in the imposition of one human will on others. It is doing away with rivalry and conflict. The theory of progress rests on the proposition that material advance is everywhere in evidence and moral and political advance will inevitably follow.

A present-day example of this version of progress is the proposition that because economic reform is occurring in communist countries, political reform is not far behind. However appealing this idea is to Western preferences and sentiments, history does not sustain such a view. Before World War II, influential theorists such as E. H. Carr linked economic planning and planned economies in Germany, the Soviet Union, and Italy with human progress. These thinkers celebrated history on the march; the totalitarian states were leading mankind to a new international order. Carr outlined his prophecy in a whole series of writings. Before the ink was dry on his *Conditions of Peace*, however, the political objectives of Hitler and Benito Mussolini were becoming clear, and he was forced to write a new introduction revising his prophecy that peace and politics inevitably follow economics.

From the communist side as well it became clear in the 1930s that the Marxian prophecy was being refuted. Marx had forecast that new regimes would emerge in which "the domination of man by man would be replaced by the administration of things." Instead, as writers such as Niebuhr discovered, the Soviet regime, which had been trumpeted as a great historic achievement in limiting the destructive impact of capitalist economic forces on the political system, was merging economic with political power. A monopoly of political power led to a monopoly of economic power. A political system whose architects had promised that monopolistic capitalism would be replaced by a new socialist economic order ushered in a comprehensive and all-powerful political order in which power was more concentrated than in the system it replaced. Far from leading to the elimination of power, Marxism augmented the concentration of power through a union of political and economic power on a scale heretofore not achieved even in authoritarian political systems.

In the Gorbachev era, the question of reform is once more being raised. By introducing *glasnost*, Gorbachev seemed to be offering political reform in advance of economic reform. Because the latter, embodied in *perestroika*, has lagged, *glasnost* is being threatened. Although the Soviets, having recognized the need for democratization, are unlikely to turn back entirely, the future of reform is still an open question as Gorbachev strives to preserve and reconstitute the union.

However, democracies, and American democracy in particular, have not escaped the harsh judgment of history on the American vision of progress. Progress was present at the creation. Not only had values imbedded in our history brought us to a new stage of political and social development, but they were exportable to peoples everywhere. The foreign policy corollary of the American dream was a form of exceptionalism that heralded the elimination of power politics on the world scene. Americans were introducing a new form of international relations. What Europeans, "cribbed and confined" within narrow boundaries, had failed to realize Americans, by avoiding "entangling alliances," were destined to achieve. We had freed ourselves of dependence on alliances and on the balance of power and, therefore, on power as a reality, a necessity, and a constraint. In the interwar period, only a handful of rogue governments made power temporarily a necessity. With their defeat, civilization could then return to a power-free world in which brave new international organizations would take the place of power politics. In such thinking, the United Nations represented an end point in world history and a culmination of the work of the authors of grand designs for peace, such as Immanuel Kant, William Penn, and Emery Reves.

This progressive vision has fallen short of fulfilling its prophecies, and the problem of power remains. The scientific approach to power offers a second vision that promises to do away with the conflicts of human life. Don Price, former dean of the Kennedy School of Government at Harvard, tests a highly provocative thesis in his *America's Unwritten Constitution: Science, Religion and Political Responsibility*. Price identifies the origins of what he calls the American unwritten constitution in certain deeply ingrained negative ideas toward authority generated in the beginning by religious dissenters in the colonies and expanded through history to include distrust of government, of ecclesiastical establishments, and ultimately of a career civil service. Such distrust, Price maintains, is reinforced by the belief in progress and a reverence for scientists, who have succeeded religious dissenters in the hierarchy of the nation's intellectual leaders. What scientists and religious dissenters have in common is the belief that society can find a way around authority and power. Whereas countries such as Britain have accepted the reality and authority of both ecclesiastical and political establishments, Americans have sought other alternatives.

Religion in America is marked by a vast proliferation of sects and denominations. Similarly, Americans in their approach to governance seek to escape the need to coordinate and balance power, preferring to substitute legalistic and reformist approaches. It is significant that Price, the author of *The Scientific Estate* and a past president of the American Association for the Advancement of Science, would raise the issue. No one would accuse him of a lack of either scientific commitment or scholarly authority. Thus, his comments are especially deserving of reflection and thought.

Who would question the application of science and the scientific method to those phenomena to which science is applicable? Profits and losses, voting behavior, hardness and softness, and metal fatigue are all subject to laboratory studies, surveys, and testing. However, to imagine that good and evil or power and powerlessness can be similarly measured, added and subtracted, and disposed of through quantification is to misjudge the nature of the many diverse forms of reality. Yet that is essentially what writers like Morton Kaplan seek to do in their theories of morality and justice. They equate the determination of right and wrong with the recognition of physical qualities like hot and cold and proclaim that until ethics takes on the attributes of physical science it is unworthy of serious discussion.

The advocates of science would thus dispose of the question of power and morality by setting aside all the uncertainty and incommensurability of power through quantifying or seeking to quantify particular elements. It may be possible to measure the voting behavior of certain demographic groups on particular issues in the same way that income and profits can be measured in studying the economy, but power and powerlessness are factors to be analyzed in context. Who twenty years ago would have predicted the devastation that terrorist groups would wreak on more highly developed societies? How could we have measured the power of Muammar El Gaddafi or Saddam Hussein? How were we to know in advance the influence of nationalist leaders such as Ho Chi Minh?

Some twenty years ago Arnold Wolfers sought to distinguish passivity and activism in international politics and compared those who sought and used power with those who were indifferent to it. He defined as points on the spectrum of world politics what he called the "pole of power" and the "pole of indifference." He placed the superpowers at one extreme and the weaker states at the other. Looking back on his distinction, we can see that its major flaw was a failure to recognize the varied forms of power, including novel instruments of power such as terrorism or oil embargoes. When science seeks to dispose of power through statistical or scientific measurements, it ignores the ever-changing character of power relations and the nearly insoluble problem of evaluating and analyzing power. It substitutes a few readily quantifiable factors, such as numbers of tanks or missiles, for an analysis of the inner dynamics of a society. It ignores the fact that the emergence of a Gorbachev may change overnight the equation of power and the political and moral factors that bear scrutiny. Whereas before World War II, analysts often underestimated elements of military power, some writers in the postwar era have substituted estimates of military strength for appraisals of political power, leading to a profound misreading of the problem of power.

The final approach that has in certain countries and eras been dominant involves the glorification, if not the sanctification, of power. According to this viewpoint, not only is power all-important, but it has spiritual and metaphysical qualities that make it the noblest of all human virtues. The German romantics, such as Heinrich von Treitschke and Nietzsche, defined power as man's highest end. According to them, only the weak and dispirited in society disparage power. Self-fulfillment flows not from submission or self-abnegation but from self-assertion. In the same way that man comes into his own through control of his environment, he realizes himself through achieving dominion over fellow human beings.

From this view of the natural and inherent tendencies of individuals, it is only a short step to the notion of collectivities and nations dominating other collectivities and nations. In the extreme, the glorification of one nation's quest for supremacy over all the rest is epitomized by Hitler's Third Reich. The concept of an *übermensch*, or super race, presupposes that one race is destined by genetics to rule over all people. The mark of collective man is *animus dominandi*. A superior nation or race is proclaimed to be deserving, whether by tradition or genetic inheritance, naturally or artificially engendered, to rule the continent or the world. With less intensity and fewer illusions, Americans have periodically spoken to one another of Manifest Destiny and the American Century, recognizing, in most cases, the voluntary character a union of democratic peoples would require. Senator Albert J. Beveridge's challenge to fellow Americans to bring civilization to benighted peoples everywhere sanctified the idea of a chosen people carrying on a crusade to bring salvation to all mankind.

With all the differences that these various forms of hegemonic power and nationalistic universalism display, each yet represents the elevation of one society or one powerful nation-state to a position of superiority over all the rest. By implication, such superiority not only is inevitable but is a moral good. Power is not to become obsolete, as in the progressive vision, or be reduced to what can be determined scientifically. Instead, its fate is to be perpetuated and carried to new moral and political heights embodied in a powerful state.

Not surprising, therefore, those who equate power with the highest moral purpose resist all promptings to consider the complexities and ambiguities of power. If power is an unqualified good, they see no reason to consider the high costs that may be involved in the exercise of it. If five million kulaks lose their lives in Stalinist Russia, their loss is justified as the fulfillment of a high moral purpose. (Stalin answered Lady Nancy Astor's question about the killings by asking about the millions killed in traffic accidents in the West, all to no constructive purpose.) If six million Jews are killed by Hitler, that act is defended by the Führer as "a necessary hygienic measure." For programs of moral depravity and human debasement, the perpetrators define their mission so that it justifies unimaginable cruelty and brutality.

These examples of differing approaches to the elimination of the problem of power offer little solace to those awaiting its early eradication or transformation. The task remains of understanding power and its varied manifestations in all the many-sided dimensions of human existence. Experience within all human communities testifies to the ubiquity of power. The literature of philosophy, religion, and politics abounds with insights on power. No one can say there is nothing to discuss, debate, or read concerning power.

The human condition provides the best laboratory for an inquiry into power. If anyone doubts the ubiquity of power he can begin by examining, as we have done, the relations between a mother and her child's new spouse. Existing relations between the mother and child and the influence she has exerted are often threatened and upset by the new spouse's invasion of the family. The rivalries and tensions in such relationships bear the pejorative name of the "mother-in-law problem." No less evident is the struggle that goes on between children and parents as the former seek emerging identities and self-esteem through testing and asserting themselves against the latter's defense of the maintenance of authority and the preservation of established family traditions and values. For families of more than one child, the phenomenon of sibling rivalries is too well known to deserve comment. Within the family, therefore, a struggle for influence and power goes on between new and old members, parents and children, siblings, different generations, and those who join a new family through divorce and remarriage. The rivalry among nations plays itself out in microcosm within the community of the family.

The contest for influence that manifests itself within the family is often even more sharply drawn in local communities. For anyone whose business or professional life is lived within adjacent legal and political jurisdictions, the competition between them for tax resources and authority is commonplace. City and county vie with one another; state and localities compete for influence and resources. Developers seek to gain variances and rezoning privileges and meet opposition from environmentalists and the residents most directly affected.

On the national level, the history of American government is a story of promoters of states' rights opposing the defenders of a strong national government. As each group pursues its ends, the struggle becomes more intense. Some historians have portrayed the Civil War as a clash between two competing political philosophies. In our day, the contest between those who favor the primacy of national jurisdiction and those who support the rights of state governments is another example. Federalism provides the framework for an ongoing competition over the right to determine the shape of American government.

Internationally, the struggle for power has been a characteristic of the modern state system since its founding. Not only rivalry among nation-states but regional competition between east and west and north and south further illustrates the pattern of struggles for power among world regions. The protracted conflict between communism and democracy is also such a contest, as is the competition between capitalism and state socialism. If anyone questions the permanence of rivalry among men and nations, the evidence of the postwar era provides an answer. Within and among states, as in human communities from the family to the global village, contests for power persist.

One final distinction that must be added to the others is the differentiation between power in general and political power. Using the definitions put forward originally by Professor Morgenthau, we can say that power refers to "man's control over the minds and actions of other men," whereas political power relates to "the mutual relations of control among the holders of public authority and between the latter and the people at large." [1] Within the United States, a struggle is waged between the several branches of government over the distribution of power and authority. Indeed, the Constitution as it pertains

1. Hans J. Morgenthau and Kenneth W. Thompson, *Politics Among Nations: The Struggle for Power and Peace* (6th ed.; New York, 1985), 32.

to the relationship between the president and Congress is best described as
"an invitation to struggle." In successive periods of American history, the
relationship between the Supreme Court and the presidency has fluctuated,
and one or the other has risen or fallen in authority. Friendships or common
origins have not determined the presence or absence of the struggle. (Chief
Justice John Marshall and President Thomas Jefferson, for example, both Vir-
ginians, waged a bitter fight over power.) Instead, the source of the struggle
has been the quest for influence and the distribution of power and authority.
For this reason, it has become commonplace for those who are assigned responsibility within government to ask for the authority to carry out such responsibilities. While these demands are understandable and realistic to a
point, authority, like power, must be claimed and defended in the ongoing
struggle for influence, as has been apparent in the relationship between the
secretary of state and the national security adviser in almost every administration. What obtains within a given political system is a fact of life in relations
among independent political systems. It is true that the international system
has characteristics of its own and can be analyzed and described as such. Yet
in the absence of a common, effective, international authority and commonly
accepted moral standards affecting and controlling political actions, it is "the
relations among the holders of political authority," namely, the nation-states,
that predominate. Their relations remain the stuff of international politics,
whether in bilateral or multilateral arrangements. Their contests for influence
preoccupy national and international statesmen (United Nations diplomats no
less than national representatives mediate conflicts among states such as the
Iran-Iraq war and the Iraqi invasion of Kuwait). If the aim of any inquiry is
to demonstrate the relevance of norms and standards of morality, it must be
done by relating such norms to the realities that prevail in a given political
system.

Thus, discussion of morality and international relations cannot proceed
realistically in isolation from the problem of power. The task is to restore the
focus to an ancient discourse that considers the interrelatedness of power and
morality. In international relations as in politics, the dynamics of power relations channels, controls, and limits the effectiveness of moral standards.

In law, scholars point to three different types of norms that are aspects
of what Roscoe Pound described as a "hierarchy of legal norms." First are
rules that can be interpreted in a narrow and inflexible sense. They admit of

no discretion. They are clearly and unequivocally defined within national and metropolitan jurisdictions. Stopping at a red light is such a rule, and so are filing income tax returns by April 15 and driving on the right-hand side of the street. Whether someone is rich or poor, driving a Cadillac or a Volkswagen, he must file on April 15 and stay on the right-hand side of the road. Rules are a vital but small part of national or domestic law and an even smaller and less effective form of international law, as recognized and ratified by separate nation-states.

Second, principles in law constitute a jumping-off place for legal reasoning. Principles are not nondiscretionary or automatic. They involve such ideas as contracts not being binding unless supported by a sufficient consideration. Something is given as a quid pro quo for commitment or promise. This fact enters into legal analysis and judgment.

Third are standards, which are vaguely worded norms for desired human conduct. The Constitution is full of them. They are subject to legislative and judicial interpretation. Because of the broad and general nature of standards, the Supreme Court often arrives at five-to-four decisions. Such standards include due process of law, the equal protection clause, unreasonable restraint of trade, and cruel and unjust punishment. To these and other standards, Justice Holmes's statement of the crystal fallacy applies: "The word is not a crystal transparent and unchanged but the skin of a living thought." The words in a standard may vary according to time and thought, but they are not expandable like an accordion. In some instances words may allow for broad areas of discretion. In other instances, they can be narrower and more precise.

Norms in international law and international morality most nearly resemble standards. They reflect a high order of generality. When a judge on the International Court of Justice or a statesman acts, he has a broad and flexible range of choice because the norms involved are highly general and open to creative determination. In treaties affecting territorial status, for example, the court must search for meanings of territorial status, as in the treaty between the Netherlands, Denmark, and West Germany, negotiated before the continental shelf had been discovered. Laws and norms cannot be simply stated where creative analysis plays so major a role in effectiveness.

In international relations, norms can restrain and guide nations and other international entities in their relationships, but such restraints are subject to the compulsion of interests and power. Thus, the United States, whose leaders before and following World War II had more to say about international law than spokesmen of most other nations, denied in 1984 that international norms applied, at least as defined by the International Court of Justice, to U.S. interests in Central America over a two-year period. In invoking the proposition that an international norm may be a lodestar to guide nations, no one should suppose that even the most law-abiding nation will seek as its guide the normative judgments of the international community if it concludes, legitimately or not, that its interests are threatened.

It is also true that international norms institutionalize an underlying consensus of values. Law cannot go beyond the degree of underlying consensus, in effect. In the words of the late judge Charles de Visscher, "neither politics nor law will ensure equilibrium in the world without the 'moral infrastructure,' " or solidarities, on which community must rest. Visscher explains further: "Every society rests at once upon material and upon moral factors. It is the resultant of solidarities active enough to call for an organization of power and sufficiently conscious of a common good to engender the idea of law and the sense of obligation." National divisions such as those separating class from class have yielded to national solidarities. Forces of solidarity and cohesion within a nation result from its resistance to external pressures and from internal sentiments of loyalty. The nation in our time has triumphed over subnational forces.

For international norms, however, Visscher has a different conclusion: "The international community has no such decisive factor of social cohesion." It can make appeals for sacrifices to a common supranational good, as in movements for universal collective security or world government, but such appeals are "hardly accessible to the immense majority of men." Nowhere else does the comparison emerge in sharper contrast than in responses where essential interests are at stake. Visscher sums up the difference in a singularly penetrating statement:

> In the State it is the vital interests, the most highly political, that evoke the supreme solidarities. The opposite is the case in the international community. There one observes minor solidarities of an economic or technical order, for example, but the nearer one approaches vital questions, such as the preservation of peace and prevention of war, the less influence the community has on its own members. Solidarities diminish

as the perils threatening it grow. The solidarities that then assert themselves turn back to their traditional home, the nation. On the rational plane, men do not deny the existence of supranational values; in the sphere of action they rarely obey any but national imperatives.[2]

Walter Lippmann, who began his writings on international relations as a Wilsonian, parted company with President Wilson over issues of morality and international relations. Lippmann criticized Wilson, saying that his norms amounted to speaking in the language of a commencement speaker who counsels the graduates to "go forward." It was equally unhelpful to call on nation-states to eradicate war as to tell a graduate to go out into the world and "go forward." Neither provided any usable guidelines or offered any direction in defining the ends to be pursued or the means needed to reach such ends. In one sense, Wilson was arguing against himself in evangelizing about these distant goals of outlawing war and substituting the common interests of mankind for national interests. As a young political scientist, he had compared the requirements of statecraft to those of a ship's pilot who, navigating into a safe harbor, had not only to keep his eye on a guiding star but also to be master of the rocks and shoals that might threaten his ship's passage. Critics such as Lloyd George and Lord John Maynard Keynes maintained that Wilson at the Paris Peace Conference was indifferent to the details of treaties and boundary disputes that were essential to progress and constituted the rocks and shoals in arriving at an international agreement.

To introduce my students in a graduate seminar to the realities of political morality, I ask them to read *Essays on Lincoln's Faith and Politics* early in the course. Published posthumously, this little book by Hans Morgenthau, with a supplement by a young religion scholar, David Hein, graphically portrays Lincoln's concern for moral and political judgments and the various settings in which choices must be made. The Civil War president made it his business to master the essentials of political and moral action in the same way he taught himself the details of weaponry and military supply. Not only was he able to understand the forces at work influencing the political decisions of others; he also achieved an unmatched objectivity and detachment about his own actions. He was able to stand back and evaluate himself, his nation, and

2. Charles de Visscher, *Theory and Reality in Public International Law*, trans. P. E. Corbett (Princeton, 1968), 94, 90, 91.

those who sought his assistance, as few leaders before or since have succeeded in doing. He achieved a profound understanding of the limits of politics and morality, at the same time recognizing what America offered to the
world in freedom and justice. Self-criticism and a clear-eyed perception of
American failings strengthened rather than weakened his capacity for leadership. The great merit of the Lincoln book is that it provides historical examples of propositions about political morality, official versus personal morality,
war and peace, and political leadership, which topics we address throughout the class. The same can be said of Morgenthau's *Purpose of American
Politics*.

From Lincoln, we turn to moral and legal reasoning. I have found students more responsive to literature that is closely linked with real-life moral
and political choices than they are with more formalistic theoretical works. In
this section, I assign works such as *The Moral Decision* or *The Sense of
Injustice,* both by the late Edmund Cahn. Cahn was a remarkable New York
University legal scholar who taught moral reasoning by reconstructing moral
and legal choices taken or not taken as illustrated in leading cases that came
before American courts. He asked readers to stand at the forks in the road
where such moral choices were made. He contrasted the choices people actually made with their sense of themselves as they were confronting their
dilemmas. In choosing, he noted, they saw themselves as embodying all virtue and morality; only they were altogether moral. They celebrated themselves and their morality. The writings of Paul Freund, Alexander M. Bickel,
and H. L. A. Hart are complementary to Cahn's analysis, providing other
examples of moral and legal reasoning.

A section follows on approaches to morality and international relations.
Here I try to introduce students to the broad sweep of the literature. I encourage them to look for a focus in the writings they explore, by asking them to
read works such as my *Masters of International Thought* or my *Traditions
and Values: American Diplomacy, 1945–1982* or Norman A. Graebner's two
treatises on American diplomacy from the founding period to World War II.
Works of this kind offer concepts and definitions by which to classify the
writings of theorists and policy makers. Beyond these writings, I invite them
to read a wide range of classical and contemporary political theorists and
international relations writers. In this segment of the course, they are responsible for defining the focus of the writer's approach, whether in Arendt's *The*

Human Condition or *The Origins of Totalitarianism*, Aron's *Peace and War*, Carr's *The Twenty Year Crisis*, or Visscher's *Theory and Reality in Public International Law*. The Carnegie Council on Ethics and International Affairs annual volume *Ethics and International Relations* combines analyses of particular approaches with an introduction to the works of different theorists.

Other areas that we discuss are the nature of morality in international relations; the role and limitations of morality in international relations; some methodological controversies; approaches in the various disciplines to morality and international relations, that is, to international law, international organizations, diplomatic analysis and history, political theology, international politics; and so forth. In each area, we examine the prevailing viewpoints in the disciplines and see what they have to teach us about international morality.

The final section of the course deals with morality in relation to leading historical and contemporary problems, including human rights, nuclear war, arms limitation or reduction, foreign assistance, country problems, the United Nations, terrorism, and national security. If one were to divide the course into two major segments, they would be theory and problems. The latter provides the testing ground for competing theories. Here the relevance of theoretical assumptions comes into play. Students combine a class presentation of their topic, whether a theory or a problem, with the writing of a formal paper. The aim is to encourage wide reading, the critical appraisal of theories, and the application of theory to an urgent contemporary problem.

Some question whether this approach is sufficiently in touch with the winds of change. Writers point to signs of an increasingly interdependent and unified world. If such claims are to reflect something more than rhetoric, two questions must be answered. The first is posed by Judge Visscher, who directs our attention to vital interests. It is one thing to trace the web of interrelationships of nations in humanitarian, social, and economic arenas. It is far more difficult to establish the impact of such interrelations on life-and-death policies where national security is involved. Moreover, the choices and actions of nations who are part of international organizations more often than not are shaped by national interests. Thus, Saudi Arabia, protecting its own interests in oil production, was the dominant force in the decisions of the Organization of Petroleum Exporting Countries (OPEC) in the 1973 oil embargo. Recent decisions by NATO reflect the interplay of U.S., British, and German foreign and defense policy interests. Therefore, the new international bodies that some see as heralding a complete transformation of international relations also provide the framework for the pursuit of historic national interests by the member states. This is only too evident in the case of the United Nations and the United Nations Educational, Scientific, and Cultural Organization (UNESCO), to say nothing of the international bodies in which North and South meet to work out a new international economic policy.

A second question is whether nations move toward wider global or regional interests through a substitution of transnational or supranational values for national values or whether they move toward these newer values, if at all, through seeking points of convergence between their separate national interests. It is clear that leading thinkers on international morality, such as Niebuhr, chose the second concept of morality. It was Niebuhr's conclusion that the Marshall Plan represented the highest possible expression of international morality because it was based on an American vital interest (containing Soviet expansion), combined with the interests of West European nations in restoring economic and political stability and well-being. It was Niebuhr's conclusion that morality based on a transvaluation of values was a utopian goal, unlikely to be realized by nation-states in any foreseeable future, whereas identifying morality based on a convergence of interests was not utopian at all.

Moral standards in international relations, then, are more likely to be realized at points where morality and power meet. Their movements need to be seen in mutual interaction. Michael Howard has pointed out that the more lofty the moral ends, the more convergence and reinforcement of nations' interests and power are required. This view is in keeping with the traditional outlook on morality and international relations. It is the premise on which the reinstating of values in politics and diplomacy must be based.

12

The Ethical Dimension in American Thinking
About Nuclear War and Peace

The subject of ethics and war is not theoretical but practical. This statement has remained true especially in the 1980s. *Turnabout* seems to be the operative term with both American and Soviet views on nuclear arms. We and they revised our positions from the 1970s to the 1980s on the Antiballistic Missile (ABM) Treaty. Within the United States, defenders of a persistent arms-control approach have become critics; those who warned us against any concessions now urge the elimination of all strategic as well as intermediate missiles. Why? What accounts for the change? What are the assumptions that guide leading spokesmen? What are their controlling views on war and peace? Never has the ordinary hard-working American citizen had more reason to be confused.

Two propositions form an appropriate starting point on nuclear ethics. The first is that historically those who focus on war tend to neglect peace and those who emphasize peace often ignore the reality of war. A second proposition is that almost every thinker who discusses war and peace intermingles considerations of ethics with views of war and peace. Philosophers justify war and peace in the language of right and wrong or good and evil for their own nations and for all mankind. Each of the two states is seen as either good or bad, right or wrong, for the human race. Thus, the question of war and peace becomes a question of morality.

Those who glorify war and value it above all other values are the romantics associated in part with a particular tradition in German military thinking. In a letter of December 11, 1880, to Johann Bluntschli, Helmut von Moltke wrote: "Perpetual peace is a dream—and not even a beautiful dream—and war is an integral part of God's ordering of the universe. In war man's noblest virtues come into play." War for the romantics not only is considered inevitable but is the pathway to man's self-fulfillment. To them, human nature is fundamentally warlike and prone to international conflict. Escape from war would require a transformation of human nature, and the romantics see only decline in such a transformation. For Spengler "man is a beast of prey who lives by attacking and killing and destroying." War is inseparable from human nature, and romantics invoke such biblical passages as Matthew 24:6, "Ye shall hear of wars and rumors of wars," to lend credence to their judgments. Some go one step further and link all human progress and social development with war. The most brazen expression of this view was that of Treitschke, who proclaimed that "all movement and all growth would disappear without war—only the exhausted, spiritless, degenerate periods of history have toyed with the idea." War is a positive good, and conflicts will persist until the end of history.

If some German thought epitomizes the romantic view of war, romanticism is absent neither from American and British thought nor from the communist outlook on war. Americans glorify figures such as General Patton and, in films, Rambo, and they remember with pride General Anthony McAuliffe's response in World War II to the German call for surrender of his 101st Airborne Division in the Battle of the Bulge: "Nuts." However, American and British romanticism about war is far more tentative and circumscribed than the German and is commonly linked with a particular war or struggle, not war in general. Its spokesmen cast their defense of war in more qualified and pragmatic terms. Often war is associated with honor, as in J. F. C. Fuller's declaration that "if honor be worth safeguarding, war sooner or later becomes inevitable, for in this world, there are always dishonorable men and if war doesn't bring nations against them, vice will triumph." Three administrations defended continuing the war in Vietnam not as an unqualified good but as a matter of honor.

Within the communist tradition broadly defined, war is considered inevitable so long as capitalism exists. Imperialism is a product of capitalism, and it brings the "have" and "have-not" nations into conflict with one another. Capitalist nations in decline act to save themselves through seeking to exploit colonial markets and in so doing clash with other imperialistic states. Because of the war-producing consequences of capitalism, communists have a missionary responsibility to change the status quo. To foster change, communism encourages revolutionary wars and wars of national liberation, goals that the Soviet Union never abandoned, even at the height of detente. In this ongoing struggle, communism, implicitly at least, recognizes the inevitability of war and conflict.

Yet communism, in contrast with the German romantics, stops short of idealizing war. In the communist version of the historical process, war may be a necessary stage to bring about national liberation. It may speed the downfall of the exploiting class or the realization of some other necessary end. But war, according to communism, constitutes a negative selection process. In war, the fit are more likely to be destroyed than the unfit. Perhaps because the Russian people have suffered such massive and staggering losses in war, the Soviet Union as the earliest and most powerful purveyor of communism has not embraced romanticism.

If romanticism glorifies war as such, certain idealists by contrast have looked on war as senseless slaughter and in its place have offered peace and nonviolence. The vision of peace and the dream of a world free of conflict have rested on a multitude of diverse and changing foundations, secular and sacred. One source in Scripture is Isaiah 2:4: "They shall beat their swords into ploughshares,/and their spears into pruning hooks;/Nations shall not lift up swords against nations;/neither shall they learn war any more." (Some biblical scholars point out that this passage refers to the last days of judgment and ought not, therefore, be identified with contemporary idealism.)

Peace for the children of the Enlightenment rests more on reason and science than on religion. Few, if any, in the Middle Ages had much faith that war and poverty could be eliminated. Social and moral reformists were to change all that. It was the spirit of the Enlightenment in the eighteenth century that ushered in a new era of thinking. We know that private citizens don't make war, they reasoned, and it follows then that war will be eradicated by bringing public acts in line with private conduct. War as viewed by a host of nineteenth-century reformers had become an anachronism, and such reasoning proved convincing to moderns. In the past, aristocratic governments had believed in power politics and practiced war. They and a handful of their successors, selfish aggressors who disrupt international harmony, still remained standing in the path of a peaceful world. Man's earlier warlike instincts have been undergoing change. Among the instruments of change are democracy and international organization, social conditioning and people-to-people relationships across national boundaries, and public recognition of the senseless waste of war. Reason tells us war is waste. Nations that go to war imagine they will obtain wide-ranging benefits. They don't. History should teach that no one gains in war, and reinforcing this lesson, morality and democracy in our time have combined to eliminate the desire and appetite for war. Religion and reason and science and economics have led men to question war and to respond to the missionaries of peace.

Further, a host of social forces and educational perspectives have inspired a new belief in the possibility of peace. Education as such and the promotion of a more rational view of the world promise an end to war. Philosopher of history Henry T. Buckle argued that "as the intellectual acquisitions of a people increase, their love of war will diminish." He went further and discovered a natural ratio between peace and war, preordaining that whenever intellectual classes are weak, military influence will be strong. For Buckle it was clear that when Russia in the mid-nineteenth century embarked on the Crimean War, it was because "Russia is warlike, not because its people are immoral but because they are unintellectual." Writing in 1913, Toynbee could judge: "War as a constructive national activity is for us a thing of the past. Between our warlike ancestors and ourselves there is a great gulf fixed." Education and its handmaiden the Industrial Revolution had created a new and more rational environment for peace.

Thus, education had broken the cycle of war by teaching new values, and closely linked with education was science. An important corollary of rationalism is the belief in a natural harmony of interests. Science had discovered that the planets were held in their orbits by a natural harmony of interests. A similar harmony had been described in Bernard Mandeville's *Fable of the Bees*. It remained for science to penetrate the social order as Adam Smith had done in the eighteenth century in describing the processes in economics by which the individual pursuing self-interest is guided, as if by a hidden hand, to serve the common good. Such harmony of interest may be temporarily obscured by the deeds of some persistent troublemaker or the atavism of power politics, but international harmony, once identified and present, will be as enduring as the harmony of the natural order, thanks to the discoveries of science.

What education and science make possible, communication enables mankind to realize in full. A shrinking globe facilitates trade and travel. Communication among peoples eliminates ignorance and distrust. The greater the contacts between national groups, the greater their mutual respect. In the eighteenth century, England and France fought with one another because they didn't know and respect one another. The English saw the French as a people of low morals, while the French viewed the English as a people without a culture. Science and social science have helped mankind see that social and human contacts break down barriers of misunderstanding and further political integration. Scholars like Professor Karl Deutsch maintain that degrees of integration can be measured scientifically by the flow of messages and communication (postcards, letters, phone calls, and telegrams) across national boundaries. However, skeptics ask if the French and Germans went to war in the nineteenth and in the first half of the twentieth century because they didn't understand one another and their objectives or because they understood one another all too well.

Finally, reformists on the left and the right find in democracy new grounds for peace. At the outset of any discussion of democracy, an important preliminary distinction between two quite different lines of argument and discourse is worth making. Democracy can be defended as the best possible form of government given human nature or as the only form of government capable of assuring the maintenance of peace. In 1796, Kant in his essay "Perpetual Peace" made the second argument, and expressions of it recur from Kant to Wilson to, ironically, Reagan. According to this view, the prospects for peace depend on the multiplication of democracies because only they cherish peace. Only nondemocratic states make war. With all their differences, Wilson and Reagan share common ground in espousing a view repeated by others before and after both world wars. Wilson argued that "national purposes have fallen more and more into the background and the common purposes of enlightened mankind have taken their place." What were these common purposes? First and foremost, they were the rights of national and ethnic groups everywhere to form their own governments, to achieve national self-determination, and to govern themselves. Having done so, they would, invoking the ancient phrase, "make war no more." The Reagan administration was equally explicit in defending the spread of democracy throughout the world by the Reagan Doctrine, asserting the inevitable link between democracy and peace.

If romantics and idealists treat war and peace in isolation, realists try to connect them. Statesmen must make tragic choices for peace almost always in the shadow of war. Whereas violence in most periods of a nation's domestic history is the exception and not the rule, war in international relations is continual and ever-present. The connection was clearly stated in the nineteenth century by Clausewitz, who wrote of war as a continuation of politics by other means. In war and peace, men seek to coerce or persuade others to do their will. War "is not merely a political act but a real political instrument, a continuation of political intercourse, a conduct of political intercourse by other means."[1] Politics is a psychological act, whereas war is primarily an act of force, yet both involve the mobilizing and using of power. Integrating this information, realism defines politics and especially international politics as a perpetual and unceasing struggle for power. However, realism chooses *not* to answer the question that romanticism and idealism answer in opposite ways.

To the question of whether war is inevitable, romanticism answers "yes" and idealism "no." Realism doesn't answer but changes the subject, insisting that neither war nor peace is inevitable but that continuing rivalry and competition intermingled with cooperation are the normal condition in political relations among states. For leaders, the choice of one or another of these viewpoints is fraught with consequences; indeed, they may lead in opposite directions. If men and states assume that harmony and cooperation are the norm, states and the people will follow unquestioningly policies based on humanitarian and moral principles. If leaders recognize that international politics is marked by continuing rivalry and competition, each nation will follow its own national interests, seeking compromises and adjustments with the interests of others. For the former, goals are likely to be absolute and global, but for the latter they are tentative, immediate, and practical. Because each nation-state lives in a pluralistic world order with more than 160 other nation-states, each with its own norms and values, the process of coping and surviving demands compromise and adjustment.

With respect to the inevitability of war and peace, realism postulates that nation-states have no choice but to live on the razor's edge of conflict. In the absence of effective universal norms, for a given nation any war that is necessary is also just, to paraphrase Machiavelli. Peace keeping in practice involves postponing conflict and playing for time more than it does adhering to abstract legal principles that outlaw war as in the Pact of Paris of 1928. Peace is a product of impending wars averted and sharp rivalries ameliorated—rivalries that might otherwise have led to war. More than forty-five years of living under the balance of terror confirms the wisdom of Toynbee's

---

1. Carl von Clausewitz, *War, Politics and Power: Selections from "On War" and "I Believe and Profess,"* ed. and trans. Edward M. Colling (Chicago, 1962), 83.

prophecy that the Soviet Union and the United States above all have needed time to learn to live on this shrinking globe. To this end, respected thinkers propose spheres of interest and buffer zones not because they are morally desirable but because they might buy time. Nations throughout the history of the modern state system from 1648 to the present have sought security, approached it through the organization of national power, encroached on or threatened the security of others, and averted conflict through some kind of rough and ready demarcation of territory or spheres of interest in which each recognized the dominant influence of the other. However much national publics, and particularly democratic publics with their strong ethnic and immigrant populations, find such divisions offensive, spheres of influence or the "principle of the fence" embodies a residual moral element. Neighborliness and brotherhood are as often served by respect for one another's boundaries as by people-to-people contacts that may become oppressive and overburdening. Politicians might also heed what philosophers write concerning distributive justice.

This discussion brings us, without benefit of anything approaching full consensus, into the nuclear age with all its awesome and perplexing problems of militarization, nuclear freezes, and hard bargaining with the Soviets. How, if at all, do the three approaches or philosophies of war and peace apply to the present? What validity is there in approaches that emphasize one or the other or that seek to unite them? What can be said about the ethical dimension? Have nuclear weapons changed everything or nothing at all or some things and not others, and, if so, what?

In the aftermath of World War II and the explosion of atomic bombs over Hiroshima and Nagasaki, it became commonplace to write that pre-nuclear thinking was obsolete. The traditional vocabulary of foreign policy no longer fit reality. Observers spoke of atomic discourse being based on an alphabet of mutual annihilation. The "absolute weapon" as defined by Bernard Brodie had changed Clausewitz's integral linkage of war and peace. Few romantics who glorify nuclear conflict remain, though a handful, including Reagan's secretary of defense Weinberger, once spoke of "prevailing" in a nuclear conflict. The one approach whose validity is most under challenge is that which looks to war as the route to man's self-fulfillment.

Despite all the claims that the debate between idealism and realism is no longer relevant and has passed from view since the 1950s and 1960s, the political and ethical issues of the nuclear age still tend to be shaped by the two viewpoints. Whatever people call themselves, whether realists or idealists, their thinking often tends to move back and forth between the poles of realism and idealism. For example, Reagan campaigned beginning in the 1960s against Strategic Arms Limitations Talks (SALT) I and SALT II but in the sixth and seventh years of his presidency talked of a denuclearized Europe and, at the Reykjavik summit conference, of a world without nuclear weapons. What has tended to happen in the nuclear age is that at different times and in different places we all tend to become idealists and realists along an ever-changing policy-making front.

Yet a hard core of basic principles sets boundaries for the tendencies of thinking of the one group, distinguishing it from the tendencies of thinking of the other group. Even in the nuclear age, realists see war and peace as being interconnected, not as Clausewitz did, but in ways that seemingly turn Clausewitz' doctrine on its head. No longer is war, except in localized and limited conflicts, a continuation of politics by other means. Rather war-making capacity, joined with other instruments of peace such as politics and diplomacy, has proven the one continuing reliable means thus far devised to prevent nuclear war. The commitment to war and to the use of weaponry is the means no longer of achieving military supremacy but of maintaining stability in peace. For over forty-five years, we have lived under a balance of terror. Even the Catholic bishops, who have spoken out strongly against nuclear weapons, recognize that the world has escaped nuclear war because of nuclear deterrence. Peace and war are linked not through one following the other in some unbroken process but through the maintenance of peace by building up and building down nuclear capacity and resources. Finally, not a world policeman or universal peace-making body but the most powerful states, those capable of launching nuclear weapons, are the guardians and custodians of nuclear peace. Therefore, realists who comprehend the need for arms limitation are understandably cautious about a denuclearized world. Ridding the world of nuclear weapons, even if it were possible, could threaten the preservation of the most successful system for preventing all-out war in the twentieth century. Yet paradoxically so vast and costly has the nuclear deterrent become that efforts at arms limitation must take the highest priority. No president or administration can fail to try, as several more obdurate ones have learned in the course of their terms of office, for mounting national deficits and political attitudes have become a spur to action. The imperative of global survival is added to the historic end of national survival as an inspiration for policy.

If realism is complex and many-sided in its views of the arms race, idealism is relatively simple. As we noted, it starts with the single and appealing proposition that war and peace must be separated: "The way to peace is peace." The world is seen as populated by both peaceful and aggressor states. The idealist's objective is to identify the former and remove the latter and in their place install democracies. Once democracy is established, a state will become peaceful, contrary to the warnings of such as the Comte de Mirabeau, who declared in the French National Assembly at the height of the French Revolution that parliamentary bodies, once passions are inflamed, can prove more bellicose than a monarch.

Education, science, communication, and democracy for the idealist are the fourfold route to peace. Education will make men reasonable about war and peace, for, as the young Walter Lippmann wrote in the first issue of the New Republic, "every sane person knows it is a greater thing to build a city than to bombard it, to plough a field than to trample it, to serve mankind than to conquer it." Yet education oftentimes tends either to abstractions or to the sponsorship of uncontrolled surges of patriotism. Educators tell us to work for justice or peace, but such words become hollow vessels lacking content. An older and wiser Lippmann wrote of Wilson and his Fourteen Points: "When Mr. Wilson began, Europe believed that the Wilson program was an American program, a thing as vital to us as Alsace-Lorraine was to France. But in the course of time the European statesmen discovered that Mr. Wilson's program was really nothing more than his gratuitous advice in a situation he did not thoroughly understand." Lippmann's conclusion was that educating others in ideals and goals can never be accomplished apart from considering political and territorial questions that in turn assume a connection between peace and war. If Wilson failed, education can hardly be seen as a panacea.

To those who say science can save us, we answer it is science that made the atomic bomb. The most memorable passage in the writings of Hans Morgenthau may be the following: "Events will . . . follow their course as though all those proposals by international commissions of experts and other rationalist-utopian devices had never been invented. . . . Yet, as a supreme irony, this school of thought attempts to monopolize for itself the virtue of being 'practical'; it treats with disdain the rare attempts to base international action on a genuine understanding of the forces determining political reality rather than on the ideal postulates of abstract reason." Lest one assume that the preference for science over politics has changed, the announcement by a large foundation of a program of grants for arms control studies is instructive. It reads that preference will be given to applicants who have not previously worked in the field but who are committed to transferring knowledge and experience from the natural and physical sciences to the subject. It puts a premium on ignorance of the substance of international politics, and to this day the fruits of such efforts, according to one leading public official, have not yielded a single contribution to the enhancement of arms control.

What has been said about the limitations of education and science could be said equally of communications and democracy. None can by itself or in mutual interrelationship rid the world of the fateful connection between war and peace. What may be needed is the moral determination and intellectual curiosity to search out the ever-changing patterns in which that connection manifests itself. A Republican and a member of the Tower Commission, General Brent Scowcroft reported he had not known a president less curious about foreign policy than Reagan. Such an observation is a more serious indictment of the president than anything resulting from the Iran-Contra hearings. This observation may explain why the president was so ill-prepared at Reykjavik and unaware of how Europeans would react to the removal of all intermediate and short-range missiles from their continent. Historically, liberal utopian internationalists and conservative isolationists have had more in common than could first be imagined. One may lead irresistibly to the other. The ethical dimension of war and peace can be summarized again in a brief comparison. The universal ethical command common to most religions is "Thou shalt not kill." Since 1648, within the nation-state system, that command has been transformed by the dictates of the national ethic into "Thou shalt kill under certain conditions the enemies of thy country." With the threat of nuclear annihilation still with us, does the rational basis exist in the 1990s for us to return to the universal ethical command?

We live at a point in time that is a meeting place of contradictions and antinomies. The nation-state has been rendered obsolete by nuclear weapons, but no effective world community has taken its place. Ideological foreign policy is a deterrent to successful diplomacy, but foreign policy not rooted in national purpose is aimless. Men seek power as the means to worthy ends, but those ends are corrupted by the pursuit of power. It is entirely possible that nations were closer to a genuine moral order in the eighteenth than in the twentieth century. In our time they meet in the international arena, each persuaded that it is the champion of the mandate of history. In such a world we seek an ethical dimension in war and peace.

Only by confronting such realities can we move toward a truer definition of the ethical dimension. We cannot achieve it by ignoring the realities of the necessary balance between East and West or North and South. We can no more seek the path of least resistance to get an unbalanced arms control agreement than we can give up the quest. We must not allow imaginary political gains, whether from those who fashion or from those who criticize arms proposals, to shape our acts. We need to steel ourselves to grapple with issues more complex than men have ever faced before, politically, militarily, and philosophically. Put in the simplest terms, the stakes are too great for us to be for or against policies because they are Republican or Democratic or because we are for or against arms agreements. Once again, more citizens and leaders, whatever their proclivities, need to make an unusually stubborn attempt to think clearly.

13

The Meeting of Ethics and Diplomacy

William Graham Sumner wrote that "the amount of superstition is not much changed, but it now attaches to politics, not to religion." To politics, we can add diplomacy. In ancient societies, men called on the gods to rid their world of conflict, evil, and suffering. If war persisted, they asked the gods to reward their side with victory. What men in their frailty could not accomplish, the gods would provide. They would protect the weak and reward virtue. If men could not safeguard justice, the gods would assure that justice was done. From ancient tribal deities to the gods who presided over the knights of the Round Table, their task ultimately was to smooth out the troubled path along which heroic men had to walk.

An opposing view of morality is rooted in classical traditions and the historic versions of the Judaeo-Christian faith. It is true that some moralists, nationalists, and religiously oriented people are tempted to make a success story out of their faith. Yet no one, least of all religious leaders, can guarantee prosperity and success, even though certain early religious movements in the colonies and the original thirteen states sought to demonstrate that outer signs of well-being were evidence of inner virtue. The twentieth-century theologian Reinhold Niebuhr wrote of two men, one who tithed from his youth and gained great wealth. That man explained his success as the product of a lifetime of religious observance. The other man, Adam Denger, by whom the young Niebuhr was employed in a grocery store in Lincoln, Illinois, generously extended credit to miners who had lost their jobs. However, the miners left Lincoln without paying their debts, and their benefactor was destroyed. In her biography of Niebuhr, June Bingham writes of the lesson that he had learned: "Mr. Denger kept believing that God would protect him if he did what was right. But God let Adam Denger go bankrupt and his young assistant grew up to preach against sentimentality and reliance on special providence."[1] When

1. June Bingham, *Courage to Change: An Introduction to the Life and Thought of Reinhold Niebuhr* (New York, 1961), 62.

Niebuhr preached against the self-serving views of those who proclaimed that God would reward them, he chose as his text the biblical passage "For He makes his sun to rise on the evil and the good and sends rain on the just and unjust."

Nothing in Scripture assures the virtuous of success or guarantees the inheritance of wealth and riches by the righteous. According to Niebuhr, it is a corruption of religion to believe that the virtuous man or the good nation will always be triumphant or that evil empires will be destroyed. Religious people too often lobby in the courts of the Almighty, endlessly proclaiming their goodness and offering their piety as proof that they deserve special favors. A more profound understanding of man and God would emphasize the tragic element in history. The unending process in diplomacy of balancing the forces of harmony and disharmony is at war with the notion that those who are good and virtuous are destined through divine intervention to inherit happiness, prosperity, and success.

A more contemporary version of the intrusion of false and superstitious notions about ethics and diplomacy is what Louis Halle has called "Pharisaism." The posturing of those who claim to be more virtuous than their fellow men is not true morality. In the parable of the Pharisee and the publican (Luke 18:10–14), those who make ostentatious display of their morality and point a finger at the iniquity of others are condemned for their false morality. Politicians and diplomats, forever denouncing the morality of others, ought as a rule to be mistrusted. By their attitudes, they would have others believe they have achieved so complete a level of morality that they are qualified to judge all others. They depend not on the gods for their morality but on their own supposed moral perfection.

Another version of morality is the morality of Manichaeism, which portrays the world in radical terms of absolute good and evil or right and wrong. Americans are early predisposed to a form of Manichaeism by childhood distinctions between good guys and bad guys or cops and robbers. The false logic of Manichaeism lies at the heart of every crusading ideology and of civilization's long chronicle, ever since the wars of religion, of unspeakable brutalities of one people against another. In the end, Manichaeism becomes a negative morality; it seeks to impose punishment and retribution on others.[2]

2. Manichaeism in its original form connected evil with the flesh and goodness with spirit.

According to the mythology of Manichaeism, a particular group or class becomes a satanic evil. For the Germans, the Jews; for the Allies, the Germans and Japanese; for the bourgeoisie, the communists and their proletarian vanguard; and for the communists, the bourgeoisie are the one evil force in the world. Once that evil has been rooted out and eradicated, peace and harmony will prevail. Not by accident, the Ayatollah Ruhollah Khomeini depicted the United States as the Great Satan in the most recent form of Manichaeism, and President George Bush denounced Saddam Hussein as another Hitler. Those who belong to groups and nations who personify evil may in the name of morality be chastised or destroyed in order that justice be done.

A reformist version of morality identifies the good with what is novel and the corrupted with continuity and past practices. Since the end of the Napoleonic Wars, ever larger groups of Western leaders have denounced diplomacy and international politics as an unhappy and outmoded stage in the progress of mankind that was bound to disappear once the historical circumstances that gave rise to it had been transformed. European diplomacy was an archaism that history would eliminate when reason and morality prevailed. For some writers, it was a particular social evil that caused the corruption of international society: colonies for Jeremy Bentham, trade barriers for Richard Cobden and Pierre-Joseph Proudhon, capitalism for Marx, and the absence of self-government for liberals. Cobden declared that in some future election, we would probably see the test of 'no foreign politics' applied to those who wish to become representatives of free constituencies. From 1934 to 1936, the Nye Committee in the Senate investigated the role of certain financial and industrial interests suspected of having been responsible for the entry of the United States into World War I. Not the requirements of the national interest but certain self-seeking groups who profited from the war were responsible for our involvement. Manufacturers of weaponry and international bankers had lured unsuspecting nations into war. According to the "devil theory," a handful of war profiteers and munitions makers were responsible for war. If the nation could rid itself of their conspiratorial and nefarious influence, peace would prevail. War would end when Congress took the profits out of war.

Underlying all such views is a deep-seated conviction that a certain group or a particular social and international order is dominated by evil forces that are responsible for the immorality of diplomacy and politics. The path to a moral international order thus is one in which the people will drive out the forces. Once they are rooted out, an ethical international system will be assured, and conflict will come to an end.

Human Nature and Diplomacy

Opposed to the essentially utopian views of these several versions of morality and diplomacy is another conception of human nature and diplomacy. According to this view, human nature has not changed since the days of classical antiquity. Politics and diplomacy bring out the harsher side of man's nature. Thucydides is therefore, as Hobbes declared in another age, "the most Politick Historiographer that ever lived."

The Melian dialogue still has relevance in an age of interdependence. Melos had remained neutral during the war between Sparta and Athens, but the Athenians, during a long truce, confronted them with an expeditionary force and called on them to join the Athenian alliance or be exterminated. When the Melians resisted, the Athenian delegation outlined its position, and Thucydides reported the ensuing dialogue. The Athenians explained that justice depends upon the power to compel; the strong do what they have the power to do, and the weak accept what they must. Even the gods will not help because they behave toward one another and toward men much as the Athenians behave toward Melos. The delegation concluded: "It is a general and necessary law of nature to rule wherever one can. This is not a law we made ourselves, nor were we the first to act on it when it was made. We found it already in existence, and we shall leave it to exist forever among those who come after us." Melos resisted and was destroyed.

Frederick the Great, king of Prussia from 1740 to 1786, in his *Origin of the Bismarck Policy* or *The Hohenzollern Doctrine and Maxims*, written for his successor to the throne, summarized his opinions on religion, morals, politics, and diplomacy, saying, "We monarchs take what we can, when we can, and we are never in the wrong, except when compelled to give up what we had taken." He wrote of religion as a stumbling block: "Religion is absolutely necessary in a State government. . . . [But] there is nothing which tyrannizes over the mind and heart so much as religion, because it agrees neither with our passions, nor with the high political views which monarch should entertain. . . . When he is about to conclude a treaty with some foreign power, if he only remembers that he is a Christian, all is lost: he will always suffer himself to be duped or imposed upon."

Frederick defended the right of each religious sect to worship and pray and seek salvation as they wished but prophesied they would never agree. Of justice, he declared, "We owe justice to our subjects as they owe us respect . . . but it is necessary to take care that we are not brought under subjection by justice itself." For Frederick, "Justice is the image of God," and so, he demanded, "who can therefore attain to so high a perfection." He invited his reader to "behold all the countries in the world, and examine if justice is administered exactly in the same manner." What troubled Frederick most was that if the trends he observed continued, one-tenth of the kingdom's subjects in the next century would be engaged in the administration of justice with "that sure and steady way of proceeding which lawyers have . . . [and] that clever manner of preserving their advantages under the appearances of the strictest equity and justice."

On statesmanship and diplomacy, Frederick reduced all moral and political practice to three principles and practices: "The first is to maintain your power, and, according to circumstances, to increase and extend it. The second is to form alliances only for your own advantage; and the third is to command fear and respect even in the most disastrous times." Harsh as his maxims seem, Frederick formulated them into a doctrine of reason of state. He warned against displaying pretensions with vanity but insisted that every ruler must have "two or three eloquent men" and leave justification for his actions to them. Only when Prussia had become more powerful would she be able to assume an air of "constancy and good faith, which, at most, [was] fit only for the greatest powers and for petty sovereigns." Of diplomats, Frederick sought "those who [had] the gift of expressing themselves in ambiguous terms and susceptible of a double meaning." He went on to say it would not be improper for a sovereign to have political locksmiths to pick locks or open doors or physicians to dispose of troublesome people who might be in the way. With regard to embassies, Frederick preferred envoys rather than ambassadors for it was difficult to find men of wealth and noble birth and "by adopting this system, you [would] save enormous sums of money every year, and, nevertheless, your affairs [would] be transacted all the same." There were cases in which embassies had to be on a scale of magnificence, as when rulers sought a political or matrimonial alliance, but such instances were exceptional. Above all, neighbors had to believe "that you [were] a dangerous monarch, who [knew] no other principle than that which leads to glory." [3]

It is tempting in the modern age to dismiss the insights of Thucydides and Frederick the Great or other political thinkers such as Hobbes, who described a state of nature involving a "war of every man against every man," or Machiavelli, who made an acute analysis of the hard realities of politics in which might makes right. Yet diplomacy in the last decade of the twentieth century is still conducted under the shadow of war and is still based on calculations of power and national interest. It is worthwhile recalling the political thought of the founding fathers. Because of man's nature and the need to remedy "the defect of better motives," the founders turned to constitutionalism as providing a system of checks and balances. They wrote of the interplay of opposite and rival interests. Because they understood the human traits of which earlier men had written, they displayed a mistrust of political power not only of other states but within their own borders. As John Adams explained it: "Our passions, ambitions, love and resentment, etc., possess so much metaphysical subtlety . . . that they insinuate themselves into the understanding and the conscience."

Nor was Adams alone in his concern about power. As we have seen, his intellectual adversary, Jefferson, with whom he was in contention during much of the period, maintained in 1798 in the Kentucky Resolutions that confidence in leaders can often prove to be not the means of freedom but the parent of despotism because free government depends as much on rivalry and competition as on confidence. It requires limited constitutions to bind down those whom a people choose to trust with power. Jefferson concluded: "In questions of power then let no more be heard of confidence in man, but bind him down from mischief by the claims of the Constitution." The exercise of power and the imposing of the will of an individual or group on others were "of all known causes the greatest promoter of corruption." However the Enlightenment may have shaped the thought of early Americans, their views reflected a sturdy realization of the hazards and reality of power. Their view of human nature was not far removed from the perspective of Blaise Pascal

---

3. Frederick the Great, *Origin of the Bismarck Policy*, European Pamphlets, No. 12 (Boston, 1870), 61, 12, 22, 23, 43, 48, 48–49, 50, 51.

("Man is neither angel nor brute, and the unfortunate thing is that he who would act the angel acts the brute"). Whatever conclusions about ethics and diplomacy may ultimately prevail, contemporaries must recognize the limitations that the more sordid and selfish aspects of human nature place on the conduct of foreign policy, including diplomacy in the nuclear age.

The Nature of Diplomacy and Morality

The most cynical view of diplomacy is the one some attribute to Sir Henry Wotton, who allegedly identified an ambassador as an honest man who is sent abroad to lie for the good of his country. The three elements that such a definition embraces are a proposition about lying in diplomacy, an implication that privately the ambassador is an honest man but publicly he is something else, and an acceptance of the inevitability of the "official lie." Moralists dismiss any reference to deceit as a necessary ingredient of diplomacy yet run the risk of moving to an opposite extreme. Sir Harold Nicolson wrote of the difference: "The worst kind of diplomatists are missionaries, fanatics and lawyers; the best kind are the reasonable and humane skeptics. Thus it is not religion which has been the main formative influence in diplomatic theory; it is common sense." Truth telling in diplomacy is limited by the fact that diplomacy is not a system of moral philosophy. It is the application, as Sir Ernest Satow wrote, of intelligence and tact "to the conduct of official relations between independent states." Honesty in diplomacy, said an experienced diplomat, doesn't mean telling everything you know.

It is evident that important differences exist between eighteenth- or nineteenth- and twentieth-century diplomacy. The former involved relationships between monarchs or members of an aristocratic elite. The latter brings together envoys of the people. In the former instance, professionals were involved in the practice of diplomacy, whereas in the latter amateurs have often been engaged. Yet with all the differences, the nature of diplomacy brings into play certain common characteristics. In describing what was needed of the twentieth-century diplomat, Nicolson called for "a man of experience, integrity and intelligence, a man, above all who is not swayed by emotion or prejudice, who is profoundly modest in all his dealings, who is guided only by a sense of public duty, and who understands the perils of cleverness and the virtues of reason, moderation, discretion and tact." Having said all this, he slyly added, "Mere clerks are not expected to exhibit all these difficult tasks at once."[4]

The crux of the matter, as certain students of diplomacy see it, is that foreign policy is conducted by governments. As a function of governmental responsibility it must serve the purposes of governments generally; as Lincoln reminded us, "its primary purpose must be to preserve the union," informed by the national interest and the dictates of national security. On this point, American scholars and writers on diplomacy differ, while nonetheless agreeing in certain conclusions regarding the nature of international relations.

Morality, Democracy, and the International System

A nation, particularly a democratic nation and more particularly the United States, tends to view its actions as taking place within a moral framework. On one hand, it sees itself as subject to certain moral limitations and judgments; on the other, it looks to national goals and historic traditions as the explanation and moral justification for its course of action. Seldom, if ever, is foreign policy defended by an argument solely for the maintenance or increase of national power or of national survival. The interpreters and defenders of a foreign policy speak rather of standing for moral purposes beyond the state: democracy or communism, freedom or equality, order or justice, and historical inevitability. Whatever cynics may say, foreign policy tends to be articulated in moral terms, even in most authoritarian regimes, whether those terms be social justice, economic equality, the overthrow of colonialism, national liberation, or putting an end to an unjust status quo.

To know that men and nations espouse goals and ends that transcend national defense or survival is a first step or approach but not a solution to the moral problem. In fact, it is more a claim than an approach; it may bespeak what George Kennan and Hans Morgenthau have called "moralism" as distinguished from "morality." Moralism is the tendency to make one moral

4. Sir Harold Nicolson, *Diplomacy* (London, 1939), 50, 45–46.

value supreme and to apply it indiscriminately, without regard to time and place; morality by comparison is the endless quest for what is right amid the complexity of competing and sometimes conflicting, sometimes compatible moral ends. Professor Paul Freund of the Harvard Law School based his 1976 Thomas Jefferson Memorial Lecture of the National Endowment for the Humanities on an aphorism of John Dalberg, Lord Acton: "When you perceive a truth, look for a balancing truth." According to Freund, we suffer in Western civilization from the decline of the ancient art of moral reasoning, the essence of which is weighing and balancing not only good and evil but competing goods.

Freedom and order, liberty and justice, economic growth and social equality, national interest and the well-being of mankind are each in themselves worthy moral ends. How much simpler moral choice would be if the leader could select one value as his guiding principle and look on the rest as secondary or instrumental. In every human community, however, the choice between right and wrong is endlessly complex and grounded in deep moral pathos. There is an inescapably tragic character to moral choice. Within the family, men all too often must choose between family interests and professional responsibilities. Loyalty to spouse and children may also conflict with caring for the needs of aging parents. Within the nation, freedoms of speech and assembly may clash with the requirements of security and order. As we have observed, the Supreme Court has declared that freedom of speech does not involve the right to cry "fire!" in a crowded theater. The right to a fair trial may collide with the right to know and the freedom of the press. Freedom of scientific inquiry apparently does not justify the secret production of a lethal weapon that might destroy the world. Even within the most developed democracy, every political and constitutional principle coexists and is related to every other principle, and each is at most a partial expression of morality; for as Niebuhr wrote, "Democracy cannot exist if there is no recognition of the fragmentary character of all systems of values which are allowed to exist within its frame."

Within the family and the democratic nation, however, forces are at work to protect fragmentary values and interests, to hold moral absolutism in check, and to prevent men from erecting a single principle into an all-controlling moral dogma. The rights of individuals are weighed against the rights of the group. Society has long-established procedures and institutions through which claims and counterclaims are weighed and adjudicated. A vast panoply of political and constitutional rights and instruments of social legislation are invoked to prevent abuses that threaten the weakest elements of society, including minorities and the powerless, little children, the infirm and the aged. Perhaps the most popular legislation in the Bush administration has been laws for assistance to the disabled. The law of love, which lies beyond the reach of large collectivities (neither political parties nor corporations nor organized churches love one another), is at least theoretically a practical possibility within the family. Even for the family, however, some form of distributive justice may prove to be man's highest moral attainment, as a loving husband and wife or devoted parents and children can attest. Justice within the family involves giving each member its due and often this process is as much a matter of calculating needs and interests as of unselfish love.

Within the nation, the Bill of Rights and the American constitutional system provide a means of mediating justice for individuals and groups, minorities and majorities, the weak and the strong. As love is mediated through justice in the family, the "higher law" principles on which the Constitution is based support the unending quest for rights within American society. The health of democracy rests finally on the possibility of minorities becoming majorities, on some approximation of justice, and on a common-sensical recognition that no single value or principle is a final guide to moral rectitude. Niebuhr explains the value of common sense: "The triumph of common sense is . . . primarily the wisdom of democracy itself which prevents [anyone's strategy] from being carried through to its logical conclusion. There is an element of truth in each position which becomes falsehood precisely when it is carried through too consistently."

The moral problem is more readily comprehended and understood as it is exemplified within the family and within democratic nations than in the fragile and embryonic community of nations. More than 160 nations make up international society, each with its own political and economic system, institutions and practices, needs and traditions. Each has its own requirements of governance, its necessities of state, its cultural and historical setting, and its rights and constraints inherent in its political and social order. For manifold reasons, the moral problem for politics among nations is even more complex than for families and democracies. By oath of office, the statesman's foremost official duty is preservation of the union, a requirement that both limits some actions and channels others along lines that may be offensive to ideas of personal morality. President Lincoln pointed out in his letter to Horace Greeley that his "primary purpose [was] to save the Union." If this goal meant freeing all the slaves, he would do so; if it meant freeing none of the slaves, he would do that; if it meant freeing some but not others, he would do that, too. His choice from the standpoint of official morality was not necessarily the choice he would have made from the standpoint of personal morality. Nor could he assure national unity without paying homage to domestic political realities.

Louis Halle in a paper delivered at a University of Virginia conference in June of 1977 on morality and foreign policy defended Lincoln's action: "Lincoln, in his Emancipation Proclamation, excluded the slaves in certain states because he needed the support of the congressmen from those states. This exclusion, although morally reprehensible in itself, made possible the eventual emancipation of all the slaves. I hold that the moralists who denounced him for this immoral act of expediency were wrong." The demands of statecraft may be even more severe than those that required Lincoln's choice, prompting the already quoted words of the Italian nationalist Cavour: "If we had done for ourselves what we did for the state, what scoundrels we would have been." Thus, in democracies no less than in aristocratic regimes, we return to the debate over official and personal moralities.

Practical Morality and Diplomacy

The prevailing approach to the ethical dimension of diplomacy, especially in liberal America, places emphasis on morality pure and simple. Oftentimes, defenders of this approach have been driven to take positions their critics call moralism and legalism. Those who question whether pure morality exists in diplomacy offer as alternatives the more proximate moral positions that are grouped under the heading of practical morality.

One such practical approach is workability, as opposed to the proclamation of abstract moral principles. Diplomatists, in contrast with international lawyers, put stress on workability: the objective of foreign policy should be as closely related to the reduction of human suffering and the promotion of as much human welfare as possible and not the unqualified triumph of abstract principle. Moral appeals to the generality of mankind or the mass of the people too often constitute not morality but Pharisaism or Manichaeism.

Whatever the short-run advantages of Pharisaism, it has foundered in the long run because an individual or a nation who claims an achieved morality that others have a duty to follow does so on the assumption of his or its having attained moral perfection. Manichaeism is a false religion that sees the world as divided between good guys and bad guys, and this disease has periodically infected American perspectives on foreign policy. Since World War I, we have divided the world into peace-loving and aggressor nations, freedom-loving and communist states, or developed and underdeveloped nations and then based foreign policy on such distinctions. The road to Vietnam lay not in the nefarious acts of the "best and the brightest," as historian David Halberstam named them, but in indiscriminate anticommunist thinking, which has often ignored the test of workability. The almost inevitable result of Manichaeism is a moral crusade, war or the threat of war, and genocide. (It is worth remembering that certain allied leaders fighting the war against Hitler, who was exterminating millions of Jews, saw the "solution" to the German problem in the extermination, in turn, of thousands of Germans.) The shortcomings of Pharisaism and Manichaeism invite the search for other standards of morality, such as workability or practical morality.

Three Traditions and the Meeting of Ethics and Diplomacy

Each of the great political traditions has its own conception of human values and the good life. In Christianity, belief in God and serving one's fellow man are uppermost in the Christian hierarchy of values. For the disciple of classical political thought, the quest for virtue in individuals and society is the highest calling. For modern political thinkers, the establishment of the best social and constitutional arrangements *within* existing societies is the foremost objective. The Christian and the classical traditions depend on certain objective values and standards outside society and the political process. The values of the two older traditions are ultimately transcendent, whereas the values of modern political thought tend to be immanent. Noteworthy exceptions are the political philosophies of the founding fathers of the American constitutional and political system.

The prospects of all three political traditions have been diminished, however, by forces at work within the present-day nation-state. Christian thought from its beginnings assumed that man necessarily and inevitably lived in two worlds, the City of Man and the City of God. The former was a transient realm of contingencies, imperfection, and sin; the latter was a timeless realm of certainty, perfection, and the good. The one was realizable here and now, the other, in eternity. The social and political order was structured to reflect, to some degree at least, the reality of the two worlds. The Christian vision provided for both a horizontal and a vertical dimension in human life, with men reaching out to one another in the social order while seeking to know God in the spiritual order. Government was the custodian of the social and political order, and citizens were enjoined to give to Caesar what was Caesar's. The church was the custodian of the spiritual order, and believers were required to serve God with what was God's.

The rise of the modern nation-state and the breakdown of the Corpus Christianum diminished, if they did not destroy, the vision of the two cities. The authority of the one universal church was undermined by the Reformation and the Renaissance. The religion of the prince within emerging political societies determined the religion of the people. Religion and patriotism tended to reinforce one another, whereas they had earlier constituted a system of checks and balances interacting with one another. If the universal Catholic church was in part responsible for the union of the two because of its tendency in the later Middle Ages to equate and make itself coextensive with the City of God, the embryonic nation-state was also responsible by becoming the repository of individual and group morality in order to assure political cohesion. Whereas the church had taught believers the commandment "Thou shalt not kill," princes and rulers taught their people "Thou shalt kill to preserve the nation-state."

Moreover, other forces were at work weakening the hold of the Christian tradition. That tradition in its historical formulation presupposed a rather simple world of sheep and shepherd. The modern era has witnessed the growth of ever more complex societies in which the individual to whom Christianity ministers is further and further removed from primary human relations with his fellow men. The Great Society has supplanted the Good

Samaritan. Christianity itself has become more and more fragmented. In America the Civil War found both sides praying to the same God and justifying their acts from the same Scriptures. During the conflict President Lincoln wrote of the tragic situation: "Each party claims to act in accordance with the will of God. Both *may* be, and one *must* be wrong. God can not be *for* and *against* the same thing at the same time." In recent days Martin Luther King, Jr., and Jerry Falwell have invoked the Scriptures to defend actions affecting millions of people in diametrically opposite ways. Maintaining a universal Christian tradition is complicated by the rise of sovereign nation-states and competing political ideologies and political religions. The nation fills the minds and hearts of men everywhere with particular experiences, particular concepts of political philosophy, particular standards of political morality, and particular goals of political action.

If the Christian tradition has been challenged by the circumstances surrounding the modern nation-state, the classical tradition is also threatened. Modernity has brought about a shift from discussions of the good man and the good state to discourse on political power and political tactics. Classical political philosophy was not unaware of the realities for good and evil in human nature. The Platonic dialogues are filled with examples of cynical and selfish men overriding reason and virtue in their political attitudes and conduct. Yet for the philosopher contemplating the human drama as a whole, reason was superior to the irrational, and virtue was the standard by which cynicism and selfishness were judged. Man could approximate his best nature by participating in the social and political order. He realized himself as a social animal.

Classicists have maintained, however, that man's fulfillment was most nearly attainable within the polity, a small-sized political community in which face-to-face political discourse occurred. By contrast, the citizen in the larger nation-state has little, if any, contact with his rulers. He is remote from the scene of urgent problems and unable to comprehend the complex issues on which he must decide. Jack Valenti, President Lyndon Johnson's closest aide, once observed that most of the nuances of nuclear questions escaped him no matter how faithfully he studied them. In the end, he was forced to search for a scientist he could trust. His comprehension required scientific and technical knowledge that only the scientific specialist could provide.

The history of modern times also throws a cloud over the argument that classicists had demonstrated the validity of reason and virtue. Wise students of political history such as Niebuhr, Butterfield, and Morgenthau have traced the influence of the irrational in politics. The German people, whose culture matched any in Europe, followed a fanatical leader, Hitler, who stirred popular emotions with slogans depicting the Germans as racially superior. Legislative assemblies, intended for prudent deliberation, became the scene of chauvinist and bellicose debate. National self-determination, which had promised satisfaction and peace to the world's people, was successfully invoked by Hitler for the annexation of the Sudetenland. Reason proved defective in anticipating the consequences of thousands of apparently rational acts. Unintended and unforeseen consequences followed seemingly rational historical acts and confounded the expected or intended results. Thus, the Protestant Reformation rested on the proposition that individuals should be free to read and interpret the Bible but caused a weakening of individualism by strengthening nationalism. The French Revolution, which promised liberty, equality, and fraternity, led to the submergence of liberty and equality in the expansion of the Napoleonic Empire.

To recite a litany of individual virtues when individuals are being swallowed up in big government, big labor, or big management seems a questionable exercise in the modern world. More germane are discussions of the problems of hard-pressed individuals seeking to reconcile competing virtues. The busy executive, for whom long hours and neglect of family are sometimes required to assure essential income and family livelihood, struggles to be a good father or mother. For the devoted parent, caring for children may necessitate overlooking his or her own parents. Being someone of virtue and principle may not be enough under these circumstances. The truly virtuous person has to "find his way through a maze of conflicting principles."

If Christian and classical thought are criticized for too much opposition to modernity and too great a faith in traditional values, modern political thought links modernity with progress. Whereas the older traditions stand in opposition to present trends, modern political theory tends to glorify and sanctify them. It glorifies the state and, more particularly, certain branches of government that it favors one after the other as the cycle turns. Transposed to the international scene, modern thought manifests an exaggerated confidence in novel institutions as instruments for transforming international politics. The rise and fall of popular enthusiasm for each successively favored institution throws into question the political judgment of modern man. It has also led some contemporary thinkers to reopen the question of the relevance of Christian and classical thought to present-day problems.

Not only has the rise of the nation-state profoundly affected the relation of the great political traditions to politics but so have the changing patterns of international politics and diplomacy. Historically, the Christian and classical political traditions assumed a consensus on values within the Christian and classical worlds. Four developments have altered the political world within which any of the historic traditions must operate. First, a worldwide system of nationalist ideologies and conflicting religious faiths has replaced the Christian Europe of which historians like Christopher Dawson wrote in tracing the formation of Western Christendom. Universal Christendom lost out to a pluralistic international system of competing nation-states and cultures. Second, the political faiths that inspire men have taken on the characteristics of the terrestrial world rather than the adornments of the heavenly city. To the extent the latter survived at all, it was as a this-world utopia. Carl Becker described the heavenly city of the eighteenth-century philosophers; Marx and Lenin elaborated a creed that identified the end of history with the Marxist classless society. Salvation was achievable here and now, and its standards were within and not outside history. The direct application of the Christian tradition to international problems was undermined by the breakdown of any consensus on values and by the disappearance of faith expressed in objective moral principles outside history.

Two other developments coincided with and reinforced these changes. They profoundly affected the relevance of the classical tradition. One of these was a consequence of the vast increase in the size of viable political units. The movement from city-states to nation-states culminated in the postwar emergence of two superpowers. That good men would create good regimes became a more difficult proposition to sustain. Good and bad men alike seized power in large collective states, claiming that only they were capable of solving the momentous social problems of great masses of people. Events that good men had prophesied were rationally impossible—events such as global depressions, world wars, and totalitarianism—followed one another in rapid succession. Large populations responded to programs whose spokesmen promised that they served all the people. If Americans had any doubt concerning the far-reaching effects of this third development, they had only to compare the deliberative processes of leaders addressing the New England town meeting with Mussolini or Hitler haranguing the Italian or German people with the claim that forty million Italians or seventy million Germans couldn't be wrong. In other words, popular sovereignty had replaced personal virtue.

A fourth development was the radical transformation of political communication. Classical political thought had maintained that personal and collective morality were indivisible. In the modern era, however, not only totalitarian rulers but democratic leaders judged what was moral and right by the interests of states. Although certain moral principles applicable to individuals survived in the eighteenth-century idea of raison d'etat, much as Machiavelli had clung to the concept of virtù, contemporary rulers maintained that whatever their personal moral standards on war or slavery, national unity and preserving the state took precedence and were controlling factors. Thus, both Christian and classical thought lost a large measure of their force in the face of far-reaching historical changes.

Modern political thought appeared to offer an alternative to the decline of the ancient traditions. Especially liberalism held out to the great mass of the people the promise of human improvement through universal public education. Today's pressing problems would yield to the workings of free society. Individuals, ever more enlightened by science and reason, would throw off human frailties and archaic political ideas and institutions that had led throughout history to conflict and war. Individual man pursuing his selfish interests would be guided nationally and internationally as if by a hidden hand to act for the common good. Nationally, the process would operate in free-market economies guaranteed to serve the general welfare. ("What is good for General Motors is good for America," a cabinet member in the Eisenhower administration declared.) Internationally, Wilson proclaimed that national self-determination would lead to a peaceful world, not dreaming that Hitler would invoke a Wilsonian principle to justify his expansionist policies. Moreover, national and international economic stagnation in the 1930s led millions of people to turn to new and more dynamic collectivist solutions.

Not only had the death knell for the effectiveness and coherence of the three great political traditions been sounded by the four developments, but the disintegration of the traditional international political order was being sped by another factor. The values that had introduced a limited degree of stability within single political communities proved ineffective on the international stage. The standards that had assured relative peace within nations proved ineffectual or largely irrelevant in international affairs. What was disallowed or dealt with as an exception to the normal processes of national societies was accepted as inevitable in international society. Whereas civil war represented the breakdown of the political order within nations, war was accepted as the continuation of diplomacy by other means in relations among nation-states.

The problem, as Niebuhr discussed it in a succession of books and articles on foreign policy, was that in international politics no single moral principle existed for the ordering of all other separate moral principles. In international politics, rough-and-ready norms such as workability and damage limitation, rather than such benign standards as the quest for the good society or for communities that made possible the individual's self-fulfillment, became the overarching principles. In the end, modern political thought, which had promised a new and better world, became an even more tragic victim to history than Christian or classical thought.

For all these reasons, the culmination of history on the international stage proved to be not the heavenly city but the nuclear age. The end of warfare that liberal political thinkers had predicted yielded to the specter of warfare as universal human destruction. Ironically, human advancement and progress have led not to the refutation of ancient political truths but to their rediscovery. Prudence has once more become the master virtue in international politics at a moment in time when anything less is a threat to human existence. But political prudence was an idea that Aristotle set forth as a guide for political practice as distinct from political contemplation. From Aristotle and Augustine through Burke to Niebuhr, Butterfield, and John Courtney Murray, prudence as an operative political principle has been kept alive not as any rigid formulation or precise definition of what was right or wrong but as a concept of practical reason. Practical morality involves the reconciliation of what is morally desirable with what is politically possible. It offers only a few absolutes but many practical possibilities. Prudence is the central precept in the ancient tradition of moral and political reasoning. It recognizes the need for moral man in an immoral world to find his way through "a maze of conflicting moral principles," no one of which reigns supreme.

National interest as a guide to diplomacy may at first glance seem remote from the ancient ideas of prudence as expressed by Christian and classical writers. Yet what political realism and practical morality have in common is the acceptance of the best solution appropriate to particular circumstances. Philosophers and reformers may offer more glittering answers to the world's problems, but it is unlikely that any other approach can come closer to a workable way of thinking. Every foreign policy decision presently has its military, political, regional, and Soviet-American or European-American or Japanese-American dimensions. Too often policy makers choose policies that apply exclusively to one or the other dimension. Prudence requires attention to multiple dimensions and an attempt to find the best possible solutions after weighing all the different factors. Tragically, the political process that brings men and women to office in the United States may not assure the capacity to think clearly in all dimensions at once. Anything less, however, could lead to disaster in American diplomacy.

Some Modest Conclusions About Morality and Diplomacy

If we assume morality makes possible the early attainment of a set of towering and novel moral principles that will transform the world, then the cynics are right that there is no ethical dimension to diplomacy. However, if such goals as workability, damage limitation, and practical morality are accepted as worthy of the name *morality,* the opposite conclusion is possible. The moral content of diplomacy is both more modest and more important than critics would suggest. The harmonizing of sometimes conflicting but potentially convergent national interests is both a moral and a political act. Drawing the poison out of a conflict as if by a poultice is an important moral aim. Framing an agreement through long and arduous diplomatic negotiations is a pursuit with enduring value, whether the end product is a formal legal treaty or a mere tacit understanding. Discovering an exit from war and an end to military conflict through truce negotiations is an essentially moral process. Settling a boundary dispute, limiting an arms race, bringing about the relaxation of tensions, and arranging cultural exchanges or trade relations are all themselves worthy purposes.

If anyone asks what is common to the quest for each of the moral purposes enumerated above, we can answer that they all can be pursued only through some form or another of diplomacy or of diplomatic and political process. Sometimes hard bargaining with a deadline may be required; other times long and protracted negotiations are needed. Whatever the form of the search for these moral ends, diplomacy and politics are vital to their attainment. For example, avoidance of Soviet occupation of Poland was such a pre-eminent value in the 1980s that Pope John Paul II and the communist military ruler of Poland made a deal that moral and political crusaders opposed instinctively. Yet an independent Poland survived and is free and democratic today. The diplomatic process may serve higher ends even when the means appear morally ambiguous. In recognizing this fact, we have moved a little closer to a more complete understanding of the ethical dimension of diplomacy.

Part IV

Persistent Problems

14

Human Rights:
Rationalism, Irrationalism, and the Contingent

In the 1960s and 1970s, the United States witnessed a renewal of interest in human rights. The beginnings of that interest go back to the 1940s and 1950s and are associated with Eleanor Roosevelt more than with any other American. In roughly comparable terms, but without the same popular commitment and respect, the mid- to late 1970s must be associated with President Jimmy Carter. The distance that separates the two symbolic figures tells a good deal about the differences in the times.

If Mrs. Roosevelt and President Carter have characteristics in common, one quality is surely a burning idealism. However different Ernest Bevin in his hardheaded realism about labor-management relations and politics may have been from the two Americans, Winston Churchill's description of Bevin nonetheless comes to mind. In the midst of a wartime debate in the House of Commons, Churchill stopped, pointed with only half-disguised admiration to the doughty Labour party leader, and declared: Look at him standing there "blinking and blazing in all his idealism." Even Mrs. Roosevelt's most outspoken foes in early postwar debates, such as John Foster Dulles, were awed by the power of her overwhelmingly inspiring idealism. Because of that quality, Dulles feared her influence on foreign policy. In her quest for a universal declaration of human rights, the luminosity of her idealism lit up the darkness of international politics. What historians and commentators remember is her sheer determination in the struggle over the declaration—a determination that in the end brought her victory. Her resoluteness was deeply rooted in an abiding faith in the people, whose fate was for her more important than the interests of states. Writers and film makers have chronicled the story of her struggle with Dulles. Millions have viewed the film's depiction of confrontations between the uncompromising idealist and the realpolitik strategist. Even that depiction, however, does scant justice to the full sweep of her vaulting idealism.

Like other Americans, I have memories of Mrs. Roosevelt, particularly of calling on her to discuss institutional needs and problems that required her sympathetic attention. In my case, the problem, which arose in the 1950s, concerned an internecine conflict within the United Nations Association (UNA) of the United States, of which she was founding chair. Professors Quincy Wright, Richard McKeon, and I were among the leaders of the Chicago branch of the UNA. We grew increasingly concerned about the seeming neglect of the Chicago program by national director Clark Eichelberger and his staff. That neglect was the more distressing because the Chicago branch contributed from a substantial fund-raising surplus to the costs of the New York office. The record of official exchanges between the two groups showed promises that were never kept, credit that was not given, and even possible irregularities in the recording of budgets.

When I appeared to discuss these issues, Mrs. Roosevelt graciously heard me out, asking a few questions, expressing some surprise, and smiling in her benign and forgiving manner until I felt embarrassed that I had presumed to trouble her. She offered to look into the problem and gave assurances that the circumstances and events I reported must have resulted from misunderstandings. I left inspired, if not reassured or reeducated. To this day, I cannot forget her warm and sympathetic reception. I also felt then and know now that the problems between the New York and Chicago offices were destined to continue, showing little evidence that anyone was undertaking to solve them.

Mrs. Roosevelt believed that the vast majority of people were good and rational. She had faith in the essential virtue and decency of mankind and thought that only various tyrannical forces within and between societies prevented that quality from emerging. Above all, she was persuaded that a good world could not remain half-free and half-slave, half-educated and half-deprived, half with medical care and half without, half-employed and half-unemployed. Rationally and from a human standpoint, it was inconceivable that societies would long deny political rights or other social and economic rights to all people. That is why she saw the American emphasis on political and civil rights and the Soviet stress on social and economic rights as essentially compatible and parts of a larger whole. In that sense she was both an idealist and a rationalist.

By the mid-1970s, the historical position of the United States had changed. With Vietnam, Americans had experienced the trauma of losing a war. History had proved we were not omnipotent. Watergate also left its mark on a people who earlier had tended to see American political virtue as untarnished by comparison with European realpolitik. The Nixon Doctrine recognized that the United States might help "lesser nations" to defend their freedom, but American boys would no longer fight other people's wars. Americans were learning within and outside the United Nations that good and rational people with differing national interests reached conclusions that were often at odds with American principles. Having commanded the support of a majority of United Nations members in the 1950s, the United States became in effect the leader of a permanent minority there. Although national power had allowed the United States to conduct policies requiring both guns and butter, Americans were coming to recognize that they no less than others lived in an economy of scarce resources. By the 1970s, informed leaders were openly discussing the *limits* of American power in the political arena.

It was such a world and this changing way of thinking that greeted the Carter presidency. As president, Jimmy Carter was described as a political liberal and an economic conservative, and if such a description fit, it rested as much on circumstances as on philosophy. Carter came to office heralded as the exemplar of a new kind of president. He had run against official Washington, as would his successor. He seemed indifferent to the need for building political coalitions. His program consisted of a checklist of promises that his colleague Stuart Eizenstat cataloged in a large book and, at the president's request, checked off as promises were kept. His own staff, and especially James Fallows, was critical that in proceeding from such a list he undertook too much too soon and failed to establish priorities. The approach was based on what was good for the country, not on what was politically possible. What was good was rational and what was rational was necessary, and thus Carter in his thinking can be identified with Eleanor Roosevelt.

In foreign policy, Carter, like Mrs. Roosevelt, was a Wilsonian, placing emphasis on declarations and the word. Following a more cynical Nixon, he and his colleagues announced that the time had come for the United States once again to *stand* for something in the world. History had placed demands on the republic. Its responsibility was to pull itself out of the mire of Watergate. Some of Carter's harshest critics asserted, however, that he believed that making a declaration was in itself the equivalent of forging and pursuing a policy.

Nowhere was this more apparent than in Carter's approach to human rights. He discovered human rights as an issue fairly late in the 1976 presidential campaign. In the early months of the Carter administration, it remained, as it had been in the campaign, more a proclamation than a carefully worked out program or policy. Because it had the characteristics of a declaration rather than a policy, the president believed he could communicate with a leading Soviet dissident without violating the main tenets of foreign policy. Nor did he see pursuit of human rights as likely to conflict with such other goals and policies as the quest for a Soviet-American arms agreement. The championing of human rights was the hallmark of a good and rational international society and thus would not clash in a rational world with the pursuit of the negotiations for SALT II. Rationally, Carter saw no incompatibility between competing policy objectives.

The problem with President Carter's approach was that the good and rational international society he envisaged had never existed. Instead, international society at best was what Hedley Bull called half-anarchic and at worst involved "the struggle of each against all." It was a society in which the parts saw themselves as more important than the whole. It was what my colleague Inis Claude has called a "topless society." Sovereignty resided with diverse and unequal nation-states. The supreme law-making and law-enforcing powers were lodged in some 160 sovereignties, not in one universal sovereign. That such a system was irrational was beside the point. If rationality means the capacity to define and achieve fundamental purposes, it was clear that sovereign states in the international system lacked such ability, either for defense or for social and economic welfare. In the first half-century of the nuclear age, the only powers that mattered in terms of the ultimate conflict were the superpowers, not the more than 100 smaller states whose survival depended on the actions of the superpowers. If sovereignty means the ability to preserve a given nation-state, that ability was equatable not with contemporary statehood but with superpower hegemony or some form of universal authority or world government.

Yet opposed both to superpower hegemony and to the creation of a universal authority were the same groupings of people who stood in the pathway of universal human rights, namely, national publics and independent nation-states. Judged by an objective and rational standard, such an organization of international society appears irrational. It is irrational if global security is the first and primary goal and irrational, as the main body of economists have argued since the days of Adam Smith, if international welfare is the goal. Whether rational or irrational, however, the international system has not changed in any fundamental or revolutionary way from the Treaty of Westphalia in 1648 to the present. It continues to provide the overall framework within which foreign policy decisions and actions are carried out. Those who exercise sovereignty may change, but the fact of sovereignty persists.

One of the tests of the durability of the international system is the paradoxical position of the newly independent nations. Leaders of Third World countries argue repeatedly that Africans and Asians had no role in the creation of the Westphalian system, which is wholly a Europe-centered system. Their cultures are not Westphalian culture. To the extent that Third World peoples participated historically in the European state system, they did so as objects, not subjects, of international law. Such a system, therefore, cannot be seen as relevant to the goals and actions of the new nations. Yet in almost every instance the first foreign policy act of new nations following independence has been to seek membership in the United Nations. While denouncing the existing international system, the new nations recognize that it alone has the means of bestowing legitimacy on them within the international community. In becoming members of the United Nations, the countries of Africa and Asia tacitly acknowledge the system's legitimacy, limited only by their ability to bring about change.

Human rights are pursued within an irrational framework in yet another respect. Although the subject of human rights clearly has a strong rhetorical content, it is also true that an effective human rights policy depends on contingencies and circumstances no one can identify before the fact. The history of civil rights in the United States demonstrates how important social and economic forces can be. Government acts "when the shoe pinches." For business and commercial interests in cities like Atlanta, "the shoe pinched" as prolonged civil rights strife continued. It was no accident that some of the most effective civil rights leadership, especially in urban centers, came from the business community. The establishment, which had long been silent, spearheaded the drive for equal opportunity. Examined solely from the standpoint of public statements, the business community initially was overlooked as an agent of social change, yet the contributions of business leaders to equal opportunity proved decisive in the end.

In part, then, Eleanor Roosevelt was right. Not only she but some rather hard-bitten realists such as Secretary Henry Stimson proceeded from the assumption, as Stimson put it, "that the way to have a friend is to be one." One can go back to Aristotle to support the proposition that persons become to some extent the image of themselves that they see in the reactions of others. In the language of classical political philosophy, man is a social animal. To assume that persons are good and rational is, within limits, to make them good and rational. Most of us have the chance over a lifetime to live in overlapping worlds and to get other perspectives. From my experience in the foundation world, I can testify that being viewed as having a responsibility and the means to be philanthropic makes one become more philanthropic and compassionate. To be seen by oneself and others as a defender of the freedom of one's country strengthens the will and resolve to sacrifice for the nation. We become what our circumstances and responsibilities require us to be.

Yet there is also something misleading about the "mirror image" view of human nature. It runs the risk of supposing there is nothing fixed and changeless about human nature. More serious still, it ignores the essential duality of man's nature, the blending of good and evil, rationality and irrationality, compassion and selfishness, vision and narrowness, good will and hostility, and sympathy and jealousy. The pairing of seemingly incompatible traits in man makes human nature a patchwork of qualities that often are at war with one another. In the end, the ambiguity of man's nature, the intertwining of goodness and self-centeredness and rationality and irrationality, constitutes the sum total of the human condition. That ambiguity manifests itself even in apparently cooperative ventures such as the common enterprise of the New York and Chicago branches of the UNA. Sometimes those who would bring such groups into harmony can depend on people's capacity for goodness and rationality but at other times whoever would lead must persuade, cajole, threaten, offer incentives, or make promises.

What is true of actions within a common framework is true a fortiori within a severely divided and fragmented world. For a newly independent state seeking to lead in the international community, past pronouncements on the obsolescence of the existing international system need not prevent that state from becoming a spokesman for human rights within the United Nations. Circumstances may inhibit leadership by other states. In the 1960s, leading Third World states such as Kenya faced troublesome dilemmas for they were dependent on the South African airlines for trade and commerce but knew that cooperation with South Africa condemned them in the eyes of other African states on grounds of ignoring human rights. Similarly, Arab states found their adherence to human rights frustrated by ancient cultural practices like the punishing of thieves by cutting off their hands. Moreover, the argument of early independence leaders such as Julius Nyerere was that however much they might defend universal political and economic freedom, Third World countries were too poor to enjoy economic systems other than planned socialist economies. Soviet leaders in superpower negotiations justified harsh actions in Afghanistan and against dissidents such as the Jews within the USSR by maintaining that the Soviet empire would unravel unless ethnic minorities were held in check.

To deny that irrationalism and contingent factors are present in the history of human rights, then, is to deny the irrationality and ambiguity of human nature and the ultimate irrationality of the international system. Yet it is within a system of nation-states, interacting with one another in accordance with certain rules and customs but with no strong system of universal central government, that the quest for human rights goes on. Because the principal units within that system are no longer able to assure the achievement of their central purposes, the system itself is becoming obsolete. However, no other system exists to take its place. In a world government, human rights could be legislated by some central body but at present, even in the developed world of Europe, there are only human rights courts and commissions, which are dependent on nation-states. Thus, political authority and international consensus are lacking for the establishment of a fully effective body of human rights law and practice. Within the present decentralized state system, it is the state, with ultimate law-giving authority, that is the source of most human rights.

The improvement of the human rights situation and the broadening of its scope within a sovereign state is in certain respects a subversive act. States and their leaders must be persuaded to overturn or change the laws they themselves have enacted. Means must be found by the international community, using methods such as threats and sanctions or the expectation of benefits, to nudge a laggard society in the direction of greater human rights. Normally, the impetus must come not from the world society itself, some of whose members fall short of human rights standards even more than those being urged to reform, but from a few leading developed countries. In the case of the Carter administration, the impetus came primarily, but not exclusively, from his administration, which tended to act independently when the United Nations was deadlocked. Thus, a single sovereign state is cast in the role of reformer of other sovereign states, which inescapably leads to its indictment as interventionist and moralistic.

To call attention to the irrationalism of the pursuit of human rights is not to question that human rights can also be grounded in rationality. Whatever the political theory on which rights are based, their foundations in reason are discoverable. Some political theorists discover the grounds for human rights in man's essential and primordial nature: "Man is born free and is everywhere in chains." Others point to the status of the individual as the source of all human rights. Others see rights assigned to the state as a means of self-preservation.

In the same way political theorists in the eighteenth and nineteenth centuries helped us understand the rational dimensions of human nature and politics, a more recent group of theorists have helped with our comprehension of the irrationality of politics and especially of international politics. They include Niebuhr, Butterfield, Carr, and Morgenthau. Their philosophies are reflected in much of contemporary dialogue. They place the emphasis on accidents and contingencies without excluding rationality. The point is that such patterns of thought are needed in any discussion of human rights. The rationalists and the idealists, however much they have contributed, tend to overlook this aspect of human rights.

15

Why Disarmament and Arms Control?

Public discourse on arms control tends to focus on technicalities and complexities. Whenever he speaks on the subject, Senator Sam Nunn warns his listeners to prepare for a rather arid and arcane discussion. Silos and throw weights, windows of vulnerability, and arguments for and against first strikes are an expanding segment of the international relations vocabulary. Not only an esoteric vocabulary but a wholly new profession has emerged to guide and shape thinking on disarmament and arms control. Those who lack the technical vocabulary and recognizable credentials are excluded from the inner circle of leaders qualified to offer judgments on arms control.

Winston Churchill was an exception to the prevailing pattern of specialization on arms control as he was an exception in other spheres of human understanding. It was not that he lacked technical knowledge. As anyone who has read his history of the war knows, Churchill in World War I and II, like Abraham Lincoln seeking to preserve the Union in the Civil War, mastered the details of weaponry and military strategy. For Churchill, as for Lincoln, weaponry was a means to an end and not necessarily the fundamental requirement for success in national defense and arms control. Nor was it the case that Churchill ignored the broader issues that were being debated on both sides of the Atlantic.

In Churchill's time, a proposal that was beginning to gain some credence and has since gained even wider support was that failing an arms agreement, leaders on both sides of the Iron Curtain should pledge never to use what Bernard Brodie called "the absolute weapon." In his era, Churchill made known his opposition to this view and sought to place it within a broad historical context. It was an argument, he said, that assumed no civilized people should use the bomb unless it was first used against them. That would amount in practice to one group of nations agreeing never to fire until they had first been shot dead. His conclusion was firm: "That seems to me undoubtedly a silly thing to say and a still more imprudent position to adopt. Moreover, such a resolve would certainly bring war nearer. The deterrent effect of the atomic bomb is at the present time almost our sole defence." [1]

By the 1980s, respected Americans such as Robert McNamara, George Kennan, McGeorge Bundy, and Gerard Smith in public statements were espousing a point of view unmistakably opposed to Churchill's credo. The popular mind, preoccupied with the mounting danger and immediacy of the nuclear threat, turned to "no first use" as an avenue for the avoidance of mutual annihilation. Although it is highly speculative and risky to indulge in the favorite indoor pastime of pundits and students of leading statesmen and thinkers, in which they ask what would "Mr. Y" have said about "issue z" if he were alive today, speculation about Churchill's view may be less hazardous. For if Churchill was persuaded of the salience of one truth concerning the Cold War, it was that peace had been preserved by the maintenance of a balance of terror.

His statements on deterrence and its relationship to the willingness to use force are too numerous to overlook. He recognized that the practical, if negative, foundations of peace he championed were anathema to those who stressed the abstract moral requirements of policy. However, he never shied away from addressing these concerns, as in his explanation of his position: "Moralists may find it a melancholy thought that peace can find no nobler foundation than mutual terror. But for my part, I shall be content if these foundations are solid, because they will give us the extra time and the new breathing space for the supreme effort which has to be made for a world settlement." [2]

It is clear then that Churchill's discourse on the prospects for a third worldwide conflict were offered before the views of historians on the last war had fully crystallized. Current history is unfolding with such breathtaking speed that comparisons with the interwar period may appear irrelevant. Churchill's comments on the risks of a third world war were offered not as reflections on some remote possibility but as though he were dealing with an impending conflict that was already upon mankind. In considering the post-

1. *Parliamentary Debates* (Hansard), House of Commons, 5th Ser., Vol. 482, December 14, 1950, p. 1368, hereinafter referred to in the notes as *PD*.

2. *Ibid.*, Vol. 473, March 28, 1950, p. 198.

war conflict, he invoked the same principles for evaluating national power and interests and the same manner of reasoning he had applied earlier in the century. Thus in his Fulton, Missouri, speech, he warned that a continued disequilibrium of power would imperil the peace and make war inevitable. The shadow of war was ever present for Churchill. When a member of the Labour opposition charged Churchill was resigned to preparing for war, he answered, "I cannot pretend that it would be possible to conduct discussions with any sense of reality . . . without the occasional use of that odious and tragic word [war]." Two years later, he reminded the British people of the reality of their situation: "We must not be in any doubt as to what is preserving the peace and security of the world at the present time. It is the power and strength of the United States." [3]

The weight of Churchill's strategic thinking always came down on the side of strength and deterrence. When his government returned to power in the early 1950s, he acknowledged that "our feeling, on assuming responsibility, is that the deterrents have increased and that as the deterrents have increased, the danger has become more unlikely." What makes deterrence credible is one side's willingness to appear ready to use force if threatened by the other side. For all these reasons, it would seem likely that Churchill would have opposed the "no first use" concept, even as he searched for new routes for ameliorating the conflict. He firmly believed that as the West maintained its strength and its evident resolve to use that strength, it would be more likely to succeed in reducing the tension. At the Lord Mayor of London's banquet, he warned of the precarious nature of the conflict: "What is the world scene as presented to us today? Mighty forces, armed with fearful weapons, are baying at each other across a gulf which, I have the feeling to-night, neither wishes and both fear to cross; but into which they may tumble and drag each other to common ruin." [4] It is entirely possible that as tensions abated, Churchill might have modified some of his views on the need to maintain a credible deterrent. But in his time he held to an outlook that appears today at odds with the view of the four Americans cited earlier who spoke out for "no first use."

3. *Ibid.*, Vol. 427, October 24, 1946, p. 1686; Winston S. Churchill, "Speech to Women's Advisory Committee of the Conservative Party, Albert Hall," April 21, 1948, in *Europe Unite*, ed. Randolph S. Churchill (London, 1950), 296.

4. London *Times*, December 7, 1951, p. 4, November 10, 1951, p. 6.

Another perspective in the forefront of present-day thinking on disarmament and arms control is the philosophy that the quest for an arms agreement should come before an approach to territorial issues and regional disputes. So central is the issue of bringing the arms race under control that some of its most prominent spokesmen have argued it must take priority over every other effort to negotiate peace. Whereas conventional wisdom had called for diplomacy aimed at the reduction of tensions as the precondition of successful arms negotiations, the dominant contemporary view is that arms talks must precede political negotiations.

Through all his writings and speeches, Churchill held uncompromisingly to the contrary position. Early in his parliamentary career he defended that viewpoint: "When you have peace you will have disarmament. . . . Europe will be secure when nations no longer feel themselves in danger as many of them do now. Then the pressure and the burden of armaments will fall away automatically."[5] After World War I, popular enthusiasm for disarmament spread throughout the population. It was an outgrowth of the widespread belief that war was an atavism and that men of good will were capable of eradicating it. One school of thought maintained, rather too simply, that men fought because they had arms. Eliminate the arms and the munition makers who produce them, and wars would disappear as slavery had in the nineteenth century. Prominent business leaders and financial tycoons set out with the same energy to do for world peace what corporate energy and efficiency had accomplished in the economic world. Andrew Carnegie in founding the Carnegie Endowment for International Peace urged its trustees to work for the elimination of war and when that had been accomplished to address themselves to the next most urgent problem. It was plausible to men such as Carnegie that the transfer of business skills and influence could bring about the same transformation in war that the "economic miracle" had wrought in the industrial revolution in the late eighteenth and early nineteenth centuries.

For Churchill, the lesson of successive disarmament conferences, all of which failed in the end, was that the direct approach to arms reductions rested on fallacious thinking. Moral energy was a driving force for these

5. *PD*, Vol. 292, July 13, 1934, p. 733.

initiatives, but political imagination was lacking. Efforts at disarmament were frustrated by the persistence of unresolved issues and problems. Speaking in Parliament, Churchill explained the differences between his thinking and the ideas of others: "The differences which arise are those of method. They arise when our sentiments come into conflict with baffling and extremely obstinate concrete obstacles."[6] Sentimentalism and an uncritical commitment to the single-minded pursuit of disarmament apart from attempts to reduce political tensions were enemies of successful arms control. Success or failure to achieve arms reduction depended on the greater realism required in dealing with political problems. Good will and noble intentions were not enough.

We need to remind ourselves of the influence and power that the disarmament approach had on the minds of men in the first third of the eighteenth century. War had become the scourge of the masses, not just of a handful of mercenaries in the service of an eighteenth-century monarch or ruler. The concomitant of the brutalization of war has been the growth of practical morality and increased respect for human life harking back to the Enlightenment and to political liberalism, an attitude not present even today in some parts of the world. Spurred on by the spirit of a more liberal age, social and political reforms led to transformations in criminal law, the improved treatment of condemned men, and electoral changes. Potentially reaching further than any of these changes was the greatest humanitarian goal of all, the outlawry of war in the Pact of Paris of 1928. To rational man, the pathway to this goal lay in the simple, unambiguous international act of outlawing or reducing the means of destruction and violence. The primary assumption underlying disarmament was that men fight because they have arms. Yet the history of disarmament conferences and pacts remains a melancholy story of numerous failures and few successes. On those rare occasions when temporary agreements have been reached, an increase rather than a reduction in armaments has resulted. This scenario was true with the Washington Treaty, or Washington Naval Agreement, of 1922 by which American, British, and Japanese production of capital ships was restricted, only to free energies and resources for a new armaments race in cruisers, destroyers, and

6. *Ibid.*, Vol. 276, March 23, 1933, p. 539.

submarines. However, when underlying political problems are adjusted or resolved, then disarmament or the regulation of armaments can result in substantial pacification.

Halfway through the interwar period, Churchill acknowledged his worries about those seeking disarmament first: "I have a sympathy with, and respect for, the well-meaning, loyal-hearted people who make up the League of Nations Union in this country, but what impresses me most about them is their long suffering and inexhaustible gullibility. Any scheme of any kind for disarmament put forward by any country, so long as it is surrounded by suitable phraseology, is hailed by them, and the speeches are cheered, and those who speak gain the need of their applause. Why do they not look down beneath the surface of European affairs to the iron realities which lie beneath?" The iron reality was the balance of power in Europe; the reality was the unresolved character of major political and territorial disputes. In an important respect, the reality was also Europe's dependence for its security on the might of the French army, a condition about which Churchill and the British Left had profound differences. In 1933, Churchill responded to political critics, saying, "If Europe enjoys peace in this year it has been under the shield of France."[7] The Left, which was pressing France to disarm or reduce its military power, was, in effect, engaged in a conspiracy bound to undermine European security. Disarmament and arms control, if they were to serve viable ends, had to be linked with political realities. In making this point, Churchill's approach, if not a voice in the wilderness, was hardly representative of mainstream thinking.

Churchill's perspective on disarmament diverged from the perspectives of those, then and now, who tend to view arms reduction in isolation from the iron realities of international politics. If he would have dissented in the 1990s from the views of prominent Americans who favor the doctrine of "no first use," he was also an exception to the prevailing school of thought that placed its faith in large international conferences. Before and following World War I, the format for disarmament conferences was dictated by the two Hague conferences, the Washington Naval Conference of 1922, the London Conference of 1930, and the Geneva Conference of 1932. With all their differences,

7. *Ibid.*, Vol. 272, November 23, 1932, pp. 79–80, 87ff.

they represent a discrete approach to disarmament. They are early examples of highly publicized international conferences. When such efforts fell short of announced goals or led to consequences that were as threatening for peace as the situation that preceded them, disarmament enthusiasts explained the failings entirely in terms of procedural defects. They reasoned that the conferences had failed or the results had been counterproductive because of insufficient diplomatic preparation, inadequate personnel, or some other unfortunate combination of circumstances.

Churchill saw the problem in more fundamental terms. He insisted that spectacular multilateral conferences for the purpose of reducing armaments could not have succeeded under any circumstances. The cause of their failure was not procedural but essential, to be found in the continuation of the struggle for power that was dividing the major participants. In the face of the publicity given conferences such as London and Geneva, Churchill sought to generate interest in more realistic alternatives. He called attention to "private interchanges in secret diplomacy between the Foreign Offices of the different countries of a friendly character—'If you will not do this, we shall not have to do that,' 'If your program did not start so early, ours would begin even later,' and so on—such as have always gone on, and may perfectly legitimately go on" and believed "a greater advance and progress toward a diminution of expenditure on armaments might have been achieved by these methods than by conferences and schemes of disarmaments which have been put forward at Geneva." [8] In place of the grand spectacle of sprawling disarmament conferences, Churchill proposed opening a continuing dialogue through normal diplomatic channels. He would devalue these large-scale conferences, reducing both methods and objectives to more limited proportions.

Throughout the interwar period, leaders placed greater faith in general or worldwide rather than in regional or local arms reduction programs. Churchill, by contrast, saw the prospect of more lasting accords resulting from negotiations between two or three nations. When the rivalries and conflicts that divided a smaller number of states were reduced, conditions for viable agreements were enhanced. Such states might come to prefer a regulated instead of

8. *Ibid.*, Vol. 276, March 23, 1933, p. 541.

an unregulated competition for power. When nations, including the two superpowers who were adversaries in the Cold War, directly confronted the underlying issues that led to conflict, they would more likely move on to arms agreements, Churchill believed.

Churchill's skepticism about world disarmament conferences was also reflected in his attitude toward international organizations in general. Some observers looked upon the structure of such organizations as a substitute for rational policy or upon international organizations as an alternative to foreign policy. Churchill knew that one could not separate the policy of an international organization from the policies of its most powerful member states. As we have observed, the actions of any large organization are likely to be the product of its members' policies and especially of those whose influence and power are greatest. In the 1930s, it was as misleading to view the League of Nations apart from the policies of France and England as it was in the late 1940s or 1950s to consider the United Nations apart from the policies of the USSR or the United States. The policies of the United States Steel Corporation determine significantly those of the National Association of Manufacturers, and Macy's policies significantly shape those of the United States Chamber of Commerce. Thus, it is fallacious to speak of organizations apart from the influence of their most powerful members. Competition goes on within the framework of any organization. This is not to suggest that the most powerful are not influenced in turn by others and by the organization as such. Not only is there a negotiating process that operates, but the sharp edges of the policies of the strongest members are blunted. The aims that the rest of the members find unacceptable are adjusted or reformulated. In all his discussions of world and regional bodies, Churchill kept the focus on their members, as in his Zurich speech in 1946, when he argued that a European union was possible only through forging a partnership between France and Germany. Both in cooperation and in competition, member states play a decisive role in the success or failure of international organizations.

Churchill carried over this perspective into his thinking on disarmament. His attitude toward large international disarmament conferences reflected his conviction that what mattered most was the relationship between important members and their success or failure in reaching political settlements and territorial agreements. When such agreements were achieved, leading to the reduction of tensions, the prospects for arms reductions were favorable. The classic example in American experience is the Rush-Bagot agreement concluded in 1816 between the United States and Canada. Until its revision in World War II, that agreement provided for the right of each nation to have three naval vessels of equal tonnage and armament for use on the Great Lakes. It remains an outstanding example of the positive function that disarmament can play. Its success, however, was dependent on the sequence in which political settlement and disarmament followed one another. Political agreement constitutes the solid foundation on which lasting arms agreements are based. It follows that disarmament can be successful when nations have first taken the step of negotiating viable political understandings. So long as they hold to mutually contradictory claims in the struggle for power, their demands for national armaments remain unresolved and contradictory.

Seen in this light, disarmament or rearmament are merely symptoms of the struggle for power. When nations have arrived at tolerable understandings about the distribution of power in their relationship, an agreement on arms reductions will reflect the easing of the burden of competition and rivalry that political accommodation has brought about. At the moment an arms agreement is reached, the relaxing of the arms race can have the result of contributing still further to the lessening of political tensions and the heightening of mutual confidence among nations.

Why Disarmament and Arms Control?

If disarmament conferences have often intensified the arms race and if Churchill was skeptical about some of the more dominant approaches in his time, we must ask the question "Why disarmament and arms control?" In the past half-century, three answers tend to recur in the responses of the world's leaders to this question. They are that arms limitations can reduce the threat of universal destruction, of economic decline, and of mounting world tensions that lead to war. Each deserves attention within the scope of Winston Churchill's thought.

In the television age, the threat of universal destruction penetrates the consciousness of almost every living person. Concern about universal annihilation stems primarily from the revolution in the nature and purpose of war.

The destructiveness of contemporary warfare has increased exponentially. The kill ratio that prevailed over centuries, symbolized by the equation of one shot for one victim, has been supplanted by the ratio of one atomic bomb for many hundreds of thousands, if not millions, of victims. Therefore, the alternatives for policy makers are no longer the same. Instead of a choice between disarmament and limited war, the practical alternatives are disarmament or suicide. It has been increasingly clear that the way to work one's will with countries such as the Soviet Union is no longer military intervention. Paradoxically, the weapons of final destruction, which must not be used, are the best assurance a major power possesses that an adversary will not use its own weapons. In the long run, Churchill was hopeful that these terrible engines of destruction might be used for peace. The London *Times* reported him as expressing precisely this hope: "This revelation of the secret of nature long mercifully withheld from man, should arouse the most solemn reflections in the mind and conscience of every human being capable of comprehension. We must indeed pray that these awful agencies will be made to conduce to peace among the nations, and that instead of wreaking measureless havoc upon the entire globe they may become a perennial fountain of world prosperity." [9]

Yet those interpreters who link Churchill with the maintenance of the status quo militarily and politically are mistaken. In surveying the world scene, he repeatedly called for change, as he did on January 4, 1947, when he compared that year with the crisis in 1938: "Certainly the scene we survey . . . bears many uncomfortable resemblances to that of 1938. Indeed, in some respects, it is even darker. The peoples of Europe have fallen immeasurably deeper into the pit of misery and confusion. Many of their cities are in ruins. Millions of their homes have been destroyed." [10] These grave conditions were a product of war in the prenuclear age, and Churchill had no illusions about the greater destructiveness, leading to universal annihilation, of the nuclear age. While he held fervently to the conviction that it would be wrong to cast the fate of the West's security adrift in an agitated and disunited world,

9. London *Times,* August 7, 1945, p. 4.
10. Winston S. Churchill, "The Highroad of the Future," *Colliers,* CXIX (January 4, 1947), 11.

as with various utopian peace plans, he always kept open the possibility of some new initiative for a political settlement or an arms agreement, especially through quiet discussions of leaders at the summit.

The second argument for arms reductions is linked with the threat of economic decline. Such diverse intellectual figures as historians Arnold Toynbee and Paul Kennedy of Yale University have warned that as nations and civilizations become overcommitted militarily, they exhaust their economic resources and begin to decline. For a nation with the ever-expanding social and economic problems of an emerging underclass, homelessness, education, and the environment, military expenditures of $300 billion and a growing budget deficit take on crisis proportions. Political leaders warn of the consequences of diverting great sums of money from productive enterprises. Studies of other civilizations reinforce the prophecies of Toynbee and Kennedy.

Churchill was the child of a historical period when leaders began to express concern over the problem. In the early 1930s, the League of Nations Secretariat reported that the average military expenditure of sixty-one leading countries over a period of four years had reached the unprecedented sum of $4 billion. The league's experts forecast that expenditures of this magnitude would contribute to the gravest economic crises and even to eventual bankruptcy. In the minds of many leaders, disarmament was becoming a compelling economic necessity.

To these warnings, Churchill responded in a characteristically unconventional way. Insofar as Britain was concerned, he sought to meet the problem with economies and greater efficiency. He became ever more vigilant in his repeated attempts to achieve maximum military efficiency for a minimum of military expenditures. He sought to meet the challenge of economic collapse but not by cutting and trimming the essential objectives of his country through arms reductions. Rather, he undertook through the husbanding of natural resources to maintain essential national security objectives. He was a dissenter to the prevailing view that world disarmament conferences could save the economy, disparaging the contribution of disarmament conferences to the economy in a House of Commons speech: "If . . . [the] expense and sacrifice involved in maintaining large armies and navies could be achieved, we should not look back to the legal reasons which have brought the Conference into being. What we have to consider is whether any useful result is actually obtained or has been obtained. I confess I have always doubted the utility of these conferences . . . in the present condition . . . of the world." [11]

A third answer to the question "Why disarmament?" is that tensions among nations increase in direct proportion to increases in armaments. If the arms race could be cut back, tensions would be eased and accommodation facilitated. Periodically, national leaders have made proposals to this effect. At the Sixth General Assembly of the United Nations, Secretary of State Dean Acheson followed the logic of this approach in a proposal for arms reduction that he argued would alleviate world tensions and thus make political discussions possible. Step one would be arms limitations, step two would be the reduction of tensions, and step three, negotiations on political and territorial issues.

For Churchill, such an approach suggested the fatal flaw in Western thinking on arms control. At its core, the approach was a case of putting the cart before the horse. He agreed with the United Nations correspondent of the *Times,* who characterized the American and Soviet proposals, saying, "There is a marked suggestion of the marketplace—perhaps of an Oriental bazaar—about these rival proposals of East and West, and most observers comment on their air of unreality, seen against the present international background." Churchill went even further to suggest that such proposals and the overall process of most interwar conferences had the effect of stimulating new tensions, so that whatever harmony had been achieved began to ebb as soon as discussions were resumed. He wrote: "There has been during these recent years a steady deterioration in the relations between different countries, a steady growth of ill-will, and a steady, indeed a rapid increase in armaments that has gone on through all these years in spite of the endless flow of oratory, or perorations, of well meaning sentiments, of banquets, which have marked this epoch." [12]

Thus, of the three answers to the question of why we pursue disarmament and arms control, Churchill laid greatest emphasis on the first, universal destruction. His perspective on the way to avert such destruction can be distinguished from the majority of doomsday prophets who attracted large fol-

11. *PD,* Vol. 265, May 13, 1932, p. 2347.
12. London *Times,* November 20, 1951, p. 4; Winston S. Churchill, *The Gathering Storm* (Boston, 1948), 102, Vol. I of Churchill, *The Second World War,* 6 vols.

lowings in his time and ours. On the issues of economic decline and disarming to reduce tensions, Churchill was more skeptical, reflecting basically his view that national security required strong military preparation and that disarming to reduce tensions was putting the cart before the horse.

The Primacy of National Interest

The concept of national interest was fundamental in Churchill's approach to foreign policy. Its importance comes into play in discussions of arms control. Efforts for universal disarmament falter and collapse because of divergent national interests. National security is dependent on factors such as a nation's geographic position, its relations with its neighbors, and its natural resources. National defense, which is the core requirement for national survival, is uniquely a matter of a nation's dependence primarily on itself. In Churchill's graphic phrase, "All history has proved the peril of being dependent upon a foreign state for home defense instead of upon one's own right arm." [13]

It has been commonplace for moralists and reformers to lecture political leaders and statesmen on the need for radical new departures in arms control. They forget what we have emphasized, that statesmen are responsible by oath of office (or its equivalent) to preserve the union and safeguard the nation's independence as formulated in the national interest. It is one thing to construct a grand design for universal disarmament; unquestionably that is an important intellectual and moral accomplishment. It is something quite different, however, to fashion concrete practical policies that are consistent with national interests. The latter is an oftentimes baffling, sometimes contentious, and always challenging political task. Not surprising, Churchill, because of his philosophy of foreign policy, assessed the more popular disarmament proposals of his time against the standard of the national interest, particularly in the years between the two world wars.

At a crucial stage in the interwar period, Churchill wrote, "I am very doubtful whether there is any use in pressing national disarmament to a point where nations think their safety is compromised, while the quarrels which

13. *PD*, Vol. 286, March 8, 1934, p. 2066.

lead to armaments and their fears are still unadjusted." For no other country was this statement more relevant than for France and its foreign policy between the wars. Churchill in Parliament defended the rationale of French policy: "As Lord Grey has recently reminded us, France, though armed to the teeth is pacifist to the core. All the countries associated with France have no wish to do anything except to maintain the *status quo.*" [14] Although France was not a threat despite its superior military strength, its negotiating strategy at the disarmament table was based on national interest. France was a land power and requirements for its defense determined its policies throughout the period. Consistently, it opposed proposals that would have limited its main sources of strength while leaving intact the elements of naval power in which others had superiority. Hugh Gibson, the American delegate to the World Disarmament Conference, made a proposal for qualitative disarmament. He called for the outlawry of so-called aggressive weapons, such as tanks, mobile guns larger than 155 mm, and gas. Immediately, the French press, which on this issue was not far removed from France's official reactions to most disarmament programs, criticized the proposal. It pointed out that Ambassador Gibson was seeking to prohibit types of weapons that were vital to land powers while leaving essentially untouched the naval power of countries like the United States and Great Britain.

France's reactions to other proposals reflected the primacy of national interest in its policy decisions. French reactions to the Hoover Plan should have been foreseen. The plan called for an overall one-third reduction in armaments. The French asked what the United States in particular was prepared to do if, despite the Kellogg-Briand Pact, war broke out. Who would defend France? As the French had anticipated, Gibson was unable to offer any security guarantees. That being so, French rejection of the plan was predictable and foreordained.

France's policy at disarmament conferences was the same regardless of the government in power. In 1932, many believed that France would be more forthcoming under the Herriot government. Delegates to the conferences soon discovered that French policy was unchanged. In practice, it was largely unaffected by who its spokesman was. Neither Joseph Paul-Boncour, who represented France at the Geneva Conference, nor Edouard Herriot, who repre-

14. *Ibid.*, Vol. 276, March 23, 1933, p. 540, Vol. 272, November 23, 1932, p. 87.

sented it at Lausanne, could hold out hope of substantial concessions in the absence of guarantees of French security.

Great Britain's policies at successive disarmament conferences also rested squarely on Britain's national interest. Although British statesmen were sometimes reticent about acknowledging the controlling influence of interests on policy, a renowned British historian assessing the discussions in 1932 was unabashedly candid. "It was natural," he wrote, "that each of the Governments . . . should bear its own national interests in mind." On the surface, Churchill appeared to give different emphasis to British practice in his proclamation in the House of Commons: "I have formed the opinion that none of the nations concerned in the Disarmament Conference except Great Britain has been prepared willingly to alter . . . its ratio . . . or impair their factor of safety." [15] If the historian spoke as an objective observer, Churchill cannot have forgotten his role as an aspiring political leader. The fact was that British proposals for naval disarmament emphasized restrictions on the building of submarines. No objective observer would claim that British delegates remained unaware that a policy suiting their interests would be entirely unacceptable to smaller naval powers under existing conditions of relative naval strength. Whereas every British proposal contained some kind of reference to the elimination of the submarine, Britain was unwilling to abandon production of key elements in its own naval strength for only minor concessions by the smaller naval powers.

The United States on at least one point was in full accord with British policy. Gibson's American draft proposals called for the same principle of restrictions on submarine construction that Britain favored. From such restrictions, the United States and Britain would suffer no loss in relative national power. Nor was the United States placing its national interest in jeopardy when it set forth a plan for disarmament based on reducing armaments to a specific proportion of each nation's budget. No one could have been unmindful of the happy convergence of this proposal with the superior wealth of the United States. In the same way, the introduction of Hoover's spectacular plan for one-third disarmament only one week before a crucial domestic election did not escape the notice of the more sophisticated European analysts. The

15. Arnold J. Toynbee, *Survey of International Affairs* (London, 1933), 237; PD, Vol. 272, November 23, 1932, p. 83.

political realities affecting American initiatives in arms reduction on which Churchill commented are not invoked to refute the genuine idealism of some of the American plans. However, no one who wishes to analyze national policies for arms limitation can afford to overlook the impact of national interests.

The same interconnection of national interests with disarmament policies is evident throughout the Cold War. The Soviet Union, whose knowledge and production of the atomic bomb was from the outset qualitatively and quantitatively inferior to the United States, called for the outlawry of that most lethal weapon, prompting Churchill's observation that he could "quite understand the Communist propaganda about barring the atomic bomb, for such a decision would leave the civilization of the world entirely at their mercy even before they had accumulated the necessary stockpile themselves." [16] The national interest required that the United States preserve its strength in the one area in which it was to remain supreme until September 29, 1949. Not only American national interest but the interests of its European allies demanded this policy. On October 11, 1948, Churchill made the allies' position on this point clear: "Of one thing I am quite sure, that if the United States were to consent, in reliance upon any paper agreement, to destroy the stock of atomic bombs which they have accumulated, they would be guilty of murdering human freedom and committing suicide themselves. . . . Nothing stands between Europe to-day and complete subjugation to communist tyranny but the atomic bomb in American possession."

What Churchill was saying was that the national interest of the United States, as well as the interests of its allies, demanded that it preserve its absolute advantage in the production of the atomic bomb, which he recognized would, in a short period of time (four years in this case), become only a relative advantage. Even when its atomic monopoly was broken, the United States would still have an advantage in its superior science and technology. On August 26, 1950, he restated his opinion: "It is indeed a melancholy thought that nothing preserves Europe from an overwhelming military attack except the devastating resources of the United States in this awful weapon. That is at the present time the sole deterrent against an aggressive Communist invasion. No wonder the Communists would like to ban it in the name of peace." [17]

16. *PD*, Vol. 477, July 5, 1950, p. 501.
17. London *Times*, August 28, 1950, p. 2.

If national interests place restraints on the quest for arms reduction, they also provide the sources for seeking convergence among nations that both compete and cooperate. One reason Churchill questioned the value of large public conferences was their tendency to highlight only the competitive aspects of armaments. In his own words, "the holding of these conferences . . . actually prevented the burden from being lightened . . . [through] the normal working of economic and financial pressures." In his references to economic pressures, he appeared to anticipate the Gorbachev era. With approaches in the 1930s, "these conferences have focused the attention of leading men of all nations upon the competitive aspect of armaments . . . [and] intensified the suspicions and anxieties of the nations." [18] Moreover, reductions in certain elements of military strength, for example, outmoded battleships in the case of the Washington Naval Agreement of 1922, invited intensified competition in smaller, faster vessels with heavy firepower, which increased the threat of conflict.

Those who would make progress in arms control, then, must recognize the link between the different defense programs of nations and their particular national security interests. The tendency is to call for reductions in those areas where rival states are strongest. The Spanish diplomat and scholar Salvador de Madariaga y Rojo recounted a fable at the February 25, 1932, meeting of the General Commission on Disarmament at Geneva. His observation had particular reference to the proposal for universal disarmament by the Russians: "The animals had met to disarm. The lion, looking sideways at the eagle, said: 'Wings must be abolished.' The eagle looking at the bull, declared: 'Horns must be abolished.' The bull, looking at the tiger, said: 'Paws, and especially claws, must be abolished.' The bear in his turn said: 'All arms must be abolished; all that is necessary is a universal embrace.' " [19]

The beginning of wisdom in any approach to arms negotiation is recognition that nations place the main elements of their national defense requirements above abstract principles on arms control. The reductions they propose are more likely to affect the relative power of others than their own. They may construct elaborate theories about offensive or aggressive and defensive weapons, but such theories have most of the characteristics of ideological

18. *PD,* Vol. 272, November 23, 1932, pp. 83–85.
19. Quoted in Toynbee, *Survey of International Affairs,* 208.

rationalizations. By outlawing the production of aggressive weapons, certain authorities argued, the sources of aggression would disappear. In practice, however, nations historically have construed as defensive those weapons in which they have an advantage and as offensive those in which rival nations have advantages. Thus, England and the United States considered the battleship a purely defensive weapon and the submarine clearly offensive. Japan maintained that aircraft carriers were offensive but not battleships or submarines. Germany proclaimed that all vessels that were forbidden to them by the Versailles Treaty were offensive, but "pocket battleships," which were permitted by the treaty, were defensive.

Churchill opposed the idea of arms control based on distinctions between offensive and defensive weapons in the strongest possible language. In doing so, he found himself arrayed against a formidable opposition to whom this popular viewpoint gave simple and reassuring answers. Not only in Britain but throughout the world, concepts of qualitative disarmament exercised a powerful appeal on opinion. Churchill recognized that it was easier to expose the fallacy of such thinking than to convince members of Parliament of its folly. He joined the debate, nonetheless: "The Foreign Secretary told us that it was difficult to divide weapons into offensive and defensive categories. It certainly is, because almost every conceivable weapon may be used in defence or offence, either by an aggressor or by the innocent victim of his assault." [20] Distinctions depended on circumstances and could not be written into policy in advance. For Churchill, it was an absurdity and a means of self-deception to spin out elaborate formulae about offensive and defensive weapons. That issue was only one aspect of the more fundamental and baffling problem of deciding on the standards for allocating types and quantities of weapons to nations seeking agreements. With both the quest for standards of equality between France and Germany in the 1930s and present-day attempts at an understanding between the United States and the Soviet Union, the search for consensus has been an unending process, sometimes resolvable only by formulae.

According to Churchill, the best chance for agreement is to identify the security requirements of the competing nations and their most vital national interests. Risks and fears, friends and foes, intentions and capabilities, natural

20. Churchill, *Gathering Storm*, 71–72.

frontiers and geographic neighbors, and historic and traditional policies and alliances all come into play. Pivotal in any such analysis is an understanding of the national interests of the several nations and their impact on arms policies. In the end, arms agreements must be grounded on the national interests of the nations and parties most directly involved.

Arms Control and the Future

Churchill's contributions to the sphere of arms control for the future rest on three controlling propositions. First, he offered principles that link foreign policy and arms control. In this area, he was an exception to prevailing thought. Too often arms control is approached in "splendid isolation" from a systematic analysis of foreign policy. Second, there is in Churchill's approach to arms control a prophetic quality that promises his thinking on major problems is likely to endure. Third, he emphasized disarmament while at the same time seeking to devalue popular approaches that stressed its exclusive and autonomous character.

In contrast with other studies of arms control, we have directly explored the connection with the underlying principles of foreign policy. Foreign policy is primarily focused on preserving the security of the nation and its people. Nations will disarm or significantly limit their arms buildups only when they feel secure. That principle was clear and unambiguous in Churchill's thinking. In the interwar years, at a time of intense public debate in Britain when his view was distinctly in the minority, he made this prediction: "Europe will be secure when nations no longer feel themselves in great danger, as many of them do now. Then the pressure and burden of armaments will fall away automatically, as they ought to have done in a long peace, and it might be quite easy to seal a movement of that character by some general agreement." [21] In this statement he seems to anticipate the changes that are taking place in the Soviet Union and Eastern Europe.

Within Britain, powerful forces and government leaders were defending an opposing viewpoint. For Sir Arthur Henderson and the government in

21. *PD*, Vol. 292, July 13, 1934, p. 733.

power, security and disarmament were interchangeable parts in the disarmament equation. Mutually interdependent, they were destined to move together. Progress in either one would facilitate success in the other. Less important than the priority given one or the other were advances on either front.

Ironically, Churchill in his approach here was closer to the French than to his own government. For the French, supported by the Polish and Romanian governments, the successful pursuit of disarmament was wholly dependent on obtaining successful guarantees of security. The French formula, endlessly proclaimed by leaders such as Aristide Briand, was that the goal of disarmament must be pursued in the three successive stages of arbitration, security, and, lastly, disarmament. One inescapably had to follow the other, and failure in the first or second stages condemned nations to seek national security through expanding their armies and national defense programs. For outsiders, such national defense buildups invited criticism, but Churchill denounced Western policies toward the French: "It was argued in odd logic that it would be immoral to disarm the vanquished unless the victors also stripped themselves of their weapons. The finger of Anglo-American reprobation was presently to be pointed at France, deprived alike of the Rhine frontier and her treaty guarantee, for maintaining, even on a greatly reduced scale, a French army based upon universal service." [22]

Churchill's approach to disarmament and arms control, as was true of his approach to every other problem, was grounded on his conception of foreign policy. For him the twin pillars of foreign policy were diplomacy and strength. In 1950, critics questioned whether concessions to the Soviets might not reflect an attitude of appeasement, but Churchill responded that it was weakness, not strength, that led Chamberlain into appeasement at Munich. In dealing with the Soviets, Churchill called for more precise definitions and explained that for him the guide was "negotiations from strength." He used an old-fashioned definition of appeasement and made it a synonym for negotiations in his declaration of December 14, 1950: "Appeasement in itself may be good or bad according to circumstances. Appeasement from weakness and fear is alike futile and fatal. Appeasement from strength is magnanimous and noble and might be the surest and perhaps the only path to peace."

Ideas and concepts such as diplomacy linked with strength were all part

22. Churchill, *Gathering Storm*, 13–14.

of Churchill's effort to construct a coherent theory or doctrine of foreign policy. He maintained that no leader could manage the complexities and contingencies of world affairs without such a theory. "Those who are possessed of a definite body of doctrine and deeply rooted convictions upon it will be in much better position to deal with the shifts and surprises of daily affairs." [23] Yet such a doctrine, as the history of world politics makes clear, is not in itself sufficient. Wise foreign policy is the outcome of a powerful and creative mind possessed of such a doctrine and comprehending the many and varied dimensions of the ever-changing world scene. Political wisdom derives from a weighing and evaluating of all the intractable elements that make up a complex situation. A leader's clarity of vision is built on a scaffolding of thought grounded on certain bedrock propositions concerning man, politics, and society. The need for a theory or doctrine of foreign policy is well stated in a paraphrase of the words of poet T. S. Eliot, who wrote that without a philosophy or a plan, wisdom will be lost in knowledge and knowledge in information.

Second, Churchill's contribution to the sphere of arms control and to the future likewise derives from the prophetic quality of his thought. Nearly forty years after the mountain peaks in Churchill's world leadership were most visible, superpower leaders are still debating the great issues he sought to define, including arms limitation, political accommodation, and economic cooperation between East and West, and the meaning and articulation of diplomacy and strength. Nations tend to judge leaders by their success in pursuing steady, principled, and pragmatic foreign policies. Successful leaders are required to look both to history and to the future. To the extent Churchill was successful in anticipating the future, his view of what was to come was rooted in the past. In World War II, as an architect of the Grand Alliance, he structured the alliance against Hitler by harking back to the lessons he chronicled in *Marlborough: His Life and Times*, his historical masterpiece of the coalition against Louis XIV. His ancestor John Churchill, Duke of Marlborough was the linchpin of the first grand alliance, which turned back France's effort to dominate Europe. First in opposing German expansionism and again in marshaling the West against Stalinist imperialism, Churchill drew on the past to meet the challenge of the future. His perspective on the future was in-

23. *Ibid.*, 210.

formed by knowledge of the past acquired both from experience and from the study of history.

Not only the past, however, but a vision of the future shaped Churchill's thinking. It can be said that both for the broad trends of national development and for the specific details of evolving international relationships, he anticipated what was to come. His view of the future of relations with the Soviets was based on a guardedly optimistic world outlook. He warned that it was a mistake to look too far ahead and spoke of concentrating on but one link in the chain of destiny at a time. Yet he believed that a political settlement could bring a resolution to the gravest disputes that divided East and West and could open the world to a brighter future, an era in which "all stands in a different setting." In describing the end of such a process, Churchill invariably put stress on the lasting, or enduring, nature of a political settlement, provided it was based on U.S. and Soviet interests.

On the specifics of an arms agreement, his comments reflected a prescient view of the future. At a time when almost every informed observer was writing of the impenetrability of Soviet national borders and the need for Soviet rulers to maintain the image of a serious external threat to justify their oppressive rule to the people, Churchill spoke of a new and revolutionary approach to inspection and control. He argued that any effective program of arms limitation would be dependent on facilities for inspection within the Soviet Union and the United States. Ways would have to be found to determine the facts of actual arms reductions. He prophesied that "what is called war talk will be swept away by an interchange of actual military facts, supported by equality between all powers . . . which are involved" and added, "That will be a great step forward in itself and may lead the way to others." [24] Whereas others doubted through most of the postwar period that a system of mutual inspection was possible, Churchill kept open the prospect. His vision achieved realization in the INF agreement signed by President Reagan and General Secretary Gorbachev and ratified by the U.S. Senate. It would be claiming too much to say that the British leader foresaw the future in the exact form of its unfolding. He did, though, hold out the benefits of an arms agreement that embodied provisions for effective internal inspection and in so doing seemed to recognize the possibilities of a new era.

24. New York *Times,* November 1, 1946, p. 15.

Third, Churchill emphasized the interconnectedness of all aspects of foreign policy. He maintained that neither arms control nor national defense could be viewed in isolation from the other aspects of foreign policy. Whereas he embraced certain strongly held views regarding a second front in World War II or opposed the unconditional surrender of the Third Reich, he understood that Britain had become a lesser partner in the alliance with the United States. The Grand Alliance imposed responsibilities and constraints on Britain. Public opinion was another reality in the formulation of foreign policy that could not be ignored. He tried to view foreign policy with all these aspects in mind, steadily and as a whole.

Of arms limitation, he wrote: "If you wish for disarmament, it will be necessary to go to the political and economic causes which lie behind the maintenance of armies and navies. There are very serious economic and political dangers . . . and antagonisms which are by no means assuaged." Arms limitation was an intelligible and realistic goal only when approached as the crowning achievement, not the first step, of a long and patient diplomatic and strategic process. If the "hideous burden" of armaments was ever to be removed, it would be by an overall approach to the relaxation of political tensions. As long as the struggle for power went unresolved and tensions remained high, rival nations were bound to pursue security through the augmentation of their power or, more specifically, through an acceleration of the arms race. The single most basic precondition for arms reduction, therefore, was a political settlement and, with it, the elimination of political grievances. Undergirding all was a broad principle that Churchill reiterated: "Here is my general principle. The removal of the just grievances of the vanquished ought to precede the disarmament of the victors. . . . Nobody keeps armaments going for fun. They keep them going for fear." [25]

In Churchill's mind, diplomacy was "the patient and skillful removal of the political causes of antagonism." Unless nations succeed in arriving at some form of understanding, whether tacit or explicit, concerning the relative distribution of world power, they cannot risk any significant reductions in their arms programs. Churchill would have agreed with the logic of a brilliantly written and wisely reasoned editorial in the *Times* on December 1, 1951, which defined the real issue in arms limitation in a single cogent sen-

25. *PD*, Vol. 265, May 13, 1932, p. 2352, Vol. 272, November 23, 1932, p. 89.

tence: "Disarmament will come, if it comes at all, only when the two leviathans have in fact achieved a rough balance of power, when they realize that they do not mean to attack each other, and when this balance and this realization can at last lead to written agreement on the debatable areas of the world." [26] In the 1990s, the two superpowers appear to be moving somewhat haltingly in the direction of this formulation, subject always to setbacks and reversals. Although the August, 1991, coup of the hard-liners was turned back by democratic forces in the Soviet Union, the weakening of the Soviet economy makes the future of the country one issue of continuing uncertainty.

Because Churchill was consistent in recognizing the relation between foreign policy and arms limitation, had a prophetic view of the future, and understood the interconnectedness of arms control with diplomacy and the balance of power and economic and social factors, his legacy endures. Disarmament depends on the lessening of tensions and the pacification of relationships among the world powers. Progress in arms control, if once made possible through changes involving these interconnected factors, can in turn mitigate other tensions and disputes. Churchill's most lasting contribution may prove to be his elaboration of a comprehensive and coherent approach to arms limitation. He came too late in one era (the era of disarmament) and too early in the next (the era of arms control) to draw all the distinctions that are required for a transitional time. He could not have foreseen that the decline of the Soviet economy would require reductions in Soviet military expenditures or the pace with which this process would occur. In fact, the willingness of both sides to accept arms limitations was driven by economic considerations. For the United States, a mounting federal budget deficit was an incentive to reduce its defense expenditures. Whatever the factors that influenced the two sides, it was clearly a historical fact that objective political and economic circumstances made possible significant progress on arms limitation, illustrating the continuing relevance of Churchill's perspective. The broad principles he set forth have relevance even in today's quest for arms control. By tracing the connections among foreign policy concerns and objective political and economic factors and the requirements of arms limitation, he bequeathed a way of thinking about arms control that is timeless.

26. London *Times*, December 1, 1951, p. 7.

16

Human Survival:
Crusade or Coherent Plan?

No one can doubt that the world stands at a crossroads. On the one side of history, the whole habitable globe lives under the Damoclean sword of thermonuclear annihilation. On the other side, mankind is threatened by the devastating effects of famine, overpopulation, resource depletion, and environmental deterioration. Men envisage the one danger in the image of a vast mushrooming cloud of total destruction, the other, in the ravages of forces that slowly but irresistibly draw life from millions of people. To ignore the double threat to human survival would be both irresponsible and unrealistic.

As we move into the 1990s, debates go on as to what constitutes the severer crisis and which is more real. Those who declare that one threat is graver than the other or speculate about the year when mass destruction from one or the other will overtake mankind speak more as seers or soothsayers than students or scientists. Whatever the prophecy, no one can afford to ignore the dark warning clouds visible on the horizon. The real issue is the search for coherent answers to two different threats, one insistent and immediate and the other long-term and in the future. Is there not risk in anyone's urging mankind to confront the one and ignore the other? Can responsible leaders afford to say the world faces only one grave peril and ignore all the others? Does not the future depend more on man's discovery of a steady course and coherent plan for meeting the challenge of each urgent problem than on merely knowing there is trouble ahead?

The Population Explosion

Questions of this kind cluster together as we begin to think about human survival. I served for nearly twenty years on the professional staff of an international technical assistance organization. The agency's most powerful leader, John D. Rockefeller III, sincerely believed that the gravest world threat was overpopulation. If he had had his way, the organization would have committed all its resources to turning back the rising curve of population growth. Whereas his father and grandfather had confronted and overcome vast odds in the industrial world, he saw his mission late in life as the use of large-scale material resources to transform the world's social order.

All of us admired his single-mindedness and dedication but doubted that any one segment of the world's urgent problems could be approached in isolation from all the others. For example, food supply and population are interconnected questions in the developing world. Moreover, it was folly to say that the nuclear problem need not concern a large organization with flexible funds that had done so much in every sphere to train qualified professionals. Looking back, we can judge it possible that the organization's retreat from supporting foreign policy and arms control studies for more than a decade may have contributed to the shortfall of trained personnel, creating a vacuum into which marched the ideologues of right and left, not surprisingly designated as "Team A" and "Team B." Harvard professor and president of the International Political Science Association Karl Deutsch warned of the pipelines being emptied of professionals in foreign policy in the 1970s. If Deutsch was right, one contributing factor may have been the flight of the foundations from this field. The cause of their defection was the elevation of population-control activities to the level of a crusade. Every other interest took second place. Foundation literature described the main goal as the "conquest" of hunger or the turning back of population growth. Falling birth rates were charted and displayed to demonstrate success, much as fund-raising graphs are used in a community chest campaign. Whenever we read a paper that calls on the world or the nation to crusade for a worthy cause to be accomplished overnight, we ought to be reminded of the campaign to rid the world of overpopulation and hunger in which a private organization was once engaged. There was something terribly pretentious and self-righteous about the whole enterprise. That is not to say that the foundation failed to make an important contribution. It did fail, however, to define and pursue a coherent set of objectives.

Conquering the World Food Problem?

The 1960s were an era of hope, particularly in the developed world, concerning the conquest of hunger. More than in any other sector of human need, with the possible exception of the conquest of infectious diseases in the 1930s and 1940s, the international community put science to work to meet a basic human need. Country-by-country programs of agricultural assistance begun in the early 1940s increased food production dramatically. Mexico, which had been using up scarce foreign exchange importing corn and wheat, became largely self-sufficient. The United States, which had never been considered a colonial power, exported trained agronomists, plant pathologists, and plant breeders to assist nations in pursuing the Green Revolution. Because the first efforts were small (the entire research budget of the Rockefeller Foundation agricultural staff in Mexico in the 1940s, exclusive of salaries, was $35,000), private assistance dominated.

Those who went abroad were not intellectuals talking about functional integration but technical specialists who practiced it. Such men talked little about an interdependent international system somewhere between traditional state sovereignty and world government. Their success depended precisely on states *not* yielding portions of their sovereignty. Gains in agricultural production were closely linked with national pride. American agricultural scientists were able to contribute precisely because the Mexicans, not the Americans, received the credit. The Office of Special Studies was a newly created unit that housed the American scientists within the Ministry of Agriculture. New varieties of corn and wheat were given Mexican names, not American or international designations. As the program progressed, fellows from abroad came to Mexico to be trained by Mexicans. Throughout the world, the remarkably successful program was known as the Mexican Agricultural Program, not the American or Rockefeller program. Eventually, the Mexicans set out to help other Latin American countries, particularly in Central America.

If we look for reasons this program succeeded whereas other attempts at increasing food production have foundered, one lesson surely is that it remained a Mexican program. Another factor was the simple, clear-cut nature of the mandate. The goal was not to assist a wide variety of "basic human needs" ramifying out through society. Instead, the aim was to increase production in a few basic food crops, namely, corn and wheat. The method for the visiting scientists was to don overalls and go into the field with the Mexicans, a practice none too common for trained Mexicans. The approach was a partnership in applied science, with both sides contributing human as well as investment capital. The visitors came to stay, learned the language, assimilated the culture, and accepted and were accepted by the Mexican people. This type of foreign assistance took the form of help in an area where the Americans had much to offer. The agricultural sciences in the United States were highly developed, thanks to the land-grant colleges. Through institutions such as the county agent system, new scientific findings were kept close to the primary consumer, the farmer in the field. However conservative their politics (including international politics), the land-grant-college agriculturalists had an inbred sense of service. Helping farmers abroad came naturally because they had helped farmers at home. Their goal was to put agriculture to work for people.

The visiting agricultural scientists brought with them enough but not too much of their national agricultural system. They insisted on training Mexican agriculturalists "to grow a crop" because they had followed the same practice at Cornell and Purdue universities, the University of Minnesota, and the Davis campus of the University of California. Wherever they went, they required experimental farms for practical agricultural exercises, sometimes drawing together unlikely combinations of plots of widely separated land. They were more practical than the British or the French but less well versed in the history and etymology of plants and crops around the world. They sought to establish in every country program a critical mass of well-trained agriculturalists working on various crops with the single goal of increasing agricultural production.

The most enduring lesson about methods is that programs that start small and grow big are more likely to succeed. The Mexican Agricultural Program was successful, at least in part, because it was integrated into the national culture. It didn't start with a global objective, such as building a world food reserve, but with the simple goal of increasing the agricultural production of those staples that mattered most in one country. It involved the efforts of doers, not conceptualizers, though basically the endeavor rested on such simple axioms as "it is better to teach a man to fish than to give him a fish." The teachers were not generalists with an incidental concern for agriculture but America's best agricultural scientists.

Once a single-country program had proven successful, others followed, appearing as spokes in a wheel. The Mexican effort began in 1943, and a cooperative program with Colombia started in 1950, followed by one in Chile in 1953. Lessons learned in one country were extended to another; trained personnel from one moved on to another. It became clear that the needs of countries were not everywhere the same. Ecuador sought to develop and improve its potato production. Rice was the focus in the Philippines. Different political systems imposed different constraints on cooperation. Some taxed imported seeds and machinery, to say nothing of the incomes of American scientists, while others were more liberal in providing incentives. As the spokes in the wheel were completed representing one region, new wheels representing cooperative programs in Asia and Africa were added. The whole effort culminated in the establishment of larger international agricultural institutes on three continents, all built on the foundations of the single-country programs but now responsive to regional and worldwide needs.

What distinguished the approach described above from other efforts was its essential character as an international functionalist enterprise. It began with an urgent need, not a theory. Different nationalities joined together, working across national boundaries on a common problem. The supranational dimensions of the activity grew out of professional and functional cooperation rather than preceding them. Cooperation in the beginning was bilateral between Americans and Mexicans. It does not follow that programs of an international organization would have been more acceptable to the Mexicans. It was professional competence in agriculture that mattered most. Unless the quality of staff members in the United Nations Food and Agriculture Organization had reflected similar competence, it is questionable they would have been as well received. Empathy and sensitivity, willingness to listen and learn, and coherence and continuity are more important than an international or multinational label.

Controlling World Population: A Complex Task

The urgency of attacking the problem of world population growth parallels the necessity of increasing the food supply. The present world population of some five billion people is expected to approach six and a half billion sometime around the year 2000. On one level, the advances that have been made in population control match those in agriculture. If anything, more agencies have been involved and more words have been written about population than about the conquest of hunger. The International Planned Parenthood Association operates in ninety-five countries. (One is tempted to ask if this is a case of spreading scarce resources too thin.) Spokesmen for population agencies have opened dialogues with highly placed leaders in countries from Canada to Brazil. World conferences have focused on population problems, a notable one having been held in Bucharest in 1974. Mexico, Colombia, Brazil, and other Catholic countries have sent delegations to conferences of parliamentarians held in countries such as Sri Lanka (Ceylon). Various consortia of organizations concentrating on population control have been formed and are active.

On a more basic level, the magnitude and complexity of the population question surpasses the problem of food. Not only is population increasing on an absolute basis, but it is concentrated in vast sprawling urban centers. In 1960, there were already sixty such cities. Mexico City, which had a population of 20 million, is projected to grow to 27 million by 2000. Of Latin America's population 60 to 70 percent is crowded together in explosively unstable urban centers. From 1960 to 1970, the labor force expanded by eight million people. In the less-developed countries, the number of people in the work force needing jobs equals the total number employed in all the industrial countries. Population pressures are reflected especially in sectors such as education. While world illiteracy rates dropped from 32 percent in 1970 to 25 percent in 1990, the absolute number of illiterate people increased from 884 million in 1970 to over a billion, and the trend is continuing.

Population programs, moreover, have fewer success stories than the Green Revolution in food production has. Four Asian countries, Taiwan, Korea, Hong Kong, and Singapore, have made more significant progress in reducing population growth rates than all other Asian societies combined. Significantly, the most dramatic achievements have occurred with defined cohorts such as the Military Dependents Program in Taiwan. At the same time, the sense of urgency about population control has been kept down both because of religious and cultural attitudes and because famine and malnutrition are viewed as more serious and immediate crises (more deaths in the Third World result from malnutrition than from any other cause). The dialogue that I recall from my own technical assistance experience with responsible leaders in African countries was repeated across the continent. I was told over and over that while representatives of private and public international agencies continually urged these leaders to devote scarce resources to population control, their most urgent and compelling problem was, as they put it, "clean water." They asked why external agencies were indifferent to such needs and why the developed countries offered them incentives, or "bribes," to redirect efforts to population programs. Was there a hidden motive verging on a conspiracy by outside forces seeking to hold down their population in order to limit their nations' power in world affairs?

However irrational such thinking appeared at the time, no serious person engaged in technical assistance could dismiss it out of hand. Population programs confronted obstacles that conquest of hunger efforts did not face. National pride and cultural practices stood in the path of successful intervention by outsiders, whether they represented the United Nations or a private foundation. The presence of such obstacles led to a broadening of the approach and to the combining of indirect and direct assistance efforts. Aid went beyond shipments of birth control materials, which often produced disappointments. For example, the wholesale supplying of large shipments of condoms and jellies was initially seen as the most effective means of controlling population growth. Then stories multiplied of primitive peoples using the jellies not for the intended purpose but to cover or paint their bodies. Greater subtlety and sophistication were required in methods of control. Sterilization campaigns worked in some cultures but caused nationalistic backlashes in others. In some cultures, the self-respect of males was bound up with their ability to produce offspring within or outside family structures. To equate social systems or to assume that family planning practices appropriate to Americans could be transferred to other cultures proved to be a fallacious approach. More indirect avenues were needed.

A prime example of the indirect approach is the one linking employment and population control. Economists and social scientists have produced statistics demonstrating that population growth is inversely related to employment opportunities for women. Working mothers bear a significantly smaller number of children than do women whose only social function is the production of offspring. Moreover, mortality rates are interconnected with population statistics. Where mortality rates are high, a large family is necessary to assure that a sufficient number of children survive to operate enterprises such as the family farm. When death rates decline, smaller-sized families are able to maintain family-oriented economies. Public health efforts, including improved sanitation, contribute indirectly to population control. Social acceptance for efforts designed to prolong human life is greater than for programs to reduce population through more direct methods. Linking public health and population control proves more in keeping with the values of indigenous societies.

The lessons of four decades of large-scale efforts at population control are that a diversified approach has a better chance of success. A packaged approach of various efforts in population control is indicated in the same way that a coherent and broad-gauged approach to the world food problem has been shown to have higher payoffs. The world food problem requires concentrated efforts to increase food production but also major attempts to improve the distribution of food products, better nutrition through improved food quality, and social reforms affecting more equitable systems of land ownership. Economics and agriculture ought to be linked. Nutrition scientists joining with plant breeders are more likely to improve the quality, as well as the quantity, of food. The goal becomes an integrated approach to meeting world food problems through adding the findings of cultural anthropologists, who can throw light on cultural preferences for crops of certain texture and appearance. (The original miracle rice, IR8, of the International Rice Research Institute in the Philippines was adapted through crossbreeding to the tastes of Indonesians, Thais, and Japanese.) Agricultural scientists introduced the concept of a "package of agricultural practices" to meet the diverse needs of different cultures, which can serve as a general model for activities in population control.

Practices in the area of population control are affected by two major theories. The first theory is that of the developed or industrial countries and emphasizes direct efforts at population control. The second theory, which many of the less-developed countries have followed, presupposes that economic development must precede population control. At world population conferences, spokesmen for the two theories, which are guided by two different sets of assumptions, have clashed. The division produced a stalemate between developed and less-developed countries at the Bucharest Conference; the cleavage of thinking has continued but has been mitigated in the present. Some progress has been made in reconciling the two viewpoints, and the influence of developed-country economic theory on the relationship between employment and population growth has helped close the gap. Much remains to be done in the future. The cutbacks in the population programs of certain private agencies have shifted greater burdens of responsibility to national and international public agencies, including the World Food Council. While the shift has assured an increase in total resources, the debate over theories and population policies has become more politicized. It would be utopian to imagine that solutions can be anything but long-term, given the nature of the population problem and the changing cultural and national context in which it must be worked out.

The Crisis of Human Survival in the Year 2000

On May 23, 1977, President Jimmy Carter directed the Council on Environmental Quality and the Department of State, working in cooperation with other appropriate agencies, to make a one-year study of the probable changes in the world's population, natural resources, and environment through the end of the century. The resulting report was published in 1980 as *The Global 2000 Report to the President: Entering the Twenty-First Century*. The new crisis in human survival becomes clear from findings in this report and more recent studies.

Population

According to the *Global 2000 Report*, the world's population will experience an enormous growth from 4.1 billion people in 1975 to a conservatively projected 6.35 billion in the year 2000. A large percentage of the population growth (92 percent) will occur in the less-developed countries, meaning that by the year 2000, of the world's 6.35 billion people, 5.0 billion will be living in the less-developed countries and 400 million males and females of the age of fifteen will have their childbearing years ahead of them.

In addition to the projected rapidly increasing population growth in the less-developed countries, the *Global 2000 Report* predicts a burgeoning movement of rural peoples to urban areas. By 2000, Mexico City will have a population of more than 35 million; Calcutta, nearly 20 million; Greater Bombay, Cairo, Jakarta, and Seoul, 15 to 20 million each; Tehran, nearly 14 million; Delhi between 13 and 14 million; and Manila, between 12 and 13 million.

This rural exodus to urban areas will understandably impose heavily increasing demands on the cities' already over-burdened services such as housing, food, water, supplies, sanitation, fire and police protection, education, and employment. Indeed, by the year 2000, the many rural people flocking to cities in the less-developed countries will be living, if they survive at all, below the level of what is currently termed "slum-living." The majority of the population in these cities will be found in settlements comprised of shacks, tents, shanties, and any structures offering a modicum of shelter.

The impact this rapid population growth will have on global per capita income will widen the present gap between today's wealthiest and poorest nations. It is estimated that by the year 2000, industrialized countries will have a per capita gross national product (GNP) of $8,500 to $11,000 (in 1975 dollars), contrasted with that of the less-developed countries, which will average less than $600. Although average annual GNP growth will be greater in these than in developed countries (4.5 percent compared with 3.3 percent), "the LDC [less-developed country] growth in gross national product develops from a very low base, and population growth in the LDCs brings per capita increases down to very modest proportions." For example, though such countries as India, Bangladesh, and Pakistan will show increases in per capita GNP, they will show nearly zero gain in per capita income because of population growth. In these countries GNP per capita is projected to remain below $200 (in 1975 dollars) by the year 2000. Further, disparities between the highest and lowest income groups in the less-developed countries will widen markedly.

Agriculture

With a dramatically increased world population and concomitant demands for more and larger food production and a greater supply of energy, we need to consider the consequent impact on the global environment. What is going to happen to agriculture, water resources, fisheries, forests, the atmosphere and climate, and species approaching extinction? The *Global 2000 Report* is not very hopeful:

> Perhaps the most serious environmental development will be an accelerating deterioration and loss of the resources for agriculture. This overall development includes soil erosion; loss of nutrients and compaction of soil erosion; increasing salinization of both irrigated land and water used for irrigation; loss of high-quality cropland to urban development; crop damage due to increasing air and water pollution; extinction of local and wild crop strains needed by plant breeders for improving cultivated varieties; and more frequent and more severe regional water shortages— especially when energy and industrial developments compete for water supplies, or where forest losses are heavy and the earth can no longer absorb, store and regulate the discharge of water.

Deterioration of soils is already occurring in the less-developed countries and is spreading desertlike conditions in dry areas and causing heavy erosion in the humid ones. "Present global losses to desertification are estimated at about 6 million hectares a year (an area about the size of Maine), including 3.2 million hectares of rangeland, 2.5 million hectares of rain fed cropland and 125 thousand hectares of irrigated farmland." Desertification, which ultimately leaves the land depleted of nutrients and useless for crops or grazing, is mainly caused by overcropping, overgrazing, and the use of woody plants for fuel. Particularly in the less-developed countries where dung is the principal source of fuel because of the lack of firewood, the land is also being robbed of its natural fertilizers.

The devastating problem of soil depletion and permanent damage to the land is not confined to the less-developed countries: it is a global problem and one the United States is also facing, particularly because of urbanization of agricultural land; salinization of irrigated land; sewage, acid rain, and industrial pollution of water resources; and accelerated use of inorganic fertilizers and pesticides. In California, for example, reportedly seventeen of twenty-five major agricultural pests are resistant to one or more types of pesticides, the natural pest-predator population having been greatly reduced.

Water

Global land depletion, naturally, has implications for water resources. As the world population soars, so does the demand on water's life-supply systems. The *Global 2000 Report* indicates increasing destruction of coastal ecosystems—destruction that will negatively affect 60 to 80 percent of commercially valuable marine life, a high-protein component of healthful human diets. The marine-life supply for human consumption will be destroyed not only by industrial and commercial pollutants but also by pollutants caused by high-yield agricultural technology, such as irrigation, commercial fertilizers, and pesticides. Another heavy contributor to water-resources pollution will be the conversion of agricultural land to urban uses as the world's rural population, unable to maintain a subsistence level, flees to cities in vain hopes of finding some means of feeding, housing, and supporting itself. Whereas water pollution in the less-developed countries is expected to increase, developed countries in the 1980s were already facing the grim problems of diminishing supplies of available water and of increasing volumes of polluted water. The United States, a chief producer of the world's food, is feeling the pinch.

Atmosphere and Climate

As present trends continue, with growth exerting increased pressure on land and water resources, so will increased pressures be exerted on forests, on the world's atmosphere and climate, and on a number of species, critically affecting the world's ability to produce food.

Air quality has already deteriorated throughout the world far below levels considered safe by the World Health Organization, particularly in urban areas in both less-developed and developed countries. It is expected to deteriorate further as greater amounts of fossil fuels, especially coal, are burned, causing a greater concentration of carbon dioxide in the earth's atmosphere. Of special concern is the warming effect on the earth caused by increased accumulations of carbon dioxide and the probable consequences of diminishing world agricultural production after 2000. The result could also change global precipitation patterns, and a 2° to 3°C rise in temperatures in the middle latitudes and an increase of 5° to 10°C in polar temperatures could lead to the eventual melting of the Greenland and Antarctic ice caps, causing a gradual rise in sea level and the abandonment of affected coastal cities.

The *Global 2000 Report* states that "even a 1°C increase in average global temperatures would make the earth's climate warmer than it has been any time in the last 1,000 years."[1] Such rapid climate changes would cause grave problems to all human adaptation endeavors, including the agricultural ones. Additionally threatening to the earth's atmosphere and globally damaging to human beings and crops is the depletion of the stratospheric ozone layer protecting the earth from devastating ultraviolet rays, which, uncontrolled, would result in a high incidence of skin cancer and a burning of crops. Principal offenders to the burning off of stratospheric ozone layers are chlorofluorocarbon emissions, nitrogen oxide emissions from both organic and inorganic nitrogen fertilizers, and possibly the effects of fuel emissions from high-altitude aircraft flights. Until 1990, few countries made efforts to control emissions from fluorocarbon aerosol-canned products. Now delegates attending a conference in London have agreed to ban chlorofluorocarbons by 2000 (developing nations by 2010), and the United States is banning hydrofluorocarbons by 2030. However, the Bush administration has taken somewhat equivocal stands at other international conferences.

Crusade or Coherent Plan?

The gravity and complexity of the problems of human survival as mankind approaches the year 2000 are greater than they were in the 1960s or 1970s. Not only has the agenda of human survival broadened to include problems in the environment, in energy, and in natural resources, but societies that had seemed to be moving ahead in food and population have fallen back. For

1. *The Global 2000 Report to the President: Entering the Twenty-First Century* (Washington, D.C., 1980), fig. 3 and pp. 13, 23–33, 37.

example, Mexico, which became self-sufficient in corn and wheat, is now a net importer of such basic food crops. Faced with the prospect of doomsday, planners and policymakers in the developing countries can choose either to embark on a crusade against the apocalypse or to search for coherent and realistic approaches to meet their problems.

Most of the evidence of past efforts to ameliorate urgent human problems suggests that coherent plans have far better prospects of success than worldwide crusades. Whatever the shortcomings and side effects of major programs in the 1960s aimed at increasing world food production, they unquestionably turned agricultural systems around in important countries and regions. Similarly, population control programs have some decades of experience on which to base future planning. The challenge with food and population is less one of constructing new approaches than of adapting existing ones to new and more urgent situations. If anything, population control has been disproportionate in some countries and for certain groups; the goal should be to spread its use to countries and groups whose growth has been left unaffected.

Most difficult of all are the environmental and energy problems that haunt mankind's future. Societies must learn to think more coherently about balancing equally worthy pairs of goals, neither of which can be overlooked. Nations must pursue a measure of economic growth while recognizing the need for environmental protection. Controls must be set up not to thwart industrial plants but to prevent pollution. Leaders need to recognize that resource depletion, including water, forests, and air, can destroy man's capacity for survival. Each human survival problem is linked with every other one. It is not enough to turn a society's resources wholly in one direction, for example, toward population control to the disregard of food, the environment, or the nuclear threat. All must be attacked along a moving front, even though one or the other may deserve priority in response to changing needs and available technology. The crisis of the year 2000 calls for new initiatives without abandoning lessons from the past. Above all, every new initiative should be part of a coherent plan.

Part V

Presidents and Conflicts of Values

17

Lincoln as Model

Religion, Values, and Choice

Having considered the principles that guide moral and political discrimination, we turn attention to the leaders who must make hard political choices, American presidents. William James wrote of varieties of religious experiences. It will come as no surprise that portraits of modern-day presidents focusing on their moral, religious, and political outlooks are just as varied, reflecting patterns in many different hues and colors. This characterization is true of a study entitled *Essays on Lincoln's Faith and Politics*. One of the authors, Professor Hans Morgenthau, considered Lincoln a believing skeptic or skeptical believer, "indifferent to religion in dogma and organization [but] . . . profoundly and consistently aware of the existential condition from which the religious impulse springs." The other, David Hein, saw Lincoln as a believer holding to a theocentric view of experience. Since our focus is on politics, Morgenthau's views are more directly relevant to our topic.

Lincoln's Faith and Politics

Morgenthau's analysis of Lincoln's faith and politics does not stem from any disrespect for religion. Indeed, he writes that "the issue that precedes all others both in time and importance is that of religion." For Morgenthau and for Lincoln, religion is not membership in a church or observance of a set of religious practices or certain professions of faith. It is rather a religious attitude that recognizes the insufficiency of man as a finite being. It seeks transcendent guidance for man in his relationship with himself, his fellow men, and the universe. In Morgenthau's words, "Religion is . . . a universal human attitude . . . of which the historic religions, religious organizations, and religious observances are but particular manifestations." Early in his life, in 1837, Lincoln wrote to his fiancée, Mary Owens: "I've never been to church yet nor probably shall not be soon. I stay away because I am conscious I should not know how to behave myself."

Early in his career, when he was running for the Illinois legislature in 1843, Lincoln was attacked both by opponents of the Episcopal church and by church members themselves. He defended himself against the former, writing to a friend, "It would astonish if not amuse, the older citizens of your Country who twelve years ago knew me as a strange(r), friendless, uneducated, penniless boy, working on a flat boat—at ten dollars per month—to learn that I have been put down here as the candidate of pride, wealth and aristocratic family distinction." His opponent was a Campbellite, and Lincoln had just married into an aristocratic southern family with Episcopal and Presbyterian ties. Lincoln found that Christians opposed him "because [he] belonged to no church, was suspected of being a deist, and had talked about fighting a duel." His critics attacked him both for being too aristocratic in his religion and for being indifferent to religion as such. What is significant, Lincoln, noting these mutually contradictory statements, did not go on to explain which criticism was correct.

Three years later, again running for the state legislature, Lincoln answered more directly to the charge of his opponent, an itinerant preacher, the Reverend Cartright, that he had scoffed at religion. In a "Handbill Replying to Charges of Infidelity," Lincoln replied, "That I am not a member of any Christian Church, is true; but I have never denied the truth of the Scriptures; and I have never spoken with intentional disrespect of religion in general, of any denomination of Christians in particular." Lincoln went on in his own defense to say:

> I do not think I could myself, be brought to support a man for office, whom I knew to be an open enemy of, and scoffer at, religion. Leaving the higher matter of eternal consequences, between him and his Maker, I do not think any man has the right thus to insult the feelings, and injure the morals, of the community in which he may live. If, then, I was guilty of such conduct, I should blame no man who should condemn me for it; but I do blame those, whoever they may be, who falsely put such a charge in circulation against me.

Morgenthau considers that this statement on religion is not a particularly fervent or even convincing profession of religious belief. Lincoln was running in 1846 in a rural county in which opposition to religion was tantamount to political suicide. Yet he is negative and defensive about religion, not positive. He says that he doesn't belong to a church, has never denied the Scriptures, and has not spoken "intentionally" in disrespect of religion. In short, his defense of his religion is that it is not as bad as it has been made out to be. For a politician, he shows striking intellectual honesty, there being not a single positive assertion of his belief in Christian doctrine. Morgenthau asserts that the name of Christ appears only once in Lincoln's printed writings, and then in a purely secular context, and that he added "under God" to the text of the Gettysburg Address only as he spoke.

Morgenthau discovered one letter by Lincoln to a relative who had written that Lincoln's father was close to death. Of the three such letters he received informing him of his father's condition, he replied to only one, saying of the others, "I could write nothing that could do any good." However, he did answer the one in these words:

> I sincerely hope Father may yet recover his health; but at all events tell him to remember to call upon, and confide in, our great, and good, and merciful Maker. . . . Say to him that if we could meet now, it is doubtful whether it would not be more painful than pleasant; but that if it be his lot to go now, he will soon have a joyous [meeting] with many loved ones gone before; and where [the rest] of us, through the help of God, hope ere-long [to join] them.

Morgenthau reflects on Lincoln's indifference in the face of his father's impending death and suggests that his fervent invocation of God's love could be seen as compensating for his own lack of filial love and human feeling. The letter, in any event, is only one of two Morgenthau could find in which detachment is replaced by religious fervor in Lincoln's articulation of his faith.

However, the story doesn't end at this point. As a statesman, Lincoln was deeply aware of the limits of his knowledge and foresight about events. On April 4, 1864, he declared, "I claim not to have controlled events, but confess plainly that events have controlled me." The sense of dependence on a higher power was not unique to him. Leaders have sought reassurance through the ages that their acts were in harmony with some divine power. The flights of birds and the entrails of animals gave clues to the divine will.

Even when others were certain of the course of history, Lincoln questioned his own ability to understand or influence God's plan. On November 15, 1861, the renowned historian George Bancroft wrote him, declaring that the "Civil War is the instrument of Divine Providence to root out social slavery; posterity will not be satisfied . . . unless . . . the war shall effect an increase of free states." Lincoln replied in quite guarded language, "The main thought in . . . your letter is one which does not escape my attention, and with which I must deal in all due caution and the best judgment I can bring to it." Lincoln's careful statement about knowing God's will was made even stronger in his response of September 13, 1862, to a group of Chicago ministers who presented an Emancipation Memorial that, they said, was based on God's revelation of his will to them:

> I am approached with the most opposite opinions and advice and that by religious men, who are equally certain that they represent the Divine will. I am sure that either the one or the other class is mistaken in that belief and perhaps in some respects both. I hope it will not be irreverent for me to say that if it is probable that God would reveal his will to others, on a point so connected with my duty, it might be supposed he would reveal it directly to me; for, unless I am more deceived in myself than I often am, it is my earnest desire to know the will of Providence in this matter. *And if I can learn what it is I will do it!* These are not, however, the days of miracles, and I suppose it will be granted that I am not to expect a direct revelation. I must study the plain physical facts of the case, ascertain what is possible and learn what appears to be wise and right.

In his second inaugural address Lincoln portrayed both sides in the Civil War as reading from the same Bible and praying to the same God. As we have seen, he went on to say that "the prayers of both could not be answered; that of neither has been answered fully." He struggled in a private *Meditation on the Divine Will* with the paradox that both sides claimed to be following the will of God and came to this conclusion: "Both may be and one must be wrong. God cannot be *for*, and *against* the same thing at the same time." By far his severest indictment, anticipated in an earlier reference we have made, was directed at those who argued from self-interest that for *some* people it was better to be slaves and that this situation reflected the will of God:

> Certainly there is no contending against the Will of God; but still there is some difficulty in ascertaining and applying it, to particular cases. For instance we will suppose the Rev. Dr. Ross has a slave named Sambo, and the question is "Is it the Will of God that Sambo shall remain a slave, or be set free?" The Almighty gives no audible answer to the question, and his revelation—the Bible—gives none—or, at most, none but such as admits of a squabble, as to its meaning. No one thinks of asking Sambo's opinion on it. So, at last, it comes to this, that Dr. Ross is to decide the question. And while he consider[s] it, he sits in the shade, with gloves on his hands, and subsists on the bread that Sambo is earning in the burning sun. If he decides that God wills Sambo to continue a slave, he thereby retains his own comfortable position; but if he decides that God wills Sambo to be free, he thereby has to walk out of the shade, throw off his gloves, and delve for his own bread. Will Dr. Ross be activated by that perfect impartiality, which has ever been considered most favorable to correct decisions? But slavery is good for some people!!! As a good thing, slavery is strikingly peculiar in this, that it is the only good thing which no man ever seeks the good of, for *himself*.
>
> Nonsense! wolves devouring lambs not because it is good for their own greedy maws, but because it [is] good for the lambs!!!

Whatever Lincoln's skepticism that men were able to know the will of God, he could not believe that God willed either slavery or the destruction of the Union. American slavery was "one of those offences which in the providence of God . . . He now wills to remove." Yet Lincoln also believed that God's will as to the time and place of the ending of slavery was unknown and unknowable. God's purpose might be different from the purposes of either party. If God willed that the war continue "until every drop of blood drawn with the lash, shall be paid by another drawn with the sword . . . the judgments of the Lord are true and righteous altogether." God knows best. With a fatalism about God's purposes that matched his skepticism about knowing God's mind, Lincoln, as the Civil War continued, told the Baltimore Presbyterian Synod that he reposed "reliance in God, knowing . . . that He would decide for the right."

Nevertheless, the fact remains that Lincoln was hesitant about proclaiming his policies represented the will of God. God governs the world by designs that can neither be known nor influenced by man. On October 26, 1862, he wrote to a Quaker lady of his continuing trust in a Providence he could not see at work:

> We are indeed going through a great trial—a fiery trial. In the very responsible position in which I happen to be placed, being a humble instrument in the hands of our Heavenly Father, as I am, and as we all are, to work out his great purposes, I have desired that all my works and acts may be according to his will, and that it might be so, I have sought his aid—but if after endeavoring to do my best in the light which he affords me, I find my efforts fail, I must believe that for some purpose unknown to me, He wills it otherwise. If I had had my way, this war would never have been commenced; If I had been allowed my way this war would have been ended before this, but we find it still continues; and we must believe that He permits it for some wise purpose of his own, mysterious and unknown to us; and though with our limited understandings we may not be able to comprehend it, yet we cannot but believe, that he who made the world still governs it.

Professor Morgenthau summed up his view of Lincoln's religious philosophy: "In one sense man is a forlorn actor on the stage of the world; for he does not know the nature of the plot and the outcome of the play written by an inaccessible author. But he is also a confident and self-sufficient actor; for he knows that there is a script, however unknown and unknowable its content, and he can do no more than act out what he believes the script to require." [1]

Antinomies and Contradictions of Leadership

Leadership is so complex and so difficult to assess and measure because almost any proposal regarding it presents a series of contradictions, tensions,

1. Hans J. Morgenthau and David Hein, *Essays on Lincoln's Faith and Politics* (Washington, D.C., 1983), 4, 6–14, 16.

and antinomies. Any proposition is almost immediately subject to qualification. In thinking about leadership, we discover that for every truth there is a balancing truth; in the application of leadership, we find that for everything there is a season. What seems appropriate and effective in one era is likely to be less effective in another.

One quickly confronts such issues when reflecting on the charismatic leader, the spiritual or political figure who inspires public attention. In the state of Illinois, as we noted earlier, it was said that one of the great misfortunes for Governor Adlai Stevenson, whose powers as a communicator were remarkable, was that in smaller groups the flow went away from rather than toward him the way it does with most charismatic and dynamic leaders. The great mass of the people was not drawn to him. It wasn't that he didn't know as much as or more than other leaders. Rather, he seemed too reserved, too distant, and too much above the crowd. He was more at home in the drawing room than on the hustings. His public relations were too formal and stiff. His demeanor ran counter to the image of a magnetic leader. He was lacking in the one sphere that some would say is essential for leadership, yet intellectually he reminded one of Lincoln.

An opposite perspective is the view that a leader must epitomize the average or common man, even the mediocre in society. Senator Roman Hruska of Nebraska gave voice to this view in defending the nomination of a supreme court justice whose appointment he justified because the man, he thought, was no better than anyone else. He asked the public if it wouldn't be more satisfied with the man in the street who was just like everybody else. Senator Hruska notwithstanding, the ideal of the leader for all seasons is a man of the people who is also a man of profound thought. Carl Schurz praised Lincoln as just such a man: "You are underrating the President. . . . I grant he lacks higher education and his manners are not in accord with European conceptions and the dignity of a chief magistrate. . . . But he is a man of profound feelings, correct and firm principles and incorruptible honesty. His motives are unquestionable and he possesses to a remarkable degree the God-given trait of the American people, sound common sense." Lincoln was in this respect a child of the people, but he was also more than that.

The concept of the charismatic leader is in tension with the notion of the leader as someone close to the people, at least as common as any of them might be. A similar tension exists between the emphasis given to other elements of greatness. Professor Morgenthau asks what constitutes greatness in any man and, more particularly, in a statesman. He quotes Emerson, who wrote that "he is great who is what he is from nature and never reminds us of others." Morgenthau discusses uniqueness in the statesman and goes on to compare it with other forms of uniqueness: Babe Ruth was a great baseball player, John Pierpont Morgan, a great banker, and so forth. These men were great because they pushed one particular human faculty, whether physical prowess, culinary creativity, or acquisition of money, to the outer limits of human potentiality; they developed one human faculty to perfection. However, Morgenthau comments, "this is a limited greatness of a functional nature"; in this case, "a man is called great" only " because he performs a particular function to perfection." There is a difference between a great baseball player or a great chef and a great man. Emerson points to this difference, writing of a great man that he must somehow be related to the rest of us. Such a man brings into our lives some promise of explanation. That is to say, a great man, in contrast to a man performing a particular function greatly, is one who approaches perfection in those qualities of mind, character, and action that illuminate the very nature of man. Not only does he illuminate the nature of man, but he also holds up a mirror to mankind's aspirations. He demonstrates in actual experience how far man can go and hence how much further than he thought possible a man who aspires to be great can go. "Great men," Emerson wrote, "speak to our wants."

In these terms Lincoln appears as a great man, combining within himself a perfection of human potentialities to be found in combination in only a few men known to history. Lincoln's statesmanship is greatness independent of success or failure. The unadorned qualities of his greatness have tended to disappear or at least become indistinct in mythological interpretations, but these are the qualities that Professor Morgenthau's book on Lincoln analyzes. [2]

Effective leadership also involves human relationships in which uniqueness, if it is present at all, must remain credible to those a leader seeks to lead. One of the recurrent topics of discussion in the early years of the civil rights movement was whether the superb United Nations leader Ralph Bunche could also be a leader for African-Americans and an example for young as-

2. *Ibid.*, 3–4.

piring minorities. The question was whether Bunche's life was so remote and beyond the experience of ordinary African-Americans that he provided them no example or leadership; he was so towering a figure that he offered no example for their lives. His image disappeared in the clouds far above them.

The notion of the visible and credible leader is in tension with another notion of leadership, one that takes on different forms and language in discussions and theories. One theory sees the leader as antileader; it is a characteristic of the effective leader that he conceals or downplays the fact he is leading. As an example, we are in the midst today of a revisionist trend of thought and writing about President Dwight D. Eisenhower and the "hidden hand" form of leadership that, according to Professor Fred Greenstein, Eisenhower practiced. He led but concealed his leadership in working through others. When he initiated a program, he said, "I have followed the recommendations of Mr. X on program Y." Another antileader, but one less respected, was President Calvin Coolidge, about whom Alice Roosevelt Longworth said, "the unsmiling Coolidge had been weaned on a pickle." Somebody else observed in the 1920s that the American people wanted nothing done and Cal obliged them completely. And another observed in a more kindly vein that "he had no ideas but he was not a nuisance." This vision of leadership stands in opposition to the image and mystery of dynamic leadership.

Attributes of Leadership

If we undertake to assess the most important attributes of leadership, the same tensions and antinomies are evident. What are the major attributes of leadership in politics? One is the role of the leader as unifier, harmonizer, and coalition builder. The White Burkett Miller Center of Public Affairs at the University of Virginia undertook a review of the presidential nominating process and invited testimony from former presidential candidates and their aides. A common bond in the late 1960s and early 1970s uniting reformers with centrists and conservatives was a consensus that the nominating process virtually guaranteed that a president would come into office lacking a coalition to govern. If experienced elected officials are excluded from the process as well as those with what former congresswoman Edith Green described as "a sense of what is possible and practical," the nation will likely bring to office a leader without the means of governing or of pursuing his policies with support from an effective political coalition. President Jimmy Carter's problems in governing stemmed in large part from the lack of a coalition for governing.

Thus, a president ought to be a leader, a harmonizer, a unifier, and a coalition builder. But what about a situation in which the task is to get the country moving again? What about the need for the president to be an antagonist and catalyst rather than a harmonizer? The person who best illustrates the role of a fighter and antagonist was the old curmudgeon in the Roosevelt administration, Harold Ickes, who continually pushed ideas that found their way into legislation. Who is the Ickes in the Bush administration? How does one resist special interests if one's only task is to harmonize? The two attributes of the leader, as unifier and as protagonist, appear to be in tension.

Further, every text refers to political courage, the ability to make decisions and defend them, as the master virtue in politics. A decision is something different from an opinion. A decision can't be put in a desk drawer and reviewed in a month or a year. Leaders are required to stand up for decisions and make hard choices. How does the quality of decisiveness relate to the need for a normalizer who restores stability and order? Walter Lippmann, with all his preference for the ideas of Adlai Stevenson, nevertheless supported Dwight D. Eisenhower for president because he said Eisenhower would restore to the American scene a sense of normality and stability. Because the public liked Ike, he would renew public confidence and the people's respect for themselves, one another, and their government. Lowering the temperature, slowing the pace in the cyclical movement of politics, either after a war or after a great social leap forward, when the American people have grown weary and fatigued, may be essential. Gerald Ford after Watergate brought peace and tranquillity, and Jimmy Carter paid tribute in his inaugural address to Ford's healing of the nation.

Another attribute of the leader is personal and political judgment. A Charlottesville friend describes her late husband as having had a single dominant virtue, the virtue of judgment. Others were brighter and more handsome or had more money, she explains, but her husband had judgment, and all the people of Charlottesville knew it. The mention of judgment is not too far removed from what political theory teaches about leadership. Because politics puts a high premium on what an Indonesian friend of mine, Soedjatmoko, called sheer blind groping, sound judgment is vital.[3] Decision making is less the search for answers in a handbook and more the instinct for what is wise and right.

In the making of political choices, the process is fundamentally different from the one in which scholars engage in their quest for truth in intellectual, philosophical, and scientific realms. Decision making means allowing facts, events, and trends to wash over you. It is listening for the rustle of events and grasping at the garments of history as they pass. It can mean settling for the less, not the more, harmful alternatives. Judgment is coherence in understanding relationships. The men and women who worked most closely with Truman talked about his decisiveness, as did the journalists, but they also talked about something else that may have been more significant. Intellectuals like Dean Acheson and other graduates of Groton and Yale said he had all the right instincts for political choices. It was his instincts, apart from pure rational deduction, that guided him to the wise and right choice.

Yet if judgment means thinking twice about decisions, the fate of Hamlet offers an opposing lesson. There is risk in the postponing of decisions in order that judgments be improved. There are dangers in allowing history to overwhelm or engulf the decision maker. The antinomy of prudent and measured judgment is the error of waiting too long. The historian Walter Johnson, with all his faith in Adlai Stevenson, nevertheless at the end of his biography on the man comes down hard on Stevenson's Hamlet-like quality. In defense of him, Johnson cites examples of the prison strike in Springfield when Stevenson was decisive and in command. However, Johnson protests too much and is too defensive.[4] Quincy Wright, professor of international law at the University of Chicago and the University of Virginia, never tired of telling a story about General Eisenhower. When Wright was adviser to Justice Robert Jackson at the Nuremberg trial, he needed funds for a certain effort. He went to Eisenhower and told him they couldn't go on with the consulting they were doing without money. Wright expected that this request would lead to a long and protracted bureaucratic procedure, but Eisenhower picked up the phone

3. Soedjatmoko was president of the United Nations University, and his writings and speeches were regularly published in the university's publications.

4. Walter Johnson, *How We Drafted Adlai Stevenson* (New York, 1955).

and explained to a subordinate that Wright and his colleagues needed funds immediately for their work. As Wright walked out the door, somebody handed him an envelope containing the money.

Thus, tensions exist between competing tendencies and forces and the leaders struggling to reconcile them. President Reagan often talked about simplifying. He observed a tendency among intellectuals and those who write about policy needlessly to complicate problems that in their essentials are simple. To the extent he succeeded, this quality of simplification may have been his foremost strength—the strength undergirding his skills in communication. However, in simplification there can often be a taint of anti-intellectualism, which in a democracy has unquestioned appeal. It was James Fallows who complained that President Carter was endlessly disposed to write every speech for the service station operator. This approach to politics throws the notion of simplifying into question. The trivialization and falsification of reality in politics can be the product of too much simplification. Television coverage based on fifteen- or thirty-second sound bites supposedly encapsulating the truth may leave the listener as ignorant as he was before viewing the thirty-second capsule.

Another attribute of leadership involves conveying hope. Whatever anyone said in disparagement of President Reagan, he gave people hope. One reason he came into office, we are told, was because in contrast with Jimmy Carter he promised a bright future. But his attitude poses problems as well. What about the Pollyannaish depiction of reality when in fact reality almost always involves an element of sacrifice and tragedy? Doesn't false hope carry the seeds of disillusionment and despair? Don't the most urgent problems require sacrifice? Have we mortgaged our children's future with the national debt? In the long run, the Norman Vincent Peales of politics may destroy lasting hope, yet the literature of politics criticizes politicians, including Carter, who offer too little hope.

There are other attributes of politics, one being detachment, that are the subject of almost every treatise on leadership. John F. Kennedy possessed a sense of detachment and a self-mocking personal style. He seemed free of all emotional involvement as he moved in and out of the cabinet room in times of crisis. Lincoln had the capacity, even in the midst of a Civil War, to view the conflict as though he were looking at it from the enemy's battle line without ever ignoring the view from his own battle line. He had the same objectivity and detachment with regard to himself and his personal appearance. He had it when he came to Washington, D.C., after his election and was serenaded. He responded to the serenaders with candor and self-irony: "I suppose I may take this as a compliment paid to me and as such please accept my thanks for it. I have reached the city of Washington under circumstances considerably differing from those under which any other man has reached it. I have reached it for the purpose of taking an official position amongst the people almost all of whom were opposed to me and are as yet opposed to me, as I suppose." Imagine any other man in this position: he has just been elected president in the face of a threatening rebellion on behalf of slavery and is coming into the District of Columbia, where slavery is legal, and finds himself serenaded by the supporters of slavery. Lincoln didn't try to gloss over the situation. He didn't offer any concessions, nor did he ask for any from his audience. On the contrary, by defining the situation in all its stark reality, he emphasized its absurdity. He looked at himself, at the crowd, and at their mutual relations and not only recognized but also articulated his extraordinary position with objectivity, saying, "I am alone; you are against me."

Or consider that the Civil War had saddled him with the crushing burden of enormous bloodletting and with long drawn out conflict, overwhelming the nation with its many international and domestic repercussions. Its course was in good measure the result of the incompetence of some of his own leaders, including the generals. On July 1, Lincoln called for 300,000 volunteers for the army, using a phrase it is difficult for us to imagine a present-day leader employing: "So as to bring this unnecessary and injurious civil war to a speedy and satisfactory conclusion."[5] Any president today fighting a war widely regarded to be unnecessary and injurious would take a different tack in calling for volunteers to fight it. Would he not rather appeal to the people to fight a necessary and beneficial, if not holy, war in order to obtain the maximum effective response? Lincoln also blended sympathy with detachment toward military deserters when he struggled with himself and with the law in trying to arrive at an approximation of justice.

If detachment is a quality of leadership, what about enthusiasm for a cause? What about the need for passion, for conviction, and for taking a stand that inspires a public response? Is there not an inherent tension between the

5. Morgenthau and Hein, *Essays on Lincoln's Faith and Politics,* 19–20.

two qualities, both of which may be essential to success in politics? Perhaps a fourfold approach to political life is needed. In his observing and judging a political situation, what is required of the statesman is that he see clearly first, the interests of his group or his country and himself, then the situation of his rival, then the rival's situation as his rival sees it, and then his own situation as the rival sees him. To see clearly means to see without passion—without the passion of pride, of hatred, and of contempt. The statesman must somehow master the paradox of wanting passionately to triumph over an enemy, of seeking to dominate that enemy to whom he feels passionately superior, while at the same time having to view his relations with that enemy with the sense of detachment and objectivity that only a few leaders attain.

As we turn to four American presidents of the postwar years, the principles set forth in this chapter may guide us in evaluating their leadership and the contradictions and conflicts of values they faced. If Lincoln, whom many consider our greatest president, faced such conflicts of values, is it any wonder that contemporary presidents are also obliged to grapple with them in the choices they make?

18

Dwight D. Eisenhower:
Military Victory Versus Political Power

In *Crusade in Europe,* General Dwight D. Eisenhower in discussing American differences with Winston Churchill wrote, "The future division of Europe did not influence our military plans for the final conquest of the country." Churchill had argued that it would have been wiser for the British armies to take Berlin and for the U.S. armies to enter Prague, as he insisted they could have done. Eisenhower maintained that Berlin, while psychologically important, was not the logical or the most desirable objective for Allied forces. He pointed out that Churchill "held that because the campaign was now approaching its end, troop maneuvers had acquired a political significance that demanded the intervention of political leaders in the development of broad operational plans." [1] Although he understood the British leader's perspective, neither he nor political leaders in the Roosevelt administration were persuaded by Churchill's thinking.

Churchill had favored a secondary invasion in the Balkans. The determining factor in his strategy was his conviction that the Germans, if pressed hard enough in the Balkans and the Mediterranean, would have to divert forces from western Europe. He also believed that a demarcation line that would allow the western sphere to extend further east would diminish the temptation for the Soviet Union to expand to fill a vacuum in central Europe. Reflecting on the debate over Balkan strategy, Churchill wrote that it constituted "the most acute difference [he] ever had with General Eisenhower." [2] Their difference stemmed in part from their respective strategic views, as Eisenhower explained:

I felt that the Prime Minister's real concern was possibly of a political rather than a military nature. He may have thought that a post war situa-

1. Dwight D. Eisenhower, *Crusade in Europe* (Garden City, N.Y., 1948), 396, 399.
2. Winston S. Churchill, *Closing the Ring* (Boston, 1951), 218, Vol. V of Churchill, *The Second World War,* 6 vols.

tion which would see the Western Allies posted in great strength in the Balkans would be far more effective in producing a stable post-hostilities world than if the Russian armies should be the ones to occupy that region. . . . I well understood that strategy can be affected by political considerations. . . . But I did insist that as long as he argued the matter on military grounds alone I could not concede validity to his arguments.[3]

Their differences may also provide a clue to the strengths and weaknesses, successes and failures of President Eisenhower in the realm of foreign policy. Historians of social thought have put forward the concept of "professional deformation" in order to help explain causes of action. Everyone is in part the product of educational, social, and professional formation, but everyone also has areas in which he is limited, or "deformed." Former secretary of state Henry Kissinger in an informal discussion touched on this point when he spoke of his own deficiencies in the realm of economics. He recounted that as secretary of state he had the most qualified advisers brief him on issues concerning the balance of payments, economic development, and the International Monetary Fund. He learned his lines and because of the prestige of his office and his considerable intellectual powers, he spoke them with unquestioned authority. However, in a moment of candor Kissinger acknowledged that he never fully grasped the stuff of economics as he did the truths of international politics. He went on to say that an American leader for whom he had great respect and whom he had once described as the American he would trust most with the powers of the presidency, Secretary of State George Shultz, displayed similar limitations in the sphere of diplomacy and international politics. He could not remember a single conversation with Shultz on diplomacy in which that highly respected economist had clearly demonstrated a primary concern or commanding grasp of the realities of world politics. Adding to these examples, we might draw from the long list of public figures who were at home in domestic politics but found international politics incomprehensible. For example, William Jennings Bryan as secretary of state under President Wilson was so frustrated and dismayed by the demands of the daily relations among nation-states that he devoted himself almost entirely to the promotion of the arbitration movement, leaving the management of foreign

3. Eisenhower, *Crusade in Europe*, 283–84.

policy to others. It would be surprising if the same limiting force was not at work for President Eisenhower.

In any event, it is worth exploring the thesis that the glory and misery, the triumphs and tragedies, of the Eisenhower presidency in foreign policy are in part attributable to the fact that understanding the harsh imperatives and recurrent truths of world politics was merely one among several guideposts for his thought. Without such an informing thesis, one cannot escape a sense of puzzlement when studying the annals of his presidency. It remains a mystery, for instance, why Eisenhower should have expressed himself with such fervor on the need to bring the arms race under control and yet seem oblivious to the consequences of actions that served the status quo but conflicted with the search for accommodation. In short, anyone who undertakes an appraisal must find some explanation for the priorities that guided choices in practice and yet appear calculated to move away from rather than toward his objective of relaxation of tensions. In a word, the political criterion to which theorists and practitioners of world politics have assigned highest priority was for Eisenhower not the governing principle of statecraft. Because of his essential integrity and past experiences, he had caught a glimpse of its importance, but it was not for him a controlling principle of action to inform and inspire all others.

On foreign policy, two authors and former colleagues of Eisenhower's, Arthur Larson and William Ewald, put stress on Eisenhower's sense of the nation's limits and his understanding of restraint and the need for international cooperation. When asked why he didn't intervene militarily in Indochina, he replied, "Nobody asked us." He recognized the importance of damage limitation, as when he sought to reestablish an immediate dialogue with the British and French after he had opposed their joint attack with Israel on Egypt. He had learned the lessons of cooperation among the Allies in World War II too well to ignore its necessity in the Cold War. More than the secretary of state, he was prepared to restore relationships among friends even when he found their actions unacceptable.

Above all, as his brother Milton explains with much eloquence, he understood that possibilities of conflict in the nuclear age were too dangerous to allow a continuing deterioration in Soviet-American relations. He wanted to focus on the necessity for trade with the Soviets in his last speech in the 1952 campaign but was overruled by party strategists. He responded enthusiastically to suggestions by liberals like Emmett Hughes for a massive program of Soviet-American cultural exchange, only to find that Secretary Dulles and State Department officials considered the plan utopian and unworkable. He invited Khrushchev to visit the United States and demonstrated his willingness to meet the Soviet leader at the summit conference table. Historians continue to debate whether his approach might have changed the course of history in the Cold War if the Paris summit had not been aborted by the shooting down and capture of Francis Gary Powers in the untimely U-2 spy plane incident. (One intimate tells the story of Ike making one last-ditch attempt to communicate with Khrushchev at Geneva, only to discover the Soviet leader had departed his conference headquarters minutes before the president walked down the hall to the Soviet delegation.) Perhaps it was Senators Walter George and Richard Russell of Georgia who influenced the president, or maybe some of Churchill's fervor for talks at the highest level had rubbed off on the president. Whatever his motivation, and some of his thought processes may be mirrored in his brother's account of the possibility of reaching an accommodation with the Soviet leader, Ike was among a handful of western chiefs-of-state who believed with Churchill that "jaw-jaw is better than war-war."

One other strength of the president has not been mentioned, and for the future of the human race it may be the most important. As few Western leaders, Eisenhower understood the devastation of war. More than most, and certainly more than latter-day civilian leaders, he took hold of the realities of nuclear war and sought to educate the public on the differences between it and conventional warfare. Thermonuclear destruction for him would be fundamentally unlike any larger-scale traditional war. He sought to check the unrealism of military and civilian leaders who spoke of "prevailing" in a nuclear war. Whatever the limitations of his own knowledge, he drew on the greater scientific authority of world-class scientists such as James R. Killian, Jr., and George B. Kistiakowsky. It was not in his makeup simply to look to scientists who happened to espouse his own viewpoint. Thus, he could hold the Pentagon in check for not only did he have as much or more military experience than they had but he knew where to turn for authoritative scientific estimates. In the words of one associate, Eisenhower knew where the bodies were buried in the Pentagon and how the dynamics of the military procurement process worked. In his much-quoted farewell, he warned of the hazards of the military-industrial complex.

If all that has been said of Eisenhower's strengths is true, the question of how we are to account for his limited successes and some of his failures remains. The most commonplace answer is to point to the intractability of the problems with which he had to grapple. No postwar leader successfully resolved the stubborn problems of the Cold War; their amelioration may have exceeded human resources. How could we expect Eisenhower to succeed where others failed?

One explanation of his administration's unsolved problems is the nature of foreign policy-making in a democracy. From Hamilton to Tocqueville to Lippmann, Morgenthau, and Kennan, informed observers have laid stress on the stubborn realities confronting those who seek to reconcile the demands of domestic politics with the imperatives of foreign policy. What early observers recognized as a troublesome obstacle to wise foreign policy had in the Cold War taken on the dimensions of an irreconcilable conflict. The two adversaries in the postwar world confronted one another not only as superpowers but as the carriers of political ideologies that were in competition for the faith of mankind throughout the world. In the Soviet Union, the government defended itself against internal opposition by depicting any external threat as requiring the perpetuation of a totalitarian regime. In the United States, the specter of crusading world communism introduced the spirit of counter-crusades into domestic politics. For a relatively moderate and reasonable president like Eisenhower, the context of domestic politics was less supportive than for more extreme spokesmen on the right or the left. For this reason, President Eisenhower discovered that moderate Democrats rallied to his side more often than right-wing Republicans. Secretary of State Dulles had vowed that he would not fall victim to critics on his political flanks like those who had destroyed the credibility of Dean Acheson, his predecessor. It is difficult to explain some of President Eisenhower's rhetoric without reference to the play of domestic politics on policy makers. A China policy that took account of the possibility of a Sino-Soviet split in the wake of the Korean War clashed with the forces of domestic politics in the 1950s, whether real or imagined. So did the possibility of a policy of rapprochement between East and West Germany in the face of the demand for a united Europe, including West Germany as a means of upholding the status quo against Soviet expansionism.

A second explanation that some historians have advanced is the thesis that whatever the strengths of Eisenhower's pattern of leadership domestically (as with his strategy vis-à-vis Senator Joseph McCarthy in not lending credibility to his name through confronting him publicly), his failure to formulate foreign policy in clear and unequivocal terms was a weakness. Political scientists have noted that presidents whose only preparation for the presidency is service in the U.S. Senate also suffer from this weakness. They tend to look for compromises and lowest common denominators in policy. They are prone to avoid taking positions until they sense where the public and the Senate are moving. They are always seeking deals and trade-offs. In a curious way, President Eisenhower's practice of leading without staking out a clear public position resembles the pattern of leadership of those who come to the presidency with only legislative experience. The tactic of political evasion, which is sometimes a virtue in domestic politics, is a source of weakness for a president who would exercise world leadership. Those who would negotiate policy are more likely than not to sound an uncertain trumpet.

A third explanation rests on the proposition that Eisenhower had an excessive faith in professionalism. The debate continues to this day whether he or Dulles was the dominant figure in determining foreign policy. Where important military and strategic questions were involved, as in the debate over U.S. intervention in Indochina, Eisenhower's views seem to have prevailed. But the president yielded to Dulles on other questions, for example, Soviet-American cultural exchange and the proposed visits by British and French leaders to Washington, D.C., to patch up a family feud following the debacle of the intervention in Suez. A more telling example may be Eisenhower's embracing of the political warfare campaign launched by C. D. Jackson and Radio Free Europe. The contrast between the cautious and prudent general and president and the flamboyant figure from *Time* and *Life* magazines could not be more striking. Who could imagine the former unleashing 11,000 balloons and 14,000,000 leaflets over Poland and Czechoslovakia to "boost the morale of the entire non-Communist population" and to fortify "spiritual resistance" until "the day of liberation" arrived. Yet Eisenhower thanked Henry Luce for the sanity the redoubtable publicist brought to his task.

Having reviewed the three possible explanations for Eisenhower's limitations in foreign policy, we return to the proposition and thesis with which we began. We ask ourselves how was it that so experienced a leader as Eisenhower could have imagined that his Atoms for Peace or Open Skies policies could bring about arms control, given the reality of the impenetrability of sovereign states, especially the Soviet Union? How could he think that simultaneously he could negotiate a political settlement with the Soviet Union based on the status quo and pursue a foreign policy of liberation? How did he reconcile in his mind the call for "massive retaliation" with his solemn warning about the "military-industrial complex"? What were the connections between his respect for the might of the Red Army and his scaling down of appropriations for the U.S. Army and half of the U.S. Navy?

The answer may lie in a certain flawed concept of the nature of international politics. Students of foreign policy today do not turn to Eisenhower for clear and coherent definitions of interest and power as they do to statesmen like Churchill. The conceptual framework within which Eisenhower thought about world politics was that of a vague, if inspiring, internationalism. He believed that the United States should lead the world, but he was never quite clear how and where. He was stronger in formulating broad, if sometimes rigid and unchanging, ends than in relating means to ends. In any debate over diplomatic strategy with Dulles, he had difficulty standing his ground. In approving Dulles' foreign policy of liberation or Jackson's political and psychological warfare, he appeared not to weigh or understand the consequences. He had dealt with national leaders throughout much of his career, yet he was strangely oblivious to the constraints imposed by national sovereignty. He understood the principle of doing what "was right for America," as General Andrew Goodpaster explains in *The Eisenhower Presidency,* but was somehow unprepared for the advantages the Soviet Union gained in the Middle East when the United States turned against its allies in the Suez crisis.[4] He acted skillfully and decisively in sending 14,000 marines into Lebanon in July of 1958 and withdrawing them in October, illustrating the dual principle Arthur Larson ascribes to him: Seek never to use force, but when you must use it, employ overwhelming force. However, he seemed less understanding of the cultural, ethnic, and sectarian divisions in Lebanon which confounded the formation of a stable national government. He was able to contrive ways in

4. Kenneth W. Thompson, ed., *The Eisenhower Presidency: Eleven Intimate Perspectives of Dwight D. Eisenhower* (Lanham, Md., 1984).

World War II to bring quarreling leaders together, but he failed to bridge the deep chasm separating East and West.

To reflect on President Eisenhower's strengths and weaknesses is in no way to detract from the quality of his leadership. A recital of his limitations leads only to a broader question. If a president with the strengths of Dwight D. Eisenhower was found wanting in some sectors at least of Cold War leadership, what will be the fate of the United States and the world in the hands of far more mediocre leaders? If he lacked the intellectual and political resources to cope with the manifold dimensions of world diplomacy, where are we to look for hope when lesser men are in the White House? It should be obvious that no more sobering question can be posed as mankind confronts the issue of human survival.

19

John F. Kennedy's Foreign Policy:
Activism Versus Pragmatism

Historians point to a tension lying at the heart of the foreign policy problems of nearly every administration, a contradiction often between two seemingly irreconcilable principles. Ultimately, such tensions imperil the success of strong presidencies and turn history's judgment against them. For Woodrow Wilson, national self-determination conflicted with the Wilsonian vision of a wider community of nation-states. Franklin D. Roosevelt failed to reconcile the goal of getting along with the Russians with an effective international security system capable of preserving the status quo. The Reagan administration failed early on to balance the largest peacetime defense buildup in the history of the United States with an effective negotiating posture in seeking some wider political settlement. Nor was the Kennedy presidency immune from the crippling effects of a basic contradiction. From its beginnings, it suffered from its own internal tensions. For the young, charismatic leader, that tension was inherent in the clash between activism and pragmatism, and nowhere was the tension greater than in foreign policy.

Kennedy's Activism

The sources of Kennedy's activism were both philosophical and personal. Philosophically, he proclaimed his activism in his inaugural address. We have it on the authority of his special counsel, Theodore C. Sorensen, that "the principal architect of the Inaugural Address was John Fitzgerald Kennedy." [1] Yet we also know that drafts for the address were solicited from strong activists such as John Kenneth Galbraith and Chester Bowles. How are we to disentangle their strains of activism from Kennedy's? Who can say that Ken-

1. Theodore C. Sorensen, *Kennedy* (New York, 1956), 241.

nedy's biographer and master draftsman may not have added to the young president's activism? Whatever the caveats to the thesis that Kennedy set the tone of the inaugural, no one can doubt that some of the activist strains were his own.

If we accept the proposition, then, that the inaugural address faithfully reflected Kennedy's intention, we see its language mirrors an imagination that was unqualifiedly activist and universalist. Who can believe that Franklin D. Roosevelt would ever have promised, "Let every nation know . . . that we shall pay any price, bear any burden, meet any hardship, support any friend, oppose any foe to assure the survival and the success of liberty"? Against what Kennedy calls the four horsemen of an imminent apocalypse—tyranny, poverty, disease, and war—"a grand and global alliance, North and South, East and West" was to be forged to "assure a more fruitful life for all mankind." The thirty-fifth president proclaimed: "In the long history of the world, only a few generations have been granted the role of defending freedom in its hour of maximum danger. I do not shrink from this responsibility. I welcome it." If we search the inaugural addresses of American presidents, we will find few that rest on a more activist philosophy.

Another Kennedy biographer, Arthur M. Schlesinger, Jr., helps us understand the roots of Kennedy's personal activism. Professor Schlesinger explains:

> Another of his qualities, in addition to intelligence and flexibility, was a tendency toward activism. You'd tell him about something, and he would listen carefully and then say, "O.K., but what do you want me to do about it?" The relationship between information and remedy was in his mind close and urgent. This was partly produced by his temperamental optimism. He really believed that with goodwill and reason . . . you could surmount, if not solve, a lot of the problems that were assailing us. . . . There was an insistent search for a remedy and an insistent pressure to do something about problems.[2]

Kennedy returned from World War II and covered the United Nation's conference in San Francisco as a Hearst reporter. However, his activist in-

2. Arthur M. Schlesinger, Jr., "A Biographer's Perspective," in *The Kennedy Presidency*, ed. Kenneth W. Thompson (Lanham, Md., 1985), 21.

stincts were not satisfied by observing and reporting. He explained what he really wanted to do: "I've loved the newspaper business but the fact is you get a feeling of frustration because you write about these things and you are really not doing much about it. I figure if I get into politics I might get a chance to do something about the system. I really would like to weigh in a little heavier." [3] He was elected to the House but was a somewhat indifferent member, introducing no more than four or five bills the entire time he was there. He changed to some degree in the Senate but more dramatically in the 1960 presidential campaign.

One consequence of Kennedy's activism was his tendency to keep too tight a grip on his administration and to get involved too early in decisions. Tommy ("the Cork") Corcoran and Benjamin Cohen compared Kennedy's activist style with Franklin D. Roosevelt's. Corcoran and Cohen believed Roosevelt reserved to himself final authority on political choices without being drawn in prematurely. Roosevelt did not involve himself in details. He chose to allow officials with competing and sometimes overlapping responsibilities to debate alternative ideas and policies. He avoided committing himself too early in the process. In contrast, Kennedy reached deep into the bureaucracy, as in his telephone calls to deputy and assistant secretaries in the State Department. He adopted a hands-on policy toward the bureaucracy and dealt directly with his subordinates. He made his presence felt throughout the executive branch, something that some of his successors, including Jimmy Carter, failed to do. He acted to make the permanent government more responsive to presidential government. He sought to translate a core idea of political scientists such as Richard Neustadt into a way of breaking through the encrustations of bureaucracy that he had criticized in the Eisenhower administration.

Yet if Schlesinger, Neustadt, and others were Kennedy's mentors in avoiding stagnation and penetrating the bureaucracy to lead, they became his critics when he chose to follow them too literally. One could not find a criticism to match in comprehensiveness Professor Schlesinger's trenchant analysis:

> The besetting sin of the New Frontier as I look back was the addiction of
> activism. I think in retrospect that there is much more to be said for the

3. Charles Bartlett, "Portrait of a Friend," in *The Kennedy Presidency*, ed. Thompson, 3.

policy of leaving things alone. The notion that every problem demands an instant remedy can get you into a lot of trouble. It is especially dangerous in foreign policy. I now think that the commitment on the part of professional diplomats to restraint, slowness, and caution probably had more wisdom than we understood at the time. A certain amount of activism was necessary to awaken the State Department from the stagnation of the Dulles years, but I think that the tendency to move in, for example, to the internal affairs of countries, to press our ideas of reform, created problems—unless handled with great tact, as indeed ambassadors like Galbraith in India, Reischauer in Japan, and Murat Williams in El Salvador did. In retrospect I place a higher value on the State Department.

Yet Kennedy's activism, as Schlesinger goes on to argue, was a product not only of his personal style but also of a historical era. The senior Schlesinger had called attention, in an article in 1939 in the *Yale Review*, to the cyclical fluctuations of politics. The ebb and flow of American history lend credence to the cyclical theory. The first two decades of the twentieth century were years of action, passion, and reform. They were the eras of Theodore Roosevelt and Woodrow Wilson. By the 1920s, a weary nation sought to consolidate its gains and rest on its oars. In 1933, Franklin D. Roosevelt and, after him, Harry S Truman gave expression to the nation's idealism in a new era of activism. For Kennedy scholars, Dwight D. Eisenhower represents the return to an era of normalization, which Kennedy undertook to supplant by "getting the nation moving again." However rough and ready the senior Schlesinger's cyclical theory may be, it points to identifiable movements in political history. In identifying the elements that make up Kennedy's activism, he sheds light on the activism of the 1960s, which provided the historical context for the young president's personal activism. "Getting America moving again," the younger Schlesinger observes, "meant in part an intellectual breakaway from a stagnation and complacency, as it seemed to us, of the Eisenhower years."[4] Two decades later, Professor Fred Greenstein, who had supported Adlai Stevenson in 1952 and 1956 against Eisenhower, was to propose that partisan criticism of Eisenhower had been overdrawn.

If the historical climate and Kennedy's personal drives and instincts help

4. Schlesinger, "A Biographer's Perspective," in *The Kennedy Presidency*, ed. Thompson, 25, 26.

to explain his activism, his followers reinforced these tendencies. They were a self-assured, if not arrogant, lot, some drawn from politics and others from journalism, with more than a sprinkling of activists from universities such as Harvard, the Massachusetts Institute of Technology (MIT), and Columbia. Some had campaigned against Eisenhower's style and policies; others had waited in the wings, not always in serene silence. More than a few were responsible for the image of Eisenhower as a "do-nothing president." Some personified the gung-ho attitude that came to be associated with the Kennedys and the active life. A friend of the Kennedys, Senator George McGovern, analyzed the role of this group: "I think they did push him on but I think they thought they were pleasing him. He set the tone and then the [activist] tough-guy mentality was something that was easy for others to manifest. . . . I remember in those early months of the Kennedy administration that it was considered quite *chic* if you were reading Mao's books on guerrilla warfare and studying the writings of Che Guevara. If you were going to be a tough-minded intellectual you had to know how to win battles." Nor was this atti-tude, as it attached to Kennedy associates, limited to counterinsurgency. It manifested itself in the vitalism of the Peace Corps, of poverty programs, of tax reform in Latin America, and with civil rights once Kennedy saw race relations as a moral issue.

Kennedy's Pragmatism

Kennedy's activism was only half the story. His advice to George McGovern when the latter was considering a second run for the Senate in 1962 provides a clue to his underlying pragmatism: "Well, if you can win, do it. If you can't win, the hell with it. Don't go out there just to be brave. If you can win, fine. But unless you are pretty sure that you are going to make it, I wouldn't attempt it again." Pragmatism involves viewing what is desirable in the light of what is possible.

Not only Senator McGovern but others close to Kennedy have written of "his capacity to stand back and look at a campaign or look at issues . . . detached from the kind of emotion that characterized other politicians." In particular, they have remarked on his style: "It wasn't that he was free of emotion but . . . [he] was a rather cool-headed, detached man who was capable of laughing at himself." McGovern spoke of "a very graceful style of operation, just the way he moved and the way he handled people" but observed that "it wasn't particularly warm and ingratiating." Burke Marshall noted Kennedy's extraordinary ability to persuade "partly by charm but mostly by . . . appealing to other people's reasoning" viewed against a background of their own interests. His was an "extraordinary detachment about problems that were just awful," but "from his personal and political point of view, he always seemed to have detachment . . . and that extraordinary composure." Marshall concluded: "I never saw him angry; I never saw him upset no matter what was going on. . . . I've heard him express exasperation, but the exasperation was at other people's passion overcoming their sense of reason." [5]

By contrast, C. Douglas Dillon dismissed the theory that Kennedy was too activist in foreign policy: "I think he was quite pragmatic and quite balanced and I don't think he would do either too much or too little." [6] According to Dillon, any failures in Kennedy's foreign policy can be attributed to inexperience, as with the debacle of the Bay of Pigs invasion. Also Dillon held Richard Neustadt responsible for leading Kennedy to think that he had to make the presidency a stronger office than Eisenhower had done, and this reinforcement led to the weakening and even the dismantling of some of the bureaucratic machinery that might have institutionalized pragmatism. Dillon's opposite number, the chairman of the Council of Economic Advisers, the late Walter H. Heller, was even more explicit. He maintained the president's practicality, particularly in economic matters: "Kennedy was a pragmatist. Kennedy's Yale speech revealed his feeling that we were getting to the point where most of the questions of economics were technical. . . . In it he said that we had reached the point where a lot of the great philosophical debates had been resolved; now we had to learn to push away those shibboleths blocking policy,

5. George McGovern, "A Senator's View," in *The Kennedy Presidency*, ed. Thompson, 44–45; Burke Marshall, "Congress, Communications and Civil Rights," in *The Kennedy Presidency*, ed. Thompson, 75–79.

6. C. Douglas Dillon, "The Kennedy Presidency: The Economic Dimension," in *The Kennedy Presidency*, ed. Thompson, 143–44.

such as worries about deficits, public debt, and rigid budget balance, and attack the problems themselves."

His approach to policy issues involving basic values resembled in part what philosophers call practical morality. He understood the need to balance conflicting values. He had been elected on a platform that emphasized the need for sacrifice by all Americans while recognizing the need for tax cuts. He told Heller: "I can't come in on a platform of sacrifice and the very first thing hand out tax cuts to people. That just won't wash." He was deeply concerned, especially after campaigning in West Virginia, with the plight of the poor and the unemployed. At the same time, he was politically bound by the balanced budget concept, saying: "Nixon will slaughter us if we go the expenditure route." He said he wished he had Eisenhower's ability to run big deficits without damaging his image as a budget balancer. Summing up, Professor Heller concludes of Kennedy: "He thought instrumentally about economic questions: How would the economic advice that we were giving him and the economic measures that we were recommending serve as instruments for his broader ends?" [7]

Some observers link pragmatism with an underlying sense of history or a strong political or religious faith. Former secretary of agriculture Orville Freeman told the story of the Cabinet's being called to the Rose Garden to review the action proposed by the working committee on the Cuban missile crisis. President Kennedy came through the French doors of the cabinet room accompanied by an African head of state, introduced him to every Cabinet member, and then escorted the visitor to his limousine. Freeman reported of the president: "You would think it was the Ides of March. He was just that relaxed and cool. There was no sense of tension or weariness. Instead, he exuded complete self-control." Kennedy returned to the cabinet room, not a hair ruffled on his head, and presided over the making of the final decision on the missiles. Freeman believed that "that kind of detachment" grew out of the president's having "a sense of acting in history." [8]

Kennedy's pragmatism and caution are also associated by some with the

7. Walter H. Heller, "John F. Kennedy and the Economy," in *The Kennedy Presidency*, ed. Thompson, 153–54, 150.

8. Orville Freeman, "A Cabinet Perspective," in *The Kennedy Presidency*, ed. Thompson, 174.

limits of his electoral mandate. Dean Rusk remembered Kennedy remained aware that he had been elected by only a few tens of thousands of votes: "He was very cautious about selecting the items on which he was prepared to do battle, particularly with the Congress. He was much more cautious than many people think, given his other attributes." Kennedy's caution may also have reflected his awareness, as he put it, that domestic questions can only lose elections but foreign policy questions can kill us.

Secretary Rusk also remembered an effort by Kennedy planners early in the administration to prepare a manual of general principles of national security policies that the president and secretary were to endorse. Rusk recalled the outcome: "When they got through with it neither President Kennedy nor I would approve it as a matter of official policy because we couldn't tell what we were approving. If you talk about policies too generally, it doesn't give you any guidance as to what you have to do tomorrow morning at 9:00. By approving general statements, you may trick yourself into thinking you have a policy when you don't." One way of defining a pragmatic approach to foreign policy is to conclude with Rusk that "some of these generalizations simply aren't guidelines of policy."[9] Since the generalizations provide so little guidance, policy makers have no choice but to proceed case by case, problem by problem, or pragmatically.

The pragmatism in Kennedy stemmed from his political nature. Charles Bartlett wrote: "Kennedy was very temperate and he was not a boiling liberal by any standpoint. I always regarded him as a sort of middle-of-the-road person. He could have been a progressive Cooper-type [former senator John Sherman Cooper] Republican just as easily as a Democrat. There was no bitterness or passion in him of a partisan nature." At least, this characterization was true before he launched his campaign in 1960. After 1960, he became something more than a diffident, intellectual politician talking intelligently and forcefully about foreign policy. His speeches became more passionate and this change helped pave the way to the presidency, but so did the remarkable practical judgment he showed in picking the key leaders for his campaign in various states. His pragmatism extended to the matter of appearance and dress. In leaving Massachusetts for the Wisconsin primary,

9. Dean Rusk, "Reflections on Foreign Policy," in *The Kennedy Presidency,* ed. Thompson, 190, 200, 201.

he asked Bartlett which overcoat he should wear, and when the latter suggested that the tweed one looked more like Wisconsin, he replied: "Now you see you are wrong. I've got to take the black one because that's the coat I always wear and the most important thing when you are in one of these things is always to be yourself."

Friends observed another practical gift, "an ability to discern quickly what people had to say that would be important to what he was trying to do." [10] He shunned conversations with people about things on which they knew very little. He always tried to find a person's area of expertise and to channel conversations in that direction. He sensed what others might know that might be useful to him. What Walter Heller said about Kennedy's use of economics could also be said about his approach to life and politics.

Arthur Schlesinger noted that "by temperament the Kennedys were not planners; they were improvisers." Kennedy, like Roosevelt, was determined not to become the prisoner of any official department or information system. He chose to work with a small staff and senior people had direct access to him. Schlesinger made this observation in comparing Kennedy's staff with the staffs of his successors:

> The Kennedy senior staff and the Johnson staff were about a third the size of the Nixon staff and the post-Nixon staffs. Arthur Link argues that there is a relationship between the size of the presidential staff and the President's personal sense of security. An insecure President like Nixon obviously wanted a praetorian guard to shield him from people he didn't like. On the other hand, Ford and Reagan both seem reasonably secure men, and they also liked large White House staffs. So I don't know to what extent the relationships between insecurity and large White House staffs can be maintained. [11]

What can be maintained is that the pragmatist in politics is likely to feel some measure of security not from the size of his staff but about his skills in the political arts, if for no other reason than that he is experienced in their use.

Perhaps Theodore Sorensen defined Kennedy's pragmatism best when

10. Bartlett, "Portrait of a Friend," in *The Kennedy Presidency,* ed. Thompson, 7, 9.

11. Schlesinger, "A Biographer's Perspective," in *The Kennedy Presidency,* ed. Thompson, 22.

he spoke of the fact that Kennedy had no grand design. He did not take office saying, "This is what I am going to do in years one, two, three and four and this is where the world will be at the end of those four years." Instead, Sorensen said, "he felt . . . that it was his responsibility to exercise the powers of the office to the fullest, to tackle each problem that arose (most of which could not be predicted in advance) with all of the vigor and skill at his command to advance the national interest."

Activism Versus Pragmatism in Foreign Policy

President Kennedy's vitality and his intellectual powers early expressed themselves in foreign policy. In the first months of his presidency he sponsored the Alliance for Progress, recast a policy to contain Fidel Castro, lobbied with African leaders, established the Peace Corps, proposed a summit conference with Khrushchev, and put forward a new test ban treaty proposal. So absorbing was his concern for Laos that he was described as taking on the functions of a "desk officer" for the ambassador in that country. He entered into personal correspondence with the leaders of other nations and spoke of the creation of a "democratic club" for Latin American leaders. He met personally with twenty-nine African leaders in less than three years. At a meeting in Toronto, he sought to induce the Canadian government to join the Organization of American States (OAS) and to give more assistance to India. He sought to speak to foreign peoples over the heads of their leaders and to all mankind. He helped develop a neutralist solution to the civil war in Laos. He offered Charles de Gaulle American assistance when his generals threatened mutiny. He urged restraint on President Habib Bourguiba of Tunisia after the bloody French assault on Bizerte. He convinced Secretary-General U Thant to continue the United Nations police action in the Congo despite the secretary-general's doubts. He played the central role in resolving the Berlin crisis and the Cuban missile crisis. He saw himself as a representative of all mankind and of generations yet unborn in these world-threatening crises. He increased the symbolic weight of his presidency in the United Nations. The more engaged he became, the more was expected of him, as when a columnist for the *Economist* wrote in June, 1961, "Unless Mr. Kennedy takes a decisive grip on the wheel, the West is in danger of bypassing one possible line of compromise after another until it reaches a dead end where neither it nor Russia has any choice except between ignominious retreat and nuclear devastation."

Pragmatism, in contrast with activism, puts emphasis on the limits of leadership and power. But Kennedy, Theodore Sorensen recorded, "was not a man who talked much about 'power' " nor presumably about its limits.[12] This reticence was a strength as he met his responsibilities, but it may also have led him astray. Vietnam was the final testing ground for Kennedy's reconciliation of activism and pragmatism, but the test results have not been evaluated yet. It remains for future historians to compose a concluding chapter to the history of Vietnam and to the key actors in what became a tragic drama. Writing of his period as ambassador there, Frederick E. Nolting delineates Kennedy's mistake in Vietnam: "The great error of the Kennedy administration was its misunderstanding of the issues involved in Vietnam in the sixties, and its reaction to those issues. More specifically [sic], the error was in its refusal to understand that the elected constitutional government of Vietnam was the best available. If we were to help South Vietnam survive at all, the only available vehicle which could sustain and carry forward the country was the government that had been in power eight years (after two elections) and which had run into a great deal of Communist-inspired trouble." [13] Ambassador Nolting's criticism of the Kennedy administration was that it encouraged a military coup without carefully measuring the consequences. Its policy in Vietnam failed because it ignored one of the tenets of pragmatism—the tenet that cautions against abandoning one alternative unless a better one exists or can be brought into being.

If one criticism of Vietnam is grounded in pragmatism, the other is centered in activism. A wiser activist course would have been either to fight from the beginning an all-out war, with American troops moving to victory, or to align the United States with nationalism and embrace Ho Chi Minh.

The Kennedy policy was to combine a version of halfhearted activism in the form of incremental involvement in Vietnam with an ill-considered

12. Theodore C. Sorensen, "Kennedy: Retrospect and Prospect," in *The Kennedy Presidency,* ed. Thompson, 296.

13. Frederick E. Nolting, "Kennedy, NATO and Southeast Asia," in *The Kennedy Presidency,* ed. Thompson, 229.

pragmatism that made a series of flawed practical choices beginning, but not ending, with the assassination of Ngo Dinh Diem. It lacked the political and cultural understanding on which either activism or pragmatism could have been based. By seeking to merge the two approaches, the policy ended by getting the worst of both worlds. Because he was blind to the irreconcilable conflict between activism and pragmatism in all its dimensions, it is doubtful if Kennedy would have changed Vietnam policy even in a second term.

What deepens the tragedy is the fact that perhaps no other postwar administration has taken as many promising initiatives at the United Nations, in Latin America and the Third World, in arms limitations, and in relations with the Soviet Union. Yet the fatal relationship between an unreconciled, and perhaps unreconcilable, activism and pragmatism in Vietnam spelled doom for the completion of its tasks. For this reason, the failures of other administrations are minor tragedies compared with the major tragedy of the Kennedy administration in Vietnam.

20

Lyndon B. Johnson:
National Interest and Collective Security

Historians and political observers, including some Johnson partisans, point to certain contradictions and tensions at the heart of his presidency. To some extent the tensions may be inherent in Lyndon B. Johnson himself. Shortly before his own death, the late justice Abe Fortas noted: "As you read the memoirs of people who were closely associated with Lyndon Johnson, you find many conflicting things. They probably all are true." This conflict may account for the fact that historians judging his presidency arrive at fundamentally opposing judgments. Robert Caro's biography paints Johnson as a leader tarnished by blemishes as man-sized as the president himself. Others find that few presidents have done more for the country, especially in education and civil rights. Yet for both sides in this historical controversy, the dark shadows of Vietnam hang over the Johnson presidency and confound every attempt at early objective evaluation.

Recognizing the controversies but sensing too the strengths of Johnson's presidency, the Miller Center from early 1984 through 1985 invited some of his close associates to visit us at the University of Virginia. We considered with them a broad range of issues concerning Lyndon Johnson: the man, his views on civil rights, his relations with the press, the economy, foreign policy, and Vietnam. We invited assessments of his role as political leader and world statesman. In one way or another, most of our discussions turned on Johnson's dilemma in Vietnam, pointing up the tensions inherent in his thought and in the ideas of many Americans about politics, international politics, and collective security.

No other problem in American foreign policy is more persistent than the discrepancies between the requirements of domestic and of international politics. Lyndon Johnson was the master craftsman of congressional politics. No other postwar Senate leader quite matched his political skills. However, American political leaders from William Jennings Bryan through James F. Byrnes to

Ronald Reagan have failed in varying degrees to translate know-how in domestic politics to international politics, and Lyndon Johnson was no exception.

Justice Fortas tried to explain one aspect of the problem as it related to Vietnam. He asked how someone with such a clear understanding of power in American politics could misunderstand its role in Vietnam. Fortas wrote, "With the Vietnam situation, it was really sort of unbelievable to [Johnson] that the application and demonstration of our nation's ever increasing and accelerating power would not cause the Communists to come to terms and to quit what they were doing and do what they ought to do instead of what they were doing." Through the skillful building of political coalitions, Johnson had organized power to achieve his ends in Congress. He had learned to use psychological pressures and the symbols of physical pressure in domestic politics. According to Fortas, Johnson in Vietnam "constantly felt that if a little more pressure were applied, the North Vietnamese and the Communists would become convinced that they were not going to win, that they would come to terms."

In summing up Johnson's predicament in the use of power, Fortas declared that "the real tragedy of President Johnson was the failure to realize that the usual results of the application of power, domestically in our own country, did not indicate that the application of an analogous force, internationally, would similarly result in changes being brought about." The Johnson administration increased the American commitment in Vietnam to 550,000 men, but the circumstances of world politics and the conditions of revolutionary nationalism nullified the effort.

Another limitation that American politicians often bring to the conduct of foreign policy is the absence of a working theory of international relations. Running through the presentations at the Miller Center was a clear and unqualified statement that Johnson was not a conceptualizer but an operator. Some commentators considered his freedom from any fixed theoretical position a strength, for it gave him room to maneuver within changing political circumstances. He was not tied down by theoretical baggage. The majority leader of the Senate understood that "what the broad statement did . . . was to narrow the area for maneuver." In Fortas' words, "He was a president who was much more comfortable with the use of a different kind of power than the power that resides in concepts and generalities." [1]

1. Abe Fortas, "The LBJ Presidency," in *The Johnson Presidency: Twenty Intimate Perspectives of Lyndon B. Johnson,* ed. Kenneth W. Thompson (Lanham, Md., 1986), 4, 11, 12, 14.

Even the most pragmatic leader, however, is never wholly free of underlying assumptions, principles, and theories. In a lecture in the Rotunda, Harry McPherson reminded us that Lyndon Johnson came to the Congress in 1937, just a year before the appeasement at Munich. The prevailing wisdom in Washington for decades after that event was that the West must avoid another Munich. "Stop the aggressor before the aggressor can climb all over you." [2] Columnists and political scientists described this philosophy as the "Munich syndrome," and in postwar American foreign policy it remained dominant until the reaction against policies in Vietnam. When President Truman gathered a small group of advisers and decision makers in Blair House following the invasion of South by North Korea, every man in the room was inspired, it was said, by a single philosophy. Aggression had to be turned back at its source if a larger and wider conflict comparable to World War II was to be prevented. The memory of Munich and its consequences was in everyone's mind the fateful night when American leaders decided to come to the aid of South Korea.

In seeking to understand the motivations for American foreign policy in Vietnam, several Miller Center speakers put forward another explanation. The weight of the commitments of other presidents, they contended, was such that no successor could disregard them. Justice Fortas believed that "Johnson pursued the Vietnamese war because of Eisenhower's position and Kennedy's position." That "inheritance affected his judgment." Fortas went on to explain the inheritance: "We are not talking about any sort of legal commitment or that he carried on because he was merely filling out President Kennedy's term. It was much more profound, much more subtle than that. . . . [and] by the time he ran and was elected in his own right the die had been cast . . . and irreversible commitments had been made." [3] Once a superpower has entered a conflict and engaged its national prestige, all the forces that influence decision making push in the direction of staying the course.

American politics was another vital force that made retreat virtually impossible for the administration. Harry McPherson described the political consequences: "Given the nature of that war, and the nature of American

---

2. Harry McPherson, "The Johnson Presidency," in *The Johnson Presidency*, ed. Thompson, 57.

3. Fortas, "The LBJ Presidency," in *The Johnson Presidency*, ed. Thompson, 13.

politics, for Lyndon Johnson to have reversed John F. Kennedy's policy and pulled out of Vietnam early on was inconceivable. It would have been political suicide to let South Vietnam fall to either the NLF [National Liberation Front] or to North Vietnam." In Johnson's mind, turning back not only would have brought down his administration but would have unleashed critics to charge that "the Democrats had lost Vietnam."

In foreign policy, the primary questions for those who resist aggression are "What is the threat?" and "Who is the enemy?" There can be little doubt that the Johnson administration saw mainland China as the dominant threat. McPherson asked himself essentially these questions and gave this response: "[Johnson] did not go in to save iron ore, oil, tin or a bunch of French Asian mandarins. He went in to try to prevent Asia from being rolled up by the Chinese Communists. That was what everybody thought was going to happen in 1963. We didn't realize that the Chinese and the Russians had already split badly, and that the Chinese and the North Vietnamese would later split so savagely."[4] If the United States had not resisted "the yellow horde," China would have overrun and captured all of Indochina.

When Lyndon Johnson became president, 16,500 troops were in Vietnam. Deterioration of the American position in Vietnam and its political position at home began to set in during the latter part of 1966. The Democrats lost some thirty-four seats in the congressional elections of that year. After that, everything was downhill. In Nicholas Katzenbach's estimation, "the great tragedy of Lyndon Johnson was Vietnam, which he didn't want," at least in part because "it wasn't within a field of . . . expertise that he felt he had."[5] He sought to buoy up his position by seeking a congressional resolution, but his associates told him that in the Congress' Gulf of Tonkin Resolution he had all the authority he needed. Johnson thought "a great big vote . . . might discourage the North Vietnamese." Katzenbach considered this proposal "a fairly naïve judgment," but it illustrated once again the confusion of domestic and international politics.

Katzenbach, when asked who applied specific pressures within the administration to escalate the war, replied, "The military primarily." It was not

4. McPherson, "The Johnson Presidency," in *The Johnson Presidency,* ed. Thompson, 54.

5. Nicholas Katzenbach, "Johnson and Foreign Policy," in *The Johnson Presidency,* ed. Thompson, 213.

that they promised results for certain increases in troop strength. Rather, the restraints on them "drove them absolutely crazy." Katzenbach's conclusion was that "it was mostly military pressure to increase" forces in Vietnam, and Johnson, like Kennedy before him, eventually responded to the pressure.

The focal point in the unresolved conflict in Johnson's foreign policy was the clash between collective security and U.S. interests in maintaining a balance of power and in cooperating with the emerging nations in Asia. As majority leader in the Senate, Johnson delivered an address before the annual meeting of the American Political Science Association in which he pronounced that collective security must be the cornerstone of American foreign policy. The bedrock principle of collective security is that the nations must band together to oppose aggression wherever it occurs: one for all and all for one. To achieve this goal, the Southeast Asia Treaty had created SEATO, a regional collective security organization. Walt Rostow observed that "a failure to honor the treaty would weaken the credibility of U.S. commitments elsewhere; and the outcome of a U.S. withdrawal would not be peace but, sooner or later, a wider war." Failure to come to the aid of any nation anywhere in the world would weaken security everywhere. The year 1964 had seen much political instability, "compounded by Indonesia's confrontation with Malaysia, its withdrawal from the United Nations, and alliance with the PRC [People's Republic of China]." In July of 1965, regular units of the North Vietnamese army entered Vietnam. President Johnson saw himself faced with the choice of accepting defeat in Southeast Asia or fighting. He chose to fight to protect not only South Vietnam but the other nations of Southeast Asia.

Rostow offers reasons Johnson's policy in Vietnam was burdened from the outset by nearly overwhelming obstacles to success. First, "Wilson and Franklin Roosevelt . . . [had] confronted both urgent domestic problems and war; but the course of events permitted them to be dealt with in sequence [whereas] Johnson faced them together from his first day of responsibility." Second, Johnson believed he could carry the Congress with him on both of these fronts. Thomas Corcoran observed that "he [knew] the players intimately" and, perhaps more important, "he [worked] at it day and night." But he underestimated the people's instincts, and therefore the Congress' as well, for a prompt and decisive resolution of conflicts in which the United States was engaged. The people were not prepared to support a protracted and indecisive war with limited objectives and mounting casualties. Third, he was determined "to conduct the war in a way that minimized the chance that any U.S. action would lead to a large engagement with Chinese Communist or Soviet forces in a nuclear age." He failed, and perhaps was bound to fail, to communicate that objective to the American people. Both hawks and doves became outspoken critics. Fourth, Rostow suggests a unique link between Johnson's domestic policy and his policy in Asia. The president concluded that Asians "wanted for themselves and their children . . . what everyone else wanted: peace, higher living standards, education, medical care," so "a sense that he was standing in support of an aspiring underdog of another race suffused Johnson's policy in Asia as much as it did his civil rights and welfare policies at home." As with Jimmy Carter's equating universal human rights with American civil rights, Johnson exaggerated the connections between American goals and the goals of Asian people. Fifth, in Rostow's concluding observation, "there was yet another strand . . . which asserted itself throughout the advanced industrial world: the reaction of a highly articulate margin of the middle class young (inflated in numbers by the post-1945 baby boom) not only against the war but also against the material values of the society . . . [and] viewing Johnson as the apotheosis of all they rejected." [6] The drumbeat of these critics brought down not only Johnson but his would-be successor, Hubert Humphrey.

American policy in Vietnam was influenced by concern over France. Senator William J. Fulbright explained our position:"We were afraid . . . after the war when Stalin was still in power and the cold war was beginning that we had to support the French or [France] would go Communist. . . . Vietnam was a side issue." It was estimated that the United States provided some two billion dollars of money and arms to the French to sustain them in Vietnam up to the time of their defeat in 1945 at Dien Bien Phu. France was seen as part of the West's collective security system. During this period, Ho Chi Minh, according to Senator Fulbright, wrote seven letters to the U.S. government, asking support on the grounds that Vietnam, like the thirteen colonies, was a colony seeking national independence. Fulbright maintained that the letters were never answered. President Eisenhower was urged to intervene

---

6. Walt Rostow, "Lyndon B. Johnson and Vietnam," in *The Johnson Presidency*, ed. Thompson, 231, 228, 232, 234, 235–36.

with troops at Dien Bien Phu, but because the British would not join him, he did not go in, foreshadowing later arguments for the principles of collective security.

Vietnam was also viewed by some as the scene of a clash of two collective political movements and systems. From this standpoint, the Vietnam War was "simply an expansion or extension of . . . the international Communist conspiracy . . . inspired by the Russians using the Chinese as a puppet government." Many people believed "if we didn't stop it in Vietnam then we'd have to stop it at Los Angeles and San Diego," so "if Vietnam fell to Communism, they would all fall." In the clash of two worldwide movements, the forms of resistance on both sides had to be collective and universal.

But collective security and resisting aggression everywhere in the world collide with other powerful social and political forces. Senator Fulbright argued this point by insisting that the day of colonialism [was] over." Moreover, American policy around the world was more restricted than British policy in the nineteenth and early twentieth centuries, which dictated that the British simply went in and "took over the country and ran it." Even in Vietnam, the United States had no such plan or intention. It simply urged good government according to its own views. Senator Fulbright concluded: "That's much more difficult than taking it over and . . . running it yourself. We have a . . . time making our own government work, let alone do it in an alien culture that has little in common with ours." [7]

It is always unfortunate in life and in politics when two goals or principles compete and conflict with one another without reconciliation. More unfortunate still is a situation in which the conflict remains permanently unresolved and is largely unrecognized by those who are involved. Beginning in the era of John Foster Dulles, some forty separate collective and bilateral security arrangements were fashioned by American foreign policy makers around the world. It was assumed that mobilizing the participants would be a relatively straightforward effort. Underestimated was the extent to which signatories would put their respective national interests first. Whereas some half-dozen nations carried most of the burden of fighting in Korea, South Vietnam and the United States were virtually alone in Vietnam.

7. Senator J. William Fulbright, "The Johnson Presidency and Vietnam," in *The Johnson Presidency,* ed. Thompson, 241, 245, 248.

Moreover, collective security was linked with the maintenance of the status quo. Movements for national independence, whether or not influenced by communist ideology, called for change in the status quo. The tides of history were dissolving the remnants of former colonial empires. If the United States was to align itself with history, it could not resist change, wherever the change occurred.

Thus, the national interest required the United States to identify its policies with the forces of change in Asia while collective security demanded pursuit of precisely the opposite goal. Historically, the one way of bringing the two objectives into harmony had been through persistent and skillful diplomacy directed toward peaceful change. Either American foreign policy was found wanting in not organizing its priorities to place accommodation above strict preservation of the status quo, or it sought peaceful change but failed because of the intractable position of its communist adversary. If the latter, the questions that Harry McPherson and others addressed at the Miller Center arise once again. Who was the adversary, and what was the threat? Apparently, policy makers in the Johnson administration saw China as the threat and Ho Chi Minh as a mere instrument of the Chinese. McPherson and others acknowledge the mistaken nature of this view, and their judgment is confirmed by the subsequent struggle between China and Vietnam.

The question that must be asked then is whether this mistaken judgment was inspired by the unresolved conflict between collective security and the national interest in the minds of American leaders. Were the commitments made to collective security, that is, to resistance to change everywhere in the world, an obstacle to any clear-eyed evaluation of the national interest? Were considerations of the national interest brushed aside on grounds that conflicts or changes on the periphery of the world balance of power would move inescapably to the center unless they were opposed at the source? Was "the newfangled view" of foreign policy, which placed international security above national interest, an invitation to make minor wars or civil wars the direct interest of the superpowers and therefore a cause of war for them?

In the nineteenth century, before the dawn of the era of collective security, conflicts in Asia and Africa occurred in areas the great powers considered "empty spaces." The dominance of one power or the other, whether Germany, France, or Britain, was determined by negotiation and treaties. War, when it broke out, was localized and limited both in duration and in number of participants. Conflicts broke out, the great powers drew a circle around the combatants, and the exit from war was facilitated by sphere-of-influence arrangements based on assessments of national interest.

No such national interest assessments were made for Vietnam. No American policy maker declared unequivocally that Vietnam was a clear and unambiguous U.S. national interest. The primacy of the collective security argument was assumed in all that was said about falling dominoes. In a brave new world with universal interests, nations were no longer seen as having to put national interest first.

What is tragic about Vietnam, then, is that the tensions and the conflicts between universal collective security and national interests remained unresolved. In fact, no one assumed such a resolution was required. Thus, the decision makers found themselves drawn ever more deeply into a conflict the rationale for which could not be explained or clarified for the American people. Collective security in the end became a unilateral American policy that was substituted for the national interest. Because other nations continued to act on their national interests broadly conceived, such a policy was doomed from the start. Neither the American public at home nor friends abroad were willing or able to do what universal collective security required.

The final aspect of the tragedy is that good and decent men with a vision of a better world were caught up in the conflict and eventually destroyed. They deserved better, and so did the nation as a whole. The United States had sought valiantly to build a security system that may have been ahead of its time.

21

Richard M. Nixon's Foreign Policy:
Continuities and Contradictions

The rediscovery and rehabilitation of Richard M. Nixon have primarily focused on Nixon's foreign policy, and it is in this area that he enjoyed his most notable successes. His conduct of foreign policy gives clues to the nature of his presidency and to the differences between national and foreign affairs. The introduction to the Miller Center volume on the Nixon presidency discusses the contradictions we have been left with: "The presidency of Richard M. Nixon stands apart from other postwar presidencies. Two images persist in the minds of most Americans. One is of a leader whose foreign policy may possibly have offered the best hope for peace with the Soviet Union. The other is of a President, disgraced and rejected by the people, boarding a helicopter to leave the White House forever."[1] How are we to reconcile these two conflicting images and viewpoints? Of the many and varied explanations of the Nixon presidency, which one is most helpful in squaring the circle with these two seemingly irreconcilable views? Are the failures of President Nixon, if they are failures, ones of policy and practice or are they the result of the perceptions Americans have of him?

One explanation that deserves scrutiny is the proposition that a president's strengths in one area may prove his downfall in another. We may ask if President Reagan's failure to explain his role in the Iran-Contra affair would have stood out in as glaring a fashion in his November, 1986, press conference if he had not until then been seen as the "Great Communicator." Does the idea of Greek tragedy and its sources bear on the problem? That is, does the virtue that makes the hero great also cause him to fall precipitously? With Richard Nixon, was his commitment to secrecy both one explanation of his success in foreign policy but also the cause of his downfall once Watergate struck? Did his capacity for homework lead him to seek too much control over the flow of events, culminating in the Watergate break-in?

1. Kenneth W. Thompson, "Introduction," in *The Nixon Presidency: Twenty-Two Intimate Perspectives of Richard M. Nixon,* ed. Kenneth W. Thompson (Lanham, Md., 1987), xi.

With Nixon, secrecy was a product of both personality and experience. Secrecy and personal isolation may have been one of the traits that led Bryce Harlow to say that "Eisenhower would never have picked [Nixon] as his favorite bridge companion." Related to his secretiveness was his apparent fear and dislike of most people and of extended social intercourse. John Ehrlichman characterized him in this way: "He's not the sort of fellow that you'd find fascinating as a next door neighbor. He wouldn't come over and play Scrabble or talk to you about a new record that he just bought. . . . His major weakness was in interpersonal relations. . . . He tended to avoid controversy by presenting an aspect of himself which he probably subconsciously calculated would be acceptable to the person he was dealing with." Ehrlichman and others have discussed Nixon's distaste for relations with some of his associates: "We've [the White House staff] got the reputation . . . of building a wall around the President. The fact is that he was down under his desk saying, 'I don't want to see those fellows,' and we were trying to pull him out."[2] He especially resisted those meetings with associates from whom he felt he had nothing to learn. His staunchest defenders attribute his keeping his distance from most people to that fact.

The majority of Nixon's intimates who participated in the Miller Center's oral history apparently believed that something deeper, some traumatic event or experience shaped his attitudes and character. Bryce Harlow asked himself: "What about so many people disliking him most of his life? There must be a reason." Harlow reports numerous conversations in which people kept saying, "I just don't like him," but were unable to explain why. Responses like these drove Harlow and his friends to distraction until finally he hit on a possible explanation: "People didn't like him for the simple reason that he didn't like people. . . . In the case of Richard Nixon, I suspect that my gifted friend somewhere in his youth, maybe when he was very young or in his teens, got badly hurt by someone he cared for very deeply or trusted totally—a parent, a relative, a dear friend, a lover, a confidante. Somewhere I figure someone hurt him badly, and from that experience and from then on he could not trust people." And by implication, they couldn't trust him. Har-

2. Bryce Harlow, "The Man and the Political Leader," in *The Nixon Presidency*, ed. Thompson, 6; John Ehrlichman, "The White House and Policy-Making," in *The Nixon Presidency*, ed. Thompson, 139, 132.

low, who would have railed against the excesses of psychohistory, admitted he had never talked with Nixon about this thesis but added that he would welcome the opportunity—an opportunity now foreclosed by Harlow's death.

Tendencies feed on one another and are mutually reinforcing, and this interdependence was true of Richard Nixon's relations with the press: "The press was hooked on an anti-Nixon drug and could never break the addiction. It was a terrible drag throughout Nixon's political career." In the 1960 campaign, he discontinued press conferences. He lived with the antagonism he engendered but could not trace it to its source. Harlow sought an answer and came closest during the 1968 campaign at a lunch with John Osborne of the *New Republic*, whom he considered the best political reporter in the capital. Harlow asked, "Just why do you hate my guy so much?" Osborne admitted to a loathing for Nixon but confessed he had no real basis for the dislike. Finally, after long reflection, he explained a possible cause: "I'll tell you one reason a reporter has trouble liking Nixon. Bryce, we've never really met him. None of us have. Do you know what we call him in the press corps— the cardboard man." Harlow asked why "the cardboard man." Osborne responded by describing his experience with the president: "He conceals himself somewhere behind a cardboard image of himself. He never comes out. I've talked to him in all kinds of ways. But I've never seen nor met the real man. I keep trying. Now, Bryce, you can't trust a man, you can't like a man . . . who hides himself from you. You suspect him."

Secrecy and distrust spread to other areas and poisoned the atmosphere. The ordinary citizen with little more than newspaper coverage sensed what was happening, but a more reliable, less impressionable source again is Harlow: "The grouping that shaped up in the 1970s—Nixon, [H. R.] Haldeman, Ehrlichman, [Charles] Colson, [Jeb Stuart] Magruder and so forth—took on an eerie quality, like the man with wax wings who flew so close to the sun that he and his son fell to the earth; these people did that. They started vying for favor on Nixon's dark side. Colson started talking about trampling his grandmother's grave for Nixon and showing he was as mean as they come. The same with Haldeman and Ehrlichman. Everybody went *macho*. It was the 'in thing' to swagger and threaten." Harlow told of a small White House meeting on campaign strategy in the spring of 1972. The group was an inside group that met semimonthly, and the president asked Harlow to attend. At one meeting, the question of the summary firing of two men in the Agriculture

Department was discussed. When Harlow asked what the men had done, he was told, "Nothing." They were a couple of innocent victims whose firings would be publicized for political purposes. Harlow, who was by then out of the government, threatened to report their design and its motivation to the president. To his surprise, the insiders dropped the plan. Later at a breakfast with Henry Kissinger at the Metropolitan Club, Harlow commented, "Henry, we are lucky it was Watergate, because if it hadn't been that, it would have been something much worse, the way things were going."

The source of the problem, which antedated the Nixon White House, went back to 1932. Watergate was bound to happen to a president sometime in the 1960s or 1970s. Bryce Harlow again gives a succinct analysis: "The sins of the fathers visiting upon their sons is what did in the Nixon generation. . . . It had been endlessly building up. . . . There had to be a reckoning. The White House had proven too powerful, too irresponsible, too independent, too self-satisfied and arrogant. It felt too big, it acted too big. It was dangerous. It had to be restrained and reformed."[3] The defects of the White House extended beyond secrecy, but it was secrecy that reinforced an atmosphere of individual arrogance and of a group standing above and outside the law.

President Nixon's distrust of the bureaucracy was well known, and he spoke of the whole structure as being "ninety-nine percent against us." Thus from the outset, his administration was destined to seek channels other than the traditional bureaucratic ones such as the Department of State. One obvious channel was the National Security Council and its adviser, but other forms of back-channel diplomacy presented themselves as well. The point is that all this indirection and more was entirely in keeping with Nixon's character and world view. As one of his political associates said, he was an introvert trying to be an extrovert. He was at his best in private meetings. In diplomacy as in politics, success may depend on one side or another imposing its will. Politics and diplomacy involve psychological relationships, not physical ones, as in the use of force. For the effective leader politics and diplomacy involve manipulating people and situations to his own ends. Of Nixon's abilities in this area, Elliot Richardson had first-hand experience: "His manipulative characteristics are things that historians will have to recreate. . . . I was a victim of

3. Harlow, "The Man and the Political Leader," in *The Nixon Presidency,* ed. Thompson, 9–10, 11, 13, 15, 16, 26.

his manipulative tendencies in the week leading up to the so-called 'Saturday Night Massacre' to a degree that I didn't even realize until months after it was all over." Moreover, he conceded, "it's hard . . . to be successfully manipulative in a situation where you are dealing with a whole lot of people who talk with each other and take notes." Nixon turned to the arenas of power because he loved to wield power, or, in Richardson's judgment, "Nixon and a handful of others over the last thirty years really have had an overriding desire to exercise power, but that is not a common characteristic in Washington," which he described as generally "a city of cocker spaniels," people desiring to be praised and admired.

Diplomacy and private negotiations require secrecy, flexibility, and a certain subtlety of mind. A sometime critic of President Nixon observed that "the distinction fundamentally between Nixon, Carter and Reagan . . . is that Nixon was capable . . . of a much greater degree of subtlety," whereas, for example, the "Reagan administration came into office in somewhat the way an individual trained to fly a fixed-wing airplane might try to take over the controls of a helicopter."[4] Reagan was capable of dealing with the likes of Clark Kerr or Helen Gahagan Douglas in state or national politics. As Lou Cannon has noted, Reagan had a sixth sense of what appealed to a majority at any given time and could deflect criticism of himself to others. He was adept at turning accusations against his accusers. Nixon had that sense in international politics, and it paid dividends in his diplomacy.

That subtlety manifested itself especially in foreign policy. American values and the overlapping grievances against, and the dislikes of, the great mass of the people for communism made Nixon's unequivocal anticommunism good politics domestically. The homogeneity of American society made a monistic approach to good and evil a possibility on the national scene. When Nixon turned to international politics, single-factor analysis and discourse went by the board. In place of communism as the sole all-consuming enemy, Nixon in foreign policy came to think in terms of dualities and sometimes antinomies, opposites that do not cancel each other out: detente and deterrence, conflict and cooperation, political tensions and peace as a process of living with conflict and arms buildups. What Nixon is saying is that interna-

4. Elliot L. Richardson, "The Paradox," in *The Nixon Presidency*, ed. Thompson, 59, 60–61, 66–67.

tional relations is not the pursuit of a single goal: "International relations are not like lunch at the club or a round of golf with friends. They are more like entering a snake pit where good intentions and good manners, adhered to slavishly in the face of your enemy's malevolence, are bound to be distinct hindrances." Closing one's eyes, one can hear the voice of Machiavelli or of Frederick the Great.

Nixon reserves some of his harshest criticisms for fellow presidents and world leaders who fail to recognize the dualities. Carter pursued detente without recognizing its linkage with deterrence. Advocates of disarmament fail to understand that wars result from unresolved political differences and territorial ambitions, not possession of arms. Complete nuclear disarmament, despite Reykjavik, is an impossible dream. And on summitry, while recognizing that face-to-face meetings may sometimes be useful, Nixon states, "No leader should meet with an adversary unless he is fully aware of his own strengths and weaknesses and those of his opponent; unless he has something he wants to bargain for and something to bargain with; and unless he is prepared to be worked over by professionals."[5] The shift in temper and perspective from Nixon's view of domestic politics to his sense of international politics is capsulated in his advice to leaders in foreign policy.

The criticism is sometimes made that President Nixon in national affairs had difficulty distinguishing between politics and governance. Given his experience in the House of Representatives, in the Senate, and as vice-president, President Nixon was perhaps the best and most experienced executive in the history of the republic. Yet few presidents have had more problems than Nixon had in establishing the balance between politics and governance. At one extreme are presidents or heads of state who assume politics has little or nothing to do with governing. From different points on the political spectrum, Herbert Hoover and Woodrow Wilson may have suffered from this illusion. Richard Nixon is said to have fallen prey to the opposite misconception. In his eyes, the law of politics was the law of the jungle, and Marquis of Queensberry's rules did not apply. Evidence mounts that he carried over this viewpoint from politics into governance. Because politics was for him a continuing struggle, red in tooth and claw, he was disposed to engage in overkill, as in his instructions to John Ehrlichman to cut off all federal money to MIT or to

5. Richard Nixon, *Real Peace* (Boston, 1984), 13.

firebomb the Brookings Institution. Ehrlichman noted that Nixon "was given to these kinds of excesses and you just simply had to know the difference." Haldeman commented that "some people give me some credit . . . and I think it was a valid function I performed—in not doing some of the things that the President wanted done." [6]

Others were less skilled in discriminating between orders that should or should not be carried out, and the example most often cited is Charles W. Colson. Ehrlichman echoed this judgment: "One place the Nixon administration got into difficulty was that there were people around who didn't know the difference. . . . They saluted and went out and did whatever they were told. . . . I wouldn't be at all surprised to learn that Colson saluted, did an about-face, and went out to collect fire bombs [to bomb Brookings]." These views may lend credence to a New York *Times* dispatch of May 29, 1987, occasioned by the release of some 267,500 pages of documents made public that day by the National Archives. In a memorandum dated January 14, 1971, from Air Force One, President Nixon wrote these instructions: "It would seem that the time is approaching when Larry O'Brien is held accountable for his retainer with Hughes [O'Brien had once done some public relations work for Howard R. Hughes]. Perhaps Colson should make a check on this." The *Times* report concludes that "many believe that Mr. Nixon's desire for information about Mr. O'Brien was behind the break-in and burglary of the Democratic party headquarters in the Watergate office and apartment complex on June 17, 1972," for which "Charles W. Colson . . . later pleaded guilty to a charge of obstructing justice and served a prison sentence." [7] Conceivably, those who took Nixon at his word were the perpetrators of Watergate.

Whatever the merits of these and other interpretations and reports, they suggest that the actions of which Richard Nixon was capable were morally and politically highly ambiguous. There follows the question whether acts of this kind are not more necessary and commonplace in the half-anarchic society that is international politics. For centuries, rulers employed court poison-

6. Ehrlichman, "The White House and Policy-Making," in *The Nixon Presidency,* ed. Thompson, 129; H. R. Haldeman, "The Nixon White House and Presidency," in *The Nixon Presidency,* ed. Thompson, 95.

7. Ehrlichman, "The White House and Policy-Making," in *The Nixon Presidency,* ed. Thompson, 129; New York *Times,* May 29, 1987, p. A19.

ers whose function was to dispose of rivals. To reiterate, the Conte de Cavour declared, "If we had done for ourselves what we did for the state, what scoundrels we would have been." It is fair to ask whether President Nixon was not better equipped to cope with such an environment than presidents who preceded and followed him.

In this connection, *Time* columnist Hugh Sidey offers two closely interrelated observations. The first involves a comparison of Lyndon B. Johnson and Nixon. The second is a revealing commentary on evil and international politics. Sidey reports President Johnson spoke of his wish to meet Chinese leaders and observed that "you never make a deal until you get two at a table." Sidey then asked him why he didn't initiate such contact. Johnson replied that his diplomats told him the time was not right. Sidey took note of the answer and later compared it to Nixon's attitude: "You know what Nixon would say if somebody told him about the diplomats' opinions; you couldn't print it. He'd just tell them to stick it in their left ear. That is what he did with China."

On the second subject, evil and international politics, Sidey recounted a conversation he had had with Nixon on the topic:

> I said, "Mr. President, it is kind of an enigma for us that in the minds of many people in the world you are the incarnate of evil. You've been thrown out of office and you've done all these bad things, and yet people are saying you have a better grasp of the world now and you are more honored for your foreign policy than anybody. On the other hand, Jimmy Carter who was a man who was supposed to be the incarnate of good, who walked among the people in his sandals and brought love, is rejected now. He is condemned and reviled. How do you explain that?" I paused and watched him. Nixon looks like an evil person. He has a hunch. On that occasion his nose and eyebrows were going up and down, and he looked evil. He took a long time to answer and it was rather incoherent but what he said was: "You've got to be a little evil to understand those people out there. You have to have known the dark side of life to understand those people. I only know half a dozen corporate chief executives that I would trust in a room with a healthy Brezhnev. Yet, I know twenty or thirty labor leaders I'd let in there." It was a view of the world. It all kind of figured. He didn't trust anybody.

Ray Price sums up the phenomenon in this way: "Americans hire presidents to look after the nation's interests in a brutal, dangerous, lawless world. . . . The worst thing a president can do is to be so paralyzed by propriety that he shrinks from bending the rules when the nation's security requires it." [8]

Richard Nixon's least praiseworthy human qualities viewed against conventional standards of virtue and good behavior in politics may have been his most important assets in foreign policy. They were reinforced by the traits of his ablest foreign-policy lieutenants, men who did not hesitate in taking liberties with virtue and truth. For those who doubt the utter ruthlessness of the National Security Council Adviser and Secretary of State Henry Kissinger, Joseph Sisco's comments are instructive: "The President gave Bill Rogers the responsibility for taking the lead in all of the Middle Eastern policy, and all the way along the book [Kissinger's memoirs] cites chapter and verse as to how Kissinger and the NSC [National Security Council] sought to undermine the policy. He was very frank about it." Sisco concludes that "one would have to cite not only the dozens of incidents that are known but the eight dozen incidents that aren't known" in relations between Kissinger's security council and the State Department and the deliberate discrediting of Secretary Rogers. Sisco credits Kissinger with being the world's foremost foreign policy talent but as having a dark side, too, about which Sisco writes at some length. It was the same dark side historians had found in Otto von Bismarck and Klemens von Metternich. It gave both important foreign policy strengths to Nixon and Kissinger and shadows that were often all the public saw in their actions.

Lenin had spoken of idealists in the West as "useful idiots" who were misled about communism and filled with illusions that Soviet leaders could exploit. Nixon held that only hard-headed policy makers were capable of responding to the Soviet threat. He quoted Charles Bohlen's comment about the Soviets: "They are pure materialists. You can no more describe them as being sincere than you could describe that table as being sincere." In Nixon's words, "We [had to] develop a policy of hard-headed detente that [would] convince Kremlin leaders that they [stood] to lose far more than they could

8. Hugh Sidey, "The Man and Foreign Policy," in *The Nixon Presidency*, ed. Thompson, 311–12; Raymond K. Price, Jr., "Nixon's Reassessment Comes Early," in *The Nixon Presidency*, ed. Thompson, 388.

possibly gain by threatening our interests." The West, and especially the United States, was handicapped in the struggle by the fact that Soviet "policy [was] one of sheer, ruthless opportunism," and in the meantime, the West struggled "to find ways to combat covert Soviet aggression that [were] in accordance with accepted rules of traditional warfare."

Even the needs of humanity were approached in this spirit. Peace in Nixon's view can never be based on mutual friendship. Its sole foundation must be "mutual respect for each other's strength." Good personal relations do not ensure good state relations, though Nixon favors annual summit meetings of the leaders of the United States and the Soviet Union. His reason, however, is wholly practical: that they take one another's measure before a crisis in order that they can respond in a more reasonable way. Anyone who would deal with the Soviet Union must understand power, because in Nixon's time the Kremlin leaders had never won a free election but they are "masters at getting and keeping power."

What Nixon finds unacceptable are the two prevailing concepts for dealing with the Soviets, which he identifies as "superhawks" and "superdoves." The superhawks call for military superiority and look forward to the collapse of the Soviet system. They forget that confrontation and isolation can strengthen a dictatorship and that a democracy cannot sustain such a policy without the hope that international tensions can be reduced. "It is irresponsible for the world's two greatest military powers not to have maximum communication and not to try to negotiate their disputes." We live in "a highly combustible atmosphere of semi-belligerency, with both sides building up armaments without restraint while firing salvos of hot rhetoric." Without negotiations, our interests could rub together in powder-keg areas such as the Middle East and set off a spark that could ignite a nuclear war.

The superdoves explain Soviet actions as stemming exclusively from fear. They excuse Soviet aggression and falsely believe that if we cut our defense budget the Soviets would do the same. The superdoves, with whom Nixon identifies President Carter before Afghanistan, do not recognize the Soviets for what they are. We do not have to convince the Soviets that we want peace, but they must know they cannot win a war. This at least was Nixon's view prior to the destruction of the Berlin Wall and the dissolution of the Soviet Union.

Opposed to the prescriptions of superhawks and superdoves, Nixon urged a policy of hard-headed detente, which combines detente with deterrence. "It is not an entente, which is an agreement between powers with common interests, nor is it a synonym for appeasement." It means not that the superpowers agree but that they profoundly disagree. "It provides a means of peacefully resolving those disagreements that can be resolved, and of living with those that cannot." From 1969 to 1974, hard-headed detente worked. Some issues, like arms control and the settlement of World War II debts, were negotiated on the basis of mutual interests. Others, such as most-favored-nation status and American grain purchases, were appealing to the Soviets and gave the United States diplomatic and political leverage. Not a single nation was lost to the Soviet bloc during this period. The Soviets backed down from establishing a submarine base in Cuba, from overthrowing King Hussein of Jordan, from supporting India's efforts to gobble up West Pakistan in 1971, and from sending Soviet forces into the Middle East during the Arab-Israeli war of 1973.

The character of hard-headed detente was best illustrated, Nixon argued, by the bombing and mining of Haiphong harbor on the eve of the 1972 summit meeting to stop the North Vietnamese offensive. Nixon indicated that these actions were vindicated by their results: "Those who did not understand hard-headed detente thought it would torpedo the summit. They were wrong. It strengthened our hand and helped pave the way for a broad range of agreements."

Why, then, did hard-headed detente fail? Why did the people turn against Nixon and Kissinger? Nixon blames the Congress and the Carter administration. Congress reduced military assistance to Vietnam, passed the War Powers Act, and denied the president the power to enforce the Paris peace accords. The Carter administration canceled and delayed major arms programs. But Nixon's explanation has to be measured against the standards he himself put forth. He had warned that leaders sometimes go to international conferences in pursuit of a good press at home. The handling of the opening to China had many of these same characteristics; Nixon claimed it was the twentieth century's greatest diplomatic triumph. Detente was oversold to the American people and invited a reaction. Friendly critics (Hans Morgenthau) warned that though nations might achieve detente on a specific problem, global detente was an illusion. Nixon knew that "history is a pathetic junkyard of broken treaties," yet he defended some of his agreements as though they guaranteed perpetual peace. He warned that "unless the superpowers [adopted] a new live-and-let-live relationship, the world [would] not see peace in this century" but did little to remove forms of confrontation that exacerbated conflict.[9]

Beyond the specifics of the ongoing conflict, neither Nixon nor Kissinger succeeded in generating public confidence in their approach and policies. Whatever the successes or failures, the American people were uneasy with Nixon's approach and perhaps always will be when leaders try to pursue policies based on concepts of realism. But neither Kissinger nor Nixon did much to reassure them that the shadowy and ambiguous course they were following had a moral purpose. Increasingly both were denounced as wholly immoral. Their secrecy and cynicism, about which Bryce Harlow spoke, turned in on them. More recently critics have challenged the soundness of some of their policies, such as refusing to seek a ban on multiple, independently targeted, reentry vehicles (MIRVs), delaying the ABM Treaty until 1972 when it could have been completed several years earlier, and accepting a numerical disadvantage in missile-launching submarines with the Soviets. They helped overthrow Salvador Allende in Chile and tied American interests to Mohammad Reza Pahlavi, the Shah of Iran.

It may be that these setbacks were inevitable, that explaining foreign policy to a mass public is impossible, but the dual judgment of the public that the Nixon policy was a combination of crafty atmospherics and cynical, Machiavellian statecraft devoid of virtù led to the repudiation of his policies. The tragedy is the deeper because few presidents and their aides have possessed geostrategic perspectives comparable to those that Nixon and Kissinger brought to foreign policy.

When all is said and done, the Nixon-Kissinger foreign policy ushered in a new era in American foreign policy. One accomplishment was the "Opening to China" registered and confirmed in the Shanghai Declaration. Another was the summit conferences with Soviet leaders, which met as American planes were dropping bombs on Haiphong. Most important, the Nixon-Kissinger foreign policy, whatever its shortcomings, demonstrated that a hard-headed, realistic approach to diplomacy was possible and could yield results.

9. Nixon, *Real Peace,* 17, 53, 76, 16, 24, 26, 28, 15.

Because an American president who was an archfoe of communism negotiated in the most serious way with leaders of the Soviet Union and China, he legitimized the process. Negotiating with the Russians became a credible feature of American foreign policy for all Nixon's successors. If an outspoken critic of the Soviet Union could parlay with Communists, it was clearly acceptable for others to follow suit. Nixon set aside ideological warfare, which was once his trademark, in order to do business with Communists.

In retrospect, however, his importance is less that of a successful negotiator and more that of a president-diplomat who pointed the way for others. It is said that President Reagan consulted the former president on foreign policy on a regular basis. Even without such consultation, Nixon's example must have been a factor in Reagan's decision to meet with Gorbachev. In this way, the Nixon era leads on to the Reagan-Gorbachev years. Nixon's debates with Kruschchev in Moscow surrounded by kitchen hardware might be said to be a preparation for *glasnost*. It is possible, therefore, to show that Nixon's policies played a role in the unfolding relations with the Soviet Union and Eastern Europe and the transforming events of 1989 and 1991.

Part VI

Whither Men and Nations

22

History as End Point or New Beginning?

Francis Fukuyama, a young State Department official with a lively interest in history, has rekindled interest in the philosophy of history with a provocative essay entitled "The End of History?" It is his thesis that the world is witnessing the triumph of liberal democracy as the end point in the evolution of political ideologies, or what he calls mankind's prevailing consciousness. The liberal state represents the final stage in political history. The two threats to liberalism as forms of human governance, communism and fascism, have both suffered defeat. Writing before the tragedy of Tiananmen Square, Fukuyama heralds the "total exhaustion" of the remaining alternatives to liberalism in the two largest communist countries and the "ineluctable spread" of liberal consumerist Western culture. He finds evidence of the dominance of liberalism in the profusion of television sets in Beijing and cooperative restaurants in Moscow.

Liberalism's victory is admittedly incomplete in the real or material world. However, because Fukuyama, like Hegel, believes that the rational is the real and that all human history has roots in a prior state of consciousness that is cause and not effect, he measures victory by the march of ideas that create the material world in their own image. Large unifying world views shape society and political and economic organization; ideas control material forces, not the reverse. If Ludwig Feuerbach and Marx turned Hegel on his head, Fukuyama seeks to restore Hegel's idealism right side up.

It may seem strange for a State Department planner to have recourse to the oftentimes impenetrable thought of Georg Wilhelm Friedrich Hegel. Yet Fukuyama defends Hegel as the earliest philosopher to speak the language of modern social science. He sees Hegel as defining history as a dialectical process with a beginning, a middle, and an end. (Critics point out that the dialectical process begins rather with a thesis that confronts its antithesis and is then resolved in a synthesis, with each synthesis becoming a new thesis for the next stage in the drama of history.) The march of history for Hegel proceeds through stages of consciousness from tribal to slave-owning to theocratic to democratic-egalitarian societies. Each stage of consciousness has produced new forms of social and political organization, culminating in a final, rational society and ideal state. The transforming moment for Fukuyama, drawing on Alexandre Kojève, the Russian émigré lecturing in Paris in the 1930s, was in 1806 when Napoleon, as the carrier of the ideas of liberty and equality, conquered the Prussian monarchy in the Battle of Jena. Napoleon's forces were the vanguard of humanity who "actualized" the principles of the French Revolution.

The liberal state after Napoleon had certain unfinished tasks (in the Marxist utopia they are called "the administration of things"), such as eliminating slavery and extending the franchise to workers, women, blacks, and other minorities. The two world wars involved the extension worldwide of the ideas of the universal liberal state. However, history reached an end point with liberalism because the ideas of the liberal state, for example, man's universal right to freedom and government by the consent of the governed, could not be improved upon or changed. In the liberal state, all conflict and contradictions are resolved. Absolute truth having being realized, generals, statesmen, and even philosophers become obsolete. Only technical and economic activity remains, along with a certain amount of tidying up. Believing this, Kojève abandoned teaching and spent the rest of his life as a bureaucrat in the European Economic Community.

Hegel, then, provides the intellectual basis for Fukuyama's defense of the primacy of ideas and human consciousness over material factors and his celebration of the victory of liberalism over Marxism.' Perhaps Fukuyama's defense is sustainable in the realm of pure thought, though serious Hegel scholars question Fukuyama's reading of Hegel. For example, the German philosopher had second thoughts on the French Revolution and its transforming effects. He found its ideology too abstract and individualistic to "actualize" the spirit of the Enlightenment and too susceptible to those abuses that surrounded the Reign of Terror. Moreover, Hegel's history is subject to two different interpretations, one, that history following the French Revolution and the Reformation was largely a matter of filling in the details, and the other, that history remains an ever-unfolding process, always seeking but never achieving fulfillment or completion.

Too much history has transpired since the French and Russian revolutions to satisfy either a contemporary Hegelian or a Marxist thinker with the end-of-history thesis. Not only revolution but world wars have twice intervened, unleashing the demoniac fury of one of the world's most culturally advanced peoples and resulting in the determined resistance of the Grand Alliance in response. Called to act as a superior race destined to rule the world, the German people who followed Hitler must have looked forward to a long-awaited victory that for them would herald the end of history. However, it was Kant among nineteenth-century German philosophers, not Hegel or Nietzsche, who prophesied perpetual peace through the spread of democracy and the resulting harmony and tranquillity. Thus, Fukuyama's choice of Hegel among nineteenth-century philosophers to support his viewpoint concerning the end of history (which he prophesies will result in societies that are passive, uninspiring, and boring) comes as something of a surprise. Incidentally, to the extent Hegel identified the end of history with a specific date and particular state, the date was 1820, not 1806, and the state was Prussia, not the conquest of Prussia at Jena. It must give pause that Fukuyama's severest critics include philosophers, such as Gertrude Himmelfarb, who remain unconvinced by Fukuyama's vision of the future and in particular his interpretation of Hegel.

The Philosophy of History and International Politics

The debate over Hegel's philosophy leads to a broader issue. Fukuyama made his argument for the end of history focusing largely on one particular philosophy, without giving much attention to differing schools of thought in the history of philosophy. We might have supposed he would have had more to say about other philosophers or philosophies. His silence prompts certain questions. Could he have feared that an approach resting on a broader perspective might weaken his dominant thesis? Would a wider field of vision detract from his single-minded focus on the idea of the end of history? Was he perhaps guided by his own ideological objectives rather than by the philosopher's search for truth? Does his essay derive from certain political objectives that he never makes explicit?

In fact, the major patterns of history are expressions of many and varied perspectives, and each historical era has had its own characteristics and dimensions. The Greeks conceived of history as the unfolding of moral principles. Ideas of virtue and the polity were the guiding light for Greek political development. For Saint Augustine in the early Middle Ages, the historical process was a spectacle that was essentially immoral. It resulted from the political consequences of original sin. According to this view, governments are composed of bands of brigands and robbers. The only hope for change is through a radical spiritual transformation of man and society. Religious truths, however, exist in a realm above and beyond history. Man is redeemed through faith and God's act of grace. This belief in objective thought carried over into later centuries though in a different form. Through much of the sixteenth, seventeenth, and eighteenth centuries, history preserved its transcendent character, but here the reference point was the transcendent principle of reason. Natural rights and the higher law are outside history as the standards by which constitutional and legislative enactments such as the Bill of Rights can be judged.

All this is changed with "progressive history," beginning with Rousseau and continued by Hegel and Marx. For Rousseau, man is born free but is everywhere in chains. If he throws off society's shackles, man will regain his pristine virtue. Instead of being informed by a transcendent principle, whether spiritual or rational, history is driven by an immanent principle of evaluation that will be realized not beyond but within history. Progressive history introduces the novel proposition that liberation from the evils history imposes is achievable here and now. For Rousseau, the will of the people— the general will—is the only measure of good and evil. The general will expresses itself within the political process. For Hegel, purpose in history finds expression in the unfolding of the idea of the world spirit (a concept that Fukuyama, for some reason, never mentions). Succeeding periods of history extending into the nineteenth century display ever-increasing progress. For Marx, history is a drama of linear moral progress within history propelled by technological and economic advances. History as Marxist science is driven irresistibly forward from one necessary stage of development to the next. Feudalism was superior to the societies that preceded it just as capitalism is superior to feudalism. Because moral evaluations rest primarily on materialist structures and values, feudalism was technologically and economically better than prefeudal systems and, therefore, morally better. No other measure of morality than the material exists in history. The realization of morality is possible within, but not outside, history. Each stage of history is necessary and inevitable; socialism is destined to follow capitalism just as capitalism succeeded feudalism. Those who truly embrace Marxism will cooperate with the Marxian historical process. Thus, Marx opposed the revolutions of 1848 because of the possibility they were premature and would have prevented the natural and historical emergence of the bourgeoisie. For similar reasons, Stalin temporarily preferred Jiang Jie-Shī [Chiang Kai-shek] to Mao Ze-dong following World War I because Maoist ideas and Mao as leader were in advance of a given stage in the Marxist design for Chinese history.

For all these reasons, it seems clear that the Marxian and Hegelian visions of history are wholly different from the visions of thinkers such as Augustine. First, moral evaluations find their place within and not outside the system. No transcendent principle of history exists. Second, the ideal state is achievable within and as a part of the historic process. In this sense, Marxism is not a philosophical but a religious system of thought, a religion, however, that is exclusively within history. The debate over the realization of goals illustrates this distinction. Communist writers maintain that Communists seek salvation within this world but that non-Communists await salvation in another world. Therefore, the Communist religion is this-worldly whereas its rivals are other-worldly. Marxism can indeed be shown to have the characteristics of a political religion: sacred texts, high holy days (holidays), priests and prophets, and ceremonial ritual. Yet it should also be clear that non-Marxians in the twentieth century sometimes hold to much the same general conception of history. While often disguised, a view that provides for fulfillment within history is also present in modern thought as it was not present in the Middle Ages. History has been transformed, but neither Marxian nor non-Marxian thinkers consider that we have reached the end point of history. Indeed, the whole thrust of both systems is antithetical to ideas of the end of history at this stage in mankind's progress. For both schools, history is an ongoing process of becoming or unfolding. Change and reform are the essence of the new history.

Modern attitudes toward war are quite revealing. For Augustine, war is the result of man's fallen nature and of original sin. No one in the Middle Ages seriously believed that war could be eliminated. Modern man, by contrast, makes a frontal attack on war. Liberalism and Marxism as philosophies of history have common roots. Both believe that the world's evils can be remedied and eliminated. History carries within its boundaries the solution to all human problems. Both see the solution to war in unambiguous terms; both would abolish and eradicate what they consider the primary cause of war, the Communists by eliminating the bourgeoisie, liberal democrats such as Wilson by eliminating the dictators. In place of the bourgeoisie and the dictators, one seeks to establish the dictatorship of the proletariat (Marx made use of Hegel's concept of the vanguard), and the other, world government in some form or another. Both viewpoints overlook the perennial struggle for power among men. Neither gives much attention to a truth that predecessors in the Middle Ages understood more profoundly, that men and societies continually find themselves in the grip of unresolved rivalries and contests for influence. Economics and technology are not the primary source of power conflicts between individuals and groups. Democracy or socialism or higher standards of living will not eliminate political conflicts, though they may change some of the ideological rationalizations that are employed.

Fukuyama seems to believe that the liberal state, because it has made possible an economic order that cannot be improved or changed, has also resolved the political problem. If he had been more inclusive in invoking a wider spectrum of philosophers of history, he might have escaped such an illusion. The missing dimension in his end-of-history discussion, surprising inasmuch as he is a State Department figure, is international politics. If the focus of Fukuyama's essay had been international politics, he might have been expected to introduce other philosophers, including Burke, Hume, Grotius, Emmerich von Vattel, or Machiavelli. Or, since his inquiry can be considered to fall within the genre of philosophy of history, he might conceivably have shown an interest in Edward Gibbon, Spengler, Toynbee, or E. A. Freeman. The latter group of historians is especially noteworthy for exploring the interconnection between general principles of history and contemporary international politics.

Inasmuch as Fukuyama eschews even passing reference to either group of thinkers, we have to assume that his purpose is less a search for truth about international politics or the philosophy of history and more the assertion of a point of view. Toynbee spoke of the true scholar as standing on the shoulders of those scholars who had gone before him. Plainly, Fukuyama shows little interest in following others. This criticism is not to deny his success as an essayist but to point out that he leaves us with the unanswered question of what his purpose really is.

Nations and the End of History

If Fukuyama shows disregard for international politics, he seems even more oblivious to the varieties of domestic politics. Do the Poles or the Hungarians or the Palestinians or the South African blacks believe that history is at an end? It seems clear that the East Germans, who have peacefully overthrown tyranny in East Berlin, are unwilling to accept the permanent status the end-of-history theory would assign to them as they survey the consequences of union with their much more highly developed partner, West Germany. Is the status quo in Northern Ireland preordained by the Hegelian thesis? Are all peoples who consider themselves oppressed condemned to endure forever their present condition? Fukuyama is prepared to acknowledge that circum-stances in the Third World may occasionally result in challenges to the liberal state, but he considers them marginal to his purpose: "Our task is not to answer exhaustively the challenges to liberalism promoted by every crackpot messiah around the world. . . . For our purposes, it matters very little what strange thoughts occur to people in Albania or Burkina Faso, for we are in-terested in . . . the common ideological heritage of mankind."

Nevertheless, it is in Asia, preeminently among non-European regions, that the triumph of the liberal state, and therefore the end of history, is indis-putable for Fukuyama. Japan, which threatened the world in World War II, has followed in the footsteps of the United States in creating a universal con-sumerist society. Throughout Asia and the Near East, other newly industrial-ized states in turn have followed Japan. Not only have countries such as South Korea and Singapore realized the status of the universal liberal state, but, Fukuyama records, "V. S. Naipaul travelling in Khomeini's Iran . . . noted the omnipresent signs advertising the products of Sony, Hitachi, and JVC, whose appeal remained virtually irresistible and gave the lie to the regime's pretensions of restoring a state based on the rule of the Shariah." In his com-mentary, one hears the same echoes that led to the Iran-Contra adventure. In summarizing developments in Asian countries, Fukuyama concludes that "consumer culture . . . has played a crucial role in fostering the spread of economic liberalism throughout Asia, and hence in promoting political liberalism as well."

The test for Fukuyama's basic thesis that political liberalism and economic liberalism are inextricably and irresistibly linked in the domestic societies of Asia came in June of 1989 in China. Apparently writing before the Chinese crackdown, he describes previous action against political dissent as mainly a matter of "necessary tactical adjustments" in a difficult political transition. He praises Deng Xiao-ping for having avoided the breakdown of political authority that had accompanied Gorbachev's *perestroika*. However long-term the political transition, he concludes, "the People's Republic of China can no longer act as a beacon for illiberal forces around the world."[1] When the twenty thousand Chinese students in the United States and Europe return to their homeland, they will demand that China respond to the democratizing trend that is sweeping Asia. What his thesis says will happen he assumes has already come about. It would be unfair to suggest that Fukuyama alone was unprepared for the events within China. Some of the ablest "China watchers" underestimated the force of reactionary elements and the extent of their actions in putting down dissent. It was hardly surprising, however, that a major sovereign nation-state would respond decisively to a substantial threat to its political authority. The monopoly of the state over the means of violence gives it overwhelming power to put down rebellions anywhere within its jurisdiction. If the government had not acted to preserve order, China would have been the exception to the rule.

Not only does Fukuyama seem not to have understood this fact about the modern nation-state and its use of violence in the face of a significant challenge to its authority, but strangely enough, he has little to say about traditional Chinese patterns of cultural conformity and political order. The maintenance of public order through "show trials" and the execution of offenders in the public square is an ancient Chinese practice. Its effectiveness in deterring civil disobedience and political deviationism is well understood. For a Westerner to be unaware of the residual influence of such traditional practices is understandable. More surprising is the failure of someone of

---

1. Francis Fukuyama, "The End of History," *National Interest*, No. 16 (Summer, 1989), 3–18.

Asian origin to anticipate that even the universal homogeneous liberal state, which has supposedly transformed history, would be subject to traditional cultural influences. We can only ask why he failed to take culture into account, noting that Fukuyama's underlying thesis about economic liberalism leading to political liberalism appears delayed of realization, if not refuted, by the most recent experiences in China.

Science, Purpose, and Politics

The earlier questions raised about international politics and the nation-state lead us back to the question of the methodological assumptions of Fukuyama's essay. In justifying his use of Hegel as the cornerstone of his study, he explains, as we have seen, that the German thinker was the first philosopher to speak the language of modern social science. He was the first to see man as a product of his social environment, but what is more important, he believed that man could transform his natural environment through the application of science and technology. If we substitute "economics" for "science and technology," we move closer to understanding the rock-bottom principle in Fukuyama's approach.

Fukuyama's approach, consciously or not, has its roots in the scientific approach to social affairs in general and politics and international politics in particular. Social science came into being because of the introduction of a revolutionary idea. Historians point out that no one in the Middle Ages believed that war or poverty could be done away with or that popular rule was a practical possibility. Technology had remained static until the invention of the steam engine. Medieval thought maintained that an ideal state, if it were ever to come about, would do so by the grace of God, not by economic planning or social engineering.

Beginning in the sixteenth century, this idea of passivity began to lose ground. Vast changes occurred in the realm of science, especially with the great discoveries of explorers concerning the earth and the universe. The medieval conception of the earth was overthrown by the great geographical discoveries. Columbus and his contemporaries brought into question the older conception of the size and boundaries of the earth. They replaced a static view with a dynamic one. What they found was at first thought of as a part of the known world but soon came to be seen as opening the door to a new and unlimited universe. In the physical sciences, comparable changes followed and contributed to a new way of thinking. In astronomy, the Ptolemaic theory prevailed until Galileo, Johannes Kepler, and Nicolaus Copernicus. For Ptolemy, the earth was the center of the universe. Galileo's evidence that the earth revolves around the sun and later discoveries changed the perspective of an earth-centered astronomy. From the standpoint of scientific discovery, human reason came to be viewed as possessing unlimited power, strengthening the confidence men had in the human mind as such. At the same time, from a philosophical and religious standpoint it became more difficult to believe that the universe had been created for man. The most profound and lasting effect was the substitution of the concept of causation for the idea of retribution, which had dominated earlier societies.

What science had begun, two other changes reinforced and solidified. One was intellectual developments in the history of philosophy. The other was the emergence of a social and economic group, the rising middle class, whose experience appeared to confirm the assumptions of the philosophers. Philosophy and political and economic developments combined to lend impetus to the emerging picture of the world. A philosophy derived from the natural sciences and the advance of technology provided intellectual justification for a new approach to social problems. In addition, the political experience of this new and influential group called the middle class seemed to prove the validity of the general philosophy. The social and political power of this class was based on economic power. Its political weapons were the amassing of wealth and the controlling of manufacturing and commerce. Its triumph was the result of its mastery of the rational interplay of social and economic forces and the replacement of retribution by causation in social thinking.

In the history of philosophy the first philosopher to give expression to the changing approach to social thought was René Descartes. In his thinking, society and nature are one and the same, and both are subject to the law of causation. The universe can be understood without reference to the divinity or to any transcendent power. It is simply a mechanism; the discipline for charting its course is mathematics. For Descartes, as for Jefferson, the divinity has no role to play except at the creation. Only in the beginning did God as "the divine watchmaker" set the universe in motion. Deism for Jefferson and scientific thought for Descartes relegated God to a single act that set society in motion. What Descartes initiated with a modern school of scientific thought has continued down to the present. Baruch Spinoza and Giambattista Vico continued the scientific tradition and expanded its influence, the latter applying science especially to the social world. By the middle of the eighteenth century, an applied social science had begun to appear. The Abbé de St. Pierre advised every French king to create a "brain trust" that would counsel the ruler. Ethics became for Rousseau, Kant, Hegel, and Auguste Comte merely a branch of the social sciences. What is and what ought to be were no longer distinguishable; what remains is only what is. In earlier political thought, the distribution of wealth was a moral question. Today, it is no longer moral but primarily scientific. Marx insisted that the economic system must be changed, because Marxist science had demonstrated there was no possibility of bringing about a better distribution of wealth under the capitalist system. Keynes was even more "scientific" than Marx, for he believed that by understanding the causes of economic maladjustment, man could perfect the economy rationally through the application of knowledge. The ethical dualism that called for the pursuit both of an ethical norm along with a realist appraisal of what is or that made a distinction between invariant principle and variant practice has passed from the realm of applied political thought. The new approach, which goes back to Descartes, seeks to transform ethics into a science that can be as exact and precise as the natural sciences and as all-determining.

Such an approach almost inevitably views the social world in an optimistic mood. Only ignorance and lack of knowledge stand between man and perfection of the social world or, in Fukuyama's case, the end of history. Any failure to reach this hoped-for development is explained as the product of cultural lag. Nevertheless, making use of the tools of modern social thought, mankind is on the way to bridging any remaining cultural lag. Until the outbreak of World War I, it was commonplace among intellectuals to believe that society was moving irresistibly toward the attainment of universal peace and prosperity. War was considered no more possible than cannibalism. For philosophers such as Herbert Spencer, war was primarily an outmoded expression of feudal society. In industrial societies, it was unnecessary because men could find other outlets for their competitive nature—outlets such as Wall Street and the stock market. Prosperity was guaranteed by economic planning.

From a comprehensive science of human behavior and the resulting perpetual peace and prosperity to the end of history may be only a brief step in mankind's social and intellectual progress. If Hegel is the first philosopher to introduce modern social science, Fukuyama is his heir carried along by the optimism of the scientific approach. Whereas scientific Marxism sees the end of history in the classless state, Fukuyama, seemingly driven by the optimism of the social sciences, finds it in the universal homogeneous liberal state. Scientific Marxism and the social sciences are linked by a sublime faith in science and progress that leaves almost no room for moral issues. In another sphere, similar thinking leads to acceptance of the logic of nuclear war—an acceptance against which philosophers such as Aron, Niebuhr, and Morgenthau have protested. Writing of the dismantling, for the first time in human history, of the balance between the creative and destructive possibilities of man's control over the forces of nature, Niebuhr makes this observation: "Progress in the field of technology is accomplished . . . through human agency. Yet it outruns human desires so that historical developments become more and more analogous to natural forces which go on their faithful way unswerved, unswerving and know not what they are." Morgenthau, in discussing the political and moral bankruptcy of contemporary debates over the two alternatives of fighting a nuclear war versus surrender, wrote that "the way out of the dilemma is to transcend the two equally unacceptable alternatives . . . and that means taking nuclear power out of the arsenal of individual nations altogether." [2] Niebuhr's and Morgenthau's views are based on a tradition alien to Descartes. They would transcend the idea of science and technology as the ultimate arbiters even as they call attention to the political ramifications of science in the service of power.

Contradictions and Illusions

It is a sign of the times, the post-Reagan era, that Fukuyama's and others' views about the end of history or the end of the Cold War should attract significant

2. Reinhold Niebuhr, *The Structure of Nations and Empires* (New York, 1949), 267–68; Sidney Hook *et al.,* "Western Values and Total War," *Commentary,* XXXII (October, 1961), 280, 285.

public attention. The Reagan years gave comfort to those who found unacceptable dire warnings of cultural and spiritual malaise. Another sign of the times is the gradual unraveling of the myth of communism as the magical solution to human problems. China, Eastern Europe, and, most noteworthy, the republics of the now-disbanded USSR are all turning to increased free enterprise and political freedom. Economic and political revolution in the Soviet Union and the decline of socialism in Eastern Europe are a measure of the emergence of the liberal idea. Dissatisfaction with negative thinking and optimism about social and political reform are important signs of change in history.

Eventually, however, the fascination with the end-of-history thesis is likely to be short-lived. For one thing, its discussion has been confined largely to one segment of the intellectual community. Cold warriors or Neoconservatives are most conspicuous in rushing alternately to its defense or to defense of themselves. Fukuyama may indeed have been prophetic in warning that those who live by ideological conflict would find the post-historical era boring and dull. They stand out among those most alarmed by Fukuyama's thesis, as is evident in Jeane Kirkpatrick's description of such debates as being "vaguely frivolous." Commentators who occupy other positions on the political spectrum have had less to say about Fukuyama for whatever reason. Perhaps those who have remained silent are uncertain how to deal with some of the contradictions and illusions in his thesis. For someone who speaks of the primacy of ideas and consciousness, Fukuyama comes down heavily on the side of materialism in organizing his evidence. It is consumerist society that is being spread around the world more than political ideas. He says relatively little about constitutionalism, checks and balances, and the separation of powers. Perhaps he believes that television sets and cooperative restaurants are more tangible than political ideas or institutions. It could also be that the defense, if not the sanctification, of free enterprise is more in keeping with his purpose. Despite his indictment of "the *Wall Street Journal* school of deterministic materialism," Fukuyama himself turns to material achievements in what seems precariously close to a non-Marxian defense of certain Marxist presuppositions. To be fair, we must admit he struggles with material and idealistic rationalizations for his view, and it is sometimes difficult to be certain which wins out.

Fukuyama's great illusion becomes evident in another area, namely, in his conception of history. Because he seeks to bring history to a close, he shows little appreciation for the interplay of contingency and change. He is closer to Spengler than to Toynbee in his deterministic outlook on history. Toynbee suspended judgment on the survival of the West whereas Spengler announced its decline. Allowing for the advance of science over superstition in political and social thought in the eighteenth century, Fukuyama expresses exaggerated confidence in a philosophy that post-nineteenth-century scientists themselves reject. Beginning with Sir Arthur Stanley Eddington and Sir James Hopwood Jeans, a new approach to science that places emphasis on probability and contingency has come into view. The modern experimental scientist leaves more room for hunches and guesswork, chance and the unexpected, trial and error, and the unanticipated and the accidental. Fukuyama seems to prefer social science thinking that reflects pre-nineteenth-century science. One wonders whether for him social science and its illusory certainties may not mask a perhaps fundamental purpose that partakes more of ideology than science. Yet he is never explicit on this point.

His other illusion is a "Common Market" concept of politics. Seemingly, he believes that the countries of Europe will no longer compete in a struggle for power once the blanket of European interdependence envelops them. Contests for influence and ideological debates may continue between the industrialized nations and the Third World, but ancient rivalries and alliances in Europe, he is sure, will disappear in the cooperative spirit of 1992. Thus, perspectives of international politics that emphasize political equilibrium or the balance of power will be archaisms for Common Market politics (if, indeed, politics as such is not eradicated). How comforting this view will be to those who worry about a reunited Germany or the instability produced by the breakup of the Soviet empire is questionable.

If Fukuyama's conclusions raise questions, his bold and audacious endeavor deserves praise. What is intriguing is that so spirited a defense of a highly provocative thesis has come not from a scholar but a State Department official. Much as the more interesting foreign policy essays in the 1950s came from journalists, public officials (several in the State Department), and theologians, Fukuyama has stirred Americans "to make an unusually stubborn attempt to think clearly" on some of the great issues. Clearly, he deserves praise and thanks for his courageous and challenging proposal, however he may inspire critics to respond.

23

Nation in Decline?

Nations are threatened and the public cut adrift from its moorings when the gulf between philosophy and politics or theory and practice becomes too great. Some respected scholars and political observers see signs of this rift in the present American scene. The four contemporary writings that we examine in this chapter address the problem of the decline of the superpowers in four quite different ways. Opposed to them, public figures express generally hostile attitudes toward such writings, denouncing those who raise the issue as prophets of doom and gloom.

The 1980s have been largely portrayed by leaders as "an era of good feelings." Raising the issue of decline has been out of keeping with this spirit. Thus, one of the nation's respected leaders, Secretary of State George Shultz, in a valedictory on January 9, 1989, sponsored by the Citizens' Network for Foreign Affairs attacked the "declinists," who, he said, "play to the darker side, to the idea that America no longer has anything to give the world." He added that "these are false prophets" who believe that great powers have declined because they were imperial or were dominated by "tradition-bound classes." America has none of these characteristics, he insisted, because American democracy has the capacity for resilience and rejuvenation.

Paul Kennedy, a Yale historian who is the author of *The Rise and Fall of the Great Powers*, reviews five centuries of international politics from the Renaissance to the Cold War, seeking answers to the question of why some nations gain and hold power whereas others fail to attain it or lose it.[1] He asks why some nations become powerful whereas others remain weak. Earlier, Oswald Spengler found an answer to this question in his pessimistic portrayal of the cyclical movement of world cultures through four historical stages of spring, summer, autumn, and winter. Cultures decline as

---

1. Paul Kennedy, *The Rise and Fall of the Great Powers: Economic Change and Military Conflict from 1500 to 2000* (New York, 1987).

they lose their vitality and organic unity and are overcome by greed and a schism of the soul.

Arnold Toynbee pointed to the rise and fall of more than twenty large civilizations occurring through a process of challenge and response. At a civilization's birth and at the point of its genesis, creative minorities inspire strong innovative responses to internal or external challenges, which process brings growth and development. Civilization comes into being through the efforts of its problem solvers. In later crises and with recurrent challenges, responses become stereotyped and routinized as the linkage between leaders and people grows blurred. Vague and amorphous reactions spawned by mimesis, or the mere imitation of past actions, replace fresh creative thrusts. Civilizations respond mechanically in ways that at most postpone the eventual decline. After repeated cycles of rout and rally, a civilization, failing to achieve coherent breakthroughs for its problems, falls into permanent decline.

The main thesis of Paul Kennedy's work is that nations prosper only when they are successful in using their economic and material power effectively and that they decline, as is often the case following a victorious war, when they are driven by hubris or insecurity to seek what he calls "imperial overstretch," thus squandering their original economic advantage. Kennedy's message is not an example of history for history's sake. His thesis would be no more than an engaging bit of modern history if his sole purpose were to help Americans comprehend historical reasons for the fall, say, of the seventeenth-century Habsburg Empire or of nineteenth-century Victorian Britain. It is true that Kennedy's monumental inquiry does suggest reasons for the growth and decline of historical societies such as the cluster of states in west-central Europe in the sixteenth century that gained world power and, by contrast, the Mogul and Ming empires that did not. His review of these chapters in world history has merit as a series of history lessons, but his goal is more than that.

The major intent of Professor Kennedy's history is to illuminate the contemporary situation of his adopted nation. The United States, like the powerful nations that have gone before, is caught on the horns of a dilemma. As the Austrian-Spanish Habsburgs in the seventeenth century required the largest army and Victorian Britain the biggest navy to defend their farflung commitments inherited in successful wars, the United States evidently needs defense forces that are increasingly larger to compete not only with the Soviet

Union but also with the most prosperous regional powers such as Japan or Germany. The question policy makers must ask, however, is whether the American economy makes all this possible or if the United States must order its actions by establishing priorities. The wealth and economic development of the United States, which surpassed everyone else's after World War II, is being challenged and may someday be eclipsed by the four major powers who make up the emerging multipower world about which former president Richard Nixon writes in *1999: Victory Without War*. Less scholarly and intellectually coherent, his work surprisingly reinforces and illustrates certain key aspects of the Yale historian's conclusions.

During and following World War II, the supremacy of the Allies, and especially the United States, was everywhere apparent. Kennedy argues that the Allies had twice the manufacturing strength, three times the "war potential," and three times the national income of the Axis powers. In wartime, the productive plant and physical output of the United States increased by more than 50 percent. The contrast with Europe was awesome. Whereas Europe and Russia were devastated by the war, the GNP of the United States rose from $88 billion in 1939 to roughly $220 billion in current dollars of 1945. While the American GNP was increasing by 50 percent, the GNP of Europe as a whole had fallen by 25 percent. From 1940 to 1944, U.S. industrial expansion rose nearly 15 percent a year, more rapidly than at any time before or since. Americans could boast the highest standard of living and per capita productivity, half the world's manufacturing productivity, two-thirds of the world's gold reserves, and one-third of the world's exports. By 1945 the material foundations for world leadership enabled the United States to support sixty-nine divisions in Europe and twenty-six in Asia and the Pacific.

It is not surprising, then, that these vastly augmented resources inspired bold declarations about the American Century by men such as Time-Life's Henry Luce. In order to fulfill its role as a world leader, the United States discovered there were more and more new frontiers of insecurity in the Cold War that it was necessary to defend and where it was necessary to draw a line. American military commitments expanded, and in May of 1965 even so prudent a leader as Dean Rusk could say: "This has become a very small planet. We have to be concerned with all of it—with all of its land, waters, atmosphere, and with surrounding space." By 1970, we had one million soldiers in thirty countries; we were part of four regional defense organizations and a participant in a fifth, had mutual defense treaties with forty-two nations, belonged to fifty-three international organizations, and provided military or economic aid to some one hundred nations around the globe. Throughout much of the period, we accomplished all this without raising taxes.

New forces that represented countervailing trends were at work, however. Paul Kennedy and Richard Nixon join in throwing the spotlight on some of them. For one, in 1955 a group of Third World nations convening in Bandung organized a movement of nonaligned nations claiming freedom from control by both the United States and the Soviet Union. Since then, global trends have continued to work against the maintenance of absolute superpower status. Whereas the United States controlled 40 percent of the world's wealth and power in 1945, there is little likelihood it will possess more than 16 to 18 percent in the future. As early as the 1960s, the United States began losing its relative share of the world's wealth, production, and trade compared with what it had in 1945. Its percentage of world manufacturing dropped from 50 to around 31 percent in 1980 and is still falling. Its average annual rate of growth of output per capita fell even more because of such combined factors as overconsumption, a low personal savings rate, and a low rate of investment in research and development, especially in the Reagan administration, with the exception of military programs.

In foreign policy, the influence of the United States and of the Soviet Union also declined. At various moments in the Cold War, leaders like Syngman Rhee and Tito had held the superpowers at bay. Despite the boasts of recent administrations that democracy is on the rise in Latin America and throughout the world, we have the word of President Nixon that "only 16 percent of the people in the world live in stable democracies." He contrasts that with communist expansion: "Until World War II, only one country with only 7 percent of the world's population had a communist government. [In the 1980s] two of the greatest powers in history, the Soviet Union and China, and over a third of the world's population [lived] under communist rule." While the hold of communism weakened, the foremost leader in bringing about change maintained until after the abortive coup in the summer of 1991 that he and his country would remain communist. The Soviet Union claimed to be producing more graduate engineers than the United States. Their space program apparently had more continuity and momentum than ours. The world is caught up in turmoil and social and political change. Although the United

States beginning in 1776 has been the true intellectual and political exemplar of revolutionary change, others periodically have claimed that mantle, as when Khrushchev told President Kennedy in Vienna in 1961 that "the continuing revolutionary process in various countries *is* the status quo, and anyone who tries to halt this process not only is altering the status quo but is an aggressor." In other words, Soviet leaders considered Soviet foreign policy to have been ordained by history to support national liberation movements around the world, an affirmation that at least some Third World intellectuals, if no longer Gorbachev himself, continue to accept.

On the last page of his work, President Nixon poses this anxious question: "Are we witnessing the twilight of the American revolution?" [2] Professor Kennedy warns that too heavy an investment in armaments, though bringing greater security in the short term, may erode the commercial competitiveness of the American economy. The nation will be less secure in the long run. For Kennedy, the scholar, history teaches that the United States will inevitably decline, but Nixon, the politician, sees the nation continuing to make history, moving onward and upward provided it is realistic about its power. Even Kennedy believes it can slow down the process of decline by managing its affairs and assessing the consequences of its military and economic programs so that the relative erosion of American power is spread over time. Imperial overstretch is what will lead to decline. The United States can fashion a better world by example, a proposal that both Kennedy and Nixon endorse. Curiously enough, the two authors, the objective philosopher of history and the often bellicose campaigner against communism, discover some important and crucial areas of agreement alongside their admittedly considerable differences.

When we compare these reflections on decline with the bold words that were spoken on the campaign trail in the presidential election of 1988, the contrast is striking. In his acceptance speech for the Republican presidential nomination, George Bush proclaimed: "My opponent's view of the world sees a long slow decline for our country. . . . But America is not in decline. America is a rising nation." The president not only sees the twentieth century as the American Century but prophesies that the twenty-first century will prove to be the second American Century. In one of his campaign speeches, Governor Michael Dukakis declared: "I am running for president because I

2. Richard Nixon, *1999: Victory Without War* (New York, 1988), 17, 33–34, 48, 321.

want to lead an America that leads the world, an America that does not settle for second-place or second-best."

Professor Joseph Nye of Harvard, a principal foreign policy adviser to Governor Dukakis, in reviewing Paul Kennedy's book in a *Foreign Policy* magazine article entitled "Understanding U.S. Strength" denounces defeatism and fervently matches Bush and Shultz word for word in deploring any thought of decline. Nye argues that external commitments are *not* sapping America's internal strength and that with a few domestic reforms and presumably the election of a Democratic administration the nation can easily adapt to the new dimensions of power: "Americans should not understate U.S. strength. Misleading historical analogies and false anxieties might prompt Americans to adopt policies of retrenchment that, ironically, could produce the results they are supposed to forestall." If the country has experienced decline, it is for the Harvard strategist a Reagan decline. The deficit, brought about by efforts ostensibly to restore American power and prestige, has led, he thinks, to the ill-considered belief that the United States cannot maintain both its domestic expansion and its international commitments. Nye therefore concludes that one should not "mistake the short-term problems arising from the Reagan period's borrowed prosperity for a symptom of long-term American decline." Only if "Americans react inappropriately . . . and inflict wounds upon themselves" will the United States be faced with decline. As Lyndon Johnson would have said, America can have both guns and butter.

By contrast, Nixon intersperses his often expansive political rhetoric with some rather sobering comparisons that offer viewpoints contrasting with those of his successors and would-be successors. He writes of the fateful choices the nation will be making in less than twelve years when the world celebrates a day that comes only once in a thousand years. We tend to forget that the United States is approaching not only a new century but a new millennium, the old one having opened on a deep sense of foreboding that God was preparing to destroy the world. Nixon is realist enough to acknowledge the dark side of the passing century (120 million people killed in 130 wars) and farsighted enough to recognize the possibility that man's power in the twenty-first century can destroy the world. Why should there be these stark differences not only between a historian and aspiring officeholders but also between a former president and aspiring candidates and their advisers, however scholarly, for the nation's highest office in the land? Why is it seen as bad politics to recognize the slightest increment of decline in the supremacy of American power?

One reason is surely that most ordinary Americans, like members of other nationalities around the world, gain their identities and self-fulfillment through pride in the preeminence of the republic to which they belong. Whatever the frustrations and disappointments of daily life, Americans are fulfilled, like the Romans before them, from knowing that they are Americans. But there is something more to the current public response. Because the dawning of the much-proclaimed American Century was precipitous after World War II and our material and military preeminence relatively short-lived compared with the British Empire, the consequences of any loss in American dominance were bound to be unsettling when decline set in. In the same way that the American people were slow to accept the idea of world leadership, evidenced by exaggerated postwar expectations for the United Nations, they now seem traumatized and confused by any sign of a relative decline in world power. The message of the Paul Kennedy and Nixon books is that what the French came to accept in the nineteenth century and the British and Germans in the twentieth century, Americans may experience sometime in the twenty-first century, if not before. On this point, the Yale historian is quite explicit and the Republican politician less direct within the context of his instinctive political rhetoric.

For those who are supremely confident that no historical analogies suggesting decline for the United States apply, it is worth remembering some events in recent history. The Korean War ended in a stalemate with boundaries being restored to the status quo ante. For the first time in twentieth-century history, the United States and its allies were defeated in a war with a minor power, North Vietnam. We had little influence on the substance or the timing of German reunification. Our ability to assist the newly independent satellite countries within the Soviet sphere is symbolized by the offer of a rather meager total of $10 million in assistance to the three Baltic states. We have thus far been unable or unwilling to act to remove Saddam Hussein from power in Iraq.

It may seem odd to select for this discussion an article rather than a book, but the lead article in the January 14, 1989, issue of the London *Economist* raised the question of whether communism is at bay. At first glance, Gorbachev appeared to be an exception to the pattern of world political leaders who dismiss as defeatist any talk of their nations' problems and any suggestion of decline. Instead, Gorbachev spoke repeatedly of failures within the Soviet Union and recited a litany of social and economic reforms essential to survival. *Perestroika* was Gorbachev's grand design for reconstructing the Soviet economy, and he showed a willingness to consider reductions in both nuclear and conventional weapons. Whether he will ultimately be successful and whether his words will be matched by deeds that transform Soviet society and substitute a defensive for a massive offensive military strategy can be confirmed only by history. Most of the debate centers on Gorbachev's survival and, secondarily, on the Soviet Union's continuing to be one of the major powers.

More than five years into the era of *glasnost* and *perestroika*, Gorbachev acknowledged that progress was slow and he had no miracles to offer. In an interview in the spring of 1988, he underscored that message: "Jesus Christ alone knew answers to all questions and knew how to feed 20,000 Jews with five loaves of bread. We don't possess that skill, we have no ready prescription to solve all our problems quickly."[3] Whatever the irony in Gorbachev's choice of words, he, more than many Western leaders in their reflections on the reported decline of the West, did not hesitate to point to Soviet failures.

On another level, however, we have it on the authority of a senior editorialist in the *Economist* that "communists have always been loath to recognise failure." The record of economic growth and well-being from health and welfare to food on the table appears to be demonstrating that market economies outproduce communist ones. Yet what one writer calls "gun-barrel Marxism" kept the spread of communism on the move into Eastern Europe in the 1940s and into the Third World in the 1960s and 1970s. "This . . . left Mr. Gorbachev with a bad case of *imperial overstretch* on top of [an] unmistakable economic mess."[4] In other words, the threat was a combination of overstretch and economic decline. Through all the discussion of reform, however, one fact went largely unnoticed. Gorbachev did not fling aside but rather grasped more tightly the banner of communism and proclaimed it would be flying proudly again. Whatever the changes that may follow *glasnost* and

3. *Newsweek*, May 30, 1988, p. 20.
4. "Communism at Bay," *Economist*, January 14, 1989, p. 15.

perestroika, for Gorbachev they were intended to serve the greater good of communism and socialism. It was the Soviet political and economic order that was flawed but not communism. It was the Soviet political and economic order but not communism that had to change, not to the end of the destruction of communism but to its fulfillment. In all his many pronouncements on restructuring and whatever the views of critics on his left and right, Gorbachev never once sounded the death knell of communism but rather promised its realization under more favorable if peaceful circumstances.

Discussions of Soviet problems as a measure of its decline are one important approach but not the end of the matter. On the one hand, the evidence was increasing that the Soviet budget deficit was likely to exceed the U.S. deficit in the 1990s according to an Associated Press news dispatch dated January 22, 1989, quoting figures published in the Soviet newspaper *Arguments and Facts* on January 21. Soviet estimates suggested the deficit could exceed 100 billion rubles or $162 billion by the 1990s, driven upward by the costs of the Chernobyl nuclear power plant disaster, and a crash program to meet shortages in housing and consumer goods and reconstruction after the Armenian earthquake. Estimates of the U.S. deficit range from $127 to $141 billion. According to Soviet research economist O. T. Bogomolov, the Soviet deficit will be 11 percent of its GNP, compared with 3 to 4 percent in the United States. Increases in the Soviet deficit result, according to Bogomolov, from the declining price of oil, the Soviet Union's primary export, and $65 billion in lost tax revenue from the anti-alcohol campaign. Armenian reconstruction costs are estimated at $13 billion and "urgent social problems" requiring additional expenditures mean the deficit has worsened.

Bogomolov's estimates are significant for at least two reasons. First, they illustrate the play of accidents and contingencies in determining the fate of nations. Second, they confirm warnings that are found in a more systematic and long-term study such as Paul Kennedy's. For while Kennedy warns of symptoms of decline on the American scene, he is even more emphatic about the USSR: "[The Soviet Union] proclaims the need for enhanced agricultural and industrial output, yet hobbles that possibility by collectivization and by heavy-handed planning. It asserts the overriding importance of world peace, yet its own massive arms buildup and its link with 'revolutionary states' (together with its revolutionary heritage) serve to increase international tensions. It claims to require absolute security along its extensive borders, yet its hitherto unyielding policy toward its neighbors' own security worsens Moscow's relations . . . and in turn makes the Russians feel 'encircled' and *less* secure." [5]

Given the Marxist emphasis on the material basis of human existence, it is ironic that the major difficulties facing the USSR have had their source in its economic substructure: agricultural productivity about one-seventh of American farming, industrial weaknesses reflected in labor and energy shortages, inferior rates of development of high-tech competence, and a toll being taken in demographics because of a steady deterioration in life expectancy and a rise in infant mortality rates since the 1970s. According to Professor Kennedy, two main political obstacles stood in the path of Gorbachev's "great leap forward": first, the entrenched position of party officials, bureaucrats, and others in the Soviet elite, all of whom enjoy a large array of privileges, and second, the very substantial share of GNP devoted to defense that siphons off vast amounts of trained manpower, scientists, machinery, and capital investment that could have been employed within the civilian economy. Thus, for Kennedy the problem of Soviet decline was even more self-evident and far-reaching than the decline of the United States. For the rest of us, the withdrawal of Soviet subsidies and its military brigade from Cuba and its agreement to stop military assistance to Afghanistan confirm Professor Kennedy's assessment. While the privileges of party officials and some Union bureaucrats may have been reduced, defense expenditures and military buildup remain difficult to estimate in 1991. Moreover, it would seem that until Yeltsin's Russia, the bureaucracy remained largely in place.

What was left unexplored in most discussions of Soviet decline was the relationship between Gorbachev's efforts at reform and history's verdict about communism. Almost a century of trial and error brought communism to its moment of truth: "Without freer markets and freer politics, communist parties cannot produce the goods. Yet these freedom-making reforms are almost certainly incompatible with communist rule." [6] It was inevitable that nationalities and ethnic groups in the Soviet Union would search not for ideas about reforming communism but for ways of using reform to escape from it. To fit all these data into the equation of the rise and fall of nations called for political imagination of the highest order.

5. Kennedy, *Rise and Fall of the Great Powers*, 488–89.
6. "Communism at Bay," *Economist*, January 14, 1989, p. 15.

A final work which chronicles the rise and fall of nations is Professor George Modelski's *Long Cycles in World Politics*, which sounds a counter-vailing theme to the ideas of Professor Kennedy.[7] It raises issues that have come to the fore in debates in the American Congress over maintaining or reducing expenditures for the navy and, more specifically, over the naval buildup of the Reagan administration. Surveying the past five centuries in the history of the modern nation-state system, Modelski argues that global wars have occurred at intervals of approximately one hundred years. Four global powers have emerged after each of these wars: Portugal, the Netherlands, Britain, and the United States. Global powers are the suppliers of order to the global system. They organize and keep coalitions intact and maintain a pres-ence in all parts of the world. They deploy forces that possess global reach. The long cycle of history is a process of global politics driven by global powers. A basic indicator of the capacity for global reach, and therefore of global power status, is the distribution of naval forces. No state has been able to overthrow the prevailing world order without first establishing command over the oceans. Modelski distinguishes between the conventional concept of world power and global powers, who for substantial periods deployed more than 10 percent of the world's capital warships in more than one sea. Capacity of this magnitude is required for global leadership.

Whereas Kennedy warns of imperial overstretch, Modelski maintains that global leadership requires global reach. Effective naval superiority over all comers is a prerequisite to leadership. First Portugal and the Netherlands, then the British navy from 1692 on, and, beginning with the battle at Midway, the United States have all maintained naval superiority, the United States most recently with approximately one-half of its deterrent power sea-based in pow-erful nuclear submarines and carrier forces. Modelski holds open the possibil-ity that new kinds of coalition building may supplant the dominance of a single global power. In the end, he returns to his primary thesis.

What is important about the Modelski treatise is its argument that world leadership is dependent on global reach, which in turn depends on naval su-periority. Great nations decline when they lose the capacity for global reach. The book is an example of the "peace through strength" thesis that has char-acterized postwar approaches to foreign policy but to a lesser extent the seri-

7. George Modelski, *Long Cycles in World Politics* (Seattle, 1987).

ous literature of international relations. It may be that the division between policy makers and the scholarly community is being healed with the emergence of the more moderate Bush administration following its success in the Persian Gulf. Then, studies of the Modelski genre may multiply, warning against military cutbacks and defending global reach.

These four writings suggest the complexity of any analysis of decline. The response to writings on decline tends to become increasingly shrill and polarized. Strong advocates and adherents of Reagan-Bush foreign policy have demanded that we go even further. Writers such as George Will and Jeane Kirkpatrick celebrate American triumphalism. Some on the left have defined themselves as better able to do what the Reagan-Bush administration has done poorly. Both groups have attacked the analysts of decline. For both, there is no choice between engagement everywhere in the world and human survival. (One specific issue is whether all aircraft carriers must be positioned on the high seas throughout the world or whether some can safely be based at home.) In Secretary Shultz's words, it's not simply a choice of engaging and taking risks or disengaging and not taking risks. He argues that either we are going to be a source of progress, stability, and harmony or we will stand aside in the face of conflict, instability, and the decline of international order. In a speech to the Citizens' Network for Foreign Affairs, Shultz denounced the "idea afloat that America is in decline, and we're in decline because we are engaged abroad." The "false prophets" call it "overextended." In a similar spirit, Secretary Dean Rusk used to argue that we had to engage with problems on the periphery of our national interest because inevitably they would move to the center. Opposed to the Shultz response is the position of former secretary of defense Clark Clifford, who has said that "this preoccupation with communism has led us to permit our country to decline." He explained: "There's been a false psychology that all we were doing was 'standing tall.' But each year our country was weakening." George Kennan believes "we are mired in the fixations of the period of 35 years ago, whereas life has moved on."[8] The debate over decline has become a debate between insiders and would-be insiders, Republicans and Democrats-in-exile, on the one hand, and a wider intellectual and political community, on the other.

The question that must be asked is whether the nature of political strug-

8. Quoted in "The Wake of the Cold War," Washington *Post,* June 14, 1988, p. D1.

gles in an age of television makes all this political rhetoric inevitable or whether an alternative outlook is possible. Are we destined to approach all the debates concerning America's place in the world with claims of military superiority and moral and political exceptionalism, coming down on the side of the proposition that we are not as other men or other nations? Have not American leaders always been subject historically to the pulls and tugs of American exceptionalism in contending with the limits of national power? Or can we draw from the American experience another view more in keeping with the challenges ahead?

What is lacking is a tragic sense of America's role in the world and of the unfolding processes of history. At the very least, leaders ought to suspend judgment on the questions of total engagement and of the American Century. If we prove superior, we need not flaunt that power. If we are suffering some measure of relative decline, the challenge is to adapt, recast priorities, regroup, and not deny that the United States like all nations is someday likely to experience some measure of decline. Lacking in present-day American leadership is the detachment and objectivity that historians associate with Abraham Lincoln, who, as we have seen, in seeking to recruit 300,000 volunteers for the Union could speak in 1862 of bringing "this unnecessary and injurious civil war to a speedy and satisfactory conclusion." Even as the supreme leader of one side in the conflict, he could on October 5, 1863, address a radical delegation from Missouri and Kansas not as a partisan but as one looking down on the strife from some stratospheric viewpoint, saying, "One side ignored the [economic] *necessity*, and magnified the evils of the system; while the other ignored the evils, and magnified the necessity; and each bitterly assailed the motives of the others." As for decline, on February 7, 1865, he recalled the heroes of the American Revolution, who symbolized an era of trial and testing in which personal ambition, rivalry, and jealousy were joined with love of freedom. Then, lesser and nobler motives were channeled into service to the republic, and Lincoln lamented the decline extending to his time: "But this state of feeling must fade, is fading, has faded with the circumstances that produced it. . . . They *were* a fortress of strength; but what invading foemen could never do, the silent artillery of time has done; the levelling of its walls."

Time had diminished "a forest of giant oaks." All that remained were the lonely trunks, shorn foliage, and mutilated limbs, and even they would disappear with the coming of the next storm. He warned sorrowfully that the pillars of the temple of liberty and the source of the nation's strength had crumbled. It is impossible to conceive a more dire formulation of a nation's thoroughgoing decline. Yet the same Lincoln acted to preserve the Union.

Lincoln went further and asked how the spirit of devotion to the Union could be restored. He reflected that passion for values had been aroused in men in the past but was being aroused no more. He reminded countrymen that survival, instead of depending on blind passion, must rest on the "the solid quarry of sober reason." It was "reason, cold, calculating, unimpassioned reason" that had to restore general intelligence, respect for the common good, morality, and reverence for the Constitution and the laws. Political reason and practical morality would make possible the support and defense of the Union. Prudence, which joined the morally desirable with the politically and materially possible, was essential. In the midst of the present strident debates over the rise and fall of nations, Lincoln's example and good counsel may be more relevant for the twenty-first century than the many latter-day declarations of pundits and political and intellectual leaders on the hustings. At the very least, we should consider it alongside the other claims and counterclaims that fill the air as we assess the fate and future of the United States. It may serve once again to preserve what is strongest and still exceptional in all that America continues to offer to the world.

It may help to link up the call from some present-day leaders to concentrate on urgent domestic problems with the argument that we must be a world leader. Often forgotten is the truth Lincoln enunciated that successes in preserving the Union and in proving that democracy could survive were the main sources of that leadership. With nations and empires threatened with dissolution and fledgling democracies embattled around the world, respect for the common good and the Constitution at home may offer more than moral preachments abroad can. If we must choose between policies based on blind passion and those based on unimpassioned reason, we should resist the former and reach out for the latter. Only by restoring the sources of the nation's strength, as Lincoln did in other times and circumstances, can we prove ourselves worthy of world leadership.

24

Living with Uncertainty

The dean of Harvard's John F. Kennedy School of Government in a commencement address compared the world upon his graduation in the early 1960s with the world of the students to whom he was speaking at Swarthmore College.. He noted differences in prevailing views of history, in concepts concerning the threat to peace and security, and in reflections on U.S. policy. For him, a Victorian Age philosophy of history of an era of unending peace and progress had been supplanted by the somber lessons of a great depression and two world wars. The symbol of the crisis perspective on history was the Cuban missile crisis, when Soviet and American policy makers confronted one another eyeball to eyeball and, as Dean Rusk observed, the other side blinked. The nature of the threat was exemplified by the U.S. policy of containment of the Soviet Union, which was the closest approximation to a coherent American foreign policy in the postwar era. If the language of Dean Robert Putnam's generation was containment, the language of the Swarthmore students was transformation, especially transformation of the Soviet Union, Eastern Europe, and a Common European Home.

No one can doubt that substantial foundations exist for a new philosophy of history rooted in a world in change. Columnists and politicians with virtual unanimity hail the end of the Cold War, and they are not alone. Gorbachev proclaims that the Warsaw Pact and NATO are no longer alliances for defense but rather international organizations for unity. The leaders of NATO at the conclusion of their June conference in 1990 described their movement from a military to a political and cultural organization, an alliance for international cooperation rather than for deterrence and defense. Throughout the Western world, a new world view, the outlines of which are unclear but the spirit of which is unquestioned, is emerging. A decade and a half ago, Hans Morgenthau predicted that the Cold War would end only when the ideological conflict ended or when the twentieth-century version of the clash of political religions in the holy-war tradition of conflicts between Catholics and Protestants or Christianity and Islam had been resolved. The Cold War would pass into history when democracy triumphed over communism or communism over democracy or when the superiority of one or the other political and ideological system became clear beyond any shadow of a doubt. In 1991, the world seems to have taken a step closer to that goal with events in the Soviet Union and Eastern Europe.

For many, including some of the most hard-bitten foes of communism, we have arrived at such a point in history. The debate is likely to be not over whether change has occurred but rather over the scope and meaning of such change. Interpreters group themselves under three prevailing schools of thought. One is the end-of-history school, which we have already discussed, another is a school that points to the beginning of a new and less threatening world, and the third is the school of continuity and change. The three are not wholly separate; inevitably the spokesmen for one cross over into the domain of the neighboring schools of thought. However, conclusions yield to the particular theory dominant in our minds.

As we have seen, Francis Fukuyama, a State Department intellectual, is the author of the end-of-history school. Prematurely, he was compared with Hegel and Marx, who identified the end of history with the world spirit embodied in the Prussian state and with the triumph of communism and the withering away of the state, respectively. Fukuyama announces the triumph of liberalism. He argues that ideas, not economics or politics, drive history. The idea of freedom is seen as victorious in *glasnost* and *perestroika* and in the victory of the forces of free enterprise in Communist China (an opinion he offered prior to the massacre in Tiananmen Square). The end-of-history view has been outdistanced by historical events for which it made no allowance, most notably the profound changes in the Soviet Union. With the decisive victory of liberalism, Fukuyuma predicts, the rest of history will be mainly a process of tidying up, of solving technical problems such as inflation or the deficit, but not a time of bold vision. Dominated by technocrats, it will be a world in which political life is boring and uninspiring. The culture will be devoid of creative ideas and great causes or stirring crusades. It will not be an era of heroic deeds and achievements.

The second school is the expression of a troubled people who for forty years lived in the shadow of a nuclear holocaust. Now the threat of 5 million troops in the Soviet and East Bloc countries and of 50,000 nuclear weapons seems to be disappearing. Nuclear arsenals on both sides of the Iron Curtain are beginning to be dismantled. The superpowers themselves are in decline. The Soviet economy is a failure and America's decline is less only by comparison, moving as we have from being a creditor to becoming a debtor nation. The superpowers in decline have lost not only the political will but the economic and military means to threaten each other, let alone to rule the world. Soviet forces have begun the process of withdrawing from Eastern Europe. The countries in eastern and central Europe, Poland, Czechoslovakia, Germany, and Hungary, over whom the Cold War has been fought are now free to tend their own gardens, hold open elections, free their economies, and become partners with the West. Those who have been on the periphery of Cold War struggles are comforted by the prospect that the Soviet Union and the United States have been too preoccupied with survival to threaten one another. For many Americans, in turn, the new history means that since the Soviet Union and international communism have been the threat, their removal guarantees global peace and security. What is surprising, many have forgotten that it has been the power and responsibility of the superpowers, and especially of the United States, that has deterred conflict and, when conflict has erupted, prevented it from spreading.

Those who have embraced the idea of continuity and change and have given support to the third school of thought are persons who look for patterns in history and lessons from the past. For them, a review of history, but especially nineteenth- and twentieth-century history, offers pointers on the major sources of conflict and cooperation, especially in Europe. Among the elements of continuity that they have identified are the following five. First, east-central Europe has been the cockpit of European wars and conflicts and of ancient and historic struggles. It has been the scene of the beginnings of two world wars. Diplomatic analysts have called it "the shatter zone." Second, since the breakup of the Austro-Hungarian Empire, the region's stability and coherence have been in doubt. Its Balkanization after World War I, driven by claims for national self-determination, left it weakened in the absence of structures to secure the economic solidarities and complementarities on which earlier economic customs unions had been built. Third, the nationality problem has persisted within Eastern Europe's multiethnic societies, exploited by predatory regimes claiming sovereignty, as with Hitler and the Sudeten Germans and Stalin and the Baltics. Fourth, throughout most of the twentieth century, Germany was the strongest power in Europe. With its seventy million highly talented and well-disciplined people, it was destined by history to rule the continent, if not the world. What history portended, however, the nations of Europe opposed and overcame. Europeans and Americans fought two world wars to turn back German hegemony. The conduct of World War II helped create a vacuum into which the power of the Soviet Union flowed, and once more Western civilization was threatened. Finally, countries in the region have suffered problems of governance that continue down to the present day. Whether ill fortune or a certain political incapacity has been the cause, nothing like British parliamentarianism or successful government by the consent of the governed is associated historically with Poland, Germany, or the Soviet Union. A certain heavy-handedness and lack of flexibility have prevailed and may continue to prevail.

Yet alongside recurrence and continuity, forces of change in history are visible. New political ideas and political systems move across the horizon. It is said that democracy is breaking out all over Europe and the world. Ideas of freedom and national identity are spreading across the region. New leaders in Czechoslovakia, Poland, Hungary, and the Russian republics constitute a metaphor for the rise of a new class to power. In some countries, intellectuals and visionaries are taking the place of Communist party officials and *nomenklatura*. Young people are in the forefront of the line of demonstrators, sometimes risking their lives in the cause of freedom. The role of labor unions striking out on an independent course and sometimes uniting with intellectuals may be more unpredictable but with Solidarity in Poland has been an important factor.

Beyond Eastern Europe, the impact of change is even more dramatic. Gorbachev, the architect of change in both the Soviet Union and Eastern Europe, was once threatened by leaders such as Boris Yeltsin and the mayors of Moscow and St. Petersburg (formerly Leningrad), who sought to carry his reforms further and faster. Following the attempted coup of August, 1991, Gorbachev joined Yeltsin and other reformers in accepting the idea of a loose confederation of an undetermined number of independent republics. Earlier Gorbachev, who had shifted the emphasis in the Soviet Union from global expansion to economic restructuring, spoke of Soviet membership in a Common European Home and proposed broadening the membership of NATO to include Eastern European countries and the Soviet Union. He envisaged a future when the still more inclusive thirty-five-nation Conference on Security and Cooperation in Europe (CSCE) would take the place of NATO and the Warsaw Pact. Growing problems in the Soviet Union make some of Gorbachev's goals seem more distant, and power has shifted to republics such as Russia and the Ukraine.

We sense we are at the beginning of an era of epochal change. No one can foresee how far it will go, because contending forces, national and international, are everywhere at work. Change is a global phenomenon. Visas are no longer required in order to cross most national boundaries in Europe. French, German, Italian, and Swiss citizens increasingly speak of themselves as good Europeans and make common cause on issues such as agricultural subsidies at economic summits, despite U.S. resistance. For many Europeans, the European community appears to be a long step toward a European Union or a Federation of Europe. What Jean Monnet and Robert Schuman began, Chancellor Helmut Kohl and his colleagues are continuing.

If the great unifying forces of change in Europe are increasingly visible on the horizon, forces of continuity also persist. Former prime minister Margaret Thatcher and her successor John Major speak in the language of traditional British foreign policy; both are more or less identified with what Europeans refer to as Thatcherism, though Major is seen as more European. Not by accident, one of Mrs. Thatcher's closest Cabinet associates warned somewhat tactlessly of the threat of a resurgent Germany, whether within or outside the European community. For his pains, he was forced to resign. Yet British anxiety over the concentration of preponderant power in a single nation-state in Europe reflects Britain's historic commitment to a balance of power. What Thatcherism makes explicit, European practice may eventually recognize, though in combination with other forces that represent change. Change and continuity are inseparably joined in the third view of history and set it apart from the philosophies that precede it.

Each of the three historical interpretations of where we stand in history has its following and inspires different policies and actions. Each guides policy choices and offers frameworks for analysis and thought. Each tempts its followers to walk precariously on the edge of a precipice threatening destruction. All three pose risks and problems, each in its own way. A world characterized by ideas of the end of history may inspire boredom and inertia, since all the great battles have been fought and all the victories won. Optimism over the consequences of a new and less threatening history leads to euphoria. Although an understanding of the intermingling of the elements of continuity and change in history can provide safeguards against both boredom and euphoria, it offers no panaceas. It requires discriminate judgments concerning the relative influence of the recurrent and the unique. It provides a way of thinking, not a copybook of answers for complex and difficult choices.

If understanding where we stand in history is the first great issue of the 1990s, the second is the definition of the nature of the threat to peace and security in the world. For the better part of the century we have been locked into a recurring debate on the theory and the practice of the Cold War. For some Americans, the threat has always been communism seeking to dominate the world. To meet this threat, true believers in anticommunist crusades have urged policies of worldwide and indiscriminate anticommunism. For others, the threat has been Russian imperialism advancing to the limits of Soviet power but targeted on areas of greatest strategic importance to the Soviet Union. To meet that threat, the United States has sought to resist Russian expansionism with a policy of containment, preferably at points of our own choosing, where U.S. national interests have been most directly engaged. That both superpowers departed on occasion from such informing theories has been less important than that these theories provided broad standards for judging the threat.

In the aftermath of the revolutions of 1989 in Eastern Europe and the precipitous decline of political stability and economic growth in the Middle East and more recently the Soviet Union, the major postwar interpretations of the nature of the threat are increasingly deficient for the 1990s. Neither worldwide communism nor Russian imperialism defines the changing nature of the threat. Today we talk of the threat as stemming from the disintegration of the Soviet economy, the failures of *perestroika*, the apparent dissolution of unity within the Soviet Union, instability in Eastern Europe and the Middle East, and the long-term problem of Germany, particularly its disproportionate power potential compared with the rest of Europe. In the long run Germany, not the Soviet Union, could be the foremost threat to the equilibrium of Europe. More immediately, however, we are anxious about transition problems from old societies we never fully understood to new societies we too hastily assume are being re-created in our own image or what we imagine is our image. Before we demand that the countries of Eastern Europe make the transition to capitalism or free enterprise overnight, we must recall American society's need from the first days of the new nation for public subsidies and state regulations of the railroads and the utilities. We remember the celebrated landgrant universities and, more recently, continuing assistance to the weakest and most vulnerable elements in society. U.S. history supports the thesis that the intermixture of state and private efforts doesn't necessarily lead to the denial of freedom.

As we rush to explain what no one had predicted, the risk is that we may settle for premature and simplistic definitions of the nature of the threat when it is in fact many-sided and complex. We need to consider that the threat will be influenced by the quality of governance, economic stability, ethnic and nationality rivalries, political unity, bureaucracy, and military developments. Each deserves attention in turn.

First, it should be obvious that problems of governance are universal. No society in the contemporary world, including American society, can afford to rest on its laurels. The United States struggles with the relationships of the three branches of government, an uncontrolled savings and loan crisis, and a mounting budget deficit. Crises are unending. Concern is even greater for governance in newly liberated countries destined to play major roles in the shaping of the post–Cold War world. Historically, few can point to particularly noteworthy achievements in the quality of governance, especially in recent years. Poland, Germany, and the Soviet Union, let alone Romania and Bulgaria, are not noted for democratic governance in the twentieth century. They are haunted by memories of the Weimar Republic suffering the trauma of psychological inferiority resulting from the Versailles Treaty or of Poland finding itself unable to govern, paralyzed by the *liberum veto*. Faced by the threatened division among members of the coalition of Solidarity and the intellectuals in Poland, the specter of Poland's historic problems of governance flashed across the nation's consciousness. In the interwar period, the Polish constitution was recast to make possible the exercise of presidential powers that was denied leaders such as General Józef Piłsudski. Yet Piłsudski's successors lacked the qualities of leadership that the new constitution legitimized. Thus, enabling constitutional provisions seem never to coincide with strong leaders willing and able to exercise them.

The uncertainties of governance in Eastern Europe and the Soviet Union, however, extend beyond their historic problems of governing themselves. In the early 1990s, the governments of Eastern Europe have been interim and transitional governments seeking to find their way from regimes controlled by the Soviet Union to independent statehood. Much as the first generation of Third World rulers after their nations achieved independence in the 1960s was composed of journalists and revolutionary intellectuals, the leaders of present-day Eastern Europe are primarily professors, playwrights, or union officials, particularly in Czechoslovakia, Poland, and Hungary. Most of them, with the possible exception of those who participated in the rise to power of Solidarity in Poland, are politically inexperienced. If, as Percy Bysshe Shelley insisted, poets are "the unacknowledged legislators of the world," their ability to govern is seldom confirmed by history. Much as the first generation of Third World leaders was replaced by men of affairs, including the military, it seems reasonable to expect a similar fate for leaders such as Václav Havel in Czechoslovakia and Tadeusz Mazowiecki in Poland. Nonetheless, political prophecy is a highly uncertain pursuit. More uncertain still is the likelihood that Eastern Europe will follow the course of Third World countries in which military regimes came to power following revolutionary governments.

A second dimension of the threat to peace and security following the revolutions of 1989 is in the realm of economics. By the late 1980s, it was already clear that the communist and socialist economic systems had fallen into disarray. Even economists sympathetic to socialist economics, to say nothing of free-market economists, cite examples of policies involving disregard of fundamental economic principles. They point to the overemphasis on the development of heavy industry and the failure to achieve currency convertibility. Paradoxically enough, given the claims made for planned economies in providing for basic individual human needs, the systems' most conspicuous failures have been in the realm of consumer goods. However, whatever legitimacy the former regimes have enjoyed in the countries of Eastern Europe has been linked with social and economic human rights of individuals to food, housing, health, and education. As subsidies for food and housing are withdrawn by successor regimes, public response takes the form of protests, strikes, and resistance. Furthermore, the new governments must deal with the plain fact that economic restructuring takes its heaviest toll on the lower classes and on working people. Not only are such changes a recipe for instability, if not revolution, but rising prices and increased inflation intensify the problem. What is true of Eastern Europe has been true a fortiori throughout the Soviet Union, where proposals for economic reform by Gorbachev and Yeltsin have offered competing strategies of economic reform.

A third factor that contributes to the threat to peace and security is ethnic and nationality rivalries. Americans are prone to translate the problems of other countries into the vocabulary of American political experience. Because American nationalism brought unity symbolized in *e pluribus unum*, its citizens too readily assumed in the 1960s that African nationalism would rapidly overcome the forces of tribalism. Only after conflicts such as the Nigerian civil war in the 1950s and 1960s did they discover how powerful were the residual tribal loyalties of Ibos, Yorubas, Hausas, and other less powerful tribal groups. The story repeated itself in East Africa, in Uganda and Kenya. While Americans were lecturing Africans on the obsolescence of tribalism, they faced ethnic conflicts within American society that challenged the concept of the nation as a melting pot. Much as Woodrow Wilson at the negotiations that led to the Treaty of Versailles had difficulty comprehending the importance of European boundary disputes, American understanding judges historic conflicts in Eastern Europe as irrational or insignificant. Conflicts based on remote historical and political interests between Romania and Hungary over Transylvania or between Bulgaria and Turkey appear irrational to most Americans. We tend to proffer solutions for such problems by invoking rather too simple versions of national self-determination, forgetting that Hitler also invoked the concept of national self-determination in his march across Europe. It may seem strange that the foremost nation, with its unrivaled success in creating a federal union, would have so little to say to the world in resolving problems such as decentralization in the Soviet Union. On the critical issue of German reunification, one might have thought the United States would have had a place at the table as the details of German membership in NATO were hammered out with the Soviet Union.

Bureaucracy is a fourth factor that could constitute a threat to European peace and security. Despite the success of the people's revolutions of 1989, bureaucracies established by communist regimes remain in place. George Kennan and others have argued that their immediate replacement by noncommunist bureaucrats may be neither necessary nor possible. Kennan appears to hope that onetime communist bureaucrats can make a successful transition to administering the programs of the new governments somewhat as in transitions in Western countries. With the election of thoroughgoing noncommunist regimes, a change may come, but even then the unanswered question is who will identify and train the needed noncommunist bureaucrats. Put quite simply, the question is how many of the present bureaucrats can and should be replaced and by whom? One answer, being forged as I write, is the abandonment of the Communist party; that is, the bureaucrat stays in place but only changes his political affiliations. However, this answer is not the only one. Others are gradually emerging as the Soviet Union changes its very structure.

The dimensions of the problem will differ from year to year and country to country. Two rather simplistic answers may be first, the traditional reactions of American politicians who discount the problem, saying that all bureaucracy is bad, and second, the rather too sanguine American expectation that a semester or year at a good public affairs school such as Harvard's John F. Kennedy School will result in a new Czech or Polish bureaucrat, if not indeed a new man. The politician's reaction is typified by antibureaucratic comments by both Reagan and Gorbachev in speeches and press conferences at summit meetings. It is also reflected in the attitudes of most recent American presidents, including John F. Kennedy and Richard M. Nixon, who condemned the stagnation of State Department bureaucrats. Yet we know that bureaucracies have with good reason been called the permanent government. They provide ways to institute or preserve programs and policies long after legislatures have acted. Therefore, they can hardly be dismissed as irrelevant to the future of Eastern Europe. Instead, they must be counted as part of the larger equation affecting peace and security.

A fifth and final factor to be thrown into the balance is military and nuclear considerations. In recent years, Gorbachev has displayed an almost reckless abandon in making proposals for arms limitations. Beginning in 1989 he apparently met growing resistance from elements in the Soviet military. If opposition had not developed, the Soviet military, measured by Pentagon standards or those of any other military establishment, would have been unique. A representative of the military sat at Gorbachev's side throughout the 1990 Washington summit. Moreover, members of the military were conspicuous both for their demeanor and their presence at the twenty-eighth Communist Party Congress. Yet failure of the military coup demonstrates that the prospect of the present military coming to power in the near future can be discounted. What is not discounted, at least by Americans such as Paul H. Nitze or Europeans such as France's foreign minister François Poncet, is the continuing threat of Soviet tanks, bridging equipment, and modernized heavy missiles. Military and political analysts warn of the risk of some twenty-seven thousand warheads, spread across eastern Germany and what remains of the Soviet empire, being unleashed in ethnic struggles. If a military threat continues to exist, its dimensions should be viewed in this light, not as large numbers of Soviet troops moving across national boundaries or as Soviet missiles being fired against nonhardened missile sites in the West. If the military and nuclear threat for which the West prepared for more than four decades has passed, conditions are lacking for justifying the claim that a military threat no longer exists. Instead, the military threat has become more decentralized and many-sided. Its exact dimensions are yet to be determined.

In summary, governance and the economies of Eastern Europe and the Soviet Union constitute a threat, as do ethnic and nationality rivalries. Bureaucracy may lead to continuing conflict, tensions, and strife, as may military and nuclear factors. Europe and the West have freed themselves from the grim prospect of conventional war leading to nuclear conflict with the Soviet empire, but the threat to peace and security remains. It would be illusory to believe that danger has passed. Its form and character and its constituent elements have changed, but the threat persists. The likelihood is that leaders in Europe and the United States will spend the balance of the 1990s trying to define a threat that is real, albeit not as simple or easily recognizable as communism or Russian imperialism.

Our discourse brings us at last to reflections on U.S. policy in such an era. Prevailing views of history and of the nature of the threat tend to be the major determinants of most proposals on foreign policy. With the political and international situation everywhere in flux, the first need in shaping policy is clearly for flexibility, resourcefulness, and openness. This need suggests a pragmatic approach to policy making, yet pragmatism itself is not enough. The strength of the Bush administration's approach to policy making, especially on Soviet-American relations, is its prudent and pragmatic world view, of which most foreign policy analysts approve. In the first year and a half what was appealing about the Bush administration is obvious. The president kept his cool. He resisted extremists of both the Right and the Left. If the administration foundered, it was when a sense of history or the understanding of a continuity of interests and objectives was required, as on the status of the city of Jerusalem. One unanswered question has been whether the largely political entourage around Secretary of State James A. Baker III has a well-grounded sense of the historic interests and objectives of the Soviets and of neighboring East European countries that persist in new guise. Will there be an equivalent use of experienced foreign policy resources such as occurred in the Kennedy administration when the president made a lifetime Sovietologist, Ambassador Llewelyn Thompson, a member of Excom (the small group who met with the president to formulate foreign policy actions)?

What worries some observers is a tendency to find reassurance in rather broad and simple formulations, such as support for NATO or the sudden shift of U.S. policy in Cambodia, which proved troubling to our Association of Southeast Asian Nations (ASEAN) allies. Some Western leaders, including Bush, have spoken of transforming NATO from a military to a political and cultural organization. Yet as the history of NATO makes clear, whatever the issues, whether the Suez crisis or Libya or the Persian Gulf, NATO has never been successful in coping with nonmilitary questions. With Europe's growing importance, extending beyond the seven or twelve members of existing international organizations, possible newcomers are seeking an alternative entry into a Common European Home. That alternative could be the CSCE with the thirty-five signatories to the Helsinki Conference or some other wider international body. However, critics question whether the CSCE will ever be more than a debating society, even though Gorbachev, Havel, and other leaders of Eastern Europe have looked to it as a means of entering more actively into the affairs of Europe.

The other worry that hangs over the changing world scene is knowing what to expect worldwide from political professionals and diplomatic amateurs. On the one hand, it is refreshing and invigorating to live in a world where Andrei Gromyko's "nyet" to every new Western proposal has been replaced by Gorbachev's and Yeltsin's bold initiatives. We also remember that the initiative on crucial issues such as the reduction of American troops in Europe came from politically oriented leaders such as Secretary of State Baker. Historically, important initiatives in American foreign policy have often come from practical politicians, and some of our best foreign policy practitioners have been non–foreign service personnel. On the other hand, foreign policy in the early 1990s, more so than in the earlier years of the Cold War, has gravitated to political professionals and diplomatic amateurs. In East and West, newcomers to the business of foreign policy are at the helm. German chancellor Kohl is a Christian Democratic party political leader, and long-time French Socialist politician François Mitterand is a lifelong practicing politician.

The records and achievements of most practical politicians making an abrupt transition to foreign policy are not necessarily encouraging. Secretary of State Jimmy Byrnes in the first years of the Truman administration proved far less successful in foreign policy than in the domestic arena. In an unguarded moment, Byrnes confessed he had difficulty distinguishing between Budapest and Bucharest. The requirements of international politics clearly differ from those of domestic politics. The problem arises because the political environment within the nation-state is one marked by moral and political consensus. Internationally, consensus is for the most part largely missing and must be created through diplomacy or the building of networks of common interest based on functional cooperation. Diplomatic agreements must register an existing situation of facts. To deal with hostile and unfriendly powers in a half-anarchic world is the stuff of international politics. With all their political virtuosity, neither Kohl nor Mitterand nor Baker has long experience in foreign policy. Only time will tell if they are able to match their impressive attainments in national politics as they cross the minefields of international politics.

Indifference to the realities and uniqueness of other cultures and politics may be the most glaring deficiency that national politicians bring to international affairs. It is equally the case that ignorance of American politics and of the need for congressional support often confounds leaders of other countries who are well schooled in foreign policy. Students of international politics warn of the high price of ignoring the constraints of domestic politics within one's own nation. A corollary is the failure to comprehend the importance of historical and cultural factors within other countries far removed from the American political scene. When international crises arise, American leaders too often are oblivious to the importance and symbolic significance of strategic lines of demarcation, as in Korea and Vietnam. The problem is compounded when those who carry responsibility believe their mastery of domestic politics is easily transferable to international politics. Even an authentic political genius such as Franklin D. Roosevelt fell prey to this tendency in believing he could charm, cajole, and persuade Stalin through the same tactics he employed with American politicians.

Two other problems confront U.S. policy makers. For almost half a century, Americans have seen the world through a single prism: relations with the Soviet Union. When local crises have erupted in the Third World, the United States has responded decisively, if not always successfully, in Korea, Lebanon, and Vietnam, always with a wary eye on the threat of Soviet intervention. No foreign policy problem anywhere in the world has been isolated from superpower conflict and the inherent danger of nuclear war. The mind-set of U.S. policy makers has been shaped by the Cold War. With the reduction, if not elimination, of the Soviet threat, leaders have struggled to construct new visions of the world. Some cling to the view that the Soviet republics with an armory of nuclear weapons remain the ultimate threat. In thirty minutes, the Soviet Union can rain nuclear annihilation on countries anywhere, thus destroying the world. An even larger body of opinion, sometimes reflected in congressional thinking and articulated by the president, holds that the danger of Soviet military action has passed and a brave new world order is at hand.

In the midst of such discussions, suddenly on August 2, 1990, Iraq invaded the desert sheikdom of Kuwait, and the harsh realities of the old world of power and conflict returned. Some 100,000 battle-hardened Iraqi troops seized the capital city of Kuwait and its rich oil fields and drove its rulers into exile. But this time the Soviet Union joined the United States. In a joint statement, Secretary of State Baker and Soviet foreign minister Eduard A. Shevardnadze condemned the invasion. Moscow, which had been Baghdad's chief arms supplier in the war against Iran, announced a suspension in the delivery of arms and military hardware to Iraq. Western European countries unanimously condemned the invasion and announced an embargo, and Britain and France joined the United States in freezing the assets of both Kuwait and Iraq in their countries. The United Nations Security Council condemned the invasion in more than a dozen resolutions, applied economic sanctions, demanded an unconditional Iraqi pullout, and called for immediate negotiations between Iraq and Kuwait. A new threat to world peace, U.S. national security, and regional stability had broken on the world.

President Bush compared the Middle East to central Europe in the 1930s when a dictator-aggressor moved across the region gobbling up one country after the other while European powers debated what to do. Scholars note the parallel with the Arab League, whose council, after days of silence, condemned the invasion, calling for Iraq's withdrawal from Kuwait, but rejected foreign intervention. Fourteen of the twenty-one members voted for condemnation, but seven abstained or spoke out against the statement. The country most threatened after Kuwait, Saudi Arabia, first hesitated to call for outside help, expressing concern that the United States and Europe might first give support but on departing would leave the country to the mercy of a stronger neighbor (Iraq had a million troops and 5,500 tanks, whereas the Saudis had 65,700 troops and 550 tanks). However, for the United States, Saudi oil represents a vital U.S. interest—an interest that the United States, without Saudi cooperation and access to its military installations, would find it difficult to defend. Not all Americans favored sending American ground forces to Saudi Arabia. Admiral William J. Crowe, former chairman of the Joint Chiefs of Staff, warned: "We can dominate the gulf from a naval standpoint. We can keep the Iraqis off the water, we can dominate them in the air. But the question of ground troops in that vast desert, that's another matter altogether."[1]

As the Middle East drama played itself out, the United States entered a new era in its foreign policy. Having defined the major threat to its interest as communism and the Soviet Union and having built a defense structure to meet that threat, it was caught off guard when the Soviet enemy became an ally in resisting the Iraqi domination of the Middle East. The shock for Americans would have been less if the words of a Yale University geostrategic thinker were better understood. In the 1940s, Nicholas Spykman wrote that the charming thing about international politics was that countries need never grow weary of their allies. They need only wait, and today's enemy will become tomorrow's friend. Following World War II, our major enemies, Germany and Japan, came to be our strong allies. Whether ally or simply no longer our adversary, the Soviet Union's relationship with the United States is in process of change, leading some to conclude that an era of global peace is at hand. We congratulate one another on having gone beyond the Cold War and speak of the prospects for a substantial peace dividend to meet domestic needs.

Although such optimism is understandable after forty-five long years of unprecedented global responsibility, the United States cannot escape the tasks

1. New York *Times*, August 4, 1990, pp. 4, 5.

of world leadership and the defense of its vital interests. Here, a second problem presents itself to American policy makers. Much as Woodrow Wilson offered Americans and the world the prospect of universal peace with the establishment of democracy and national self-determination, Reagan administration officials had announced that democracy was breaking out everywhere in the world. Unfortunately, the expected convergence between American vital interests and democracy is almost never complete. In Kuwait and Saudi Arabia, as well as in other Gulf states, our allies remain monarchs and royal families. The demonstrations against these regimes involve the masses, however such movements are initiated and orchestrated and by whom inspired. The initial muted response of Arab states in the Gulf crisis reflected popular interest in subduing the oil-rich monarchies of the region. Thomas L. Friedman observed that "for many younger generation Arabs from the poorer Arab states, seeing the wealthy Kuwaitis defeated is a source of enjoyment, not distress." Equally enjoyable for Iran, for example, were the rising oil prices that OPEC forced on the world through insisting that the Kuwaitis curtail overproduction, which was depressing the price of oil. Delays after the war by the Emir of Kuwait to establish a more democratic regime revived criticism in the region.

One source of the Gulf conflict seems indisputable, whatever may be true of the relations among Arab states. The United States permitted, facilitated, and encouraged the augmentation of Iraqi power in the region, oblivious to the growing threat to the balance of power. It gave direct assistance to Saddam Hussein throughout the 1980s, long after Iran ceased being the principal threat to regional stability. We in no way discouraged the Germans, Chinese, or French from continuing military and other assistance. From January to July of 1990, participants in the policy review process in the Bush administration either failed to throw up warning signs or the signals were disregarded, whether from bureaucratic inertia or indecision on policy. On the eve of the invasion of Kuwait, the U.S. ambassador in Iraq reportedly reassured Saddam that the United States had no opinion on territorial disputes in the region. We vacillated as late as July 31 on the sale and transfer to Iraq of computerized equipment by a Brazilian company. The Commerce Department ignored warnings by its own staff on technology transfers. Then, on August 2, Saddam invaded Kuwait.

Future historians may find that some aspects of this account require revision. A longer view may provide new perspectives. What is unlikely to change, despite historical judgments on some of the details, is the dominance of political and strategic factors in the crisis. In much the same manner that the conduct of the final phase of World War II left the Soviet Union overwhelmingly the most powerful force in eastern and central, if not all of, Europe, Iraq emerged from the Iran-Iraq war supremely powerful in the Middle East. Not only Saddam but some of his predecessors had told Western observers, including myself, that if Iran or Syria should ever falter as frontline states in the struggle against Israel, Iraq would prove itself the most uncompromising and hard-line state in the region. In the early spring of 1990 reservists assigned to the Pentagon for temporary duty reported 100,000 Iraqi troops massing on the borders of Kuwait. The handwriting was on the wall.

Throughout those months silence reigned in the Bush administration, which was preoccupied with change in the Soviet Union and with transformation in Eastern Europe and was proclaiming once again the coming of a brave new world order. Not until Iraqi troops crossed into Kuwait did the president and his principal aides warn the American public. When the warning came, it took on the formalistic and legalistic language of the 1990s: aggression, Munich, Hitler, and collective security. Missing was any reference to the destruction of the balance of power in the region, perhaps because the administration had contributed to that destruction. That military men with a strategic sense, such as General Brent Scowcroft, Admiral William Crowe, and General H. Norman Schwarzkopf, and not President Bush or Secretary Baker were the voices who warned of threats to the balance of power remains a significant point. It is as though Bush administration officials, much like Rip Van Winkle, had slept through the late 1940s and 1950s when the language of containment and of the restoration of a balance of power was the prevailing response to the Soviet threat. The principles of international law and international organization are principles of the 1930s, which postwar policy makers made secondary to the rebuilding of stability and equilibrium in Europe and Asia.

Not only were the timeless principles of political stability and strategic equilibrium ignored in forging U.S. policy in the Gulf, but few gave much thought to the aftermath of war. It is true that a handful of Senate critics warned that war must be a last resort. They urged that sanctions, which had shown signs of weakening Iraq's national power and capacity, be given more time. However, even critics failed to question whether the Bush administration had defined not only its objectives in war but also its objectives for peace. The course of events in two world wars should have taught leaders that too often Americans win the war but lose the peace. It was hardly sufficient to reiterate endlessly that driving Saddam out of Kuwait and forcing him to free the hostages were our objectives. If anyone thought seriously about what the United States should do with Saddam after the war or about how to protect the Kurds and the Shiites in Iraq from a weakened but still powerful Iraqi army, we have not yet seen the evidence. Americans seemed totally unprepared for the harsh treatment of the minority populations in Iraq.

Theorists of international relations are inherently cautious about the consequences of revolution and war. Even theorists who in their framework put emphasis on coercion and power politics see dangers in the use of disproportionate force. They stress that war and peace are closely linked. The way wars are fought determines the prospects for peace. If the Bush administration gave serious thought to these interrelationships, it was hardly evident in the last stage of the war, the pursuit of a cease-fire, or the understanding of the challenges of the peace. Not peace and harmony but cruelty and brutality by the Republican Guards and Iraq's armies followed nearly one hundred years of war in the region, leaving the future of the Middle East even more in doubt.

For many Americans the struggle with the Soviet Union has often been a misunderstood conflict. The Middle East has a several-thousand-years history of wars and rivalries. Relations within the region are continually undermined by long-standing jealousies and shifting alliances. While the existence of Israel as a strong, functioning democracy remains, in Churchill's phrase, "an event in world history," Israel is also a permanent impediment to rapprochement between Arab states and the West. In the region, optimists predicted an eventual realignment of states to counterbalance the power of Iraq, whose army was once larger than the combined forces of Britain and France. But for Americans, persuaded that democracy is sweeping the world and bringing peace in its wake, likely U.S. allies are not democracies but medieval regimes such as Iran and Syria and monarchies such as Saudi Arabia, the United Arab Emirates, and Kuwait.

Therefore, the struggle for peace in the world continues apace even though the scene has changed. The immediate threat is a fifty-three-year-old dictator of whom one Soviet commentator wrote, "We created this monster with our arms sales." They did it with help, it must be added, from the United States, whose tilt toward Iraq in the Iran-Iraq war continued through the 1980s. Overnight, Iraq has replaced Iran as the most disliked country for Americans. As policy makers prepare to live with uncertainty in the world's most troubled region, whose oil remains essential to the United States and the West, it will not do to be guided merely by sentiment and passions. U.S. policy must find the firm ground of U.S. national interests if its actions are to have any chance of safeguarding the well-being of the United States and the West and of limiting the spread of conflict that might otherwise light the fuse of the most fateful of world wars. Nowhere are the choices for U.S. policy makers more difficult and the possibilities of political prediction more uncertain. We must learn to live in a world where the nature of the threat has changed and the means of responding must change not over decades but seemingly overnight. It is difficult to conceive of a greater challenge over the whole history of American foreign policy.

Index